CORNISH STUDIES

Second Series

ELEVEN

INSTITUTE OF CORNISH STUDIES

University *of* Exeter
IN CORNWALL

EDITOR'S NOTE

Cornish Studies (second series) exists to reflect current research conducted internationally in the inter-disciplinary field of Cornish Studies.
It is edited by Professor Philip Payton, Director of the Institute of
Cornish Studies at the University of Exeter, and is published by the
University of Exeter Press. The opinions expressed in *Cornish Studies*
are those of individual authors and are not necessarily those of the
editor or publisher. The support of Cornwall County Council is grate-
fully acknowledged.

Cover illustration: A.L. Rowse revisits his old Elementary School at
Carclaze, near St Austell, Cornwall (reproduced by kind permission of
Grindley Studios of Tregrehan).

CORNISH STUDIES

Second Series

ELEVEN

Edited by

Philip Payton

UNIVERSITY
of
EXETER
PRESS

First published in 2003 by
University of Exeter Press
Reed Hall, Streatham Drive
Exeter, Devon EX4 4QR
UK
www.ex.ac.uk/uep/

British Library Cataloguing in Publication Data
A catalogue record for this book is
available from the British Library

ISBN 0 85989 747 8
ISSN 1352-271X

Typeset in 10/12pt Times by Kestrel Data, Exeter

Printed and bound in Great Britain by
Antony Rowe Ltd, Chippenham

Contents

REVIEW ARTICLE

INTRODUCTION

A familiar theme in this series has been the extent to which Cornish Studies, as an area of academic activity, has in the last decade or so been able both to learn from and to contribute to major scholarly debates. As this series attests, and as *Cornish Studies: Ten* (2002) evidenced in detail, nowhere has this been more apparent than in our engagement with 'the new British historiography', where Cornish historians and political scientists have sought to locate consideration of Cornwall and the Cornish within debates about the processes of state formation and the perpetuation of 'difference' within the British Isles —or the 'Atlantic Archipelago' as it is now more properly designated within academic circles.

The publication in 2002 of Mark Stoyle's *West Britons: Cornish Identities and the Early Modern British State* demonstrated the growing maturity of this engagement, an intervention whose impact was felt far beyond the traditional bounds of the 'Cornish Studies community', ensuring that for practitioners of the 'new British historiography'— whoever and wherever they might be—Cornwall and the Cornish would no longer be hidden from the historian's gaze by the hitherto dominant 'four nations' approach to Archipelagic history. Implicit in this experience was the view that Cornwall and the Cornish had come late to the Archipelagic debate, overlooked in the simplistic 'four nations' analysis that had first emerged, and only latterly—courtesy of Mark Stoyle and others—making an eleventh-hour entry, clinging pluckily to the coat-tails of John Morrill, Steven G. Ellis and other distinguished proponents of the genre.

However, there is an important paradox here, for if we cast our gaze back beyond the current fashion for Archipelagic history, a product principally of the 1980s and 1990s, we can detect in the 1940s and 1950s surprisingly early traces of what we would now recognize as an Archipelagic approach to the study of the history of these islands. But more than this, we find that Cornwall and the Cornish, despite

their apparent Johnny-come-lately status in the current debate,
featured strongly in these early, tentative steps towards a new British
historiography, so much so that when in 1955 it was asserted by one
historian that 'the sixteenth century saw the great awakening for all the
island peoples', the Cornish were given due consideration as one
of these separate peoples alongside the English, Scots, Welsh and
Irish. This perceptive historian was, of course, A.L. Rowse. Given his
Cornish birth and sensibilities, it is not surprising that Rowse sought to
identify the Cornish as one of the constituent peoples of these islands,
and indeed we may go further to suggest that it was the influence
of this deeply ingrained Cornish background that allowed him to
formulate a view of the formation and expansion of the English State
that admitted a 'Celtic dimension' and had room for the experience of
the other, non-English peoples of the isles at this critical juncture in
their collective histories. What is surprising, perhaps, is that nearly fifty
years on historians of the early modern period have largely forgotten
the pioneering work of A.L. Rowse and, in so doing, have until Stoyle's
very recent intervention also overlooked the place of Cornwall and the
Cornish.

The publication of this volume (December 2003) coincides almost
exactly with the hundredth anniversary of A.L. Rowse's birth, and it is
a fitting opportunity to commence reassessment of his contribution to
the writing of British and Cornish history. As intimated above, it
is argued here that Rowse is an oft-overlooked progenitor of the
new British historiography and its Archipelagic debate. Although
remarkably ahead of his time in a number of areas, by the time J.G.A.
Pocock made his impassioned plea in 1975 for a new approach to the
study of British history, Rowse's early contribution was already being
forgotten, Rowse having abandoned mainstream history for the
controversial realms of Shakespeare, his academic reputation already
dented as a result of the way in which he promoted his own opinions
and denigrated those of others. As a result, Rowse's early contribution
was (along with Cornwall and the Cornish) routinely overlooked as a
new generation of historians emerged to respond to Pocock's *cri de
coeur* and begin the re-fashioning of British history.

It is only following Rowse's death that commentators have sought
to assess his contribution to British life and letters, and it is only now
that we are in a position to gauge the extent to which he was an
original (even prophetic) precursor of the current Archipelagic school.
As is shown here, Rowse was a remarkably early advocate of 'holistic'
history, of history that attempted the fusion of the 'local' with the
'national', and of history written from 'the bottom up'—all approaches
that have become *de rigeur* since the 1960s. Intriguingly, Rowse also

displayed an early interest in the emergence of nationalism and regionalism in modern Western states, posing searching questions about the rise of separatist sentiment in Quebec, Wales, Brittany, even Cornwall, at a time when most contemporary historians and political scientists were content to subscribe to a scholarly conventional wisdom which assumed the fundamental homogeneity of the liberal-democratic state and its attendant 'civic culture'.

In the end, Rowse had neither the inclination nor the time to devote to the study of the potential re-formulation of modern Western states in response to nationalist and regionalist demands (in extreme old age he retreated firmly to his Shakespearean comforts). It has been left to a new generation of scholars to consider Cornwall's place in the evolving territorial compact of the United Kingdom. In this volume, for example, Mark Sandford, a specialist in regional government in the Constitution Unit at University College London's School of Public Policy, examines the prospects for a Cornish Assembly against the background of the government's recent White Paper. In earlier publications, notably his and Paul McQuail's *Unexplored Territory: Elected Regional Assemblies in England* (London, 2001), Sandford has alighted on the 'Cornish problem', noting that although Cornwall is for regional government purposes considered an integral part of a wider 'South-West', it is in fact the one territory to express widespread interest in the prospects of regional government: but on the basis of a 'Cornwall-only' region. A petition of 50,000 names calling for a Cornish Assembly was presented to the government in 2001, and in the subsequent consultation period following the publication of the White Paper, submissions were dominated by those from Cornwall.

It is this conundrum, the enthusiasm in Cornwall for a Cornish Assembly and the inability of the government to conceive of Cornwall in any terms other than an integral South-West, that fascinates Sandford. As Sandford puts it: 'Cornwall is different. It is something of an enigma to the current government, because it simply does not fit within the government's vision of what regional government in "England" is.' Moreover, he argues, there is in government thinking a strong division between the 'devolution' afforded Scotland and Wales (and Northern Ireland) and the altogether different prospect of 'regional government within England', a division that is of crucial significance from the perspective of central government but which is rarely recognized or understood in Cornish circles.

Indeed, the basic tenets of Cornwall's claim for separate or privileged treatment—Celtic origins and historical identity—are themselves not understood (or are anathema) in Labour circles, in marked contrast (for instance) to the North-East of England where there is a recent and powerful history of alignment between regional aspirations and Labour Party policy. The North-East, after all, has long been a focus of traditional working-class Labour-voting trade unionism, in marked contrast to Cornwall with its limited Labour movement and a distinctly individualistic political culture based on the Liberal/ Methodist nexus, the Independent tradition in local government, and a small but serious and persistent nationalist party (Mebyon Kernow). Sandford argues that it is this difference in political culture that informs the difference in governmental attitudes towards the North-East and Cornwall. Using the telling analogy of the very different perceptions and treatment of the two regions in recent television programmes, Sandford concludes that 'at an extreme, it is represented by the difference between *Our Friends in the North* and *Wild West*'.

As Sandford suggests, the Cornish political culture that he identifies is, even if imperfectly understood by central government, of long-standing, reflecting the legacy of Cornwall's nineteenth-century hey-day when the Liberal/Methodist nexus arose as a significant feature of Cornish identity. The late Brian Elvins, as Edwin Jaggard demonstrated in his insightful and affectionate memoir in *Cornish Studies: Ten*, was one of a group of historians and political scientists who in recent years did much to elucidate this political culture and to explain the rise of Cornish Liberalism. In this volume, in an article prepared shortly before his death, Elvins returns again to this theme, furnishing the second part of his major study 'Cornwall's Newspaper War', his in-depth analysis of the long-running rivalry between the Tory *Royal Cornwall Gazette* and the eventual victor, the *West Briton*.

Taking as his period for this second article (the first appeared in *Cornish Studies: Nine*, 2001) the twenty years or so after the Great Reform Act of 1832, Elvins examines the relative fortunes of the two newspapers over time, taking into account the effects of changing political climates and both local Cornish and UK national events and personalities. Although he stops short of describing the *West Briton* as a Radical newspaper (indeed, he identifies some decidedly con- servative editorial opinion), he considers that it was essentially Reformist, with a strong and growing Whig-Liberal and Nonconformist flavour throughout the period. The *Royal Cornwall Gazette* was, by contrast, both Tory and Anglican, and it was this latter, religious factor (Elvins argues) that condemned the *Gazette* to play second-fiddle in terms of influence and circulation numbers, even when political fortunes seemed to be running against the Liberals. Indeed, the *West Briton* did much to articulate and mobilize political support for Non- conformist principles (such as opposition to the payment of tithes), enhancing the Liberal/Methodist nexus and consequently drawing the ire of the *Gazette* on a range of issues where the *West Briton* was seen to be supporting 'Nonconformist' causes, such as emigration.

As Elvins reflects, Nonconformity, especially Methodism (in its several guises), had become the religion of the majority of the Cornish people by the middle of the nineteenth century, a major component of the Cornish identity and a powerful determinant of group and individual attitudes and behaviour. Integral to this was the sometimes overt social, theological and political divide between Nonconformity and Anglicanism, not least when expressed in hostile exchanges between the *West Briton* and the *Royal Cornwall Gazette*, a division which survived intact into the twentieth century and (some might argue) to a degree into the twenty-first. Be that as it may, the division was an important determinant of contrasting behaviour in Cornwall in the early part of the First World War, the news of the outbreak of conflict in the summer of 1914 being met equivocally with mixed emotions, in contrast to the often uncritical exuberance experienced elsewhere. Although there were enthusiastic scenes at St Ives as the Royal Naval Reserve and the Royal Naval Volunteer Reserve (the latter formed in 1903) were mobilized, and although recruiting for the Royal Navy continued to run strongly in Cornwall, there was a complexity of Cornish opinion which, as Stuart Dalley argues in his article, differed from the supposed responses elsewhere in Britain.

As Dalley demonstrates, there were certainly difficulties in persuading many Cornishmen to join the British Army in the early days of the Great War, and echoes of the Boer War (which had sharply divided Cornish society) were heard as early anti-war feeling made itself evident, especially in Nonconformist circles. In contrast to the wild, jingoistic scenes evidenced at recruiting rallies elsewhere, audiences in Cornwall were more circumspect. As Joseph Hocking observed approvingly in May 1915: 'the Cornish are the most difficult to move. They are not stolid; they are stony. They will listen keenly, intelligently, critically, and show no sign . . . They regard it as a kind of weakness to manifest anything in the nature of enthusiasm, and they act accordingly.' Dalley also suggests that when the Cornish did exhibit 'patriotic' sentiment, this was often more of a humanitarian than a martial nature, a notable example being the considerable efforts made in Cornwall to look after Belgian refugees. Ultimately, as the war dragged on, more and more Cornish people became embroiled (and a great many lost their lives), with early anti-war sentiment melting away (as in the case of Sir Arthur Quiller-Couch). But, Dalley insists, the Great War never had quite the immediacy and impact that the Boer War had had in Cornwall. As the *Cornishman* newspaper opined as late as 1950: 'In 1939 the old men of St Just and Camborne had a clearer memory of Ladysmith and Spion Kop than of that long terrible struggle on the Somme'.

If there are detectable antecedents in the Cornwalls described by Brian Elvins and Stuart Dalley of the 'enigmatic', 'individualistic' Cornwall encountered today by Mark Sandford, not least in the enduring influence of the Liberal/Methodist nexus, then we might also observe that Sandford's insightful dichotomy of regional perceptions— *Our Friends in the North* versus *Wild West*—has a relevance in cultural circles that extends far beyond the party political. For example, while North-Eastern 'Geordie' accents are deemed appropriate and acceptable for a range of television commentaries, from Channel Four's *Big Brother* to the BBC2 documentary *Fighting the War*, Cornish accents occur but occasionally—and then usually in parodying, rustic 'mumerset' tones such as those in the Dawn French situation comedy *Wild West*. Here we see not only the governmental prejudices detected by Sandford but a wider set of British popular perceptions (mainly, but not exclusively, metropolitan) which amount to a construction or imagining of Cornwall that is reflected routinely in film and television. This, as Alan M. Kent demonstrates in his article in this collection, has had a profound effect on those who would make films or television programmes in Cornwall, including the fledgling, indigenous Cornish film industry.

Kent's contribution represents the first major, critical synthesis of film and television in Cornwall. It engages with concerns raised within 'new' Cornish Studies, and tackles wider issues of 'authenticity' and 'heritage' that have emerged elsewhere in film and cultural studies. In characteristic fashion, Kent ranges far and wide in pursuit of his material, noting the often telling comparative cases of Ireland, Wales and Scotland, and providing a brief but comprehensive history of film and television in Cornwall. In his review he alights specifically on three well-known films located in Cornwall, the controversial *Straw Dogs* (1971) which caused an outcry when first screened, and the more recent *Blue Juice* (1995) and *Saving Grace* (1999). *Straw Dogs* portrayed the Cornish as uncouth, menacing, provincial, full of a dark Celtic violence and malignance. The later films, however, were more balanced. As Kent acknowledges, *Blue Juice*, set in a Cornish surfing community, 'succeeds on several levels' and exhibits a degree of 'authenticity', even if 'for many [Cornish] viewers . . . the representation of Cornwall is too rose-tinted', while *Saving Grace*, though still concerned with the 'other' and the 'exotic', at least demonstrates that 'a larger-scale production can produce a legitimate and populist cinematic vision of Cornwall, which does not patronize the Cornish'.

Patrick Laviolette is, like Kent, concerned with representations

and constructions of Cornwall and, like Sandford, he is drawn by
'Cornwall's enigmas or contradictions'. In his article in this volume,
he 'offers various materialist and ethnographic interpretations of the
meaning behind certain images and depictions of Cornwall', showing
how familiar spaces (such as the home, gardens and public murals) and
visual artefacts (such as tourist brochures, postcards and the Cornish
national tartan) both shape and are shaped by the diversity of Cornish
identities. An anthroplogist, Laviolette conducted his fieldwork in
Cornwall between May 1998 and October 1999, living and working
alongside a disparate group of informants who ranged from amateur
footballers and artists to landscape gardeners and tourists, some
of whom were 'Cornish' and others 'in-migrants' or 'outsiders'. Part of
his research, for instance, was based around a sample of 105 homes
throughout Cornwall, where he sought to discover whether residents
displayed local landscape representations (paintings or photographs) in
their homes, finding that occupation, gender, class and other elements
of personal identity played crucial roles in determining what was or was
not on view. He interviewed people to gain their reactions to murals,
such as those that grace gable ends in Callington, and asked landscape
gardeners why they thought Cornish gardens such Heligan, Trebah
and Trelissick were important icons of Cornish identity.

From this kaleidoscope of impressions, Laviolette detects the
central importance of the production, consumption and awareness of
visual cultures in the formulation of social identities in Cornwall. As he
concludes, '[e]ven though not everyone is directly drawn to the Cornish
peninsula because of its artistic associations, a kind of visual metaphor
for the expression of cultural distinction nevertheless exists'. Here
individuals, locals as well as in-migrants or tourists, can appreciate and
appropriate the landscape they encounter, and contextualize within it
their own lifeworld. To take one specific icon in the Cornish landscape,
this is exactly the role (or one of the roles) performed by the church at
Gunwalloe on the Lizard.

As Graham Busby shows in his article, Gunwalloe is now by any
accepted definition a 'heritage visitor attraction', part of the general
trend in modern British tourism towards the seeking out of parish
churches (à la Betjeman or Jenkins) as well as cathedrals, but also a
specifically 'Cornish' destination for those intent on discovering 'a true
Cornish treasure' (as one visitor has termed it). Examining data in the
visitors' books at Gunwalloe, Busby identifies the motives, impressions
and experiences of those who visit (and often re-visit) the church. As
Busby explains, it is dedicated to St Winwaloe, a Cornu-Breton 'Celtic
saint', and (for many visitors) is redolent of an Anglo-Catholic Celtic
Revivalism in which the Diocese (of Truro) is seen as 'Celtic', an

inheritor of the ancient 'Celtic Church' and 'Celtic Christianity', almost
as if it were an independent see within the Anglican Communion.
Father Sandys Wason was the Anglo-Catholic incumbent of Gunwalloe
from 1902 until 1920: in 2000 one visitor wrote that the church 'Keeps
the faith which Fr. Sandy [*sic*] Wason taught here—bless his soul, rest
in peace'.

The relationship between the Celtic Revival and the Anglican
Church in Cornwall in the years 1870 to 1930 is the subject of David
Everett's article. Like Busby, he draws attention to the particular
qualities of the Anglican Church in Cornwall, especially the relationship between Celtic Revivalism and Anglo-Catholicism, and he
describes the movement which in the nineteenth century led to the
creation of the new diocese and the foundation of its cathedral in
Truro. His principal intention, however, is to identify and describe the
contribution of individual Anglicans in the period, those who not only
helped to reinvent the Anglican Church in Cornwall but also assisted in
projects such as the revival of the Cornish language and the foundation
of the Cornish Gorsedd. Henry Jenner, son of the incumbent of St
Columb Major, is one such figure. Generally acknowledged as the
Father of the Cornish Revival, it was Jenner who, almost one hundred
years ago, published in 1904 his *A Handbook of the Cornish Language*.
But there were other significant early Anglican Celtic Revivalists,
notably Wadislas Somerville Lach-Szyrma, onetime vicar of Newlyn,
who diligently sought out remnants of the spoken Cornish language
and busied himself in the study of the antiquities of West Penwith.
Today, when it is fashionable in some nationalist circles to defend
Methodism as symbolic of the modern Cornish identity and to eye the
Anglican Church in Cornwall suspiciously as an agent of English
intrusion, it is instructive to recall Lach-Szyrma's late nineteenth-
century perspective. In his experience, the Methodists thought the
Cornish language 'carnal: and wicked (which does not affect our old-
fashioned church people) and that "it does not pay"'.

As Everett concludes, the completion of Truro Cathedral represented the triumph of Anglican renewal in Cornwall, a movement that
had successfully articulated Cornwall's Celtic identity as part of its
strategy to create a separate Cornish diocese and had subsumed Celtic
Revivalism within its Anglo-Catholic world view. Although, by the
1930s, the individual personalities associated with this movement were
passing away one by one, the influence endured and is recognized
readily today. Paradoxically, as John Beckett and David Windsor
observe in their contribution, while the drive to achieve a separate
Cornish diocese in the nineteenth century was driven by Celtic
Revivalism and a Cornish awareness of their own ethnic identity, Truro

was a beneficiary not only of this desire for ecclesiastical expression of separate identity but of a parallel (and thoroughly English) phenomenon of raising the seats of new sees to 'city' status. Thus the town became the 'City of Truro'!

The work of the Celtic Revivalists, of course, drew attention to the fate of Cornwall's only recently deceased Cornish language and laid the foundations for its revival in the twentieth century. The Revivalists also prompted a renewed scholarly interest in the Cornish language, an interest which shows no sign of abating and which, indeed, has experienced redoubled enthusiasm in the opening years of the new millennium. This enthusiasm is reflected in this volume, where Matthew Spriggs, the distinguished Australian archaeologist who has been working for some years on the social history of the Cornish language, presents a major examination of where and when Cornish was spoken. Refreshingly, Spriggs is anxious to discuss the fate of Cornish against the wider context of language shift within England and, deploying his archaeologist's perspective, is able to draw upon the work of Hines and others to show how English so completely supplanted the earlier British speech—except in Cornwall, whose late subjection (at the hands of Athelstan) ensured the survival of Cornish ethnicity and with it the Cornish language. Interestingly, Spriggs's perspective lends further academic weight to the growing view that Athelstan's accommodation of Cornwall was not the benign and altruistic process inferred by an earlier generation of anglocentric historians but was the result of *realpolitik*: the Cornish, no longer a threat, could safely be left alone, in contrast to their compatriots who had only recently been evicted from Exeter (and perhaps the rest of Devon) in a process that Spriggs suggests may have been something akin to what we would recognize in today's world as 'ethnic cleansing'.

Be that as it may, Spriggs's exhaustive investigation, drawing upon his own meticulous research, together with that of other Cornish-language scholars, including the place-name specialist Oliver Padel, offers an important synthesis of existing and new knowledge, mapping as accurately as the evidence will allow the historical fortunes of the Cornish language and listing and interpreting all principal attestations. It is a process that confirms some existing assumptions but which also offers some surprising new perspectives. In the latter he is aided by the work of Julyan Holmes, who, complementing Spriggs's investigation, focuses specifically on East Cornwall, suggesting that this sub-region is deserving of greater attention than it has been afforded hitherto and that the survival of the Cornish language there was both later and more complex in nature than is generally acknowledged.

This interest in where and when Cornish was spoken is matched by a sustained interest in the historical documents of the language itself, and recently there has been a return to the so-called 'Tregear Homilies', first noticed in 1949. This re-examination has been precipitated in part by Charles Penglase, who, in an article in *Etudes Celtiques*, has published evidence from Tregear which he interprets as showing that a medieval Bible in the Cornish language must once have existed. D.H. Frost is another scholar to have returned to the Tregear Homilies in detail, focusing in his article in this volume on the so-called 'Thirteenth Homily', *Sacrament an Alter*, which is not (unlike the others) a translation of Bishop Bonner's work and is not even in Tregear's hand. He considers that it may have been the work of one Thomas Stephyn and that it was not a homily or sermon but rather a *catena*, a collection of patristic quotations from the Fathers of the early Church. Malte W. Tschirschky, prompted by the Penglase article, also returns in this volume to the Tregear Homilies but this time with the intention of demonstrating that Penglase's conclusions regarding a putative medieval Cornish Bible are unwarranted. Agreeing with Penglase that the apparent Middle Cornish 'archaisms' in Tregear's texts are evidence of an appeal to 'higher authority', he argues that this authority is not a Cornish Bible but rather the Catholic Church itself, the resort to archaic language in specific biblical quotations designed to evoke the authority of the pre-Reformation era.

Intriguingly, the renewed debates and disagreements regarding the Tregear Homilies are mirrored in a wider controversy regarding the nature of sixteenth-century Cornwall. The year 2003 has witnessed the publication of two books purporting to be the successors of A.L. Rowse's *Tudor Cornwall*—John Chynoweth's own (unimaginatively titled) *Tudor Cornwall* and J.P.D. Cooper's *Propaganda and the Tudor State*. In a stimulating review article, Bernard Deacon concentrates on the latter volume, identifying it as a 'Kernowsceptic' reaction to the recent work of Mark Stoyle but revealing a range of shortcomings, from flawed and weakly presented arguments to the 'just plain wrong'. Moreover, Cooper also displays 'a serious lack of historical imagination', a severe disappointment for those Cornish historians who—a century after the birth of A.L. Rowse—have alighted upon the significance of Rowse's early contributions to the writing of 'new' British and Cornish history, and are now attempting to locate Cornwall and the Cornish very firmly as a constituent territory and people within the 'Atlantic Archipelago'.

Professor Philip Payton
Director, Institute of Cornish Studies,
University of Exeter, Truro, Cornwall.

'I WAS BEFORE MY TIME, CAUGHT BETWIXT AND BETWEEN': A.L. ROWSE AND THE WRITING OF BRITISH AND CORNISH HISTORY

Philip Payton

INTRODUCTION

'[T]he sixteenth century saw the great awakening for all the island peoples.'[1] Today, this assessment is at the heart of the 'new British historiography', a new approach to the writing of British history which eschews hitherto dominant anglocentric perspectives and stresses instead the individual but complementary roles of the constituent territories of the British Isles—or rather, in the parlance of the new British historiography, of the 'Atlantic Archipelago'. Nowhere has this approach been more significant than in the study of the early modern period, the years from the end of the fifteenth century until the late seventeenth or thereabouts, when (as the above quotation suggests) the state-building activities of England (and, to a lesser extent, Scotland) brought the several peoples of these islands into vigorous contact as they coalesced and reacted to the processes of state formation.

Historians such as John Morrill and Steven G. Ellis, in tackling this era, have abandoned the old anglocentricity but have also sought to transcend the limitations of compartmentalized English, Welsh, Irish and Scottish histories by taking a 'holistic' view of the development of the Atlantic Archipelago.[2] Although the resultant 'four nations' (England, Wales, Ireland, Scotland) view of British history has to some observers appeared unnecessarily simplistic and constrained, in practice it has proved sufficiently flexible to accommodate, indeed encourage, new approaches to regional history, enabling historians to set regional distinctiveness within the experience of the Archipelago as a whole. Helen M. Jewell, for example, in her *The North–South Divide*, has examined the origins of Northern consciousness within the English State, arguing that the North existed as a distinct culture zone long before the industrial revolution re-invented its separate identity.[3] Closer to home, and even more profoundly, Mark Stoyle's *West Britons: Cornish Identities and the Early Modern British State* has fundamentally subverted the 'four nations' approach by establishing Cornwall incontrovertibly as one of the component territories and the Cornish as one of the constituent peoples of the Atlantic Archipelago.[4] But, far from refuting the basic tenets of the new British historiography, Stoyle's intervention, in revealing the limitations of an assumed 'four nations' history, has brought a renewed freshness, subtlety and vitality to the Archipelagic debate.

From this perspective, there is a certain paradox in Stoyle's contribution. As Stoyle himself remarks, Cornwall has come late to the Archipelagic debate, for too long hidden from the historian's gaze by the 'four nations'. But, we might also observe, Cornwall's eventual appearance centre stage courtesy of *West Britons* was critical because it allowed Stoyle to inject that very freshness and renewed sophistication that have taken the debate forward. And yet there is an even greater paradox, for the quotation above, so much the epitome of the new British historiography and its Archipelagic debate in the late 1980s and 1990s, was in fact penned almost half a century ago by a historian who had Cornwall and the Cornish very much in view as he ventured to describe the contacts and collisions of the peoples and places of these islands in the early modern period. That historian was A.L. Rowse. The purpose of this article, then, is to return to the work of A.L. Rowse to discover anew his early, tentative but in several respects crucial contribution to the formulation of the new British historiography, an inquiry which focuses initially on his (in several respects) prophetic volume *The Expansion of Elizabethan England*, published in 1955, but also ranges across a portfolio of other work, notably *Tudor Cornwall*, which reveals the extent to which his early concern for history that is 'holistic'—able to reconcile the 'local' with the 'national', written from the 'bottom up', and recognizes the 'Celtic' component in Britain and its diaspora—anticipates many of today's preoccupations.

FROM POCOCK TO *THE ISLES*
Ironically, it is not just that Rowse's role as a forerunner of the new British historiography has been routinely forgotten; rather, it has for the most part been denied altogether. For example, Norman Davies, in

his monumental volume *The Isles*, a lengthy synthesis of Archipelagic perspectives, published in 1999, dismissed Rowse as an '[e]ven more Anglocentric' Tudor historian than the anglophile Geoffrey Elton, accusing him of doing 'little to further the cause either of Cornwall or of non-English perspectives' in the writing of British history. Indeed, 'Rowse's somewhat patronizing approach to Cornwall presented a little land of strange names, exotic saints, and curious antiquities which should thank God for being overrun by the English'.[5] In Cornwall itself, Rowse has a determined band of admirers and apologists, anxious to defend its hero's achievements and revere his memory, together with a smaller but only slightly less vociferous coterie of detractors keen to echo Davies's withering condemnation.[6]

For the rest, outside of Cornwall and in the wider academy there is a great silence, with only occasionally a glimmer or hint that the name of Rowse might be relevant in this discussion. Even so, for the discerning observer the continuing influence of Rowse is unmistakable if unspoken and such acknowledgement as there was before Stoyle's intervention of Cornwall's place in the Atlantic Archipelago was due almost entirely to Rowse's elaboration of the Cornish experience in his *Tudor Cornwall* and its wider contextualization in *The Expansion of Elizabethan England*. How else, for example, would one explain Steven G. Ellis's confident assertions regarding Cornwall in his pathfinding article 'Not Mere English' in 1988, where he describes 'the extension of English law and language in Ireland, Scotland, Wales and Cornwall from the mid 1530s onwards' and notes that within the Tudor State 'Cornwall, with its separate language, exhibited special features'?[7] Equally, Hugh Kearney's treatment of Cornwall in his 1989 book *The British Isles*, where he observes 'Celtic-speaking Cornwall, which was incorporated into "England", governmentally if not culturally',[8] smacks strongly of Rowse's influence, though one searches without success for mention of Rowse in the notes and 'selected reading list'.

Mark Stoyle, more explicitly, in his 1997 article 'Cornish Rebellions 1497–1648' recalled the comparative importance of Rowse's work, noting that 'A. L. Rowse has described the 1549 rising as Cornwall's equivalent of the Scottish '45 and the comparison seems an apt one'.[9] More significant still, Michael Hechter in his *Internal Colonialism: The Celtic Fringe in British National Development*, published in 1975 before the current rush of Archipelagic history, observed that the territorial extent of the United Kingdom had occurred through a lengthy period of territorial interactions and annexations. He considered that Rowse had had an early and pivotal role in elucidating this process, citing a telling article in a 1957 edition of the *William and Mary Quarterly* by Rowse and remarking with considerable insight and historiographical sophistication that 'Rowse is quite well aware of the fact that his own Cornish origins were indispensable to this view of British history'.[10] But although like Rowse an early advocate of what we would recognize now as an Archipelagic approach to British history, Hechter has (again like Rowse) not been generally accepted into the community of Archipelagic writers, partly because his own academic domain is sociology and political science rather than history proper, and partly because his 'internal colonialism' thesis has endured sustained savaging from other scholars, notably Jim Bulpitt in his masterly *Territory and Power in the United Kingdom*.[11] Rather like Rowse, Hechter has been seen by many as a maverick and an outsider, and his identification of Rowse as a forerunner of the new British historiography has, therefore, gone largely unnoticed and unremarked.

And so, despite these fleeting and fragmentary evidences, implicit and very occasionally explicit, of Rowse's influence, there has been no place for him and no acknowledgement of his contribution in the principal historiographical texts of recent years. For example, there is no mention of Rowse in Glen Burgess's lengthy and otherwise illuminating Introduction to his important collection *The New British History*, published, like Davies's tome, in 1999. Ironically, looking back to try to identify the founding fathers (or mothers) of the new British historiography, Burgess alights briefly on the work of Dame Veronica Wedgwood, who '[i]n one of her essays . . . managed deftly to weave a British dimension into an account of the causes of the English Civil War'.[12] The irony is that Wedgwood and Rowse were once great friends and collaborators; she, when an undergraduate student at Lady Margaret Hall, was one of his first and (he averred) best pupils. They saw each other frequently when Rowse was in London during the 1930s (she even encouraged him to write a play about Elizabeth I and was complimentary about his poetry), and she wrote an enthusiastic review of his *The Spirit of English History*, published in 1943.[13] As an editorial assistant at Jonathan Cape, Rowse's first publisher, Wedgwood remained in almost constant contact with her former mentor, a friendship that did not turn sour until 1969 when, in the space of a few months, Wedgwood had had the temerity to doubt Rowse's identification of the 'Dark Lady' of Shakespeare's sonnets *and* had been awarded the Order of Merit which Rowse had imagined was rightly his.[14] But in their closeness over many decades, as like-minded friends and as professional historians with similar interests, it is at least possible that some of Rowse's early ideas about a 'British dimension' might have rubbed off on his erstwhile student, especially on occasions such as those when together they visited Boconnoc and the Civil War sites of East Cornwall. In the academy today, of course, as Burgess evidences, it is Wedgwood and not Rowse that historians choose to remember and respect. This, amongst other things, helps to explain why Steven G. Ellis in his otherwise excellent article 'Tudor Northumberland: British History in an English County', a contribution to a recent collection of Archipelagic essays, conspicuously fails to note the comparative relevance of Rowse's *Tudor Cornwall*, an omission echoed elsewhere in his chapter 'The Tudor Borderlands, 1485–1603' in John Morrill's *The Oxford Illustrated History of Tudor and Stuart Britain*.[15]

Be that as it may, Burgess and others like him searching for the origins of the new British historiography have settled almost unanimously upon the New Zealand historian J.G.A. (John) Pocock, who in an address to the New Zealand Historical Association in 1973 made 'a plea for a new subject', a plea that was published subsequently in New Zealand, British and American academic journals over the next decade.[16] Notwithstanding the brief acknowledgement of Wedgwood's earlier influence, this posits the new British historiography as a remarkably recent phenomenon, still hardly more than a quarter of a century old, beginning hesitantly in the mid-1970s, finding its feet in contributions such as Steven G. Ellis's article 'Not Mere English: The British Perspective 1400–1650' in 1988 and Hugh Kearney's *The British Isles: A History of Four Nations* in 1989, gaining maturity in collections like Bradshaw's and Morrill's *The British Problem c.1534–1707: State Formation in the Atlantic Archipelago* in 1996, and culminating (perhaps) in Norman Davies's *The Isles* on the eve of the Millennium.[17]

As Burgess observed, '[t]he British history for which Pocock called was a long time in coming'. However, '[w]hen it did come, it bore only partial resemblance to the vision that Pocock's wizardry had so beguiling conjured from nothing [*sic*]'.[18] For what Pocock had envisaged was not only a new approach to the study of these islands but one which took the story of the several British peoples beyond the Archipelago to America, South Africa, Australia and (of course) his native New Zealand, a broad panorama that would first explain the coalescence of peoples in the Archipelago and then trace the export and impact of this multi-threaded 'Britishness' in the New World. As Pocock explained, the new British history 'should start with what I have called the Atlantic archipelago'.[19] But it ought not be 'confined to the island that the cartographers have called "Britain"'. Rather, he said, it should extend to and encompass the enigmatic, ambiguous, partly colonial relationship between Ireland on the one hand and the several British peoples and the emerging British State on the other, and then extend still further 'into oceanic, American and global dimensions'.[20]

THE ARCHIPELAGIC ROWSE

As Burgess remarks, the new approaches to British history that have appeared have not generally been like this and, despite the very recent emergence of a 'British world' perspective from the editorial pens of Carl Bridge and Kent Fedorowich (which seeks to establish a global project much like that which Pocock had in mind),[21] the method of those Archipelagic historians who have looked beyond these islands has more often than not been to construct European comparisons—to compare the processes of state formation in the Archipelago with those on the Continent itself. While pointing to many pertinent and important comparisons and contrasts between the Archipelagic and Continental experiences, this has had the effect, critics might argue, of deflecting the historian's gaze from the rest of 'the British problem' —its diasporic context. Paradoxically, just as Rowse's early contribution to the formulation of Archipelagic perspectives has been overlooked, denied or plain forgotten, so his equally early insistence on a perspective that took the experience of the British peoples first to Ireland and then on to the New World has been likewise disregarded. Here, for example, is A.L. Rowse's assessment in his *The Expansion of Elizabethan England* of the processes of state formation in the Tudor period:

> The subject of this volume is the expansion of that society, both by the state and by individual enterprise, first into the margin of backward societies at home—Cornwall, Wales, the Borders, with the sweep of a sickle on the map: into Ireland, where the process involved conquest and colonization; then across the oceans, to our first contacts with Russia, the Canadian North—the tenacious search for a North-East or North-West Passage to the riches of Eastern trade— our emergence into the Pacific, the search for *Terra Australis* (the ultimate discovery of Australia may be seen as a distant product of the Elizabethan age) . . . the first projects and attempts at the colonization of North America.[22]

Of course, it may be objected that the very title of Rowse's book betrays unionist (even imperialist) predispositions, with his ingrained anglophilia never far beneath the surface and his adherence to the Whig tradition of English history worn firmly on his sleeve—all of which is anathema to Archipelagic history as practised today. The phrase 'backward societies' is value-laden and pejorative, and who today could write innocently of 'the discovery of Australia'? Elsewhere there is language that would offend the sensibilities of Norman Davies (and many others) and give credence to his stinging criticisms of Rowse. We learn, for example, that in Scotland the embryonic Scottish State had to deal with 'Celtic chaos', while in Ireland there was the 'deplorable spectacle of a Celtic civilization in part medieval and in part pre-medieval . . . in a stage of rapid social decomposition'. The Borders of Scotland and England were characterized by 'the primitive conditions of life'. Wales had been rescued by the Tudors 'from the disaster of Owen Glendower's rebellion', while 'Cornwall was brought inevitably, and profitably, into the mainstream of English life'. But there was Cornish resistance to this English intrusion: 'One recognizes the familiar symptoms—how boring they are!—of anti-English feeling'.[23]

These dismissive and uncomfortable words surely reflect the fact that, as argued elsewhere, *The Expansion of Elizabethan England* was researched and written at the time of Rowse's disaffection and disappointment, most especially in the aftermath of his failed political career and his keen sense of 'rejection' by Cornwall and the Cornish people.[24] It is also worth noting that his more assured advocacy of things Cornish and Celtic came much later, in the evening of his career when he had retired to his Cornish home at Trenarren, near St Austell. However, despite our objections today to the attitudes and language so uncomfortably apparent in his book, in the context of his time (immediate post-war) and place (Oxford), Rowse's approach is already a significant departure from what was then anglocentric orthodoxy in the writing of English/British history. Obscured by his obvious approval of the actual process of English expansionism, was his understanding that state formation in these islands, though dominated by English imperatives, involved a series of complex relationships between the several territorial components of the isles, not least as they coalesced and reacted to those state-forming activities. Moreover, long before Pocock's (largely unheeded) call for a British history that sought first to understand the Archipelago and then, armed with understanding, to proceed to 'oceanic, American and global dimensions', Rowse was already there, arguing for just such a juxtaposition. There was also, long before the appearance of Mark Stoyle on the scholarly stage, recognition in Rowse of Cornwall and the Cornish as distinctive and integral in the Archipelagic story.

Indeed, Rowse's apparently anglocentric title serves to disguise the radical structure of his book and his method, for the crucial first four chapters are devoted not (as one would have expected of his time and place) to the English 'centre', the hub of the expansionist imperative, but rather to the Archipelagic reactions of Scotland, Cornwall, Wales and Ireland to England's state-forming aspirations and activities. Remarkably, there is brief acknowledgement too of the state-building efforts of Scotland, which, even as the English State looked to consolidate and secure the Borders, sought to bring the Gaelic Highlands and Islands more firmly within Edinburgh's Lowland sway. There was even a comparative word about Brittany, that 'Celtic duchy'[25] as Rowse dubbed it, which was increasingly the object of French state-building attentions in this period, a recognition on Rowse's part that Continental comparisons might be instructive but an acknowledgement too that in those days of state-building flux Brittany was still—culturally, economically, even politically—somewhere on the edge of the Archipelagic world.

Should all this seem suspiciously like an *ipse post facto* attempt to attribute to Rowse an originality and prophetic vision that in fact (detractors might argue) he did not possess, then it is useful to consider the contemporary reaction to his book. Rowse himself, in September 1944, wrote to the Warden of All Souls, submitting for approval his research plans for the future, intimating the genesis of what would become his Elizabethan trilogy (of which *The Expansion of Elizabethan England* was to be a part): 'the main direction of my reading and research continues to be the Elizabethan Age. And I want to write what will be a really big book, a kind of successor to *Tudor Cornwall*, on the whole Elizabethan Age in all its aspects, political and economic, social and literary; in fact a portrait of a whole society.'[26] Actually, what Rowse achieved was something rather more than this. His friend and mentor, G.M. Trevelyan, welcomed *The Expansion of Elizabethan England*, writing that 'I enjoyed it very much, particularly the part about Cornwall, which was an excellent introduction to the subject of the expansion of England'.[27] But the real significance of the work was recognized by Sir John Neale, doyen of Tudor historians, who wrote to Rowse from his home in Beaconsfield in June 1955, shortly after *The Expansion of Elizabethan England* was published. He knew at once that Rowse's approach was novel, ground-breaking, the decision to commence his study with the Celtic lands an insightful flash of brilliance which would change the way in which the history of these islands was considered: 'I admire its conception. The approach through the Celtic lands was an inspiration. It is fresh; it is absolutely right; and artistically it unifies the whole story. It gives one a new grasp of the age ... You have reason to be very proud indeed.'[28]

This was praise indeed, for Neale was then at the height of his powers and the pinnacle of his profession, having begun his career at

University College London in 1919 and, by way of the Chair of Modern History at Manchester, gone on in 1927 to be Astor Professor of English History at University College. On his retirement in 1956 he was appointed Emeritus Professor. For many years he presided over the Tudor Studies seminar group (of which Rowse was a member) at the Institute of Historical Studies, and it was there that new ideas were raised and debated. Not surprisingly, for a time Rowse exercised some influence within the group, and when in 1961 colleagues published a *festschrift* in honour of Neale it aimed to review 'recent trends in Tudor political and social historiography' in which, amongst other things, '[o]ur Irish, Scottish and Welsh contributors have enabled us to include something of the complex story of the relations between the four peoples who occupy these islands'.[29] This was, as it were, proto-Archipelagic language, an indication perhaps of Neale's developing taste and the influence of Rowse upon him, although there is in the book but one fleeting mention of Cornwall and no contribution from Rowse (though there is a piece by W.G. Hoskins on Exeter's Elizabethan merchants). By this time, perhaps, Rowse was already moving on, no longer the intimate of the lead thinkers in the field, no longer able to persuade and cajole in the way he had before, heading inexorably into other areas (notably Shakespearean) and (although the third volume of the trilogy was not published until 1971–2) away from serious history—a theme that will be elaborated further below. The Archipelagic legacy remained, though not fully grasped until years later, but Rowse's role was already being forgotten.

TUDOR ROWSE

But before we leap ahead to the latter-day Rowse we should return to his earlier work, most especially his *Tudor Cornwall*, first published in 1941 and indisputably his greatest book. In the Preface to this remarkable work, Rowse explained that *Tudor Cornwall*, the fruit of a dozen years' research (interrupted as they were by political distractions when a Labour candidate in Cornwall and by illness), had been conceived initially as a study of the Reformation in Cornwall: what it meant, where it had come from, and how it had affected society. But these inquiries led him soon to other fields—economic, political, military, cultural, and so on—and to his growing conviction that 'the time has come in our historical writing for a synthesis of local and national history'. And, recognizing the particular value of Cornwall as a case study in attempting this convergence of the 'local' and the 'national', he added: 'Perhaps a Cornishman may be forgiven for thinking that no area would prove more intrinsically interesting or historically fruitful than Cornwall in the Tudor age'.[30]

So *Tudor Cornwall* was to be much more than mere local history, nothing less than an attempt to elucidate Cornish society in all its complexity against the background of the influences and intrusions of 'national' (English) affairs in the Tudor era. It was, after all, a turbulent period of change, upheaval and danger, one which witnessed the growing centralization and outward expansion of the English State (both these trends impinged upon the life of Cornwall), culminating in the great confrontation with Spain—in which Cornwall was also to play its role. In Rowse's own words:

> From being a far-away, insignificant corner of the land, sunk in its dream of the Celtic past, with its own inner life of legends and superstitions and fears, its memories of Arthur and Mark and Tristan, lapped in religion and the cult of the saints, it was forced in the course of the Elizabethan age into the front-line of the great sea-struggle with Spain. Inevitably, the small backward-looking society struggled against the process: the Rebellions of 1497 and 1549 were to Cornwall what the '15 and '45 were to the Highlands.[31]

Behind the veneer of pejorative language that offends the early twenty-first-century eye (but is more or less symptomatic of mid-twentieth-century scholarship)—the inevitability and futility of the 'backward-looking' society's resistance to change; the implied redundancy of the old Celtic periphery, Catholic Cornwall as much as Gaelic Scotland—is the historiographical innovation inherent in Rowse's approach. The *Sunday Times*, in its review of *Tudor Cornwall* in December 1941, caught well the spirit of the book: 'He [Rowse] tells of the change from the Cornwall of the Wars of the Roses, wild, unruly, un-English, and defiant, to the Cornwall of Elizabeth's latter years, patriotic and Protestant, a bulwark of the realm, its turbulent energy pouring out through its seaports to attack the Spaniard'.[32] But the *Times Literary Supplement*, in its review, detected something more: '[a] sense that Cornwall was being exploited for the benefit of foreigners runs through the whole of Mr Rowse's book, and was undoubtedly present to the Cornish mind in this age'.[33] Between them, the reviews had captured the complexity of Rowse's portrait, the transformation wrought by English intrusion but also its trauma, not only the redirection of Cornwall's 'turbulent energy' but also the lingering sense of exploitation and resentment that endured throughout the period, surviving even the Reformation and the wars with Spain. Here we see, perhaps, the influence of Mary Coate (of which more below), but what is especially apparent is Rowse's attempt to match the 'local' to the 'national', to explore the interaction of the two and the impact of the one upon the other.

Rowse was already a devotee of 'total history', the bringing together of the various strands of historical writing in the manner advocated by his hero Trevelyan, a position he made plain in his *The Use of History*, first published in 1946, where he insisted that there was now an 'impulse towards this kind of total history—giving an account of a society in all its aspects, it geographical environment, the land system and its industries, the governmental and administrative system, the social structure, the political events, the social, religious and cultural life'.[34] In the 1940s this was hardly a conservative approach to the study of history, and especially innovative was the recognition that historical writing should encompass much more than the deeds of the great men and women of the State's 'centre'. But if this was innovative in the 1940s, then it was positively radical almost two decades before when in 1927, as a young scholar still fresh to his subject, he argued for an interpretative 'total history' which would pull obsessive historians away from the minutiae of unceasing and never to be written-up research and force them into wide-ranging, generalizing literary expression:

> it is apparent that the supremacy of research in schools of English history has lasted long enough, and what is needed is a return to synoptic writing . . . Research must go forward all the time, but the exigencies of research have for too long determined historical style. We must expect, therefore, from the new movement a greater breadth of conception, a nobler treatment of subject, which will restore the literary graces which have almost ceased to adorn recent work.[35]

If all this seemed somewhat obscure (the young Rowse had yet to develop the 'easy reading' style for which he was later appreciated), he went on to explain:

> It will no longer be sufficient to describe the minute happenings in the small circle of a governing class under the impression that this is the history of England; and it will become clearer that the history that we read is only the record of changes in the distribution of power within the ruling classes. We shall have to plumb the depths of society in order to reach rock bottom; and upon that foundation we must begin to rear the structure upwards, and give up the attempt to build from the top downwards.[36]

ROWSE THE ANTI-ANTIQUARIAN

Here we can detect Rowse the socialist (anticipating Eric Hobsbawm, perhaps, or E.P. Thompson) but we also see unmistakable signs of the 'holistic' and 'history from below' approaches which became fashionable in the 1960s. E.P. Thompson's essay 'History From Below' in the *Times Literary Supplement* in 1966 is often credited as the 'real starting point'[37] to this movement in historical writing, but, as we have seen already, Rowse was toying with such ideas years before. Indeed, in an apparently unpublished manuscript 'Local and National History', prepared not long after the Second World War, Rowse returned to his favourite subject of the relationship between the 'local' and the 'national', arguing not only for their fusion in a 'total history' but for the relevance of this fusion in attempting history from 'the bottom upwards' (as he termed it). *Tudor Cornwall*, he thought, had provided the model and the inspiration for such work:

> What is new in all this, what is so fascinating *now*, is to watch the way in which this local material is being used to illuminate the history of the nation, of our people as a whole: we are watching the marriage of local and national history, observing the fertilisation of one with the other. It is bringing about a deepening of our nation's history: we no longer think of it as just the narrative of political events on the top surface; we try to carry along in our minds all the layers of the cake, all the strata of society from the bottom upwards.[38]

Lest this be seen as something less lofty than traditional history (or what today we might term 'dumbing down'), Rowse was quick to insist that this new approach to historical writing was intrinsically more difficult: 'Of course that makes history harder to write, almost impossible on the grand scale'. The answer, therefore, was 'to portray society in miniature, to take a particular area at a significant time, a subject that has some homogeneity—like Tudor Cornwall or Wales, Reformation Yorkshire or Lancashire, Medieval Kent or East Anglia in the Civil War'.[39] In considering how such a task might be accomplished, Rowse turned to local history, a field dominated for so long by those who were (in Rowse's estimation) harmless antiquarians: men and women who had done much to record in infinite detail all the incidentals of their parishes. Now, however, local history was to be called upon to fulfil an altogether more important task; Rowse smiled upon the antiquarians but thought their time had passed:

Local history has for long been a favourite subject of study
all up and down the country. I love those generations of
antiquarians who have done so much to recover and keep
alive the story of their parishes, their families, their counties
and towns. I see them—clergymen up from the country with
their Gladstone bags . . . to work at the British Museum
or Public Record Office; passionate and often whiskered
antiquarian ladies and gentlemen who cared so hotly for
learned subjects that the bodies to which they belonged—like
the Devonshire Association—were sometimes riven by their
quarrels; or quiet county gentlemen in their gilt and calf-
bound libraries looking out on the acres of their ancestors
—libraries and acres now alike dispersed, the species
vanished.[40]

But now local history, to ensure its continuing relevance and its
engagement with professional history, had to abandon its antiquarian
past and participate in the grander project for which Rowse wished to
prepare it:

there is no doubt that a change has come over the study of
local history—it has got a new breath of inspiration: I should
say that it is the most promising field of the lot, where some of
the best and most fruitful work is being done . . . In my view it
offers far better returns than those over-cultivated and too
much trodden areas—diplomatic history, the endless works
being poured out, the interminable discussions on the history
of the two World Wars. When you think of the innumerable
books written about Napoleon, think of the libraries that will
be written about Hitler![41]

As it happened, Rowse was to be disappointed in his aim, for there
was to be no mass realignment in the writing of local history (notwithstanding the indefatigable efforts of the Leicester school), much of
which continued more or less as it had before. Every now and again
Rowse would emerge to call for a study of Tudor this or Stuart that or
somewhere in the Civil War, but it was not until the appearance of the
much later work of David Underdown (more of which below) that he
felt that his urgings were at last being heeded. By then, as argued
above, Rowse had in any case drifted away from mainstream history, so
much so that later writers on local history (rather like the architects of
the new British historiography and the Archipelagic debate) habitually
forgot his pioneering work. Remarkably, and refreshingly, John D.

Marshall in his *The Tyranny of the Discrete: A Discussion of the
Problems of Local History in England*, published in 1997 (the year of
Rowse's death), admitted this omission and belatedly, as it were,
restored Rowse to something like his position as a progenitor
of post-antiquarian local history. Like Rowse so many years before,
Marshall argued for a new direction for local history, noting that in the
previous forty or fifty years the practice of local history research and
writing had not lived up to the expectations of its academic advocates:
'In standard and style of approach it has clearly disappointed the
proponents of people's history, history from the grass-roots'.[42]

Criticizing antiquarian local historians who beavered away in local
record offices with no real aim other than the amassing of 'facts' about
their preferred localities, Marshall in an earlier (1992) article had
regretted that 'there have been few successful attempts to look at
regions holistically',[43] noting the relatively few volumes (mostly in
the area of regional economic history) that came anywhere near the
mark. In *The Tyranny of the Discrete* Marshall returned to this article,
explaining that in his survey of those successful histories he had
unfortunately overlooked the much earlier work of Rowse: 'One major
work not there noticed is Rowse, A.L. (1941), *Tudor Cornwall: Portrait
of a Society*, which is essentially "political" in approach, while
it attempts at the same time to do justice to economic and social
factors'.[44]

ROWSE, HENDERSON, COATE AND 'Q'

Significantly, Rowse's interest in local history was due in the first place
to the influence of his close friend Charles Henderson, whom he met in
1928. In later years Rowse would insist that Henderson was really 'an
antiquarian' and 'not a historian', distancing himself from Henderson's
youthful enthusiasm for collecting ancient documents and enthusing
over the obscure, writing in 1976 that 'he did not finish much in the way
of books', his principal contribution being 'a voluminous mass of
notes'. As Rowse explained, 'He was really an antiquary—an
honourable title—rather than an historian . . . folk in Cornwall do not
know that; nor that, when he died, he was actually turning away from
his intense, rather parochial, concentration on Cornwall, perhaps in
the process of development towards becoming an historian'.[45] However, it was Henderson who had alerted Rowse to the possibilities of
local history in Cornwall. Well-connected and well-off, certainly when
compared to the young Rowse, Henderson had the means to explore
Cornwall and was welcomed to the muniment rooms of almost all its
great houses, something impossible for the working-class Rowse until
Henderson had made the necessary introductions. Thus it was that

Rowse had his first taste of a 'country-house weekend with Charles Henderson at Penmount' and, accompanied by Henderson, 'Sunday lunch at Killagordan, sequestered Queen Anne House deep in the valley . . . [t]ea with the Masefields at Mawnan . . . [s]upper at Lis Escop with Bishop Frere'.[46]

Often driven by Charles's sister Chrys in the Hendersons' motor car, Henderson and Rowse toured the length and breadth of Cornwall, and Rowse was deeply impressed by his companion's apparent knowledge of every church, farm, lane, stream and bridge from the Scillies to the Tamar. It was this topographical intimacy, the willingness to step beyond the record office and into the field, that (Rowse considered) gave Henderson's antiquarianism its particular innovative quality, something that promised a fresh approach to local history—if only Henderson could be persuaded to write it all up. Hitherto, Rowse had not considered seriously the possibilities of Cornish research that might be significant or sophisticated enough to stand up in the national and international arenas. In any event, 'I wasn't interested; Cornish history was not my subject, history in general, literature, and politics were'.[47] Furthermore, it was Sir Arthur Quiller-Couch, the immortal 'Q', who had thus far guided the young Rowse, an influence that had helped him on the road to Oxford but had also led him firmly in the direction of literature: 'My interests were as much literary as historical; I thought of Q as my model and mentor'.[48] Henderson, however, emerged as a new, in some respects stronger influence, unveiling for Rowse a hidden Cornwall that had been beyond his view and whetting his appetite for Cornish research. Henderson's main interest was medieval, so that without any sense of rivalry or intrusion Rowse could happily concentrate on the Tudor period. Moreover, Henderson introduced Rowse to the difficult but essential world of paleography. As Rowse observed: 'I came to manu-scripts rather late . . . [u]nlike my early friend and mentor, Charles Henderson, the leading antiquary of his time, who was up to his knees in manuscripts from the time he was a boy'. And so, '[a]ctually I learned my A.B.C. of Elizabethan handwriting from a transcript that Charles Henderson made from a document in the City Library in Exeter, by systematically comparing the two'.[49]

When Charles Henderson died suddenly and unexpectedly on his honeymoon in Rome in 1933, aged only 33, Rowse was devastated. Already convinced by Henderson of the intrinsic value (as well as fascination) of Cornish research, Rowse saw it as his duty to take up where Henderson had left off, to bring the worth and inter-national relevance of Cornish history to the academic world and to the informed reading public: 'When he died so young, at thirty-three, I was heartbroken—it worked out strangely that I should become his inheritor. He was essentially a medievalist, not attracted to the Tudor period. It fell to me to write *Tudor Cornwall*, and to dedicate it to his memory—since I was determined to do everything I could to keep it green.'[50] Rowse also collaborated with Charles's widow, Isobel, to publish in 1935 an edited collection of Henderson's *Essays in Cornish History*, to which 'Q' contributed an elegant Preface, and in 1937 the Royal Institution of Cornwall published Henderson's *History of Constantine*, lightly edited by Canon G.H. Doble.[51] This latter book had been in the making for some years, Constantine being amongst Henderson's favourite Cornish parishes and easily accessible when he was living at Falmouth and later at Penmount. To the modern eye it is a strange volume, the greater part (no doubt the earliest to be written) strongly in traditional antiquarian style, with its painstakingly detailed account of church and vicars and manors. The final (and much shorter) part ventures somewhat into the realm of social history and into the modern period, with short essays on education, Nonconformity and the several industries of the parish. But there is only one page devoted to copper mining, and there is no mention at all of Constantine's great nineteenth-century industry, granite quarrying, or of the craft trade unionism and the emigration of skilled workers that it engendered.

However, there was perhaps just enough 'history from below' in this to satisfy Rowse, and he was certainly delighted when the *History of Constantine* posthumously saw the light of day, writing loyally and enthusiastically in the *Spectator*: 'The book is a model of what a parish-history should be; it is most thorough, based at every point upon documents in public or private hands, the whole picture made living and real by Charles Henderson's genius for topography, his loving knowledge of every field and building and road, every feature in the Cornish landscape'.[52] In a sense, Rowse may have used the *History of Constantine* as a model or inspiration for his own *St Austell: Church: Town: Parish*, published in 1960, although Rowse's book is altogether more integrated, with a leavening of grass-roots history and a much fuller picture of the modern, industrial period (not least the china clay industry into which Rowse had been born).[53] John McManners, in his obituary of Rowse in the *Proceedings of the British Academy*, thought *St Austell* 'a gem of local history writing'[54] but for Rowse it was actually a sideshow, if not a distraction, a momentary departure from other tasks to help the parish church in its fund-raising efforts. 'Local' history, for Rowse, to be important should be more than parish history, able to contribute to the 'national' in the way that *Tudor Cornwall* had.

In this conviction, articulated time and again over many years, we see the influence not so much of Charles Henderson but of Mary

Coate, who had reached much the same intellectual position during the 1930s, exemplified in her *Cornwall in the Great Civil War and Interregnum, 1642–1660*, published in 1933, the year of Henderson's death.[55] Mary Coate was, like Veronica Wedgwood, at Lady Margaret Hall, and was likewise an early friend of Rowse. He recalled how 'congenial [it] was meeting Mary Coate, who was writing her book *Cornwall in the Civil War*. A good historian, she was a dedicated Tory, a devoted teacher, who handed on pupils for me to teach.'[56] He also lent her books,[57] and a measure of their closeness was the fact that, when Rowse lay gravely ill from a stomach operation and his mother was summoned from Cornwall, it was Mary Coate who offered to meet her from the train.[58] A further connection was that Noreen Sweet, Rowse's lifelong friend, had for a time taught English at Truro High School for Girls when Dora Coate, Mary's sister, was headmistress there.[59] Years later, Rowse chose to emphasize in his Foreword to the *History* of the school that 'I was a great friend at the University [Oxford] of her sister, Mary Coate, admirable historian of Cornwall during the Civil War'.[60]

When Coate's book first appeared, Rowse wrote an approving review for *Devon and Cornwall Notes and Queries*.[61] He thought the volume perhaps 'the most important single contribution to Cornish history that has been made'. From Rowse, this was praise indeed: 'But it is more than that: it is a valuable contribution to the history of England'. Here Rowse was echoing Coate's belief in the symbiotic relationship between the 'local' and the 'national' in the Civil War, 'this dualism between the visible political changes at the centre and the unvarying life of the countryside'[62] as she chose to describe it: [t]he history of Cornwall in this period has more than a local interest and importance. It belongs to the realm of the historian rather than of the antiquarian'.[63]

Indeed, Rowse was at pains to remind his readers in another review that what Coate had found in the Civil War in Cornwall was also true of the earlier period, when the intrusion of the Tudor State in Cornish affairs had had profound consequences for both Cornwall and England: 'a century that saw an army of Cornishmen march from one end of the country to the other in 1497, until it met with defeat only upon Blackheath, and that witnessed the dangerous Rebellion of 1549, which paralysed government for a time and ultimately led to the downfall of the Protector Somerset'.[64] Here there was also more than a hint of Cornish particularism, something that Coate had made plain in her book where she sought to explain the devotion of the ordinary folk to the Royalist cause in terms of 'the passionate attachment of the Cornish to their own county and their own race' and a 'local patriotism,

born of racial difference and geographical isolation'.[65] It is not difficult
to imagine that Rowse and Coate (and Wedgwood) swapped notes and
exchanged ideas on such matters, the one influencing the other, and if
we can detect in Rowse an early advocate of an Archipelagic approach
to British and Cornish history then we must also acknowledge the place
of Mary Coate in crafting his views. To be sure, it is the influence of
Coate the historian, and not Henderson the antiquarian nor 'Q' the
literary mentor, that we see in Rowse's confident characterization of
the Cornish at the beginning of the Tudor period. Cornwall was then,
he said,

> a homogeneous society of its own, defined by language
> and having a common heritage underneath, like Brittany or
> Wales or Ireland, reaching back beyond Normans and Saxons,
> beyond even Romans in these islands, to an antiquity of which
> its people were still dimly conscious. Some memory of all this
> they carried in the legends of the race that haunted them.
> They remembered that they were a conquered people.[66]

CELTIC ROWSE

The Cornwall that Rowse thus describes is the 'Celtic Cornwall' of his
historical imagination. Indeed, all the while that Rowse was writing of
English history and extolling England's greatness, he was mindful
of a countervailing and component 'Celtic' existence, a sensibility
sharpened by his view of Cornwall as a land of 'difference' and given
breadth by his Archipelagic interpretation of the processes of state
formation in these isles. Notwithstanding his enthusiasm for all things
English he was a self-confessed 'Celt', always on the lookout for the
opportunity to stress the 'Celtic' in British history. For example, in
a patriotic radio broadcast in 1940, designed no doubt to evoke
Britain's glory and to strengthen resolve in that darkest hour, he spoke
of the 'spirit of English adventure' but immediately offered a
corrective:

> That leads me to another point. We say the 'British Empire'
> —you know it was a Welshman who coined the phrase in the
> sixteenth century, the distinguished geographer, Dr Dee. And
> I suppose I ought to say 'the spirit of British adventure', not
> merely English. For I think the greatness and variety of its
> record is partly due to the different elements, the different
> contributions of temperament and character, of English,
> Scots, Welsh, and Irish: it has made it all the richer.[67]

Similarly, in 1943 Rowse could note that '[n]ineteenth-century historians were apt to regard us simply as an Anglo-Saxon folk; in fact we are really an Anglo-Celtic people'.[68] He also asserted that the Celtic component of English make-up was much greater than popularly imagined, making the English in 'racial' composition far nearer to the French and less close to the Germans than was generally supposed. This was, no doubt, a welcome message at the height of the war, and although it reflected Rowse's by now deeply ingrained hostility to all things German, it also revealed his genuine conviction that the 'Celtic component' of both Britain and England mattered and was important in any historical elucidation of these islands. It was a conviction that Rowse carried with him over the years, evidenced (for example) in an aside in his discussion of the Victorian historian James Froude, where he not only berated Froude for his 'Teutonist' [*sic*] and anti-Celtic sentiments ('A Celt myself . . . [I] can rise above these prejudices') but reaffirmed his belief in an 'Anglo-Celtic England (for we must not overlook Wales and the West of the island)'.[69] The concept of an Anglo-Celtic England, of course, was comfortable and attractive for Rowse or any other Cornish person faced with the 'in England but not of England' ambiguity of Cornish identity, especially if they relied (as Rowse did) upon the patronage of England for their advancement.

Be that as it may, Rowse's insistence upon a 'Celtic component' represented a recognition on his part of the possibility of non-English perspectives in the writing of British history, a demand for consideration of the 'Celtic' in the make-up of Cornwall, England and Britain that complemented both his Archipelagic view of state formation in these isles and his regard for the necessary reconciliation of the 'local' with the 'national'. But this assessment is in one respect too easy, too neat, for while it gives due acknowledgement to Rowse in the development of these ideas, it avoids the uncomfortable fact that underpinning Rowse's construction of the 'Celtic' was a good deal of racial stereotyping. In the pre-1945 era, when scholars could get away with sweeping generalizations about 'national characteristics', it perhaps did not matter too much, but after the war—with the experience of the Hitler years still fresh in memory and with the emergence of more sophisticated understandings of ethnicity and ethnic identity—Rowse's continued resort to stereotypical characterizations was increasingly unsatisfactory. While his continual self-ascription of 'Celtic' attitudes, foibles and failings might be indulged, even enjoyed, his attempts to perpetuate outdated stereotypes were met with less tolerance. The 1971 Pelican edition of his *The Use of History* revealed what must have been a gentle (?) tussle between Rowse and his editor, Rowse's insistence upon the continued discussion of 'racial characteristics' tempered by a new demand for 'scientific ethnology'. The resultant compromise is not entirely convincing:

> Nothing is more remarkable to a discerning student of British history than the dualism of English and Celtic characteristics in the people: the extremism, the vivacity and temperament of the one, the reliability, the dogged qualities, the imagination, the sense of moderation of the other . . . Anyone with discernment can observe these strains coming out in our people and their history; and we can say that without involving ourselves in the crudities of racialism. The stock counts for something, and a scientific ethnology is the way to assess it.[70]

ROWSE AND THE 'WITHDRAWAL INTO HIS FORTRESS OF PRIDE'

By this time, however, Rowse was already a very different writer from the man who had penned *Tudor Cornwall* thirty years before. Returning to his first love, English literature, the domain of the 'dear Q' whose memory he cherished, Rowse had increasingly turned away from mainstream history and into literary work. Shakespeare, in particular, whose quintessential 'Englishness' and central place in the canon of English literature appealed to Rowse's anglophilia, was a favourite subject. Complementing his historical research into the Elizabethan period, Rowse's work on Shakespeare resulted in a string of publications, from his *William Shakespeare: A Biography* in 1963 (an instant popular success, which was massively reviewed in both Britain and America and had sold 200,000 in hard covers by 1965) to *My View of Shakespeare*, which appeared in 1996, not long before his death.[71] From the start, his Shakespearean following was as much popular as academic. Popular enthusiasm held up for as long as he cared to write books on the subject but his academic credibility was severely dented by the furore over his supposed discovery of the identity of the 'Dark Lady' of the sonnets, not merely because critics found flaws in his circumstantial evidence but as a result of the way in which Rowse defended himself—denouncing his critics and refusing to acknowledge any weakness or uncertainties in his argument.

By this time, in McManners's estimation, there was 'a fatal flaw in his temperament which was insidiously taking him over', Rowse's work (and scholarly conduct) exhibiting a 'deterioration', accompanied by a 'withdrawal into his fortress of pride'. McManners thought that

Rowse's injudicious responses to the Dark Lady criticisms 'made him a laughing stock' in academic circles, resulting in his 'frantic industry, perhaps desperate to reinforce his tarnished credentials'.[72] Part of this 'frantic industry' was the turning out of historical 'potboilers' and lightweight volumes, such as his *Story of Britain* produced for the retail chain Marks & Spencer in 1979, none of which did much to restore his reputation within the academic community.[73] But there were some works of real worth amongst this outpouring. In *Court and Country: Studies in Tudor History,* for example, published in 1987, and which included some Cornish material, Rowse returned in assured manner to familiar territory.[74] Earlier, in 1969, a more radical departure had been his *The Cornish in America*, published on both sides of the Atlantic.[75] Unlike *The Cornish Miner in America*,[76] produced just two years before by his friend A.C. Todd, which concentrated on a specific occupational group (and therefore specific geographical areas), Rowse's volume was truly panoramic in scale and nature, sweeping across the whole of the country and encompassing several centuries, in a sense linking up with *The Expansion of Elizabethan England* and returning in the early part of the book to some of the themes first addressed a decade before in his *The Elizabethans and America*, which, as he put it, had had 'a West Country bias'.[77]

McManners thought that Rowse had been 'breaking new ground with a study of Cornish emigration to America'[78] and in many ways he had, *The Cornish in America* (along with the work of A.C. Todd and, a little later, John Rowe) laying the foundations for a rich tradition of Cornish emigration studies which still shows no sign of abating.[79] Indeed, having identified in earlier work the particular place of the Cornish as a people in 'the making of Britain', he was in this book (in the manner later advocated by Pocock) taking his perspective overseas, tracing in the New World the nature and impact of Cornish ethnicity transplanted. But Rowse was by now 'fair game' for academic snipers, and *The Cornish in America* was the target of a devastating attack in the *Times Literary Supplement* by an American professor, Denis Brogan, who condemned it as 'filiopietistic' and sneered at its supposed reliance on 'telephone books and simple works of reference. This is not what I would call serious research.'[80] Fretful notes of reassurance from old friends like F.L. Harris and A.C. Todd could not console Rowse, who wrote directly to Brogan to tell him what he thought of his review.[81] Brogan was unrepentant, replying: 'I'm sorry to have caused you distress or anger but the gap between us is unbridgeable. I dislike, for professional reasons, the kind of book you wrote.' Indeed, '[t]he fact that you do it better than most people could do makes it all the more dangerous. I can't see any reason why the

Cornish in America should not be studied in a numerate and if you like sociological fashion like other ethnic groups.'[82]

Already scornful of 'sociological fashion' in historical writing, Rowse had had his worst fears confirmed by Brogan. Thereafter, there were to be no half-measures in his opposition to 'sociological history'. 'Why do I not subscribe to the exaggerated esteem for sociological history which is fashionable among academics today?', he asked rhetorically, '[m]y reason is that history is a portrait of life as it is lived, in all its subtlety, its fluidity and variableness, and this cannot be caught and rendered in sociological generalisations'. Moreover, '[t]he rigidifying of life into abstract concepts yields dubious results', for 'history is not a theoretical subject'.[83] Rowse later widened this view to include criticism of a variety of other historians of whom he did not approve or with whom he had crossed swords, writing in *Historians I Have Known* in 1995 that he did not care for Arnold 'Toynbee's attempt to sociologise history' and that R.H. Tawney the arch 'theorist' finally tired of the conceptual—'So much for historical theorising . . . Tawney eventually gave a halt to it as serving no purpose'. And as for Hugh Trevor-Roper (Lord Dacre), 'if one is addicted to pushing forward a thesis one is liable to go wrong'.[84]

For Rowse, who had devoted so much time, even after abandoning the politics of the Left, to arguing that the rigour and clarity of Marxian analysis were indispensable to a proper understanding of history, this contempt for 'theory' was a considerable retreat from a position once stoutly defended. Moroever, despite the years he had given over to writing *about* history—calling for the reconciliation of the 'local' with the 'national', for history to be written from the 'bottom up', and so on—he was now entirely of the view that such activity was the preserve of the second-rate: '[r]eally distinguished historians do not waste time discussing how to write history . . . they get on with the job. They leave it to the not so good at it to discuss how it should be done.'[85]

Such an attitude contributed to the prevailing conventional wisdom, elaborated by McManners, that Rowse was now little more than a marginalized eccentric whose views were not be taken seriously: '[h]is mind retained its acuity, but his lunatic self-importance was subverting his scholarly judgement'.[86] Rowse's attitude also meant that he had intentionally distanced himself from historiographical debate, which he now saw as worthless, so much so that when Pocock began his call for new Archipelagic approaches and Marshall criticized antiquarian local history, he was not merely silent but plainly not interested. He was by then, of course, an old man. But, paradoxically, age did not prevent him from time to time, when it suited him to do so, dusting off his old concerns, returning briefly to those passions of years ago, and then (having made his point) retreating once more to his 'fortress of pride'. For example, he applauded the newly emergent 'younger and (better) historians of the Civil War, putting behind them the out-dated theses of Christopher Hill, Trevor-Roper, Lawrence Stone and company'.[87] He welcomed John Morrill's *Cheshire 1630– 1660*, which appeared in 1974, but was most enthusiastic about David Underdown's *Somerset in the Civil War and Interregnum*, which had been published twelve months before. There were in Underdown's title shades of Mary Coate, but more than this: 'Mr Underdown's book on Somerset during the Civil War and its aftermath is quite first-class, a model of how these things should be done'.[88] Here, at last, was someone responding to the challenges he had set years before, reconciling the 'local' with the 'national' and dealing with his subject from the 'bottom up'. Underdown, for his part, devoted a series of books and articles to popular behaviour and politics in Civil War Somerset, Dorset and Wiltshire, culminating in his widely regarded *Revel, Riot and Rebellion*.[89]

DR ROWSE AND CORNISH NATIONALISM

Underdown, in turn, influenced the writing of Mark Stoyle, who produced first (in 1994) his *Loyalty and Locality: Popular Allegiance in Devon during the English Civil War*,[90] before moving more explicitly into the area of Cornish identities and the forging of the early modern British State. Although Rowse did not live to see *West Britons*, Stoyle's all-important and crowning contribution, which restored Cornwall and the Cornish to their 'rightful' place in the Archipelagic debate, he had been much impressed by Stoyle's article '"Sir Richard Grenville's Creatures": The New Cornish Tertia, 1644–46' in *Cornish Studies: Four* in 1996, in the late evening of his life expressing pleasure that the themes that had captivated him of old were gaining a new popularity.[91] Earlier, although privately expressing misgivings that *The Making of Modern Cornwall*, published in 1992, was dangerously close to the 'sociological history' he so abhorred, he was gracious enough to pen a favourable appreciation in the *English Historical Review*, though attributing the recent resurgence of territorial politics in the United Kingdom not to an enduring centre–periphery relationship but rather to what he considered to be the disintegration of the governing classes.[92] As he had already observed elsewhere, '[a] feature of the twentieth century has been the resurgence of the Celtic peoples, now that the unifying influence of the old governing class has broken down: one sees it in Ireland and Gaelic Scotland, Wales and Brittany, even in my own "little land" of Cornwall'.[93]

This view was, in effect, Rowse's last (albeit fleeting) contribution

to the writing of British and Cornish history, a brief flirtation with the
contemporary history of the United Kingdom (and other Western
states) in which he reflected upon the causes of 'disintegration' and the
rise of regionalism and nationalism, a phenomenon which (as he was
well aware) threatened at least partially to undo the state-formation
processes of the early modern period that he had chronicled so
many years before. In his collection *The Little Land of Cornwall*,
published in 1987, his article 'Dr Johnson and Cornish Nationalism'
was a not-so-tongue-in-cheek examination of Samuel Johnson's
humorous eighteenth-century 'comparison' of American and Cornish
calls for independence, in which he (Rowse) revealed his own atavistic
sympathy for the claims of Cornish nationalism.[94] As early as
December 1968 he had been thinking of writing an article on '[w]hy
there is this present growth of Cornishness, of Cornish national
feeling',[95] and in the following year, reflecting on the effect of the
disintegration of the old governing class and of what we would
we today call 'globalization', he told one American newspaper: 'Ah,
the cosmopolitan sameness of life . . . [i]t's responsible for the
recrudescence of nationalism among the smaller peoples—the rise of
Brittany against de Gaulle, the trouble brewing for England in Wales,
the revival of the Cornish language in Cornwall'.[96]

His growing sympathy for the aspirations of 'smaller peoples' also
reflected his ultimate disappointment with England and the English.
Having invested so much time and energy in admiring and celebrating
all things English, England's loss of Empire and decline of international influence after 1945 distressed him deeply, as did what he took
to be England's descent into economic failure, strikes, social collapse
and moral bankruptcy. In 1979, before Thatcher's rise to power that
year, all his worst fears seemed to have been realized, as he pondered
again England's historical relationships with her Archipelagic neigh-
bours: 'No wonder there has been a residual hatred of the English
among the Welsh—and, as a Cornishman, I am certainly not starry-
eyed about the English or very sympathetic about the fate they have
called down upon themselves today'.[98]

CONCLUSION

In the end, Rowse had neither the inclination nor the energy to pursue
what might have been a renewed contribution to the debate about the
relationships between the several peoples of these islands, and his
insights into Cornish nationalism and the resurgence of territorial
politics in the United Kingdom did not go much further than incidental
observation and comment. Ultimately, he had no desire to become
embroiled in the study of contemporary history and politics, for

England had gone to waste already, and in extreme old age he contented himself with his favourite subjects—especially Shakespeare, the subject of his final book, entitled, aptly enough, *My View of Shakespeare*, published the year before his death and 'Dedicated to HRH the Prince of Wales [Duke of Cornwall] in our common devotion to William Shakespeare'.

By then, in any case, Rowse, long since retired from All Souls and well beyond the reach of current academic debate, was seen by the academy as irrelevant. John McManners's assessment reflected the views of many: 'Outrageous and wounding in controversy, he finished up being regarded as an eccentric . . . an impossible figure whose insults no one took seriously'. Moreover, '[s]uch academic friends as corresponded with him put up with his overweening self-esteem and denigration of others because they sensed his inner loneliness and saw that he himself was the chief victim of his outrageous performances'.[98] Put alongside Norman Davies's resounding condemnation, especially the accusation that Rowse had done nothing for Cornwall or for non-English perspectives, there seems little room in this for his redemption. But this would be, unforgivably, to forget Rowse's pioneering work, much of it before, during and just after the Second World War, which had anticipated in no small measure the preoccupations of the current generation of historians, starting with the fad for history from 'the bottom up' in the late 1960s, 1970s and 1980s and culminating in the 'Archipelagic' history of today.

Of course, we must accept that Rowse was a product of his time and place, and critics might well argue that he was in fact writing an 'enriched English history'[99] rather than a genuinely *British* history (an accusation that John Morrill, in a not altogether dissimilar context, has levelled against Conrad Russell), one which never quite escaped its anglophile assumptions or (notwithstanding his castigation of Froude) could never restrain its pejorative assessment of 'Celtic attributes'. And yet, in his defence, Mark Stoyle, a leading figure in both the 'new British historiography' and its Cornish off-spring, has observed that Rowse's early contributions have not 'received the recognition they deserved from the new breed of early modern British historians',[100] an indication that it is time for us look afresh at the work of Rowse and ponder anew his contribution to the writing of British (and Cornish) history.

The recent emergence of something like the 'Rowse industry' that he had himself predicted back in the 1970s may herald his posthumous rehabilitation in academic circles, although it must be said that in recent commentaries, including Richard Ollard's impressive contributions, there is yet little sign of this.[101] But the final word, perhaps,

should go to A.L. Rowse himself, who came to recognize eventually
that his work had been well before its time, tackling issues and
suggesting new methods before the academy was fully prepared to
accept them, and yet by turns forgotten or derided when at last these
novelties were in vogue. As he once put it, in a different context, 'I was
before my time, caught betwixt and between'.[102]

NOTES AND REFERENCES

1. A.L. Rowse, *The Expansion of Elizabethan England*, London, 1955, repub. 1973, p. 45.
2. See, for example, Brendan Bradshaw and John Morrill (eds), *The British Problem c1534–1707*, London, 1996, and Steven G. Ellis and Sarah Barber (eds), *Conquest and Union: Fashioning a British State 1485–1725*, London, 1995.
3. Helen Jewell, *The North–South Divide: The Origins of Northern Consciousness in England*, Manchester, 1994.
4. Mark Stoyle, *West Britons: Cornish Identities and the Early Modern British State*, Exeter, 2002.
5. Norman Davies, *The Isles: A History*, London, 1999, p. 976.
6. For a brief discussion of Rowse's Cornish supporters, see Philip Payton, *A Vision of Cornwall*, Fowey, 2002, pp. 103–5; for an example of a detractor, see John Angarrack, *Breaking the Chains*, Camborne, 1999, and John Angarrack, *Our Future is History: Identity, Law and the Cornish Question*, Bodmin, 2002.
7. Steven G. Ellis, 'Not Mere English: The British Perspective 1400–1650', *History Today*, December 1988.
8. Hugh Kearney, *The British Isles: A History of Four Nations*, Cambridge, 1989, p. 70.
9. Mark Stoyle, 'Cornish Rebellions 1497–1648', *History Today*, May 1997.
10. Michael Hechter, *Internal Colonialism: The Celtic Fringe in British National Development 1536–1966*, London, 1975, p. 63.
11. Jim Bulpitt, *Territory and Power in the United Kingdom*, Manchester, 1983, pp. 37–44.
12. Glen Burgess (ed.), *The New British History: Founding a Modern State 1603–1715*, London, 1999, p. 7.
13. A.L. Rowse, *The Spirit of English History*, London, 1943.
14. See Richard Ollard, *A Man of Contradictions: A Life of A.L. Rowse*, London, 1999, pp. 87, 174, 245–6, 269.
15. Steven G. Ellis, 'Tudor Northumberland: British History in an English County', in S.J. Connolly (ed.), *Kingdoms United? Great Britain and Ireland since 1500: Integration and Diversity*, Dublin, 1999, pp. 29–42; Steven G. Ellis, 'The Tudor Borderlands, 1485–1603', in John Morrill (ed.), *The Oxford Illustrated History of Tudor and Stuart Britain*, Oxford, 1996, pp. 53–73.
16. See Burgess, 1999, pp. 8–9; for a corroborating view, see Raphael Samuel, *Island Stories: Unravelling Britain—Theatres of Memory,*

Volume II, London, 1998, pp. 25–7. The Pocock essays are: J.G.A. Pocock, 'British History: A Plea for a New Subject', *New Zealand Journal of History*, 8, 1974, reprinted in *Journal of Modern History*, 47, 1975, pp. 601–28, and J.G.A. Pocock, 'The Limits and Divisions of British History: In Search of the Unknown Subject', *American Historical Review*, 87, 1982, pp. 311–36.

17. Ellis, 1988; Kearney, 1989; Bradshaw and Morrill, 1996; Davies, 1999.
18. Burgess, 1999, pp. 8–9.
19. Pocock, 1975, p. 606.
20. Pocock, 1982, p. 312.
21. Carl Bridge and Kent Fedorowich (eds), *The British World: Diaspora, Culture and Identity*, London, 2003.
22. Rowse, 1955 and 1973, p. 6.
23. Rowse, 1955 and 1973, pp. 18–19, 22, 45, 60, 139.
24. Payton, 2002.
25. Rowse, 1955 and 1973, p. 18.
26. University of Exeter Rowse Collection, Box 37, Confidential Report to the Warden of All Souls: 14 September 1944.
27. Rowse Collection, Correspondence, Letter from G.M. Trevelyan, 14 November 1955.
28. Rowse Collection, Correspondence, Letter from Sir John Neale, 12 June 1955.
29. S.T. Bindoff, J. Hurstfield and C.H. Williams (eds), *Elizabethan Government and Society: Essays Presented to Sir John Neale*, London, 1961, p. vi.
30. A.L. Rowse, *Tudor Cornwall: Portrait of a Society*, London, 1941, p. 10.
31. Rowse, 1941, p. 9.
32. *Sunday Times*, 28 December 1941.
33. *Times Literary Supplement*, 27 September 1941.
34. A.L. Rowse, *The Use of History*, London, 1946, repub. 1971, p. 51.
35. A.L. Rowse, *On History*, London, 1927, pp. 30–1.
36. Rowse, 1927, pp. 36–7.
37. Jeremy Black and Donald M. MacRaild, *Studying History*, London, 1997, p. 109.
38. Rowse Collection, Box 52, unpub. MS 'Local and National History'.
39. Rowse Collection, Box 52, unpub. MS 'Local'.
40. Rowse Collection, Box 52, unpub. MS 'Local'.
41. Rowse Collection, Box 52, unpub. MS 'Local'.
42. J.D. Marshall, *The Tyranny of the Discrete: A Discussion of the Problems of Local History in England*, Aldershot, 1997, p. 49.
43. Marshall, 1997, p. 105; here Marshall is echoing his J.D. Marshall, 'Proving Ground or the Creation of Regional Identity? The Origins and Problems of Regional History in Britain', in P. Swan and D. Foster (eds), *Essays in Regional and Local History*, Beverly, 1992, pp. 1–26.
44. Marshall, 1997, p. 107.
45. A.L. Rowse, *A Cornishman Abroad*, London, 1976, pp. 198–99.
46. A.L. Rowse, *A Man of the Thirties*, London, 1979a, pp. 127–8.
47. Rowse, 1979a, p. 16.

48. Rowse, 1976, p. 199.
49. Rowse Collection, unpub. MS, 'Experiences with Manuscripts'.
50. Rowse, 1979a, p. 16.
51. Charles Henderson, *Essays in Cornish History*, ed. A.L. Rowse and M.I. Henderson, Oxford, 1935, repub. Truro, 1963; Charles Henderson, *A History of the Parish of Constantine in Cornwall*, ed. G.H. Doble, Truro, 1937 (the short title *History of Constantine* appears on the frontispiece).
52. *Spectator*, 4 March 1938.
53. A.L. Rowse, *St Austell: Church: Town: Parish*, St Austell, 1960.
54. John McManners, 'Alfred Leslie Rowse, 1903–1997', in *Proceedings of the British Academy: 105: 1999: Lectures and Memoirs*, Oxford, 2000, p. 552.
55. Mary Coate, *Cornwall in the Great Civil War and Interregnum, 1642–1660*, Oxford, 1933, repub. Truro, 1963.
56. Rowse, 1979a, p. 111.
57. Rowse Collection, Box 237, MS 113/2/5/4, MSS from Notebooks 1928–84, 1928.
58. Ollard, 1999, p. 57.
59. Rowse Collection, Correspondence, Undated Letter from Noreen Sweet, later gloss by A.L. Rowse.
60. A.L. Rowse, 'Foreword', *History of Truro High School for Girls*, Truro, n.d., p. xii.
61. Rowse Collection, Box 37, Clippings, excerpt from *Devon and Cornwall Notes and Queries*, n.d. c.1933.
62. Cited in A.L. Rowse, *West Country Stories*, London, 1945, p. 148.
63. Cited in Rowse, 1945, p. 129.
64. Rowse, 1945b, p. 129.
65. Coate, 1933 and 1963, p. 351.
66. Rowse, 1941, p. 20.
67. Rowse, *The English Spirit: Essays in History and Literature*, London, 1944, p. 55.
68. A.L. Rowse, 1943, p. 12.
69. A.L. Rowse, *Froude the Historian: Victorian Man of Letters*, Gloucester, 1987, pp. 75–6, 78.
70. Rowse, 1946 and 71, p. 75.
71. A.L. Rowse, *William Shakespeare: A Biography*, London, 1963; A.L. Rowse, *My View of Shakespeare*, London, 1996. The estimation of sales is in Sydney Cauveren (ed.), *A.L. Rowse: A Bibliophile's Extensive Bibliography*, Folkstone, 2000, p. 18.
72. McManners, 2000, pp. 544, 548.
73. A.L. Rowse, *Story of Britain*, London, 1979b.
74. A.L. Rowse, *Court and Country: Studies in Tudor History*, Brighton, 1967a.
75. A.L. Rowse, *The Cornish in America*, London, 1969.
76. A.C. Todd, *The Cornish Miner in America*, Truro, 1967b.
77. A.L. Rowse, *The Elizabethans and America*, London, 1959, p. 38.
78. McManners, 2000, p. 552.

79. See, for example, Philip Payton, *The Cornish Overseas*, Fowey, 1999; John Rowe's principal contribution is: *The Hard-rock Men: Cornish Immigrants and the North American Mining Frontier*, Liverpool, 1974.
80. *Times Literary Supplement*, 24 July 1969.
81. Rowse Collection, Box 208a, Correspondence and MSS Fragments, Postcard from F.L. Harris dated 30 September 1969; Rowse Collection, Correspondence, Letter from A.C. Todd dated 27 September 1969.
82. Rowse Collection, Box 208a, Letter from Denis Brogan dated 4 October 1969.
83. A.L. Rowse, *Portraits and Views: Literary and Historical*, London, 1979c, pp. 125–6.
84. A.L. Rowse, *Historians I Have Known*, London, 1995, pp. 56, 57, 95, 101.
85. Rowse, 1979c, p. 116.
86. McManners, 2000, p. 547.
87. A.L. Rowse, *Discoveries and Reviews*, London, 1975, p. 163.
88. *Books and Bookmen*, July 1973.
89. David Underdown, *Somerset in the Civil War and Interregnum*, Newton Abbot, 1974; David Underdown, *Revel, Riot and Rebellion*, Oxford, 1985.
90. Mark Stoyle, *Loyalty and Locality: Popular Allegiance in Devon during the English Civil War*, Exeter, 1994.
91. Mark Stoyle, '"Sir Richard Grenville's Creatures": The New Cornish Tertia, 1644–46', in Philip Payton (ed.), *Cornish Studies: Four*, Exeter, 1996; although complaining that his eyesight was failing, Rowse readily undertook the reading of Stoyle's article as external referee.
92. Philip Payton, *The Making of Modern Cornwall: Historical Experience and the Persistence of 'Difference'*, Redruth, 1992; *English Historical Review*, June 1995, p. 816.
93. A.L. Rowse, *The Little Land of Cornwall*, Gloucester, 1986, repub. Redruth, 1992, pp. 297–8.
94. Rowse, 1986 and 1992, pp. 299–301.
95. Rowse Collection, Journal 30, 28 December 1968.
96. Rowse Collection, Box 35, Cuttings, article in unidentified American newspaper, 1969.
97. Rowse, 1979c, p. 148.
98. McManners, 2000, p. 545.
99. John Morrill, *The Nature of the English Revolution*, London, 1993, p. 260.
100. Stoyle, 2002, p. 4.
101. Ollard, 1999; Richard Ollard (ed.), *The Diaries of A.L. Rowse*, London, 2003.
102. Rowse, 1979a, p. 181.

A CORNISH ASSEMBLY? PROSPECTS FOR DEVOLUTION IN THE DUCHY

Mark Sandford

INTRODUCTION

'Prospects for devolution', as a subject, suffers greatly in the far South-West due to the lack of discussion of devolution crossing the Tamar. On the west side there tends to be an air of defiance—nothing other than a strong devolved assembly for Cornwall should be on anyone's agenda. On the east side, meanwhile, there is often an air of incredulity at the idea. A set of rather predictable objections are trotted out—Cornwall is too small, too nationalist, too poor, too far away.[1] But at the same time there is a very wide gap, both metaphorically and actually, between views of what 'devolution' actually means, and what it implies for the future government of a territory, on either side of the Tamar. So for that reason, in this article I want not just to focus on devolution in the Duchy, but to make some wider comments about the future of devolution in the UK as a whole, and to explain where I see the Cornish question fitting into the development of government policy on devolution as it stands now and as it develops over the next five to ten years.

The territorial issue of Cornwall is different. It is something of an enigma to the current government, because it simply does not fit within the Government's vision of what regional government in 'England' is. There is a strong line drawn, both in the government's thinking and in the reality of legislation, between two policy processes—one called 'devolution', which took place in Scotland, Northern Ireland, and Wales, and one called 'regional government in England'. 'Devolution' saw new, democratically elected institutions superimposed on to territorial offices, which had long been in existence to administer the non-English parts of the Union. The arguments in favour of devolution were far easier to put in territories which have long been recognized as being distinct by the very structure of UK administration. The creation of the Scottish Office in the 1880s was an admission that Scotland was no longer 'North Britain', as it was encouraged to become in the eighteenth century, but a discrete—if not separate—part of the UK's national territory. Thus, proponents of home rule were more easily able to ask: if Scotland has administrative devolution, why not political devolution? It was a demand which became, little by little, impossible to resist.

The fact that administrative offices already existed in Scotland and Wales also meant that the powers of the new democratic institutions created in 1999 were in effect already defined. Proponents were able to avoid being distracted by long and tiring arguments over the exact extent of the power of the Parliament and Assembly.[2] The territorial offices carried out most of the sub-national administration, which proved that all their functions *could* be carried out at the sub-national level: thus there was no real argument for repatriating those functions to the UK government. There can be little doubt that the advancement of the debate by the Scottish Constitutional Convention whilst Labour was in opposition was pivotal, both because the Convention carried out the groundwork and because the Opposition committed to the policy at a time when it owed favours to its supporters. A government that is two years into its second term *ipso facto* does not owe favours in the same way.

Regional government within 'England'—including Cornwall—was an entirely different matter. Although England has long been administered through a group of regions by a wide range of executive agencies, regional offices, and non-departmental public bodies, all of these offices and agencies remained part of England-wide central government departments, and thus were part of the mini-empire of a Cabinet minister (not to mention the fact that most of their boundaries were entirely different from one another).[3] Therefore, establishing any form of regional government within England means chipping away at these mini-empires—in other words, it means turkeys, in the form of Cabinet ministers, voting for Christmas. This is why it has taken five years of the Labour government to put together any proposals at all on English regional government. It also explains why the proposals in the White Paper, *Your Region, Your Choice*, are so weak—an issue discussed further below.

Because of the need to avoid alienating political interests, in the

form of certain Cabinet ministers, the Labour government has con-
tinually promoted regional governance—in the form of the Regional
Development Agencies—on the grounds that regional development is
good for the economy.[4] Regionalism has, as it were, clung on to the
coat-tails of bread-and-butter issues. That link provides the motive
power behind the policy existing: this is why the regional agenda in the
first five years of this government has been limited to the creation of
Regional Development Agencies and the extension of the power and
reach of the Government Offices for the Regions. The nature of the
government's priorities meant that the executive power of regional
agencies came first, and democratic accountability came second.
Democracy was perceived not to add value: if anything, it removed
value.

Secondly, and more importantly, regional development and
regionalism have been part of *national* government policy, not a means
to the devolution, to lower levels, of *political* power to forge distinct
policy paths (which was the case in Scotland and Wales). The flavour of
the White Paper *Your Region, Your Choice* is quite clear in this regard.
There is a clause in the Greater London Authority Act obliging the
Mayor of London to follow strategies that are 'consistent with national
policy'.[5] The fact that regionalism has been part of national policy also
helps to explain why the issue of regional boundaries has been of low
interest to the government. Future elected regions are not perceived as
political entities but as democratically elected administrative ones—
much closer to local than to national government in their character.
If their purpose is efficient administration as opposed to political
pluralism (not to mention recognition of territorial identity), then it
does indeed follow that the precise shape of the regional boundaries is
of only minor significance.

CORNWALL AND LABOUR-ISM
However, there is a deeper sense in which Cornwall does not fit
the government's regional agenda. This is in the nature of Cornish
regionalism, or demands for autonomy, itself. It is instructive to compare Cornwall with the North-East, which has long been considered
the 'vanguard' region in the movement towards English regional
government. The two areas are similar in that they are a long way from
London and fare poorly on economic and social indicators. But their
economic and cultural backgrounds, and histories, are quite different.
Cornwall has a very strong identity based upon its Celtic origins,
surrounding the Cornish language and a variety of distinctive cultural
markers.[6] Its economy has been in decline for over a century, during
which time tin and copper mining have gradually given way entirely to

the traditional occupations of farming and fishing, and tourism has grown enormously. Besides this, there is a strong perceived tradition of Cornish individualism. This is reflected by, amongst other things, a traditionally strong Methodist church and a marked tendency to vote for the third party, the Liberals/Liberal Democrats, in national elections and to vote for Independents at local government level (while most other county councils are dominated by the political parties). There is also a nationalist party of long standing, Mebyon Kernow, which acquitted itself moderately well in the 2003 local elections.

The North-East, meanwhile, has long enjoyed *some form* of territorial identity—principally an occupation-based one revolving around heavy industry on Tyneside and mining-village communalism. Territorial identity of 'the North' generally goes back hundreds of years. Shields refers to literary treatment of it as follows:

> The Northern Working Class [*sic*] is an invention cast as the foreign 'other' of the socially constructed orderliness of the British nation centred around London. Class imagery . . . collapses into spatial imagery[7] . . . A nostalgic discourse of tradition valorises the North as the homeland of a traditional British Working Class [*sic*] and the culture associated with it.[8]

This diffuse identity revolved around the lived reality of heavy industry. Identity related to the large industrial cities, Newcastle/Tyneside, Liverpool/Merseyside, Leeds, Manchester. Stephen Caunce points out that the large cities of the North even now are similar in size and importance, leading, he argues, to a tendency for inhabitants of Manchester to be more familiar with London than with Leeds or Middlesbrough.[9] But a *regional* identity dates from only the last ten years, representing the response of certain individuals on the Left to the powerlessness experienced by industrial England under the Thatcher governments.[10] What has historically characterized the North-East is union activism, voting Labour (and hence exercising some parliamentary power through its bloc of MPs), and recent, large-scale industrial decline. Regional consciousness relates to the Labour movement, working-class communities and heavy industry, rather than any historical preconceptions of the North-East as a distinct entity.

This type of regionalism strikes a far more sympathetic note with the Labour Party and the Labour movement than the regionalism of Cornwall does. It is far less easy for the Labour movement—and indeed Whitehall—to take seriously a very small territory, with a small population, a distinct identity based on a group of ethnic markers (language, cultural distinctiveness, territoriality, and even nationalism), and with an economy characterized by small-scale enterprise, relatively weak unions, and a recent history of small-scale industrial production. My hypothesis is that this distinction feeds into differing attitudes to the two territories within central government. This difference is reflected in attitudes across a swathe of UK society: at an extreme, it is represented by the difference between *Our Friends in the North* and *Wild West*.

The Labour Party and Whitehall have long been able to agree that territorial or sub-national identity, and smallness, are undesirable. Smallness is perceived as the opposite of success in terms of effective trade and business, economic development and political power. Territorial identity runs contrary to long-established strains of internationalism, opposition to nationalism, and support for a strong, redistributing, central state within the Labour movement.[11] These traditional concerns drove the substantial opposition to devolution by much of the Labour Party in the 1970s, and the Attlee government's dismissal of a petition of *one million* signatures calling for a Scottish assembly in the 1940s. These long-established trends explain the tenacity of the frame of mind which prevents a serious analysis of the territorial issue within Cornwall. London-based commentators, officials and politicians have so far had almost nothing to offer but patronizing, belittling and dismissive statements about the Cornish question; perhaps remarks about Cornwall are the last acceptable face of metropolitan prejudice.

At the same time, there are good political reasons why the government does not want to look again at boundary issues. From the perspective of London, and most of England, to see a single county gaining the powers of a regional government is bound to inspire calls for similar treatment for other areas: Cumbria, Lincolnshire, Essex, even Devon. The government would need to take a position, and stick to it, of 'Cornish exceptionalism': in other words, declaring that Cornwall was sufficiently 'different' to warrant such an assembly, and that other counties in the UK were not sufficiently 'different' to follow its lead. This would require a remarkable *volte-face*, of the kind which governments are not known for unless they are subject to considerable political pressure. And the government has not, so far, shown itself to be vulnerable to this pressure.

THE WHITE PAPER

The reaction of most campaigners for regional government to the White Paper *Your Region, Your Choice* has been 'it's not much, but we're delighted to have anything at all'. Certainly in the 'vanguard regions' of the North-East and North-West, this has been the line taken by both the Regional Chambers and the Constitutional Conventions. In the North-East, too, it has been the line taken by most local government leaders, many of whom are Labour and are in favour of regional government by personal and political conviction. The White Paper proposals are viewed as a good starting point—with the implicit hope that the regions will be offered more in a short space of time.[12]

Despite a personal conviction in favour of strong elected regional government, I am very concerned that the government is proposing a form of regional assembly that might turn out to be worse than useless, for three reasons. Firstly, their powers, and their financial and policy freedoms, are incredibly tightly drawn. A comparison can be drawn with the Scotland and Wales devolution acts of the 1970s, which were much criticized at the time for enumerating, at great length, every single power that was to be transferred to the proposed Scottish Assembly [*sic*] and Welsh Assembly. The respective Secretaries of State were also to be permitted fairly wide veto powers over the legislation and policy of those bodies. This very controlling approach was a major factor in support for the assemblies being lost—both because of the electorate's distrust of the intentions of central government and because of the potential for disputes between UK government and national assembly.

By contrast with the current devolved bodies in Scotland and Wales, the proposed regional assemblies in England will be subject to considerable reserve powers of the Secretary of State to change policies or strategy intentions that the government does not like. (This is not to mention the fact that they will be responsible for only some 3 per cent of public expenditure in their region.) One of the reasons for the success of devolution in Scotland and Wales has been that Westminster has not interfered at all with the policy directions taken in any of the three devolved institutions.[13] The government practising non-interference has been vital for the legitimacy of those institutions to take root—surveys repeatedly show that the Scots and Welsh have become more in favour of devolution since it took place, even though there is no great love for the politicians who run the Parliament and Assembly.[14]

The government's White Paper is full of radical rhetoric on the need for regional assemblies to take a lead role in improving life chances and economic circumstances within their region. The rhetoric is strangely at odds with the actual powers and budgets on offer. The White Paper claims that the regional assembly can exercise control on a wide range of policies by writing strategies:

- Regional Economic Development Strategy
- Regional Spatial Strategy (replacing RPG)
- Regional Transport Strategy
- Regional Cultural Strategy
- Sustainable Development Framework
- Regional Housing Strategy
- Regional Waste Strategy
- Framework for Employment and Skills Action
- Health Improvement Strategy
- Biodiversity Strategy[15]

Though the jury remains out both on how strategies actually work and on whether they work, in London the strategic planning powers of the Mayor have failed to have any appreciable effect so far. Instead, the parts of the Greater London Authority which have seen changes since the Mayor's election in 2000 are the parts over which he has direct executive control: buses and fireworks.[16]

Second is the issue of public support for the proposed regional assemblies. At the present time it seems quite possible that a referendum will take place in mid-2004 on whether to establish a regional assembly in the North-East, and possibly in the North-West. At that time the electorate in those regions will be faced with a proposed reorganization of local government into unitary authorities. In a full public debate, the government will face an uphill struggle to convince the electorate that the powers of a Regional Development Agency, a hotch-potch of funding for housing provision, the regional tourist board, public health and the right to chair the committee monitoring EU Structural Fund expenditure constitutes a package of powers which will make any difference to anyone's life.

If and when a proper public debate develops in the North-East and the North-West, the limitations of the proposals will become increasingly clear. Apart from the very limited powers, and the need for costly and no doubt rancorous reorganization of two-tier local government areas, assemblies will have to agree 'six to ten high-level targets' with the government—effectively a public service agreement. In short, they will have very little room for manoeuvre. There has to be a strong likelihood that the electorate of the North-East will reject the proposals—much as the electorate of Wales did in 1978. In both cases there was interest in some form of devolution, but not the kind offered. A lost referendum in the vanguard region will kill the policy stone dead for a generation.

Thirdly, for all of the reasons above, there is merit in the claims of those who oppose regional government *per se* that the regional assemblies *proposed by the government* are an extra layer of bureaucracy which will add no appreciable value.[17] Regional assemblies will consist of a new army of strategy-writers—far more costly and potentially wasteful than an extra layer of elected politicians —who will need to be kept informed and consulted about any new initiatives in the region. There will be almost no reduction in the huge number of quangos and executive agencies which currently spend public money in and for the regions in a totally unaccountable fashion. The Greater London Authority was expected to need about 250 staff: it has just reached 600.[18] And most of its work is producing strategies and research reports. As a university researcher, I will be the last person to decry spending money on research, but it is not necessary to elect a regional assembly for that purpose.

Regional assemblies should be taking over the executive powers that already exist in the regions. They can achieve more, and become more valuable, the more powers they have. A new regional structure with merely 'influencing' and 'strategic' powers will achieve nothing significant except to revive the Labour Party's reputation for creating bureaucracy. Unless the government revisits the powers in the White Paper, my feeling is that the policy will fail—whether or not referendums are won.

A CORNISH ASSEMBLY IN THE STRANGE WORLD OF REGIONALISM

How do the prospects for a Cornish Assembly fit into this wobbly, waffly regional policy? In 2002 I was commissioned to produce a report fleshing out three models for regional devolution in the standard South-West region.[19] Model number 2 envisioned a six-county South-West regional assembly alongside, and distinct from, a Cornish Assembly. The report was very much the first word on the issue and not the last: it did not explore complex issues about exactly how government by either of those institutions would take place. But it found that there were no insurmountable obstacles to a Cornish Assembly being brought into existence under the policy as set out in the White Paper.

This sounds like significantly positive news for those in favour of a Cornish Assembly. But that statement should immediately be qualified. There are a number of unanswered questions about such an assembly, and disincentives against the government creating one.

Firstly, in the case of Cornwall, the thinness of the powers on offer to elected assemblies is a particular problem. On the basis of current budgets, the report estimates that a Cornish Assembly under this model would have a regular budget of approximately £40 million.[20] To this would be added any remaining Objective 1 funds—but in the long term this model of assembly will have a very small budget. Although, proportionately, this will be an equivalent level of funding to any other regional assemblies that are set up, there is an additional issue of *scale*. With such a small *amount* of money it will be very difficult to make a significant impact on any policy at all. The sum of £40 million would be a useful addition to the existing funds available to Cornish government, but this does not constitute a reason for creating a new body to administer it. Local government in Cornwall administers something like £440 million today: how far could an Assembly influence other (supposedly subordinate) levels of government that spend ten times the amount that it does?

Secondly, staff would have to be relocated to Truro from a variety of locations such as Exeter and Bristol. This would cost time and money and would interrupt the various agencies that are the subjects of this transfer from doing their jobs. It is hard to gauge how much of a problem this would be, but it will be a disincentive to the government considering the policy. The issue of scale may also be a problem for staffing: if very small numbers of staff are to be transferred to a Cornish Assembly, will extra staff—meaning a proportionately higher administrative cost—have to be hired? These are real and not rhetorical questions. They have not yet been answered, because the Cornish question has so far been ignored instead of challenged by government. But they do need to be answered. It is not sufficient to point to the fact that smaller regions and states than Cornwall exist in Europe and to ask how they manage. The answer might be 'very badly'; some of these very small places may have very poor public services or be ill-equipped to deal with serious policy challenges (Iceland, for instance, is notorious for copying new policies from the larger Scandinavian countries).

FUNCTIONS OF THE CORNISH ASSEMBLY
First and foremost, the Cornish Assembly would chair the committee which would allocate Objective 1 funding. It would appoint a board to a Cornish Development Agency, which would take over the functions of the South-West Regional Development Agency as exercised in Cornwall. It would draw up Regional Planning Guidance for Cornwall. It would allocate some funds for public and housing association housing in Cornwall, a job that is currently done by the Government Office for the South-West in Bristol and the Housing Corporation in Exeter. It would take over a regional tourist board for Cornwall, possibly also the functions of the Arts Council, and certain English Heritage functions. It would most likely take on the responsibility for

the Cornish language following its designation in 2002, a function which obviously has no counterpart elsewhere in 'England'.

It would also have the responsibility to write the ten strategies listed earlier. This is a factor where Cornwall's small scale may be an advantage. There would be one assembly and a very small number of local authorities. Other regions will have at least fifteen local authorities with diverse interests, with whom they will have to negotiate strategies. A Cornish Assembly would have only three or four local authorities within its territory. This would make negotiation much easier, purely because of the ease of getting all of the relevant people in one room. This sounds like a banal point, but it is inevitable that partnership is easier when there are fewer partners—politics is no exception to this rule.

The government has stated that a unitary local government structure must exist under any elected regional assemblies.[21] It would be irrational to create a unitary authority covering all of Cornwall: this would lead to two political assemblies covering the same area. And current wisdom states that unitary authorities must have populations of 100,000 or more, ruling out a structure based on the six district councils.[22] It seems likely that the existing districts would be merged, either into two or three unitary authorities. As the current pattern of local strategic partnerships and Primary Care Trusts matches that of three unitary authorities, this pattern is the most obvious choice. The Scilly Isles, meanwhile, would surely be maintained in their current, unique position.

PROSPECTS FOR A CORNISH ASSEMBLY

This model of a Cornish Assembly is not available under the Regional Assemblies (Preparations) Bill that is being speedily passed through Parliament. Clause 26 of the Bill states that 'a region is a region (except London) as defined in the Regional Development Agencies Act 1998'.[23] That Act defines the current, standard boundaries of the regions. It specifies that the Secretary of State can make an order changing regional boundaries, but that he or she may not make an order creating a larger number of regions overall than already exist. Therefore, unless an amendment is added to the current Bill, permitting a greater number of regions than currently exists, this Bill closes the door (at least for the time being) on a Cornish Assembly.

It is possible that that amendment could be added to the second Regional Assemblies Bill. This will be passed after the first referendums, and will set out the powers, functions and structures of the assemblies.[24] The present shape of policy makes this unlikely.

A GOVERNMENT OF CORNWALL BILL?

However, there is a possible alternative to both of these tricky situations. This is to pilot through Parliament a Government of Cornwall Bill, to deal singly and solely with creating a Cornish Assembly. I want to stress that this suggestion is mine, and not that of the Cornish Constitutional Convention, which is leading the campaign for a Cornish Assembly. There are sound political reasons for the Convention not to suggest such a move: as the political scene stands, it is valuable for the Convention to make common cause with other regions rather than to pursue a path of 'Cornish exceptionalism'. If the Cornish Constitutional Convention is seen to want to design an entirely different road to regional government from the one that exists currently, this could imply that campaigners for regionalism in Cornwall are not able or willing to be serious political players—that they want simply to go their own way without reference to realities.

Yet there are many reasons why a Government of Cornwall Bill could prove an attractive proposition. Firstly, it would solve the issue referred to earlier, of a Cornish Assembly setting a precedent for every other county in 'England'. A separate Bill for Cornwall would implicitly classify Cornwall as a 'special case' region, accompanied by descriptions (or, for the less charitable, rhetoric) of its cultural and ethnic distinctiveness. This would remove Cornwall from the confines of the English regional debate—and, given the drawbacks of that debate as described above, that could be a considerable advantage.

Secondly, this Bill would be able to ensure that local government reform took place in an appropriate manner for Cornwall. Either a small number of unitary authorities could be created, or a more radical alternative involving readjustment of the division of functions between local and regional authorities could be considered.[25] This Bill would also enable the Cornish Assembly to be elected by the Single Transferable Vote mechanism,[26] instead of the Additional Member System proposed by the government—if the electorate were amenable. This alternative relates to the distinctive political preferences expressed in Cornish elections.

Thirdly, this Bill could potentially bypass the problem referred to above, of a White Paper-model Cornish Assembly having very few powers and a very thin budget. The existence of a Government of Cornwall Bill would enable the debate over powers to be reopened. Somewhat paradoxically, in light of the common claims that Cornwall is too small to do certain things, the smallness of the powers and budget of a White Paper-model Assembly leads to a case for more powers rather than fewer to a Cornish Assembly. There is an implicit link between this idea and the 'devolution settlement' in Scotland and Wales: a bespoke devolution Bill, in recognition of cultural distinctiveness and economic underperformance, and the need for a strong portfolio of devolved powers to address aspirations in both areas.

So, for instance, a Government of Cornwall Bill could legislate for the 'repatriation' of services and powers that have for some time been run on a Devon-and-Cornwall basis: the ambulance and police services, the Learning and Skills Council, and the Small Business Service. There is no *prima facie* reason why these services should be run from outside Cornwall. Cumbria, with the same population and similar issues of remoteness to those of Cornwall, has its own police and ambulance services, its own Learning and Skills Council, and its own division of Business Link.

Secondly, in the long term it ought to become feasible to channel funding for the Combined Universities of Cornwall through a Cornish Assembly, much as funding for the federal University of Wales (and University of Glamorgan) is channelled through the Higher Education Funding Council for Wales. With a co-ordinated steer from the Cornish Assembly, synergies should be possible with the rest of the Objective 1 programme.

Thirdly, the wide range of quangos which were left out of the proposals in the White Paper could be reviewed for the Government of Cornwall Bill. For instance, the three trunk roads in Cornwall that are currently looked after by the Highways Agency could be handled by a Cornish highways authority. The various grant-giving functions currently exercised within the Government Office South-West, based in Bristol but with a branch office in Truro, could be transferred to the Cornish Assembly. Bodmin's Environment Agency office, the Countryside Agency and English Nature are other candidates. The newly created organizations Creative Kernow and Heritage Kernow could become what are known in Wales as Assembly Sponsored Public Bodies, distributing funding to a range of creative, heritage and language organizations. They would, however, be accountable to democratically elected representatives and there would be a clear, overarching strategic plan determining their decisions. A radical Bill might also channel funding for local government and the National Health Service through the Assembly.[27]

Such a range of functions would bring this model of a Cornish Assembly close to the range available to the National Assembly for Wales, and would bring its budget up towards £1 billion or more. This is a much more exciting vision (assuming that the electorate in Cornwall were to elect people who spent that money wisely). This represents a far greater degree of control in Cornwall, of Cornwall, by

Cornwall. And it would not be dependent upon progress in English regions to make it happen.

As things stand, the government does not appear to be interested in such a proposition. Although the proposed redrawing of parliamentary boundaries may cause Labour some difficulties locally, the government does not lose many votes in Cornwall, and hence does not lose much sleep over its constitutional demands. There are no readily apparent levers of power available to campaigners for a Cornish Assembly to force the government to listen to their demands. Despite best intentions, most governments ignore those who have no power.

THE WIDER PERSPECTIVE
It was the intention to situate this article in the wider purpose of regionalism: something which is hard to visualize through technical debates over the minutiae of functions. It is very tempting for in-terested parties simply to view regional government as a game of administrative musical chairs—take this and that from Whitehall and give it to the regional government, add in three executive agencies, two quangos and stir. Regionalism has to be about more than this if it is to do what it has failed to do so far: impact on people's lives.

Although their definitions are hazy, 'devolution' and 'regional government' differ conceptually from what we know as 'local govern-ment'. The great advantage of regional government and devolution in the UK is that it is a greenfield site—it presents us with a chance to create a new and very different kind of government. (This is a good reason to be patient about its establishment.) After all, if regionalism is simply viewed as a management reorganization of existing functions, this will simply lead to another set of advocates in 25 years' time telling us that there is yet another type of government reorganization whose time has come and which we all ought to embrace as the future, because you can't stop progress, and that you surely must appreciate the sublime methods by which this new reorganization redraws boundaries.

To have a discernible effect on people's lives, regional government needs to become more than an administrative fad. It needs to become outward-looking, towards its electorate, not focused purely upon how best it can administer a bag of 'functions'. This means that an Assembly needs to do two things. Firstly, it needs to have the means and the inclination to go beyond keeping its allocated administrative functions moving. It needs to think through new ways of solving problems, looking at new ways in which government can help to improve the quality of life. In London, for instance, the GLA could add considerable value through co-ordinating the improvement of London's infrastructure. But it hasn't the means and it hasn't the power—which leads to a loss of public interest and a conviction that governments are a waste of time, except for when they make things worse.

The second priority for regional governments—linked to the first—is to draw in their electorates. This is the real meaning of 'partnership'—to give a sense that the regional government is not just there to get in the way, or to produce documents, but to improve people's lives. It is possible that Cornwall will have advantages here. Territories with strong identities can often make use of 'motivational resources', which essentially means in this case that people are prepared to go the extra mile for the sake of making a good life in Cornwall. And there is the advantage of small scale. In Cornwall, there are never going to be many people involved in government. Michael Keating has suggested, in *Nations Against the State*, that:

> Small nations and regions may have some advantages in coping with and adapting quickly to a changing external environment, given certain characteristics. One is a small decision-making elite, with a high degree of interaction and mutual trust. Another is a capacity for creating social capital and solving collective action problems to produce positive sum outcomes.[28]

In short, a regional assembly needs to be able to inspire people to all pull in the same direction. To succeed, it has not merely to take over a series of decisions that already are being made, but to make them differently: to answer the question 'Cornish boys are fishermen and Cornish boys are miners too, but now the fish and tin are gone, what are Cornish boys—and girls—to do?'.

This aspiration can and should link Cornwall to the other nations and regions of the United Kingdom. This aspiration—to do things differently under strong regions, to use them as a greenfield site for a new form of governance—is too rarely used as part of the case in favour of regional government. This possibility, whether it occurs under a strong regional government or a weak one, is the best argument for devolution, whether in the Duchy or elsewhere.

NOTES AND REFERENCES

1. See, for instance, DTLR/Cabinet Office, *Your Region, Your Choice*, 2002, p. 48; County Labour Party of Cornwall press release, November 2001; Jonathan Wallace, *Devolution by Evolution*, Centre for Reform no. 25,

2001; see also Stephen Tindale, *Devolution on Demand: Options for the English Regions and London*, London, 1996, for two paragraphs favourable to the Cornish case (pp. 16–17) which were omitted from the final version of the paper in Stephen Tindale (ed.), *The State and The Nations: The Politics of Devolution*, London, 1996.

2. See Scottish Constitutional Convention, *Scotland's Parliament, Scotland's Right*, Edinburgh, 1995; Graham Leicester, *Scotland's Parliament: Fundamentals of a New Scotland Act*, London, 1995.

3. See Brian Hogwood, *Mapping the Regions: Boundaries, Co-ordination and Government*, York, 1995, for a description of the heterogeneity of English regional boundaries, which has become markedly out of date in the last eight years; David Marquand and John Tomaney, *Democratising England*, London, 2000; Mark Sandford and Paul McQuail, *Unexplored Territory: Elected Regional Assemblies in England*, London, 2001, pp. 26–31; John Tomaney and Peter Hetherington, *Monitoring the English Regions*, London, November 2001, p. 6 (quote of Stephen Byers MP); Performance and Innovation Unit, *Reaching Out*, London, 2000.

4. See Gordon Brown's speech at Manchester University on 29 January 2001, quoted in John Tomaney, 'Reshaping the English Regions', in Alan Trench (ed.), *The State of the Nations 2001*, Thorverton, 2001, p. 109, as one of the best-known examples of this trend.

5. Greater London Authority Act 1999, s41 (5) (a). One can reasonably expect a similar clause in the Bill to set up English regional assemblies.

6. See Mark Stoyle, *West Britons: Cornish Identities and the Early Modern British State* Exeter, 2002; Philip Payton, *The Making of Modern Cornwall: Historical Experience and the Persistence of Difference*, Truro, 1992; Philip Payton, *A Vision of Cornwall*, Fowey, 2002.

7. Rob Shields, *Places on the Margin*, London, 1991, p. 218.

8. Shields, 1991, p. 229.

9. Stephen Caunce, 'Urban Systems, Identity and Development in Lancashire and Yorkshire: A Complex Question', in Neville Kirk (ed.), *Northern Identities*, Aldershot, 2000.

10. It is likely that the use that the Thatcher and Major governments made of the UK's highly centralized polity explains the relatively uncommon pattern within the UK of the Left being broadly supportive of regional government and the Right being strongly opposed. Typically regional powers have been strengthened by the Right in countries such as France and Italy; the USA's 'New Federalism' came under Ronald Reagan.

11. For a similar argument, see Chris Lanigan, 'Region-Building in the North-East: Regional Identity and Regionalist Politics', in John Tomaney and Neil Ward (eds), *A Region in Transition: North East England at the Millennium*, Aldershot, 2001: for an up-to-date version of this view, see David Walker, 'Why Inequality Will Scupper Regional Government', *Guardian*, 9 May 2002.

12. There is, however, a strong view that the current proposals should be strengthened: see for instance John Adams and John Tomaney, *Restoring the Balance: Strengthening the Government's Proposals for Regional*

Assemblies, London, 2002, from two advocates and campaigners. See also Mark Sandford, *A Commentary on the Regional Government White Paper*, London, 2002.

13. Despite the Alun Michael affair in Wales, which was consistently (and rightly) excoriated at the time as an attempt to impose central control on a new democratic body, actual interference in Scottish and Welsh *policy* by Westminster has been negligible. Whether this would still be true when different parties are in government in either place remains to be seen. The omens are good at present: when one considers the amount of policy divergence that has taken place, and the UK Labour government's reputation for centralism, it is commendable that the UK government has not been tempted to interfere.

14. Electoral Commission, *Wales Votes? Public Attitudes Towards Assembly Elections*, London, 2002. This study shows that despite political apathy the institution is still perceived as important in Wales: support for greater powers has grown since 1999.

15. DTLR/Cabinet Office, 2002, p. 36

16. Scott Greer and Mark Sandford, *Fixing London*, London, 2003, pp. 16-17.

17. This includes the Conservative Party, UK Independence Party, and much of the national press: for instance, Peter Riddell, 'Political Patchwork is No Comfort for Town Halls', *The Times*, 10 May 2002; Simon Jenkins, 'Save the Counties, Not Compass-Point Regions', *The Times*, 10 May 2002; the *Daily Telegraph* leader column, 'Scotland's Sorry Precedent', 10 May 2002.

18. A consultancy report, John O'Brien, Peter Wallace and Jeroen Weimar, *The Greater London Authority: Organisational Structure*, London, 1999, gives the figure of 250.

19. Mark Sandford, *The Cornish Question: Devolution in the South-West Region*, London, 2002.

20. There are several assumptions built into this figure: it assumes a Cornish Assembly taking 10 per cent of current South-West Region budgets (except for that of SWRDA, 20 per cent of whose money is spent in Cornwall), and assumes no change in current funding formulas for the English regions. It is possible that Cornwall's social and economic statistics would justify a higher level of funding.

21. DTLR/Cabinet Office, 2002, pp. 65–6.

22. This current wisdom is rarely committed to paper, but can be roughly deduced from the results of the review of local government during the 1990s.

23. Regional Assemblies (Preparations) Bill 2003.

24. The author has heard reports of off-the-record discussions indicating that, if boundaries were to be changed, the second Bill would be the preferred opportunity. This would accord with the government's priority of getting at least one assembly up and running before the next general election.

25. Early papers produced by the Cornish Constitutional Convention indicated support for a far more decentralized form of local government. Cornwall has no major cities, containing some 12–15 towns of

15,000–25,000 people. Interviews conducted by the author indicated some disaffection with the current district councils, which cover 2–4 of these towns each and thus encourage intra-district rivalry. Under a Government of Cornwall Bill it might be possible to create far smaller units of local government (as exist in Northern Ireland, which has 26 district councils for 1.6 million people, with a smaller range of powers than English local government).

26. See the paper on 'Electoral Arrangements' by the Cornish Constitutional Convention, at www.senedhkernow.freeuk.com/otherdocuments.html.

27. It would also be possible for a Government of Cornwall Bill to address the issues of Cornish constitutionalism, defended by the unilaterally re-formed Cornish Stannary Parliament amongst others. Several ancient royal charters give support to the concept that Cornwall was and possibly is constitutionally distinct from the rest of 'England' through the existence of the Duchy. None of these have been recognized by current administrative arrangements, and British law at present might be able to sidestep a direct challenge on these issues, as it does not recognize the idea of inalienable laws and has a very foggy relationship with the Queen and the Duke of Cornwall (as witnessed by the Paul Burrell trial of late 2002). It would be a brave government which addressed these issues.

28. Michael Keating, *Nations against the State: The New Politics of Nationalism in Quebec, Catalonia and Scotland*, Basingstoke, 2001, p. 67.

CORNWALL'S NEWSPAPER WAR: THE POLITICAL RIVALRY BETWEEN THE *ROYAL CORNWALL GAZETTE* AND THE *WEST BRITON* PART TWO 1832–1855

Brian Elvins

INTRODUCTION

In the 21 years of rivalry between the *Royal Cornwall Gazette* and the *West Briton* after 1810, it had been the latter which had challenged the pre-eminent position of the *Gazette*. After 1831, the roles were reversed, the *Gazette* seeking to recover the ground which by that time it had so clearly lost. In one respect it is easier to investigate the rivalry because of the availability, for the first time, of the number of official government stamps issued to the two papers.[1] Donald Reed, in his excellent study of newspapers and public opinion in the North of England, has given a cautionary note on the Stamp Tax Returns. He emphasizes that 'before 1836 they cannot be generally relied upon as the number of stamps credited to each newspaper depended on arbitrary assessments made by paper agents. In 1836 each paper was given a distinctive die and thereafter the stamp returns can be taken as an approximate guide to newspaper sales.'[2] For comparative purposes, however, they provide an effective guide to the relative position of the two Cornish papers. The figures, as shown in the appendix, provide stark evidence of the difficulty facing the *Gazette*, owned since 1819 by Thomas Richard Gillet Jnr and edited by his father, Thomas Gillet Senior.

The year's total of 27,000 for 1831 even declined in the following

years. By contrast the *West Briton* showed an increase to 52,200 by
1833. In round figures, therefore, the *Gazette*'s circulation was only half
that of the *West Briton*'s 1,000 a week.

As far as one can tell, the first mention of any figures in the papers
themselves was not until August 1833. The *West Briton* printed an
extract of a Parliamentary Return 'An Account of Stamps issued to
each provincial newspaper in England in the year ending 1 April 1833',
quoting correctly the two papers' figures. The *Gazette*, perhaps quite
naturally, does not appear to have referred to them at all. The Return
also indicated that the *West Briton* had a substantial lead in the number
of advertisements in the year—1,679 as opposed to 1,305 in the
Gazette. In terms of advertising revenue, however, the latter did not lag
too far behind. In the calendar year of 1832, the amount of duty (3s 6d
for each advert) paid by the *Gazette* was £228 7s 6d, that by the *West
Briton* £293 16s 6d. It was revenue from advertisements that kept the
Gazette in business, for its circulation dropped in 1834 to 18,000 or only
350 a week.[3] It is necessary, therefore, to examine the tactics it pursued
in its efforts at recovery and to judge how successful they were,
especially when the political climate favoured the Conservatives. How
did the *West Briton* respond to the challenge? Did factors other than
political, such as religious allegiance, play a role in deciding the out-
come and what was the significance of the *West Briton*'s triumph for
Cornish politics?

'THE INSTITUTIONS OF THE COUNTRY WOULD BE SUBVERTED'

There could certainly be no boasts by the *Gazette*, in the post 1832-
period, of its superiority, as in the past. It even admitted that 'we are at
present on the losing side'. Instead it concentrated on the general
political position and on the situation in the two new county divisions
of East and West Cornwall as a way of attacking the *West Briton* and
hopefully weakening its support in Cornwall. Essentially it staked its
hopes of recovery more than anything else on an improvement in the
fortunes of the Conservatives nationally. The two alarms which it
sounded were that following the Reform Act 'the institutions of the
country would be subverted' and also that 'the Liberals will move
heaven and earth to send to Parliament men pledged to the total
abolition of the Corn Laws'.[4]

Specific legislation of the Whig government also came in for
criticism. The proposal to abolish slavery in the British Empire would
'inflict great evil on the West Indian proprietors . . . and do no good to
the slaves'. It attacked the proposed Church reforms but most of all it
found a fruitful field for criticism in the Poor Law Amendment Bill.

After first stating that 'we do not see that there is much to object to in the measure', the *Gazette*'s editor reacted to the growing public hostility that the measure aroused, by swinging round to opposition. The paper objected to the diminution of local control in favour of increased centralization and to the new workhouse system which 'is made up of cruelty and oppression towards those on whom poverty has already laid her heavy hand'.[5] On the question of tithe reform, though it was extremely cautious, torn between concern for the Church of England and the knowledge that many Cornish farmers felt it was a matter demanding urgent reform.[6]

As regards the Cornish electoral scene, the *Gazette* was aghast at the prospect of all four county seats being occupied by what it termed 'Whig-Radicals'. Denouncing it as 'outrageous and contrary to all ideas of common justice', it accused them 'of attempting to ride roughshod over Cornwall' and alleged that the Liberals in the two divisions were plotting together to deprive the Conservatives of their fair share in the representation: 'Supposing the Tories are in a minority in Cornwall why should they be unrepresented? Their bitterest opponents must allow that they are more than one quarter of the electors of Cornwall.'[7] It hoped desperately that Ld Valletort, the son of Earl Mt Edgcumbe, and Sir Richard Vyvyan, the former Tory county MP 1826–30, would come forward to contest, respectively, the East and West Cornwall divisions. Continuing its animosity against Edward Pendarves for his part in the original foundation of the *West Briton*, the *Gazette* made him its main target, standing as he was for re-election in the West division. He was subjected to a long hostile attack in September 1832, as an MP 'without influence in Parliament beyond his own vote, yet he has managed to persuade the Whigs and Lord Grey that he is a person of tremendous consequence in Cornwall'. Equally such supporters as the Davey and Williams families—'the mining agents and speculators of Redruth and Gwennap'—were accused of unfair electoral tactics: 'They play the part of petty tyrants and threaten the dependent miner with dismissal and the small shopkeeper of a cessation of custom if they suspect them of leaning to the side of the landed interest'.[8]

After all four Liberal candidates—Pendarves, Sir Charles Lemon, Sir William Molesworth and William Trelawny—had been returned unopposed in December, the *Gazette* gave prominence to any of their subsequent votes in Parliament which, it felt, might be unpopular in Cornwall. Highlighting the fact that Molesworth was the only one of the four to vote for the abolition of the Corn Laws, it concluded 'the farmers [of East Cornwall] will notice it'. Likewise on another agricultural issue—the defeat of a motion for the abolition of the Malt Tax—it remarked 'Let the East Cornwall farmers enquire what part their representative—Sir W Molesworth—took in these divisions and also Mr Pendarves'. In June 1834, too, it emphasized that Molesworth and his colleague Trelawny 'voted in favour of the motion for the spoliation of the Irish Church'.[9]

By the summer of 1834, the *Gazette* was convinced that its tactics had been successful: 'The people of Cornwall are an unsophisticated people and many of them who voted for Radical Reform at the last election are now firmly convinced that they should have given their support to upright Conservative characters'. When an election was called in the autumn, the paper had hopes that the Conservatives would gain a seat in the West division through Lord Boscawen Rose, the only son of Earl Falmouth. Inevitably it concentrated its attack upon Pendarves: 'He appears in Parliament for himself alone; all is subordinated to that original design of advancing his own greatness'.[10] The *Gazette*'s disappointment, therefore, was great when Boscawen Rose, after an initial canvass, decided to retire before the election. This feeling was made worse by the unopposed return of Molesworth and Trelawny in East Cornwall, following the refusal of John Tremayne—a former county MP 1806–26—to stand against them. Only Lemon of the four MPs was exempt from the paper's strictures. In April 1835, it commented favourably on his vote against a Whig motion for appropriation of the Irish Church's properties: 'We held it to be impossible that Sir C Lemon should be the ally of the 40 Catholics who gave this majority to Lord John Russell'. As for the others who voted in favour, it added: 'With Mr Pendarves all questions have a common insignificance but as they bear on the all important circumstance of his friends regaining office. As to Sir W Molesworth, he is far too refined to adopt a creed while Sir W Trelawny merely exhibited an amiable regard for the closing faith of his father.'[11]

Less than a week after this editorial, the *Gazette* suffered a severe setback with the sudden death, on 15 April 1835, of Thomas Gillet Jnr, its proprietor. Gillet, who was only 39, died at Wells in Somerset, collapsing after getting out of the mail coach and walking with other passengers up the steep hill leading out of the city. According to the report, he suffered 'an attack of asthma . . . and instantly expired'. The tragedy was that he was on his way to London to complete plans for improving the paper by increasing its size.[12]

SUPPORTING THE WHIGS?

The challenge for Edward Budd, the *West Briton*'s editor since 1810, was less daunting than that which faced the *Gazette*'s editor, but it was nevertheless a stiff one. First and foremost he had to maintain the lead which the paper had attained over its rival. All the statistical evidence indicates he was successful in so doing. We have already referred to the figures for 1831 to 1833, while the last year of Budd's editorship in 1835 saw an increase to a new high of 56,000. With advertisements—the lifeblood of any paper—also showing a substantial lead over the *Gazette*, the *West Briton* could be increased in size without any change in the 7d price. The original size in 1810 had been 20 x 15 inches. In January 1832 it announced an increase to 23 x 15, later modified to 22 x 16.[13] In July 1835 it instituted a further increase to 24 x 18 on the grounds that 'being placed in point of circulation and advertisements at the head of the periodical press in Cornwall, the necessity of enlarging our paper has for some time been a subject of serious consideration . . . the demands of our subscribers left us no alternative'. It hotly denied that it had been forced into the move by any plans of Gillet to increase the size of the *Gazette*. While accepting that 'our contemporary is very naturally desirous of improving his paper in order if possible to increase his circulation', it made the startling statement that 'the *West Briton* and the *Cornwall Gazette* have long ceased to be rivals. We each have a distinct line of politics, supported by perfectly distinct parties and we are very far from wishing it should be otherwise.'[14] While one can understand what Budd meant, the essential fact remained that the papers were still the rivals they had been since 1810 for readers and their political loyalty.

Although parliamentary reform—the *West Briton*'s original *raison d'être*—had been achieved in 1832, Budd maintained the paper's political position. In his words, 'Unless the abuses of the corrupt system which have so long cursed this country be rectified, the privilege granted by the Reform Act will be worthless'. It was still a paper campaigning for political reform, Budd remaining committed, for example, to triennial parliaments. In addition, as early as the spring of 1833, he dropped his long-standing objection to voting by ballot: 'If it would ensure secrecy it must afford protection to those who require it. If it would not . . . it may be safely conceded to the popular wish as a very harmless matter.' In the same spirit, he strongly supported the need to reform the borough corporations. The paper provided detailed coverage over four successive weeks of the investigations of the Municipal Corporation Commission into such Cornish boroughs as Liskeard, Looe, Truro, Lostwithiel and Bodmin, concluding that 'It is utterly impossible that under a Reformed Parliament, Corporate Bodies should continue to exist under their present footing'.[15]

The paper equally gave prominence in its columns to demands for a whole range of other reforms. These included the abolition of slavery, tithe reform, reform of the Irish Church, reform of the poor law system, Church reform and the removal of the grievances of the

Dissenters such as the right of admission into universities and the abolition of church rates. It maintained that 'to the principle of each, no reasonable objection can be made'. It was equally strenuous in its demand for retrenchment by government: 'The Reform Bill is merely the means of accomplishing an end—that end is good and cheap government', and subsequently demanding that the Whig government must go further with their reductions 'or they by no means meet the expectations of the people'. As Donald Read has reflected in his study of the North of England papers, the difficulty here is to decide whether the *West Briton* was merely following the public in these demands or whether, as had been the case with parliamentary reform after 1810, it was actually creating public opinion. The number of reported meetings and petitions drawn up on these matters suggest the first. However, the very prominence given to them in the paper indicates that the *West Briton* still felt it had a major role to play in moulding the views of its Cornish readers.[16]

It was probably its awareness of public expectation that influenced the paper's attitude to the new Whig government, an attitude that may be described as one of qualified support: 'Should it appear that Grey and his colleagues are about to disappoint the just hopes of the Country, we shall be unreserved in our censure'. In subsequent editorials it pleaded with those readers disappointed with the slow pace of reform to give ministers more time, while equally contending that the government must no longer attempt to conciliate the Tory peers in the Lords. When Melbourne replaced Grey as Prime Minister, it declared that the government 'must adopt a more decided course and propose and carry through such measures as will satisfy the just expectations of the People, leaving it to the Peers to reject or adopt them', even hinting at the need for measures against the House of Lords.[17]

Knowing how crucial the support of the Cornish farmers had been to the election triumphs of the Reformers in 1826 and 1831, Budd was very concerned to reassure them over the Corn Laws. In particular, he felt it important to counter the *Gazette*'s claim (4 August 1832) that they were under threat. In long editorials over the following two weeks, he argued that 'the only alteration desired by the Reformers of this County at least' was the substitution of a fixed duty for the 1828 sliding scale. 'The agriculturists' true interest is to obtain a fixed duty proportioned to the average difference between the cost of cultivation here and on the Continent; that being the full amount of protection, which in a manufacturing country like this, can possibly be obtained by agriculture, the prosperity of which depends on that demand for its products which a prosperous manufacturing population will supply.'

More editorials on the same lines followed in the autumn and in the following year.[18]

Budd was equally aware of the strong feelings among farmers for the abolition or commutation of tithes, for there were certainly more meetings on this issue in Cornwall than any other. He provided full coverage in the paper and devoted many editorials to the matter.[19] Although appearing to side with the tithe owners—'a demand for total extinction cannot be a claim of right'—the paper's sympathies were with those demanding reform. It declared that 'the wisest thing the Tithe owners can do is to consent to terms of a fair and liberal character as shall disarm the hostility of the great bulk of the Tithe payers who belong to a class that are always unwilling to push matters to extremities'. It also felt that the question could not be separated from that of Church reform, expressing support for the view that 'Dissenters should not have to pay tithes to keep up a different church'.[20]

A LIBERAL STRONGHOLD?

Budd's other concern was to help ensure Cornwall became a Liberal stronghold. The potential for achieving this had been evident for some time and had been demonstrated in 1831 when the Reform candidates Pendarves and Lemon had easily won both county seats in a four-cornered contest with the Tories. Budd was anxious to continue the momentum into the post Reform Act period. When it appeared that no contest would occur in East Cornwall in 1832, with the seats being shared between the two parties, he gave the paper's support to moves to find a second candidate: 'If the great body of Reformers in the East division are resolved to return two Reformers, the means are in their own power'. He gave access to correspondents as well as providing full reports of different meetings on the matter. How far all this had been arranged with party leaders is impossible to tell but the result was that one of the original members of the Reform group, Trelawny, agreed to stand, if assisted financially by the voters. The paper urged the formation of district committees to ensure that potential voters were registered under the new procedures and had paid the requisite 1s fee. It repeatedly provided information on the registration process and the progress of the Liberal candidates in both divisions. It covered Trelawny's campaign in great detail and equally alerted readers in West Cornwall to a possible Tory challenge from Vyvyan. When it became known that he was standing for Bristol and there would be no contest in either division, it boasted 'Cornwall will enjoy the proud distinction of sending four Reformers to the first Reform Parliament. It amply repays the toils, anxieties and often apparently hopeless of the

Reformers . . . for more than twenty years.'[21] In 1835 the *West Briton* was again very much alive to a possible challenge to the Liberal supremacy in West Cornwall from Boscawen Rose. Declaring that 'the Reformers must once more "buckle on the armour"', Budd gave strong backing to Pendarves and Lemon, emphasizing in several editions that they were standing on a joint ticket. 'It is true that a set is made against Mr Pendarves but the best, the only effectual way of securing him is to vote for him and Sir Charles . . . Vote for our late members unitedly regardless of who may be at the top of the poll.'[22]

After the election Budd focused the attention of his readers on the registration of voters. In his view, 'the decisive struggle will take place in the Registration Courts', and consequently he threw the paper's weight behind a campaign to convert the *ad hoc* Reform Committees in the divisions into formal registration organizations. In June, it publicized the calling of meetings in Bodmin, Redruth, Truro, Helston and Penzance to establish such bodies, gave full details of the resolutions agreed and welcomed the actual Reform Associations which resulted. It repeatedly emphasized the fact that 20 July was the last day for would-be voters to have their names inserted on the local overseers list. It reported in detail, in the autumn, the proceedings of the Registration Courts under the Revising Barristers, with Budd claiming at their conclusion that the Reformers had done extremely well in both divisions.[23]

Budd's death on 22 December 1835 after 'a painful and protracted illness' was announced in the last issue of the *West Briton* for the year in a short piece surrounded by a heavy black border. Proclaiming that 'With great mental powers, unshaken steadiness of purpose, unbending spirit and untiring zeal, he maintained for a quarter of a century the high and honourable character of a fearless advocate of the Divine Rights of Englishmen' (though Budd was an Irishman), it concluded that 'he had the satisfaction of seeing consummated most of the great measures he had advocated as a public journalist; Abolition of Slavery, Repeal of the Test and Corporation Acts, Emancipation of Catholics, Establishment of a Reformed Representation and finally the enactment of a statute for reforming Municipal Corporations'.[24]

His contribution to the success of the *West Briton*, over the 25 years he had been editor, was immense and the full column tribute to him on 1 January 1836 was not exaggerating in its remarks. 'The ties which connected Edward Budd as Editor with his readers and this county were not of an ordinary nature . . . He respected his readers, he loved his paper . . . Nor were his labours without fruit and rewards. Every successive year brought him fresh accessions of strength. During the year now closed public approbation was more than commonly liberal in its rewards. The subscribers of the *West Briton*, numerous before, have greatly increased.'[25] Just as significant, too, had been his contribution to the popularity of the Reform/Liberal cause in Cornwall, for the two aspects were inseparable. He had first gained and then retained the loyalty of his readers and that in turn had helped towards the unquestioned supremacy of the Liberals at the time of his death. Support was most solid in the predominantly mining areas of West Cornwall—a fact emphasized by the unopposed return of Pendarves and Lemon in the two elections. Equally farming opinion, which had first swung behind the Reformers in the early 1820s, was still loyal, not least because Budd had always supported the need for protection for agriculture. This helped to ensure that the much more agricultural East division was also Liberal, with Molesworth and Trelawny, too, returned unopposed. Along with John Colman Rashleigh, the founder of the Reform group, Budd can be justly described as one of the key figures in the making of nineteenth-century Cornish Liberalism.

THE *GAZETTE* AFTER GILLET

The deaths of the two rival editors in April and December of the same year inevitably had significant consequences for the two papers. These coincided with the government decision in 1836 to reduce the Stamp Duty from the 1815 figure of 4d to 1d. This meant there was scope for a reduction in the 7d price charged by both papers. The *Gazette* expressed its dislike of the proposal, since 'there are taxes which might be better given up than the duty on newspapers'. It only reduced its price to 4½d, claiming that it would sustain a loss which could only be made up by increased demand. The *West Briton*, by contrast, welcomed the proposal, arguing that 'the public have a right to expect that proprietors will evince a readiness . . . to render political information accessible to every man, however poor he may be'. It reduced its price, on 16 September, to 4d. Although 'well aware that this price will not cover the cost of stamps, paper, printing and distribution etc, we confidently expect that our already extensive circulation will be greatly increased in consequence of the new low price and that our present large number of Adverts will be augmented as a result of the increase in circulation'.[26]

The expectation was fulfilled. The Stamp Return for 1836 itself was 63,300, an increase of some 6,500 on Budd's last year, but the increase in 1837 was a dramatic one, by more than 80 per cent, to 115,500. The *Gazette*, by contrast, only raised its 1836 figure of 26,700 —itself a decrease on the previous year—to 28,733, one-quarter of the *West Briton*'s.

From the scanty information available, it is difficult to unravel the changes at the *Gazette* after the death of Gillet. Nigel Tangye, in his useful *Gazetter and Finding List of Cornwall Newspapers*, provides the following list of succeeding editors:[27]

From 25 April 1835	Louisa Elizabeth Gillet, widow
30 October 1835	Edward Wintour
4 December 1835	James Gillet
14 April 1837	Frederic George Carrington
28 April 1837	George Wilkinson Kneebone
5 January 1849	George Wilkinson Kneebone

However, there are difficulties in accepting this list as it stands. It is perfectly possible that Mrs Gillet, who was the daughter of a Truro printer, John Carthew, took over editorial responsibility for a while as the *Gazette* was her property. She seems to have carried on her father's business after his death. James Gillet was most likely her brother-in-law, formerly a Captain in the Tower Hamlets Militia and who later died unmarried at Mylor in 1867. Frederic Carrington (1816–64) was clearly connected with newspapers, being editor and proprietor of the *Gloucestershire Chronicle* for several years. However, F.C. Boase suggests he merely contributed articles to the *Gazette*. There are problems with the remaining two named by Tangye. It has not been possible to discover any detail about Edward Wintour, while the little that has been gleaned on George Kneebone—certainly a Cornish name—indicates that he was the printer and publisher of the *Gazette* rather than its editor.[28]

Tangye's list, moreover, omits mention of three others who definitely acted as editors after 1835. First the death notice of Gillet Jnr in the *Gazette*, 25 April 1835, was penned by Thomas Gillet Snr—'it is a father who must speak of it here'—and he stated that 'the paper will hereafter be carried on for the exclusive benefit of Mr Gillet's widow and children . . . The management of the concern and the principal share of its labours will fall upon the writer of this notice.' He also pledged himself 'to the maintenance of those principles which THIS PAPER has so long and consistently advocated'. How long Gillet Snr performed this role is unknown for he was already 72 years of age. He died at Mylor in 1850 aged 87.[29]

Secondly, the *Gazette* on 2 June 1837 stated in a Notice to Correspondents that 'the editor of this paper is H Doubleday and to whom all communications should be addressed'.[30] Again it is not known how long he was editor, though, according to *Collectanea Cornubiensia*, there was a Henry Doubleday listed in 1839 as an actuary with the Truro Savings Bank. Doubleday's appointment appears to have coincided with a change of ownership, following its sale by Mrs Gillet. The *West Briton*, on 26 May 1837, mentioned that 'a new crowd of Cornish gentle-men have taken over the management of the *Gazette*'. This provoked the *Gazette* into an attack on its rival for 'enquiring after the *Gazette*'s internal organization'. Asserting that 'the proprietor of this paper is no man of straw', it admitted 'that we receive help is not denied . . . We have as much right to do so at the outset of our labours and until a little experience has determined our ability to dispense with it.'[31] It seems most likely that this new proprietor was, in fact, George Kneebone, while the financial help mentioned came from Earl Falmouth. The latter, writing to Peel, the Conservative leader, in May 1839, on the political situation in West Cornwall— 'perhaps the most Radical in the Kingdom'—referred to his 'expense and exertion to prevent almost the extinction of Conservative feelings and representation. It was thus that the only sound press was for some time kept alive and it is well known how far that conduced to the return of one member for East Cornwall.'[32]

Thirdly, it is incontrovertible that the *Gazette* had from 1841 onwards another new editor, again not mentioned by Tangye. This was Edward Osler, who was in charge of the paper until his death in 1863.[33]

Whoever was in charge, responded to the improvements made to the *West Briton* in July 1835 by increasing the size of the *Gazette* in September 1835, and again in August 1837 when the size became the same as that of its rival—24 x 18 inches with seven columns to a page. At the same time it reduced its price by ½d to 4d. On its circulation, it claimed that 'among those whose suffrages must determine the election for the County, the *Gazette* has a circulation as extensive as that of its more boastful opponent [whilst] we allow that in that class which can contribute nothing to the success of any contest, the *West Briton* may somewhat outnumber us'. (Two weeks later it referred slightingly to 'the people who read the *West Briton* or hear it read'.) In 1837 it actually published for the first time the Stamp Tax Returns. Admitting that the *West Briton*'s circulation 'is at present greater than our own', it placed the blame on Gillet for not increasing the size of the paper and reducing its price when the *West Briton* had done. It claimed, however, that though 'its restoration has been very gradual, it has been steadfast', and shortly after even boasted 'we shall soon be on an equal footing'.[34] In the light of the actual returns for 1837, which showed the *West Briton* on 115,500, over four times larger than the *Gazette* (28,733), such claims were rather 'whistling in the wind'. The thought which arises is whether the frequent changes at the *Gazette* contributed to its inferior position or whether they reflected the feeling of the editors that the position could not be reversed.

THE *WEST BRITON* AFTER BUDD

The change-over at the *West Briton* following Budd's death was, by contrast, smooth. It would appear that the Heard family—widow Mrs Elizabeth (died 1867 aged 79) and her second son Edward Goodridge Heard—became the proprietors as well as the printers and publishers.[35] The new editor, Joseph Thomas, like Budd, was not a Cornishman, having been born in Cheshire in 1791. More significantly, Budd, the Wesleyan lay preacher, was succeeded by a man who had been a full-time Wesleyan minister at Liskeard as well as of a British congregation in Normandy. His newspaper experience had begun as editor of the *Welshman* at Carmarthen following 'a severe illness which completely shattered his health [and] compelled [him] to relinquish the laborious profession of a Methodist preacher'. He was to be editor of the *West Briton* for eleven years till his retirement in 1847 (not 1862 as Tangye implies in his list, for Thomas died at Bridge Cottage, Truro, in September 1857).

'His clearness of head, his sound judgement and a practical acuteness . . . formed valuable qualifications for the conducting of a newspaper'. However, 'the feeble state of his health prevented him from taking much active part in the more laborious department of an Editor's duty, that of original writing'.[36] In these circumstances it would seem that the editorial line came from the pen of others, such as Isaac Latimer. He became the chief reporter in 1837, having previously been a reporter in the Midlands and in London for the *Morning Chronicle* at the same time as Charles Dickens was reporting for the paper. Latimer, as Philip Payton has detailed in his works, was also active as an agent for encouraging prospective emigrants for South Australia and other Antipodean colonies.[37]

Thomas inherited a strong successful paper, which was still, as the opening editorial of 1836 proclaimed, 'the unflinching advocate of Reform, of Good Government, of Civil and Religious Liberty throughout the world'. The Stamp Tax figures demonstrate the paper's success in maintaining its pre-eminence in Cornwall. After the Stamp Duty reduction to 1d in 1836, the 1837 figure was an all-time high and despite a decline the following two years its lead over the *Gazette* was still substantial. One notable feature of Thomas's editorship was the much more overt use of the Stamp Tax figures for publicity purposes. Issues regularly appeared containing the month-by-month figures for the previous six or twelve months, often with comment on the paper's lead. For example, it boasted on 17 June 1836, 'We are not only first in point of circulation in Cornwall but our circulation is equal to that of all the other papers in the County with the exception of some 300–400 copies weekly'. On other occasions it rubbed salt in the wound by boasting that while its circulation had risen to 1,600–1,700 a week, that of the *Gazette* was only a third of that, languishing on 500–600. Or it published the amount of Advertisement Duty paid to the government (reduced to 1s 6d each advert in 1833). For the three-year-period to Janiary 1840, the *West Briton*'s bill was £752 0s 6d, that of the *Gazette* £497 15s 6d.[38]

In these circumstances, the *Gazette*'s main hope was that the national swing towards Conservatism would have an effect in Cornwall. Certainly after the stimulus given by Peel's 1st Ministry of 1834–35, the Conservatives were revived while the Whig government of Melbourne ran into difficulties because of growing divisions between Radicals and Whigs, defections to the Conservatives, a declining majority in Parliament and problems over legislation such as the Poor Law Amendment Act. In Cornwall, difficulties for the Reformers escalated, producing a swing towards the Conservatives in both divisions. In East Cornwall, Molesworth, after publicly quarrelling with older leading Reformers such as Sir Colman Rashleigh, announced his decision not to stand again, while in the 1837 election Trelawny lost his seat, being pushed into third place. Worse was to follow. In 1841 Lord Eliot (son of Earl St Germans) and William Rashleigh Jnr of Menabilly captured both seats for the Conservatives. John Trelawny, much more Radical than his father, came bottom of the poll, over 1,000 votes behind. Likewise in the Western division, the Conservatives gained one of the seats in 1841. At the last moment, Lemon decided not to risk a contest so Boscawen Rose was returned unopposed. This meant that three of the four county seats were Conservative: a dramatic turnaround from 1832.

The *Gazette*, confident that 'if we take reasonable advantage of the rising Conservatism in the County', it could be on equal terms with the *West Briton*, played an aggressive part in the election campaigns. It gave much publicity and support to Eliot's cause in 1837, exploited to the full the differences in the Reform ranks and in particular targeted for attack the second Whig candidate, Sir Hussey Vivian, a former general. He was subjected to fierce and consistent attacks in the paper from two correspondents with the pseudonyms 'Miles' and 'Old Miner'. The first sought to embarrass Vivian over his military pension, while the latter alleged that the family smelting firm of Vivian and Co. at Swansea favoured reducing the import duty on foreign copper to the detriment of Cornish mines. The joint attack lasting several months was very effective and, in fact, reminiscent of similar correspondence in the early days of the rivalry between the papers. The paper was equally vigorous in the 1841 campaign. It laid much emphasis on the issue of the Corn Laws, urging Cornish farmers to oppose any alteration, while also attacking Pendarves and Lemon in the West division for supporting the abolition of the Duchy Coinage Duty on tin, and castigating them as 'unworthy representatives of the County and unfaithful guardians of its interests'.[39]

The *Gazette* was optimistic that its aggressive political line would pay off: 'we look for a further improvement in our circulation commensurate with the efforts we are making and with the growing Conservatism of the County'. It made more frequent references to the Stamp Return figures as they showed an improvement in the fortunes of the paper (1838 45,000, 1839 48,000). At the end of 1840 its circulation was its highest ever, 53,500, and since the *West Briton* had dropped to 88,500, the gap between the two was at its narrowest. It boasted in its New Year editorial of 1841 that its supply of stamps was up to 5,000 a month and concluded 'Our circulation has steadily increased year after year until it has nearly doubled the amount at which it stood about four years ago when we undertook the management'.[40]

That year the paper acquired a new editor. Edward Osler had an unusual background for a newspaper editor. He had been born in Falmouth in 1798, and after being apprenticed to a surgeon in the town had gone to Guy's Hospital in London for formal medical training. He qualified in 1818 as a MRCS, and was Resident House Surgeon in Swansea Infirmary for six years before becoming a surgeon in the Royal Navy in 1825. His duties took him to the West Indies where his growing literary talents led to him composing and later publishing (1830) *A Voyage: Poems Written at Sea and in the West Indies*. After his return he produced, in 1835, a *Life of Viscount Exmouth*, a biography of a prominent eighteenth-century naval figure, Edward Pellew, a fellow Cornishman. By 1837 he had returned to Cornwall, marrying his second wife, Sarah, at St Gluvias Parish Church, Penryn. She was the sister of the Rev. Atkinson, master of the Classical School in Falmouth.[41]

A 'DEMOCRATIC REPUBLIC'?, A 'DISSENTING NEWSPAPER'?

The *Gazette*'s claim that the *West Briton* wanted Britain to become 'a democratic republic' was wide of the mark. However, there is little doubt that, after 1836, the latter did become more Radical in its views, strongly supporting demands for more parliamentary reform in the shape of the ballot and triennial parliaments. While these were no more than what Budd had advocated, the paper, under Thomas, also favoured an extension of the right to vote since 'the measure would go far to re-unite all branches of Reformers and give life and spirit to the Liberal cause'.[42] However, the biggest policy shift was on the Corn Laws. As early as May 1836, only five months after Budd's death, the paper printed its first editorial denouncing them: 'they have assuredly failed . . . the course of recent events has shown that the prosperity of agriculture depends more on the general prospects of the trade of the country than on any statute Parliament may enact'. Similar editorials followed over the next few years. The paper also gave favourable reports of lectures given by James Acland, employed by the Anti Corn Law League (ACLL), at places such as Redruth, where it claimed 2,000 attended the meeting. Such support lends credence to the *Gazette*'s repeated claim that Thomas was a member of the League's council. John Trelawny's candidacy in East Cornwall received strong support from the *West Briton* as he too favoured free trade and had a Radical political agenda. No wonder the *Gazette* exclaimed after the 1841 election that 'The *West Briton* has committed itself to those who glory in the name of Radical'.[43]

With Liberalism apparently in the doldrums in Cornwall, it might have been expected that the *West Briton*'s circulation would have suffered accordingly. Intriguingly, that does not appear to have been the case. It is true that there was, for three years, a drop in the figures from the high point of 1837, but in 1841, the year of Liberal election defeat, they recovered to 101,000—remaining around that level for the next few years. The onset of the economic depression in the late 1930's—the prelude to the period known as the Hungry Forties—may account for the initial decrease as it is clear that the *West Briton* had a wider readership among the lower classes. It is also likely that while the free trade policy of the paper offended Cornish farmers, it found favour with the many non-farming elements in the population. The paper's argument that cheaper corn would benefit the consumer was one which, inevitably, had more and more appeal in the years of economic depression. As the writer of a long letter on 'Cornwall and the Corn Laws' explained, 'The County is not a manufacturing one but yet the interests of the vast majority of its inhabitants are identified with the masses of the North and Midlands; an immense population maintained from other sources entirely independent of the cultivators of the soil . . . The poor miner, labourer and fisherman can hardly contrive to keep body and soul together.'[44]

It may be, too, that influences other than politics were at work in persuading the Cornish reading public to favour the *West Briton* rather than the *Gazette*. The key factor, indeed, was most likely to have been religion. It was abundantly clear, by the early nineteenth century, that Nonconformist bodies, especially Methodists, commanded far greater support within Cornwall than did the Anglican Church. The Religious Census of 1851 provides statistical evidence of general religious allegiance and even if the figures have limitations, nevertheless, as

Alan Everitt has stated, 'the number of "sittings" available in church and chapel . . . provide at least some kind of rough indication of denominational strength'. According to his table, in Cornwall, the Nonconformists with 166,529 sittings out of a total of 261,684 had the highest percentage (64 per cent) of all 41 'English county' areas. The popularity of the Bible Christians and Wesleyan Methodists was also reflected in the number of places of worship, with the two far outnumbering the Church of England.[45]

We have noted previously, in the early days of the *West Briton*, Budd's support for the Nonconformist demand for equality with the Anglicans by the Repeal of the Test and Corporation Acts in 1828. In the 1830s their efforts to make that legal equality into a practical reality, by the abolition of church rates, the reform of Tithes and the admission of Dissenters into universities, had his support, though not the demand for Disestablishment. Budd declared at the opening of the new parliamentary session in January 1834, 'Church Reform must come first', expressing the hope that the clergy would not oppose it for that 'would augment the opponents of the Establishment'. The paper reported Dissenter meetings at Liskeard and Launceston where removal of grievances were demanded, highlighted the vote of the four county MPs on the admission of Dissenters, and declared about the Bill for the abolition of church rates, 'to the principle no reasonable objection can be made'.[46]

The importance politically, both to voters and candidates, of such Nonconformist demands is evident in a number of ways. John Penhallow Peters, the leader of the Cornish yeomanry, called for public support for Pendarves and Lemon on the grounds that 'a real amendment of the abuses that have crept into the Church can only be obtained from honest and genuine Reformers'. Pendarves, in his address, supported 'Reform of the Established Church in Ireland and England and the removal of disqualities on the Dissenters'. Lemon thought it important, on the hustings, to defend his votes on the Dissenters (University) Bill. His explanation that having voted in favour on the second reading, he felt it necessary to vote against on the third reading because of the omission of certain clauses, was greeted with 'boos' by the crowd.[47] Again in 1837, he felt impelled to defend his position on the abolition of church rates. His vote against the appropriation of the surplus revenues of the Irish Church earned him Budd's editorial disapproval: 'it has surprised and grieved us. We know . . . he would resist and we think properly, any proposition for appropriating Church property in England but we were not prepared for him viewing the sinecure Church of Ireland in the same light.'[48]

As a former Wesleyan minister, Thomas was just as committed as

Budd to backing Nonconformist demands. An editorial, 28 April 1837, maintained the paper's support for the measure to abolish church rates, while a month later another expressed 'regret' at Lemon's votes on the issue. The paper praised William Trelawny for stating in his election address in 1837 that 'in vain has the conscientious Dissenter pleaded for relief from the exaction of Church Rates'. John Trelawny's address in 1841 met with the paper's approval on the same grounds. When the question of the Maynooth grant (a government subsidy to a Catholic seminary in Ireland) came up in the mid-1840s, the *West Briton* revealed its Nonconformist sympathies by admitting that it wanted the grant abolished because 'the money should come from the Irish Church of England'.[49]

The obituary notice on Thomas in 1857 emphasized that 'on all political matters his opinions were thoroughly liberal and on questions connected with religious liberty in particular, his interest was always peculiarly keen and his views decided'. However, 'his mind was entirely free from any tinge of narrowness or bigotry'. As a result, in the early 1840s, he became 'averse to the ecclesiastical administration of Wesleyism', which he regarded as incompatible with 'those more enlarged ideas of Christian liberty to which he had become attached'. He, therefore, ceased to hold communion with the Wesleyan body during the last 12–15 years of his life.[50]

Nevertheless, under Thomas, the *West Briton* became so identified with the Nonconformists that the Bishop of Exeter, Henry Philpotts, was even led to accuse it of being 'a Dissenting Newspaper'. After the *West Briton* denied the charge, the *Gazette* quoted, with obvious relish, a letter from a 'Churchman', who declared: 'If the fact of a paper being edited by a professional dissenter, conducted on dissenting principles, having a large majority of dissenters among its proprietors and its columns week after week teeming with offensive attacks on the Church and its ministers does not make it "a dissenting newspaper", what does!'[51] The opposition of the *Gazette* on religious as well as political issues could be guaranteed. If the *West Briton* pushed the Non-conformist cause, the *Gazette* was equally strong in its support of the Church of England. It consistently opposed all the proposed Church reforms of the Whigs, arguing that they would lead to 'the confiscation of Church property'. It implored West Cornwall electors in 1835 to refuse their votes for any candidate 'who will not give satisfactory assurances of his support for the Established Church against any measure calculated to impair its stability'. Likewise, in 1837, it railed against 'Church assailing, free trading' Liberal candidates.[52]

The *Gazette*'s support for the Church of England was even more marked after Osler became its editor in 1841. He had been brought up in Falmouth as a Baptist but after his return from the West Indies in the early 1830s had joined the Church of England. In 1836 he was on the staff in London and Bath of the Society for Promoting Christian Knowledge, producing first *Church and Dissent Considered in their Practical Influence* and then *Church and King*—the latter brought out in twelve separate numbers between November 1836 and August 1837 and dedicated to the Bath Conservative Association which paid him for its production.[53] Osler developed strong views on the role of the Church in society, envisaging for it a prominent position. An excellent insight into his views was laid out in a private letter, which, by good fortune, has survived in the Rashleigh Mss in the County Record Office. Writing to William Rashleigh in March 1857:

> I am more and more convinced that the Church is the only Conservative Power. Property, station etc are Conservative principles but they all imply the elevation of the few and the subordination of the many. To reconcile the Masses to this inferiority, we need a Real Power in which all have an equal interest and which possesses an authoritative claim to their obedience, reverence and love.
> The Democracy of the country is becoming more and more paramount and the question is, who shall guide it? I believe the Church to be the only Power equal to control it. I think I see how existing institutions may be worked to effect this object.[54]

The Bishop of Exeter's remark about the *West Briton* could be countered, therefore, by describing the *Gazette* as an Anglican paper.

If, indeed, religious affiliation was as influential as political views in dictating readership of the two papers, then the reason for the *Gazette*'s failure to rival the *West Briton* in circulation becomes clear. The fact that the Anglicans in Cornwall were in a permanent minority compared to the Nonconformists meant that the *Gazette* could never hope to attract as many readers as its rival, whichever editor was in charge and whatever policies were pursued. It is perhaps in this context that Budd's remark in July 1835 about the papers being each 'supported by perfectly distinct parties' makes sense. It helps, too, to explain why even with a Conservative government in power after 1841, the *Gazette* failed to make much impact on the *West Briton*'s circulation lead. As was evident in 1840–1, the popularity of Conservative support for the Corn Laws and their general election victory might have led to a narrowing of the circulation gap but never to the point where the *West Briton*'s predominance was really threatened.

NEWSPAPER RIVALRY AND THE CORN LAWS

The fierce rivalry between the papers after 1841 focused on the emotive topic of protectionism and the continued existence of the Corn Laws. The *West Briton*, although first supporting the Whig scheme for a fixed duty, became openly more in favour of complete repeal, while the *Gazette* remained passionately protectionist. The issue featured in the pages of both papers on a regular tit-for-tat basis. Likewise, just as the first gave sympathetic coverage to the activities of the ACLL, so the *Gazette* dismissed its efforts as ineffective and accused Thomas of 'wearing the livery of the League'.[55] The topic also influenced their attitude to the new Conservative Prime Minister, Sir Robert Peel, his budgets and finally, of course, the Repeal of the Corn Laws in 1846. It is instructive to note the changes of attitude which took place.[56]

Despite stating 'we are not blind admirers of Sir R Peel', the *Gazette* regarded him favourably, even referring to him in 1844 as 'unquestionably a very great man' for 'the fruits of his wise administration have been peace and honour . . . and that essential element of strength, financial prosperity'. It accepted the new sliding scale for the Corn Law in 1842, arguing 'there was nothing to fear'. However it strongly opposed the general tariff changes which related to tin since 'the consequence to Cornwall may be frightful'.[57] The *West Briton*, by contrast, was not in favour of the sliding scale, expressed its dislike of the introduction of income tax and, like the *Gazette*, held that the reduction in the duty on imported tin 'must be altered'. It accused Peel of having 'deceived all sections of the party' and of being guilty of both 'expediency' and 'duplicity'. Yet it had to admit that by the general tariff changes 'the minister has done more to advance Free Trade principles . . . than was ever done before'.[58]

By 1845 attitudes began to be reversed. The *Gazette* attacked 'the free trade mania' of the government over its budget proposals, denounced Peel for his decision to endow the Maynooth College in Ireland and warned that 'Conservatives will sacrifice not their principles to their leader but the leader to their principles'.[59] On the other hand the *West Briton* found itself increasingly in favour of the economic measures since 'they have sealed the fate of the protective system'. It had shifted its position on the Corn Laws to one of total repeal, arguing constantly in editorials that it was only a matter of time before repeal took place for 'the leading statesmen of all parties are avowed Free Traders so it is found impossible by every administration to carry on government without acting on these principles'.[60]

When the final crisis developed in the autumn of 1845, the positions of the papers were almost totally reversed. The *Gazette* was unrestrained in its denunciation of Peel's 'arrogance' and 'betrayal of the people and the Church'. It argued, in issue after issue, that repeal would ruin the small farmer, be particularly harmful in Cornwall, where the average size farm was only 83 acres, and that 'high farming was only practicable for individuals'. After Peel's fall from office, it called for a general election so protectionist candidates could 'fight the battle for protection' again and 'extinguish nominal Conservatives'.[61] The *West Briton*, in contrast, became friendly to Peel in its editorials. It favoured him 'taking the responsibility of bringing this question to a settlement', even subsequently praising 'his masterly speech' in the House. Although preferring immediate repeal to the three-year phasing out of the duty, it commended Peel's measure in successive issues and contended that farming had nothing to fear about foreign competition: 'the energies of Englishmen freed from the shackles of a mistaken policy, will maintain them in their position as the first and greatest producers in the world'. When Peel fell in late June, the paper did not express much regret but welcomed the return of Russell and the Whigs, merely adding that 'Peel has broken the old party ties . . . has destroyed for a time his own political power and rendered it difficult for the government of the country to be carried on'.[62]

On 24 July 1846, the 37th anniversary of its foundation, the *West Briton*, as if in celebration of the triumph of the free trade cause it had advocated for the previous decade, announced the paper was being enlarged. The extension to 32 lengthened columns was, it claimed, 'necessary because the increase in advertisements was encroaching upon news'. Its average weekly sale was 2,500, or 130,000 a year: 'the largest sheet at its price in the West of England'. In fact, the Stamp Tax returns for the year gave it a slightly higher figure of 135,500—an increase of 27,500 on the previous year. This was a striking vindication of its position on the protectionist issue. The *Gazette* had only managed an increase of 3,500. It is little wonder that the *West Briton* boasted that 'the Liberal Press as the exponent and in some measure the guide of public opinion has risen to an undisputed supremacy. The Old Tory prints are becoming obsolete. They must reform or perish.'[63]

In fact, under Osler, the *Gazette* did fight back. By January 1849 the paper had been increased from four to eight pages with a total of 40 columns—price 4½d and a further change in January 1851 to 48 columns; changes which seem to have had some success, given the Stamp Tax figures for 1850, 1851, and 1852.[64] This success was assisted by political events in Cornwall, characterized by a backlash among East Cornwall farmers because of falling corn prices. There was a strong tide for a return to some form of protection, which resulted in the successful candidacy of Nicholas Kendall of Pelyn in the 1852 election, at the expense of the moderate Protectionist MP William Pole Carew, first elected unopposed in 1845.[65]

The *West Briton*, however, was able to respond under its new editor, Gordon Taylor Brown, who replaced Thomas on his retirement in 1847. While circulation did suffer some decline at first, recovery was effected after changes in the paper's format. First there was an increase in size to 28 x 22 inches, followed, in January 1851, by an increase to eight pages instead of four since 'it must continue to be the leading journal of the County'. This was accompanied by an ½d increase in price, making it the same as the *Gazette*. In justification the editorial claimed that the old price was 'below that of the majority of provincial papers of the former size of the *West Briton* and nothing but the liberal support we received in the form of advertisements enabled us to publish at that rate'.[66]

With both papers the same, in terms of price and size, the *West Briton* easily beat off this latest challenge from the *Gazette*. In fact, by June 1855, when the Stamp Tax was finally abolished, the paper was forging ahead. While the *Gazette* had dropped back to 70,000 after the peak of 1852, the *West Briton* had leapt to a new high of 161,000 and was still rising. Indeed, news of its success reached beyond the Tamar. Liberals in West Somerset in 1858 were puzzled by their lack of electoral success in the division, despite the fact that the three local Liberal papers all owned by one proprietor 'had an aggregate circulation of 3600, more than any other proprietor in Somerset'. As the investigation, which they set up, acknowledged, 'throughout the whole West of England, there is only one that sends out a larger number—the Proprietor of the *West Briton*!'.[67]

CONCLUSION

The rivalry between the two papers over the 45 years after the *West Briton*'s foundation in 1810 had embraced the whole gamut of political issues and especially those of parliamentary reform and protection. It had even extended, as Philip Payton has shown in his recent comprehensive study, *The Cornish Overseas*, to opposing attitudes to the emigration of the Cornish people. The *Gazette* was critical of 'the rage for emigration', and of the *West Briton* for encouraging it. As early as May 1819, it remarked: 'We have every reason to believe that most of [these wholesale emigrations] are instigated by interested parties who dextrously avail themselves of the discontent excited in the minds of the ignorant by a certain class of our public writers'. It was especially opposed to emigration to the USA—'neither the deluders nor the deluded can so easily pretend that they are departing to a land flowing with milk and honey'—taking the view that if people had to emigrate, they should at least go to a British colony.[68] In contrast to the *Gazette*'s 'patronising contempt', as Payton has characterized its attitude to would-be emigrants, the *West Briton* emerged as a supporter of emigration for those Cornish desirous of leaving for economic, political or religious reasons. Whenever, therefore, it referred to 'the rage for emigration', as it frequently did, it did so in sympathetic terms. Indeed, it actually acted 'as a source of practical information and as a conduit for applications for free or assisted passages'. This was especially so after Latimer joined the paper in 1837, given his involvement in the subject.[69]

It had always been a rivalry, too, characterized on both sides by deeply held views and often involving personal abuse by the editors, of each other or of political opponents. The papers had been at the heart of the political battle— a fact well illustrated by a rare example of physical violence in 1850, when Brown, the *West Briton*'s editor, was attacked by the High Sheriff of the County, Sir Samuel Spry, wielding a horse whip! Brown's offence had been to print in his paper a complaint from Pendarves that Spry had read out, at a county meeting on distress in agriculture, only a part of his letter explaining why he declined to attend and that 'the portion which had been read unfairly represented his sentiments'. Spry, in turn, had responded with a letter to the *Gazette*'s editor, complaining of Pendarves' discourtesy in not writing to him about the matter. The *West Briton*'s description of Spry's letter as 'a strange piece of impertinence' and of 'the meanness and petty spirit of the writer' then provoked the assault on Brown.[70]

Although the circulation war had been clearly won by the *West Briton*, nevertheless the rivalry continued for the next 100 years until 1951 when the *Gazette* was taken over by its competitor. By the second half of the nineteenth century, however, it was considerably diluted by the rise of newspapers in other Cornish towns serving a more local readership than the whole of Cornwall. Penzance, for example, could boast of two papers of its own—the *Penzance Gazette* (1839) and the *Cornish Telegraph* (1851), with Stamp Tax returns in 1854 of 8,450 and 17,000 a year respectively.[71] Towns such as Falmouth, Bodmin, St Austell, Launceston and Redruth followed suit, so there was no longer a clear-cut two-paper rivalry in Cornwall.[72] Still, one might suggest that it had helped in the making, perhaps one should say strengthening, of the distinct and distinctive Cornish society with its 'individualistic and independent aspects of behaviour' so well described by Philip Payton in his recent authoritative survey of Cornwall, or what Sir Richard Vyvyan, in a striking phrase, referred to as 'an independence of character which is almost republican (although there is universal attachment to the Queen)'.[73]

Moreover, in an age without radio or television, the rivalry had been immensely valuable in the political education of the readers of the papers. Over the years they had been introduced to a whole range of political issues and provided with detailed information on both sides of any argument in the effort to influence their views and political preferences. As the Stamp Tax had been scaled down from its 1815 level of 4d, so the circulation of the papers had increased, opening up to a wider and wider readership. The fact that the two papers dominated the scene in Cornwall meant that the public's views tended to be polarized into two opposing political camps. After 1830, increasingly that became a reflection of the religious divide in Cornwall between Nonconformist and Church of England, as well as actually adding to it even further.

What was the significance of the *West Briton*'s triumph in the circulation battle? Its role, as it stated in 1846, had been twofold: 'as the exponent and in some measure the guide of public opinion'. It is conventional, as was done here earlier, to call the *West Briton* a Radical paper, but strictly speaking this is only valid in comparison with the *Gazette*. Its political position as a Reform/Liberal paper was one of an essentially moderate non-Radical type. Like the papers in the North of England, sympathetic to the ACLL and representative primarily of the middle class, it disapproved strongly of the Chartist agitation and the six demands of their Charter (1838).[74] Socially, too, it was not at all Radical. In 1847 it even attacked the 'non-political' food riots in Cornwall on the grounds that 'the constitution of society was ordained by God'.[75]

However, the paper had helped to mould as well as to reflect the political views of its readers and thus had contributed in no small measure to the Liberal supremacy in Cornwall which was established by the middle of the century. By 1847 three of the four county seats were again Liberal. As well as the safe West Cornwall seats, held by Pendarves and Lemon, one seat had been recovered from the Conservatives in the East division. Thomas Agar-Robartes (1808–82) of Lanhydrock had actually gained the seat without a contest, but when one occurred in 1852, he came top of the poll. He held the seat without difficulty until his retirement in 1868. In that year the Liberals won both seats, and although they were pulled back to one seat in 1874, both were won in 1880, and held till the county divisions were abolished in 1885.[76] Such was the long-term political legacy of the original founders of the *West Briton*: Walker, Rashleigh, Pendarves and Glynn, as well as its main editor from 1810 to 1835, Edward Budd. Their names deserve to be better known in the history of Liberalism in Cornwall.

APPENDIX: NEWSPAPER STAMP RETURNS

	Royal Cornwall Gazette	*West Briton*
1831	27,000	50,900
1832	24,000	50,700
1833	24,000	52,200
1834	18,000	38,400
1835	28,500	56,800
1836	26,700	63,300
1837	28,733	115,500
1838	45,000	93,500
1839	48,000	98,000
1840	53,500	88,500
1841	58,200	101,000
1842	54,000	105,000
1843	47,000	97,000
1844	51,500	102,000
1845	50,000	108,000
1846	53,500	135,500
1847	54,000	132,500
1848	50,000	124,000
1849	52,500	110,000
1850	65,000	132,500
1851	68,500	116,200
1852	71,500	141,500
1853	—	—
1854	70,000	161,000

Source: Public Record Office, IR 69.

NOTES AND REFERENCES

1. See Appendix. Figures from the Inland Revenue, Somerset House, now located at Public Record Office, IR 69.
2. Donald Read, *Press and the People 1790–1850*, London, 1961, p. 209.
3. *West Briton*, 26 July, 9 August 1833.
4. *Royal Cornwall Gazette*, 4 August 1832, 5 January 1833, 4 January 1834.
5. *Royal Cornwall Gazette*, 18 May 1833, 15 November 1834 (slavery), 29 June, 28 December 1833, 11 January 1834 (Church reform), 26 April, 19 May, 24 May, 5 July, 23 August 1834 (poor law).
6. *Royal Cornwall Gazette*, 29 April 1833, 9 August, 1 November 1834.
7. *Royal Cornwall Gazette*, 11 August, 8 September, 20 October 1832.
8. *Royal Cornwall Gazette*, 15 September 1832.

9. *Royal Cornwall Gazette*, 25 May 1833, 8 March, 7 June 1834. For details of Molesworth (1810–55), see Alison Adburgham, *A Radical Aristocrat: Sir William Molesworth of Pencarrow*, Padstow, 1990, although its account of the political scene in Cornwall is rather deficient.

10. *Royal Cornwall Gazette*, 16 August 1834, 10 January 1835.

11. *Royal Cornwall Gazette*, 17 January, 11 April 1835. It should be explained that Trelawny's father, Rev Sir Harry, 7th Baronet, left the Anglican Church for the Roman Catholic Church, being ordained as a priest in 1830. On his death in February 1834, William assumed the title as 8th Baronet.

12. *Royal Cornwall Gazette*, 25 April 1835, for obituary notice, which referred to him as 'the editor and proprietor'. The *West Briton* in its later report of the event (21 August) called him 'the son of the editor of the *Gazette*'.

13. *West Briton*, 6 January 1832.

14. *West Briton*, 15 July, 21 August 1835.

15. *West Briton*, 15 June 1832, 1 March, 3 May, 27 September, 4, 11, 18 October 1833, 23 May 1834.

16. *West Briton*, 15 June 1832, 26 April 1833, 2 May 1834; Read, 1961, Ch. 5.

17. *West Briton*, 1 February, 3, 31 May, 14, 21 June, 19 July, 9 August 1833, 18 July, 22 August 1834.

18. *West Briton*, 10, 17 August 1832, 22 November 1833, 14 March 1834.

19. *West Briton*, 10 August 1832, 26 April, 12 July, 13 December 1833, 3, 17, 24 January 1834.

20. *West Briton*, 27 December 1833, 24, 31 January 1834.

21. *West Briton*, 29 June, 20 July, 10, 17, 31 August, 14, 21, 28 September, 12 October 1832.

22. *West Briton*, 19, 26 December 1834, 9 January 1835.

23. *West Briton*, 6 February, 5, 12, 19, 26 June, 17 July, 25 September, 2, 23 October, 13 November 1835. The three associations set up were the East Cornwall Reform Association headed by Colman Rashleigh, the West Cornwall Reform Association under Humphrey Willyams, and a separate Redruth Reform Association under its chairman Michael Williams.

24. *West Briton*, 25 December 1835.

25. *West Briton*, 1 January 1836.

26. *Royal Cornwall Gazette*, 24 June, 16 September; *West Briton*, 1, 8 July, 16 September 1836.

27. Nigel Tangye, *Cornwall Newspapers in 18th and 19th Century*, Redruth, 1980.

28. The main bibliographical sources have been G.C. Boase and W.P. Courtney, *Bibliotheca Cornubiensis*, 1874–82, G.C. Boase, *Collectanea Cornubiensia*, 1890; F. Boase, *Modern English Biography*, 1892–1921; and *DNB*.

29. *Royal Cornwall Gazette*, 25 April 1835; Boase, 1890.

30. *Royal Cornwall Gazette*, 2 June 1837.

31. *West Briton*, 26 May, 2 June 1837.

32. British Library, Add Mss 40426 fos 283–7, Lord Falmouth to Sir R. Peel, 9, 19 May 1839.

33. Boase and Courtney, 1874, p. 416; Boase, 1890, p. 644, Boase, 1892–1921, Vol. II, p. 1270; *DNB*, Vol. XIV, p. 1206.

34. *Royal Cornwall Gazette*, 4 September 1835, 15, 29 July 1836, 11 August, 29 September, 6 October 1837.

35. Claude Berry, *The West Briton in Nine Reigns*, Truro, 1955, repeated in the 150th anniversary supplement of the paper on 20 July 1960. Berry was of course editor of the paper himself from 1947. John McFarlane Heard —another son—was listed as manager of the paper on 2 August 1850.

36. *West Briton*, 25 September 1857, obituary notice.

37. Berry, 1955; Philip Payton, *The Cornish Miner in Australia*, Redruth, 1984, pp. 12–15; Philip Payton, *The Cornish Overseas*, Fowey, 1999, pp. 87–90. In 1844 Latimer moved to Plymouth where he edited and owned the *Plymouth Journal*, before founding and controlling for nearly 30 years the *Western Daily Mercury*.

38. *West Briton*, 1 January, 22 July 1836, 4 November 1837 17 July 1840; for examples of circulation figures see issues of 17 June 1836, 22 September 1837, 12 January, 25 May 1838, 1 March 1839, 17 July 1840. The figures for duty paid in 1837 were: *West Briton*, £239 18s 6d, the *Gazette*, £158 6s 6d, (*West Briton*, 17 August 1838).

39. *Royal Cornwall Gazette*, 6 October 1837, 28 December 1838. The letters from Miles and Old Miner began in the *Gazette* on 24 March, continuing through the election till 15 September. For the Duchy Coinage Duty question, see John Rowe, *Cornwall in the Age of the Industrial Revolution*, Liverpool, 1953, pp. 202–3.

40. *Royal Cornwall Gazette*, 19 January, 1 June 1838, 4 January 1839, 1 January 1841.

41. Osler, whose life of Exmouth was even translated into Russian in 1857, was most likely a member of the Osler family that Payton, 1999, p. 78, has identified as being involved in an emigration scheme to Cape Colony, South Africa, in 1820.

42. *Royal Cornwall Gazette*, 20 April 1838, *West Briton*, 31 May 1839.

43. *West Briton*, 6 May 1836, 25 January, 8 February, 7, 14 June 1839, 4 June 1841; *Royal Cornwall Gazette*, 16 July 1841, 3 March 1843.

44. *West Briton*, 23 November 1838.

45. Alan Everitt, 'Nonconformity in Country Parishes', in Joan Thirsk (ed.), *Agricultural History Review Supplement*, 18, 1970, p. 180; Peter Hayden, 'Culture Creed and Conflict: Methodism and Politics in Cornwall 1832–1979', Ph.D. thesis, University of Liverpool, 1982, quoted by Edwin Jaggard in 'Liberals and Conservatives in West Cornwall', in P. Payton (ed.), *Cornish Studies: One*, Exeter, 1993, p. 20. The totals were: Wesleyan Methodists 251, Bible Christians 94, Church of England 121.

46. *West Briton*, 3 January, 21 February, 25 April, 2 May 1834.

47. *West Briton*, 12, 19 December 1834, 16 January 1835.

48. *West Briton*, 7 July 1837, 10 April 1835.

49. *West Briton*, 28 April, 19 May, 7 July, 1837, 4 June 1841, 25 April 1845.

50. *West Briton*, 25 September 1857, obituary notice.

51. *Royal Cornwall Gazette*, 15 November 1844; John A. Phillips in his study,

Electoral Behaviour in Unreformed England, Princeton, 1982, found that religious divisions played a greater role in deciding political partisanship than any other social or economic distinction.

52. *Royal Cornwall Gazette*, 12 April 1832, 20 December 1834, 21 July 1837.
53. *Royal Cornwall Gazette*, 13 March 1863, obituary notice. See note 33 for other sources on Osler.
54. Cornwall Record Office (CRO), Rashleigh Mss DD, R.E. Osler to W. Rashleigh, 12 March. No year is given but it is clearly 1857 from internal references to Nicholas Kendall's candidacy for East Cornwall and the death of Mr Meredith. J.H. Meredith, an associate of Kendall, died 12 March 1857 (Boase, 1890, p. 1019).
55. *West Briton*, 21 April, 6 October 1843; *Royal Cornwall Gazette*, 13 January, 17 February, 3 March 1843. In the 9 February 1844 issue, it referred to 'that organ of the League, the *West Briton*'.
56. Read, 1961, ch. 5 for a similar shift in attitude among the northern newspapers.
57. *Royal Cornwall Gazette*, 25 March, 6 May, 3 June 1842, 28 June 1844; Rowe, 1953, pp. 204–5.
58. *West Briton*, 18 February, 25 March, 15 April, 26 August, 23 December 1842.
59. *Royal Cornwall Gazette*, 21 February, 4, 11 April 1845.
60. *West Briton*, 4 April, 20 June 1845. In editorials such as 5 November 1841 and 6 January 1843, it increasingly stressed the misery caused by the Corn Laws to ordinary people because of high food prices.
61. *Royal Cornwall Gazette*, 19 December 1845, 2 January ('No Minister that ever ruled England arrogated such exclusive personal importance'), 20 February, 6 March, 24 April, 17 July, 21 August 1846.
62. *West Briton*, 2, 30 January, 6 February, 26 June 1846.
63. *West Briton*, 24 July 1846.
64. *Royal Cornwall Gazette*, January 1849, 3 January 1851.
65. See issues of both the newspapers, 1850, 1851, 1852, for the background to the election, July 1852.
66. *West Briton*, 3 January 1851. More needs to be known on Brown; he is not mentioned at all in either Boase and Courtney, 1874, or Boase, 1890.
67. Asa Briggs, *The Age of Improvement*, London, 1958, p. 427; Somerset Record Office, Taunton, Sanford Mss DD/SF/3733, document dated 1 January 1858. The Sanfords of Nynehead, near Wellington, were prominent Liberals, Edward Ayshford Sanford being county MP 1830–41.
68. *Royal Cornwall Gazette*, 22 May, 3, 20 July 1819; Payton, 1999, ch. 3 esp. pp. 71, 78.
69. *West Briton*, 2 April 1832, 17 February 1843; Payton, 1999, pp. 72, 87.
70. *West Briton*, 2 August 1850. The trial at Cornwall Assizes found Spry guilty. The county meeting, held on 12 February, was reported in the *West Briton*, 15 February 1850.
71. Berry in the *West Briton*, 20 July 1960. Both papers had, over the years, taken over other local papers. The *West Briton* had absorbed the *Cornish Guardian* in 1835, commenting (17 April): 'After a fair experiment of two

years it has been ascertained that the County will not support two journals of decidedly Liberal politics'. On 21 August 1840, the *Royal Cornwall Gazette* announced 'the *Falmouth Express* is now incorporated into the paper'.

72. For other Cornish newspapers, see Tangye's Finding List, 1980, and the more accurate and recent *Bibliography of British Newspapers: Cornwall*, ed. Jean Rowles, British Library 1991.

73. P. Payton, *Cornwall*, Fowey, 1996, p. 214; CRO Vyvyan Mss 22.M/BO/36/46 Sir R. Vyvyan to Lord Churston, 4 January 1864.

74. Read, 1961, for his study of Manchester, Sheffield and Leeds papers. For the *West Briton*'s attitude to Chartism in Cornwall see issues of 22 February, 15 March, 5 April, 3, 17 May 1839, 24 January 1840, 16 April 1841, 23 February 1844.

75. *West Briton*, 11 June 1847. For a full account of the riots which lasted from late January to June, see Rowe, 1953, pp. 157–62. In the initial stages, the *Gazette*'s editor had been fairly sympathetic: 'When the utmost food they can procure is not enough to give them strength for their work, while their families at home are pinched with want, we cannot wonder if they meet, not to riot and threaten, but to satisfy themselves that their present sufferings are unavoidable' (22 January 1847).

76. J. Vincent and M. Stenton (eds), *McCalmont's Parliamentary Poll Book 1832–1910*, Brighton, 1971.

THE RESPONSE IN CORNWALL TO THE OUTBREAK OF THE FIRST WORLD WAR

Stuart Dalley

INTRODUCTION

On 4 August 1914 the British government finally ended weeks of speculation and declared war on Germany. Alone in his office that afternoon, Prime Minister Herbert Asquith wept as he told his wife: 'It's all up'.[1] The Foreign Secretary, Sir Edward Grey, famously compared the war 'to the lamps going out all over Europe', adding: 'We shall not see them lit again in our lifetime'.[2] Nevertheless, whilst some politicians, including the German Kaiser himself, seemed deeply shaken by the scale of events that was unfolding, a euphoric and patriotic fervour had swept through the people of Europe. Whilst chants of 'we want war' and 'God save the king' were heard around Buckingham Palace and Whitehall, similar scenes were being acted out across Europe as major cities buzzed with excitement and anticipation.

The abundant recollections of people enthusiastically greeting the news of war have since been used to support the belief that war was warmly welcomed across Europe in 1914. Yet, there is a growing amount of evidence that seeks to qualify this belief and to question whether it is all too often based on the reactions of the people in major metropolitan areas of these countries, rather than the more peripheral and rural parts. These metropolitan reactions are then used to illustrate the response of the 'British', 'French' or 'German' people.

By investigating the response in Cornwall to the outbreak of the First World War, this article aims to fill some gaps in our knowledge of how different parts of Britain responded to the war. For a number of reasons, Cornwall is a particularly interesting example of how a peripheral and largely rural region responded to the news of war. Its distinctness is reinforced by strong traditions of Nonconformity, especially Methodism, and Liberalism. Though pacifism does not form part of the doctrine of Methodism, unlike Quakerism for example, it has in the past had a streak of pacifism and was blamed in some parts of Wales for low recruiting figures throughout the course of the First World War.[3] This article seeks to understand whether people in Cornwall reacted differently to the news of war than did people elsewhere. This will then allow us to ascertain whether Cornwall did or did not conform to what is supposedly the national—or indeed European—'norm' of jingoistic patriotism.

WAR ENTHUSIASM IN CORNWALL

If the initial news of the outbreak of war was greeted throughout Europe with joyous celebrations and large gatherings in major metropolitan areas, this did not extend to Cornwall. Indeed, the *Cornish Guardian* on 7 August reported on the 'absence of gaiety' in Newquay since the declaration of war. Horse shows, wrestling matches and other Bank Holiday attractions had seen low attendance because, it was claimed, 'people did not feel like amusement'.[4] There was a low turnout too at the Newlyn carnival as people, concerned about the unfolding crisis, 'refrained from festivities'.[5] A week before, the *West Briton* had declared that 'the supreme surprise is the enthusiasm with which a proportion of the population of every country receives the news that war has been declared'.[6]

What is most striking about the response in Cornwall to the outbreak of the war is the difficulty in finding evidence to suggest that news of the war was popularly received. To many in Cornwall, unconcerned with the intricacies of European power politics, the outbreak of war came as a complete surprise. Writing in her diary on 9 August, Elsie Stephens of Penryn commented on how 'everything has come on us like a sudden thunderstorm'.[7] Nevertheless, it is from the very earliest days of the war that the variety of responses to the war from different sections of Cornwall's diverse population becomes apparent. Two groups stand out in Cornwall for their support of the war: the seafaring communities and the Methodists. A third group, the Anglicans, also supported the war, though given their minority religious status in Cornwall, evidence of their reaction is less easy to find.

Whilst Cornwall did not witness scenes of spontaneous celebration at the news of war, Cornwall's coastal communities are notable as being one of the only groups where signs of explicit war enthusiasm can actually be found. These scenes of enthusiasm occurred mainly in the opening days of the war with the call-up of the Royal Naval Reserve and the Royal Naval Volunteer Reserve. Thus, when Britain declared war at the beginning of August, thousands of fishermen and other seafarers across Cornwall were soon issued with their call-up papers and told to report immediately to Devonport.[8] The departure of these men was the cause for great excitement in fishing ports across Cornwall. Nevertheless, it was seemingly in St Ives where the scenes of greatest excitement occurred. Two thousand people, both locals and some holidaymakers, are reported to have lined the streets of the town in scenes of 'great enthusiasm' as the naval reservists departed. 'God save the King' and 'Auld Lang Syne' were sung as the reserves marched through the streets and the crowds waved union flags, handkerchiefs, hats and caps.[9]

Despite the fact that the naval reserves would be called up at various stages throughout the war as they came of age or were needed as replacements, scenes such as those witnessed at St Ives would not be repeated. They are a reflection of the early enthusiasm for the war to be found in these communities before hostilities began to exact their heavy toll. Indeed, by October the government's Inspector of Fisheries, Stephen Reynolds, who spent much of his time in the Cornish fishing ports, could write: 'It seems incredible that war can be on at all in this peaceful and beautiful Cornwall'.[10] The enthusiastic reaction of these communities early on reflects, in part, the fact that they were used to sending their young men away as reservists at times of national emergency. Arthur Quiller-Couch, known in Cornwall and beyond as 'Q', Professor of English Literature at Cambridge University, founder member of Cowethas Kelto-Kernuak (The Cornish Celtic Society) and one-time president of the Bodmin Liberal Association, later commented: 'Nothing could surpass the readiness, unless it were the cheerfulness, with which all the Reservists answered the instant call'.[11] Many men in these communities had had sustained contact with Royal Navy and military service. It had been estimated at one time that men from Cornwall and Devon made up two-thirds of the Royal Navy's total manpower.[12] The lives of the men in these villages were tied up with the Royal Navy from an early age, even if they were never actually called upon to serve. Their early years would be spent learning the ways of the sea and young children from these villages would spend their time distinguishing the different types of battleship that had set out from Plymouth to carry out their speed tests off the south Cornish coast. They had far more contact, both direct and indirect, with the British military than other communities in Cornwall. This sustained contact with the military had instilled in them a readiness and willingness to fight when war came, and when that war came in August of 1914 they marched eagerly away.

Whilst scenes of excitement were witnessed immediately in Cornish seafaring communities, the response from Cornwall's pulpits was not so immediate, but they would soon come to endorse and support the war. Among Methodists, the Boer War had led to much soul-searching, but the soldier was still seen as a remote and brave person defending the outposts of the British Empire and Christian civilization. Most Methodists accepted the necessity of the South African War and the need for British victory. However, more will be said later of the reactions of Cornish Methodists to the war with regards to recruiting; as the dominant religious group in the county their response to the war more generally must be examined. Their reaction and the role they played in recruiting campaigns demonstrates that what may have been said about the effects of Nonconformity on the response to the war in parts of Wales, highlighted above, does not necessarily apply to Cornwall. Nevertheless, some Methodists did harbour initial reservations about the war. The Wesleyan Superintendent Minister of Helston reacted with horror to the news of its outbreak, whilst the Reverend G.A. Bennetts, preaching at St Austell, encouraged people to do 'all they could to conquer the war spirit'.[13]

These views, however, were short-lived. One of the earliest reactions of some Methodists was to suggest that moral and social corruptness had brought about the conflict. G.A. Bennetts, who had earlier pleaded for peace, believed that the war was the judgement of God and he raged against the short skirts, foul language and drunkenness that he claimed to see and hear on the streets of St Austell.[14] The view of the war as the product of man's immorality lasted in Methodist circles until November when, with reports of German atrocities in Belgium reaching Britain, Methodist ministers started to take a stronger pro-war line and saw the necessity of the conflict. They became less inclined to blame human immorality or to confine the blame to the invidious activities of the Kaiser and his militaristic entourage.

From the beginning of the war there was a belief among Methodists that would get steadily stronger as the war progressed. This belief revolved around the idea that the war was a just crusade and that the bloodletting that it was causing was a necessary purge of the human soul. Many also spoke of it in Darwinian terms believing that the fittest would survive to form the basis of a new and stronger race. Before this, however, it was necessary to have destruction and sacrifice before peace could rise from the ruins. Whilst this view was spreading by the autumn, some ministers had spoken of it from the outset. Preaching in August at the Zion United Methodist Church in St Austell, W.J.

Nicholls had said that though he hated war, Britain had entered it with a clear conscience and 'would defeat the lustful purposes of men in high places, and that out of the cauldron of fire and flames, the world would produce a new order in which war between civilised nations should be an utter impossibility and the brotherhood of man should be universally recognised'.[15] This view was to be echoed on a number of occasions in the autumn and winter of 1914 and into 1915.

Some ministers spoke of their fears if Britain should lose and urged their congregations to remember the seriousness of what they were up against. The Rev. Dr F.B. Meyer had claimed that the only way peace could be achieved was to 'shatter militarism and the German Emperor',[16] whilst in the spring of 1915, with the war still raging, J.H. Cartwright had reminded his congregation in Marazion that the war against the devil and all his works should be waged with same ferocity as the war against 'the German and all his works'.[17] Other ministers spoke to their followers of the bravery and chivalry of the British soldiers compared with their German counterparts who were quite prepared to injure civilians and damage property.

Thus, what is clear from the views of Methodist ministers is that they openly supported the war and were prepared to try to infuse a more patriotic feeling into their congregations. Any suggestions that they lacked war spirit or loyalty to the country are simply not true. From the available evidence they actually stand out for their pro-war opinions. Nevertheless, when writing of the response of the 'Methodists', several factors must be borne in mind before it is accepted that Methodists unequivocally supported the war. Unlike Anglicanism, Methodism has a strong tradition of lay preachers taking the services at local chapels. Though they did receive some training, they could almost be described as amateurs. Many Methodist ministers would have five or six chapels for which they were responsible, and as they could not be in several places at once, they used lay preachers to take services when they were absent. The difficulty, as far as this article is concerned, in understanding the response of the Methodists is that newspapers only report the sermons given by the actual ministers, not the lay preachers. It is possible that the views of ministers were not really that of lay preachers or their congregations. Methodist ministers tended to have the same type of middle-class educated backgrounds as their Anglican counterparts and were thus more likely to conform to the official government line and not to speak out against the war. Furthermore, although it is not always possible to know the precise backgrounds of the ministers, many of them were not actually Cornish. Lay preachers, however, were arguably more reflective of local opinion. They were local people who did not have 'establishment' backgrounds and were thus more likely to speak out against the war than the ministers were. Evidence for their opinions, however, is very hard to find. One example though is that of the congregation at Falmouth Wesley Church. Each member of the congregation, at the outbreak of the war, signed the following letter:

> To the right honourable Sir Edward Grey,—We, the under-signed, view with horror the terrible outrage to humanity and the menacing challenge to Christianity involved in a European war. We desire to strengthen by every means in our power the strenuous efforts you are making to limit the war by pledging and maintaining our peaceable relations with the nations of Europe whilst reserving our freedom to give every peace as opportunity affords.[18]

Examples of the actions and beliefs of congregations, as opposed to ministers' personal views, are extremely difficult to find; yet their importance should not be discounted. It is distinctly possible that below the official rhetoric of the Methodists, there lies a current of opposition to the war. That newspapers did not print many examples of dissension may be due to their own choice of what should appear in the newspaper, rather than reflecting lack of Methodist opposition. It may be suggested that newspapers did not print them because, as will become clearer later in this article, Cornwall was already being accused of not being patriotic enough and editors did not want this view reinforced in their newspaper columns.

Some anxiety already existed that Cornwall was being neglected and forgotten by the central government. This, in combination with the less than enthusiastic response with which the war was met in some parts of the county, may have led some editors to try to assert the fact that Cornwall supported the war and was as patriotic as the rest of the country. Anything that suggested otherwise would be left out of the newspaper. The issue of the response of lay preachers and the actual congregations is an important dimension to the response of the Methodists and it is unfortunate that it cannot be illustrated further. It is also important in that comments made by men like Colonel Williams, Commander of the 3rd Battalion of the Duke of Cornwall's Light Infantry, may not have been totally groundless. Williams, speaking at Trewennack (near Helston) in March 1915, had blamed the lack of enthusiasm in Cornwall on the Nonconformist conscience. Though the editor of the *Cornish Guardian* called his remarks 'ill-advised',[19] and the Congregationalist minister D. Lewys-Thomas said that he was 'impatient with the vulgar sneers at the

Nonconformist conscience, the veiled insinuation of the lack of loyalty and patriotism',[20] it may be that the colonel was reflecting on what he had heard from Methodists who were not the ministers whose comments regularly appeared in the local newspapers.

Cornish Anglicans also responded to the outbreak of war in a very similar way to the Methodists and it is not necessary to repeat much of what has already been said above. Indeed, on occasions, the war actually pulled the two closer together and some Methodists expressed concerns that doctrinal differences between Nonconformists and Anglicans were actually being erased. Others Methodists spoke of the development of a 'non-ecclesiastical Christianity'. Joint prayer meetings attended by Nonconformists and Anglicans were also held on several occasions, such as that in St Austell on 3 January 1915.[21]

Given their minority status in Cornwall, evidence for the response of Anglicans is much more difficult to find than it is for Methodists. After all, 'Cornish folk were not on the whole enamoured of the ways of the church which had neglected its people for so long'.[22] The Bishop of Exeter, visiting Cornwall at the end of the nineteenth century, was appalled by the apathy and indifference of the clergy there who seemed to spend most of their time hunting. In 1896 when the Rev. Reginald Hobhouse's successor arrived to take over at St Ive parish church near Lostwithiel, he was shocked to discover that in a parish of 900 people, no more than 26 could be regarded as Anglican.[23] Mary Moore, daughter of the Bishop of Truro, also speaks of the 'poor' and 'lonely' existence of the clergy 'in remote villages where most people were Nonconformists'.[24]

Nevertheless, it would seem that, much like their Nonconformist counterparts, many Anglicans had initial reservations about the war which were soon cast aside with reports of German atrocities in Belgium and the growing seriousness of the conflict. Clearly they did not expect war to break out in August of 1914 and were taken aback when Britain issued its ultimatum to Germany. The Bishop of Truro, Winfred Burrows, had been planning to go to Canada on 7 August where he was due to preach at the General Synod of the Canadian Church in Vancouver. In parishes across Cornwall prayers were said in the days leading up to war not only for peace in Ireland and for the Welsh Church, but also 'for those who are spending their holidays in Cornwall, that they may gain refreshment of body and mind'.[25] There was seemingly no sense of the impending crisis. However, when war was declared the bishop immediately cancelled his planned trip and called for special weekly services of intercession in every church in addition to the usual daily offices. He suggested that bells should be rung daily to recall hearers to prayer for those serving in the forces.

The bishop believed that the people of Cornwall stood in front of God 'innocent, penitent, suppliant, united, resolute and trustful'. Echoing some Methodists, he said: 'The war was forced upon us but we could hardly doubt that God was chastising us for our sins . . . We were resolute to fight for our country, our freedom, our Empire, and our lives, until . . . we came through to the end.'[26]

Anglicans, much like Methodist ministers, seemed to have done all they could to help the war effort. Numerous Belgian refugees arrived in Treverbyn parish early in 1915 to be looked after by the local clergy, whilst the Bishop of Truro also received some to stay at his home at Lis Escop. The bishop also allowed injured Dominion officers, who had no family in Britain, to stay at his home after they had left hospital. Thus, the available evidence for the response of Cornish Anglicans confirms the rather unsurprising fact that Cornish Anglicans, apart from one exception that will be mentioned later, considered the war to be a just cause. There is no suggestion that they objected to the war's outbreak or condemned its conduct as the casualty lists mounted in the early months of 1915. Nor were they ever, unlike the Nonconformists, accused of lacking in patriotism or of shirking in their duty to the country.

OPPOSITION TO WAR

When Britain announced its declaration of war on Germany, Arthur Quiller-Couch had just returned to his home town of Fowey. He was a very well known local figure and until 1912 had been President of the Liberal Association in East Cornwall. He had resigned over government proposals for the detention of the medically unfit which, he believed, ran counter to his liberal and humane principles. Quiller-Couch was among the first in Cornwall to express his grave reservations about the war. In a letter to the *West Briton*, which was also sent to a number of other local newspapers, he had written:

> As a nation of honest men, we must stand by our engage-
> ments . . . It is madness, nevertheless, which commits England
> to this foolish balance of power, and may call out Englishmen
> to die, fighting Germans (with whom they have no quarrel)
> for a set of Serbs in whom they have no interest. The whole
> business, in short, is merely monstrous.[27]

People in Cornwall at this time had great reason to express con-cern at the coming of war. In many ways it is not surprising that people there did not share in the great enthusiasm which is supposed to have been so apparent elsewhere in the country. The Rev. Bernard Walke, vicar at St Hilary near Penzance, himself an opponent of the war, wrote of the day that war was declared:

> It was very hot that Sunday night and the church was crowded with men and women, many of whom I had never seen there before . . . Some were there, as animals will herd together in the face of a common danger, to find assurance in the midst of a crowd; others came to seek for God and to discover an escape from the destruction they felt to be overtaking them.[28]

The war had an immediate and devastating effect on three of the county's main industries and caused much unemployment. On 17 August the *West Briton* had warned of the effect the war would have on the county:

> Three industries in the county are heavy sufferers at present —china clay, tin mining and fishing . . . Germany and Russia took enormous quantities of china clay from Cornwall and the closing of those markets for a time is a disaster to the district . . . Tin mining is inconvenienced only because the London Metal Market is closed and there is no quoted price for the metal . . . The fishing industry is hindered in three ways. Men are taken for the Naval Reserve, those that remain at home are restricted in their operations at sea, and the best markets show the effects of a general depression.[29]

In 1914, Cornish tin mining had long since past its heyday of the mid-nineteenth century and only a handful of mines remained in operation. Those that did remain had, since the turn of the century, faced fierce competition from the tin mines of Bolivia, Malaya and, after 1905, Nigeria. As the Cornish mining industry went into serious decline, Cornish miners began, once again, to search for richer mineral fields abroad.[30]

Though the Cornish tin industry struggled on, despite the mass emigration of miners and competition from abroad, it was to be the outbreak of the First World War that dealt one of the final blows to the industry. The year 1914 would, for tin-mining interests, be remembered as one of the disaster years to rank alongside those of 1874 and 1896. The first signs of the impending crisis came in 1913 when, in the autumn, the price of tin on the London market fell from £288 in January to £184 by July.[31] This was followed by the sale of Great Dowgas mine in September, which was reckoned to be among the best equipped mines in the county. Work in the mines at Carn Brea and

Botallack was suspended in early 1914, and by June of that year the price of tin had dropped to £139 per ton. With the outbreak of war in August, the situation for Cornish mines became critical. With the London Metal Market closed, sales of tin had to be postponed and no ticketings (sales of tin) were held in Redruth for nine weeks. As a result of this, the mines at Wheal Bellen, Porthledden and Cape Cornwall all had to lay off their workforce and cease production. By September they were followed by Dolcoath, Botallack, Wheal Jane, Boswin, Mulberry and Wheal Hampton, which all suspended or totally ceased operations. The mining crisis continued into 1915 when the St Ives Consolidated mine was wound up in April, leaving a deficit estimated at £14,000. Most of the plant was then shifted to the company's Wolfram Camp mines in Queensland, Australia.

Though there can be little doubt of the scale of the problem that the war brought to Cornwall's mines, the major problem is finding evidence to suggest an anti-war feeling among tin-mining interests and among the miners themselves. However, despite the lack of direct evidence, it is very difficult to believe that hundreds of men who had just lost their jobs and mining interests who were making no money due to the cancellations of ticketings did not express some type of reservation about the war. The only real evidence of anti-war feeling among miners will be addressed below, when their response to volunteering is considered. Though the tin price would rise again during the war and miners would be re-employed in order to produce the wolfram necessary for armaments production, it is distinctly possible that there was a strong feeling against the war and its impact upon tin mining.

The Cornish clay-mining industry was also hit hard by the outbreak of war, which seriously impacted on the previously flourishing trade. Only the previous year the clay-mining industry had been seriously affected by a general strike of its workers. At one point the strike had turned violent and special riot police, more used to rampaging mobs, had to be drafted in from Bristol and South Wales to control the strikers. Nevertheless, many people, including some strikers who had joined due to the threat of reprisals from fellow workers should they not get involved, saw the strike as totally unnecessary. The clay-mining industry was very prosperous and had avoided the unrest and strikes that had beset other British industries in 1911 and 1912. However, a small group of workers had stirred up trouble by highlighting the fact that clay miners were not getting their fair share of the profits that were being generated. It was pointed out, for example, that coal miners were paid more than clay miners even though the price of coal was only 9s 6d per ton, compared with 20s for clay.[32]

By the outbreak of the war the clay industry had fully recovered from the strike of the previous summer and was enjoying boom conditions. Given the surge in demand following the strike, producers had huge stocks of clay ready to be exported abroad. Nevertheless, when news of the war broke most of these orders were immediately cancelled. Clay destined for France, Russia, Germany, Belgium and the Netherlands would never leave port. By 10 August, a mere six days after Britain's declaration of war, several clay companies, including those of Carn Stents, West of England and Great Beam, had practically closed down, whilst others had introduced a shorter working week. The situation for the industry had become so serious that by 20 August the *West Briton* claimed that one thousand clay miners had lost their jobs since the outbreak of war. Local papers testify to the devastating impact that the war had upon the industry, with weekly reports of the depression and unemployment to be found in those areas around St Austell. Nor, unlike tin mining, would the situation improve for clay mining as the war continued. Indeed, it became worse. By 1917 clay production, which in the boom year of 1912 had reached 860,649 tons, had now sunk to 463,632 tons.[33]

The importance of the devastating impact of the outbreak of war on Cornish industry lies in the fact that it would be highly unlikely that not one single person adversely affected spoke out against the war. Though there is a total lack of evidence to indicate any hostility from these sectors, the possibility should not be discounted. The disruptions caused to Cornish trade and jobs may have played a key part in explaining the less than enthusiastic reception with which the war was greeted in some quarters. Many people already felt that they were poorly paid and the war had brought yet more misery for them. Newspapers sometimes printed statements made by local people which had been overheard by someone else, who had then written to a newspaper to express their disgust at such views. One person, it was reported, had claimed that: 'We should be as well off under the Germans as we are now. We have to work for our living now, and for poor pay, and it should not be worse under the Germans.'[34]

Whilst a number of prominent individuals in Cornwall opposed the outbreak of war, or at the very least held deep reservations about it, special mention must be made of one certain individual. That individual was Emily Hobhouse, who was born at the Rectory of St Ive near Liskeard on 9 April 1860. She deserves special mention not only because of her opposition to the war, but also because she was one of the few females in Cornwall at this time whose opinions were actually taken seriously. Indeed, later in the First World War her pacifist activities were seen as so threatening to British interests that she was constantly under the supervision of the Home Office, or of the Foreign Office when she was abroad. After a spell in the United States in the late nineteenth century where she worked helping alleviate the poor conditions of Cornish miners, she returned to Britain to work with the Women's Industrial Council in London, which was concerned mainly with the exploitation of working children. During the Boer War she became Secretary of the Women's Branch of the South African Conciliation Committee and help to set up a relief fund for women and children who had found themselves without homes and food due to the war. She also made a tour of British refugee camps in South Africa and was appalled by the conditions in which the prisoners were kept. She returned to Britain in May 1901 and immediately set about addressing audiences throughout Britain, writing letters to newspapers and attempting to get audiences with senior British politicians in order to highlight the plight of those interned in British camps. It is her work in South Africa for which she is best known and her efforts to raise money and awareness of the conditions there did little to enamour her to the British government. It considered her to be an interfering menace and refused to give her permission to land at Cape Town when she returned again in October 1901. Though Miss Hobhouse is more famous for her activities in South Africa, her opposition to the First World War and her attempts at uniting people against it are still very important. On 1 August, with war looming in Britain, Miss Hobhouse wrote a letter to the *Manchester Guardian* endorsing that newspaper's demand for neutrality. She wrote:

> Few English people have seen war in its nakedness, hence the thoughtless cries for it. They know nothing of the poverty, destruction, disease, pain, misery and mortality which follows in its trail. I have seen all this and more and my experience adds force to my appeal to all lovers of humanity to avert the horror that is threatened.[35]

Shortly before Britain declared war, Miss Hobhouse wrote to Lloyd George asking him to avoid war and said that declaring war on Germany would ruin his life's work. She also wrote to her friend Jan Smuts in South Africa begging him not to get his country involved. From her home in Bude, Miss Hobhouse took to supporting the efforts of women throughout Europe to mitigate the effects of the war. In October she addressed an open letter to women throughout Europe outlining the devastation caused by war and highlighting how, a hundred years ago, men had fought for freedom and independence. 'War failed to secure those objectives then', she wrote, 'can we reasonably suppose it will do so now?'[36] During the spring and summer of 1915, sometimes with the help of the Quaker Relief Detachment, she visited France, Italy, where she normally spent her winters, and Switzerland. She also played a part, along with Dr Aletta Jacobs, Holland's first female doctor, in establishing an international committee which they called 'Women for a Permanent Peace'. In her travels throughout Europe, once again to the great annoyance of the British government, she spread the word of peace and reconciliation.

Miss Hobhouse would keep up her campaign for peace for the duration of the war and even managed, in June 1916, to get an audience in Berlin with the German Minister for Foreign Affairs, Gottlieb von Jagow. The Foreign Office and the British government seethed when they found out and her passport was promptly confiscated.

Thus, a number of prominent individuals in Cornwall opposed the outbreak of war, even if some of them, like Arthur Quiller-Couch, would soon come to help organize Cornwall's war effort by addressing recruitment marches and helping to raise and pay for the equipping of a new battalion of the Duke of Cornwall's Light Infantry. Nevertheless, whilst educated and respected individuals such as these have left books and memoirs that testify to their feelings about the war, the mass of Cornish folk at this time have, unsurprisingly, left little evidence of their views. It has, however, been suggested above that many of these people would have had good reason to oppose the war. It is possible that this, at least partly, accounts for the lack of enthusiasm to be found in the county that was so often commented upon in the newspapers. However, there is one area of response to the outbreak of the war about which it is easier to gauge the general mood of people in Cornwall at that time. That area is the response of men to Kitchener's call for volunteers to supplement Britain's small regular army.

RECRUITMENT IN CORNWALL FOR KITCHENER'S NEW ARMY

Whilst the responses of the groups mentioned above are essential in forming an opinion of how Cornwall reacted to news of the war, there can be no better measure of war enthusiasm than the willingness of men to volunteer for military service. Once again, however, although it is possible to talk in general terms about the willingness of Cornishmen to volunteer, the diversity of Cornish society must be borne in mind. Attention needs to be paid to the major employment sectors and to address the reasons why men in each of these sectors may, or may not, have been willing to fight. The major employment sectors in Cornwall at this time were those of mining (tin and clay), agriculture and fishing. There was also a nascent tourist industry, but in 1914 this was still a very small employer. Each of Cornwall's major employment sectors had its own distinct identity, history and traditions and these have to be appreciated in order to understand the response to volunteering. Thus, whilst the overall response to volunteering will be examined, each individual group will be analysed as a separate case.

On 7 August 1914 Lord Kitchener addressed a letter to the Lord Lieutenants and Chairmen of Territorial Force County Associations throughout Britain indicating his intention to enlist at least 100,000 men and asking for their help in achieving this. His request for men was answered throughout Britain with astounding enthusiasm as men flocked to join the British forces in unprecedented numbers. The War Office was totally unprepared for the deluge of young men eager to volunteer for military service. This flood of volunteers into the British forces has now come to form part of the mythology of the First World War and it is often held up as the prime example of war enthusiasm. If volunteering is one of the key manifestations of war enthusiasm, then once again Cornwall's enthusiasm for the war can be questioned. The apparent unwillingness of men in Cornwall to fight would plague the county throughout the period under consideration here. At the end of August, the *West Briton* claimed that whilst 'in some large towns men are joining in large numbers . . . Cornwall in the week for which records have been published was surprisingly backward, less than seventy men joining. One hopes that this will be rapidly improved before the next lot of figures are issued'.[37] Figures, however, did not improve, and Cornish newspapers attest to the problem of volunteering in the county with regular letters from members of the public rounding on those young men who should be at the front, as well as publishing the figures released by the Parliamentary Recruiting Committee (PRC) which were rarely flattering to Cornwall.[38]

Newspapers frequently reported the poor attendance at recruit-ment meetings or how, after a series of rousing speeches by officers and local dignitaries, only one or two men came forward.[39] A major recruiting march around Cornwall by the 3rd Battalion of the Duke of Cornwall's Light Infantry in March and April 1915 was a dismal failure despite bands and patriotic appeals to the young men. At Troon the marchers were ridiculed and shouted at by local men. When Colonel Williams asked why they had not enlisted, 'they simply laughed and jeered at us'. The marchers were also abused and shouted at when they reached Illogan. Mr T.W. Dobson, speaking during the march at Wendron, said he regretted the need for the march to take place but 'it is because Cornwall has not been as patriotic . . . as certain other towns and districts. For some reason . . . Cornwall has not rallied around the British standard.'[40]

Whilst there is a wealth of evidence indicating an unwillingness among many in Cornwall to volunteer, what should concern us most is why this should be. If men everywhere else in the country really did flock to join up, then the reasons why this should not be so in Cornwall need to be explored further. For this to be done, attention must be paid to the different employment sectors in Cornwall. All of these have different reasons for their unwillingness to volunteer, though some of these are very difficult to pinpoint precisely. Whilst some at the time may have raised the idea that Cornwall's unenthusiastic response was due to the 'Celtic temperament', such abstract notions need not detain us here, for there are other more easily identifiable reasons for the reluctance in Cornwall to fight.

According to a survey carried out by the Miners' Federation of Great Britain shortly after the outbreak of war, 115,000 of its members had already volunteered. By the middle of 1915, more than 230,000 miners across Britain had volunteered, with Glamorgan, Durham, Northumberland and some Scottish coalfields registering extremely high rates of enlistment.[41] One commentator believed that miners 'seem to have been moved to remarkable enthusiasm for the war and they enlisted by the thousands after hearing stories of the British fighting and the destruction of Belgian towns'.[42] However, whilst miners throughout Britain rushed to sign up, Cornish tin miners were less than enthusiastic. Indeed, volunteering rates in Cornwall appear to indicate a particularly poor response in the county's industrial areas. In February 1915 the chairman of the Mining Division Recruiting Committee reported that volunteering rates there were the worst he knew in Cornwall. Even the recruitment march by the 3rd Battalion, mentioned above, failed to stir the miners to a sense of duty. 'At Porkellis', reported the *Royal Cornwall Gazette*, 'not one of the many young miners who listened to the band could be aroused to a sense of their duty.' Colonel Williams, addressing an audience mainly composed of miners at Wendron, called them 'a damned disgrace'. He claimed:

> The Welsh miner was putting his king and country before his own little miserable local affairs. Why can't you follow the lead of your brother miners in Wales? Why can't you follow that example? It is a crying shame you men in Cornwall should see your brother miners going and laying down their lives, and that you will not go and back them up.[43]

Yet the lack of enthusiasm for the war found among miners already had its precedents. To some, the response of Cornish miners in 1914 to the demands of their country for duty and sacrifice simply echoed their response in 1895 and 1899–1902 at the time of the Jameson Raid and the Boer War. As has been highlighted above, thousands of young Cornishmen had emigrated to South Africa throughout the nineteenth century so that by the time of the First World War there were possibly more Cornish miners in South Africa than there were in Cornwall. Such was their reluctance to become involved in the political affairs of South Africa that in both 1895 and 1899 many of them fled the country to return to the safety of Cornwall. Others moved on to other mining areas in Australia and the United States. This lead to attacks on them as unpatriotic cowards.

Whilst some miners had fled South Africa for Cornwall in 1895 and 1899, the reverse was sometimes the case in 1914 and 1915. Many Cornish miners, keen to avoid the pressures upon them to volunteer, left for South Africa, whilst others, it was reported, had gone to the United States. Such was the scale of emigration to South Africa that by December 1915 the Cornish Association of South Africa was moved to condemn the actions of those arriving there:

> It seems incomprehensible to us that young able-bodied men should desert their country at a time when it is fighting for its very existence. The Association intends if the offence continues to approach the Chamber of Mines and invite them to refuse any employment to eligible men arriving in that country from England and have every reason to believe that the Chamber will comply with their request.[44]

Rates of volunteering were not very good among Cornish clay miners either. Nevertheless, whilst it is not always possible to be precise about the reasons for the unwillingness of some tin miners to volunteer, it is easier to highlight a key factor behind the resistance of clay miners to volunteer. Quite simply, they had not yet forgiven the government, or rather the 'establishment', for the brutal suppression of their strike the previous year. They were certainly not going to join up and fight a war for them now. This is apparent time and again in reports of recruitment meetings held in clay-mining areas. Unlike tin miners, many of whom it can be suggested eventually volunteered because they had lost their jobs due to the depression in the tin-mining industry, clay miners steadfastly refused to volunteer despite the mass cancellation of clay orders and the resultant high unemployment. Even the editor of the *Cornish Guardian* was forced to admit that 'recruiting in Cornwall generally, and the clay district particularly, has not been up to expectations'.[45] Arthur Quiller-Couch recognized this lack of enthusiasm and, despite his numerous addresses to them, was forced to admit that they were still 'nursing a major grievance due to the authorities bringing in corps from outside and prepared to use martial force to break the strike'.[46] The Rev Booth Coventry, Primitive Methodist Minister, speaking at a recruitment meeting for clay miners in November 1914 was met with shouts of 'What about twelve months ago? We don't forget',[47] whilst Alfred Browning Lyne was told by one clay miner: 'Let the gentry go and fight, what is it to do with us?'[48]

Recruitment also proved difficult in rural areas of Cornwall where 'the idea of war was a new thing . . . while that of a General levy to meet an unrealised energy lay remoter yet and far beyond the country-side's horizon'.[49] Nevertheless, numbers of volunteers could often be proportionally greater than in the towns. Agricultural labourers had a greater economic incentive to volunteer. In his editorial column of the *Cornish Guardian*, Alfred Browning Lyne believed that 'men who have been engaged on the land are joining up in bigger proportion than those in industrial centres, because the inducement in regard to the matter of pay is bigger in their case than it is with the others'.[50] Nevertheless, volunteering in rural areas could still be very slack, especially during the opening days of the war due to the need for men to be available to collect the harvest. Farmers could not, at this stage, afford to lose men to the forces and many protested into 1915 about the damage that losing men would do to their business. One farmer writing to the *Royal Cornwall Gazette* claimed that 'farmers' sons were well justified in staying at home keeping things together'. He believed that 'in many instances these sons are the stay of the farm, and many people forget that if we want to reap next year, the work on the farm must be accomplished in the winter'.[51] Not only was recruitment often inhibited in these places because of the need to carry on vital work, but many commentators also believed that many people in these remote rural locations did not fully understand the gravity of the situation. It may also be that they did not really care. Living far from major population centres they were often ignorant of events happening else-where.

The Cornish writer Joseph Hocking said he was astounded at the level of ignorance in the rural districts: 'The ignorance as to the causes and aims of the war is appalling . . . Owing to the fact that they are so far from the centre of things the people do not realise the tremendous issues at stake.'[52] He also repeated a story he had been told about how, in one remote Cornish village, a postman had been asked to resolve a dispute between a man and wife over whether Lord Kitchener was

British or German! It was also likely that some agricultural labourers did not volunteer for one reason that has also been attributed to the lack of enthusiasm from tin and clay miners. An article in the *Royal Cornwall Gazette* stated that: 'For scores, perhaps hundreds of years past, it has been regarded by Cornish folk—the working-class particularly—as a "low down thing" to enlist as a soldier. It was the fashion . . . even for a ne'er do well to be regarded as having taken one step lower in the social scale.'[53]

However, volunteering rates in some rural districts were among the highest in Cornwall. This may be due to the ability of landed families to exert some pressure on those who worked their land, as well as the fact that church-going tended to be higher in Cornwall's rural areas than its industrial centres.[54] As farmers were one of the groups that formed the backbone of Methodism in Cornwall at this time, they could therefore be influenced into volunteering by those many Methodist ministers who urged men to go and fight. By May 1915 it was reported to the May Synod of the Wesleyan Cornwall District that 80,000 'followers of John Wesley are engaged with the forces'. This referred only to Wesleyan Methodists. The United Methodists reported that they too had 12,500 of their number in the forces.[55] Landed families also seemed to be able to pressure their workers to follow their lead and this arguably accounts for such high recruiting figures in rural areas such as St Michael Caerhays or on the estate of Lord Falmouth.

Nevertheless, despite the rather pessimistic reports about volunteering in Cornwall at this time, the situation was not as straightforward as it may first appear. Clearly recruitment was problematic in Cornwall and one local newspaper was probably correct in its assertion that: 'Men who have spoken at recruiting meetings in West Cornwall and are acquainted with other parts of the country in the same way, state that here the men are more difficult to move . . . Why is it that the calls of this war are so callously heard by hundreds of young men in Cornwall?'[56]

Nevertheless, there are a number of factors that militate against the wholesale castigation of Cornishmen for their unwillingness to volunteer. Whilst some parts of Cornwall saw more volunteering than others, such as the east, the overall extent of Cornwall's initial contribution to the British war effort was greater than some contemporary commentators were prepared to acknowledge. It would appear that, all too often, observers were overly focused on volunteers for the army when, in fact, many Cornishmen joined the Royal Navy. This was true even of those that did not come from coastal communities. Many men in the county stepped forward to answer the Navy's demands for recruits. In May 1915 the Royal Navy had recognized the need for more recruits and had decided that 'special efforts [were] to be made to recruit ord. seamen for the period of hostilities age 19 to 30, with a minimum height of 5'4", chest 35" '. Volunteers up to the age of 38 would also be accepted provided that they had previous sea experience.[57] Most people in Cornwall at this time, judging by the letters and editorial columns of the local newspapers, seemed to accept that whilst Cornishmen were slack in volunteering to join the Army, they were much keener to join the Navy, which was seen as more acceptable. The *West Briton* wrote of 'places in the county . . . where calls for the Army are unheeded by youths and young men who are really anxious to join the Navy'.[58] One of those young men was Alfred Williams, who, whilst not exactly typical of the average Cornish youth at the time (not many young men in Cornwall could claim that their brother had driven his Rolls Royce at 'shocking' speeds through the country lanes near Redruth), later wrote in his memoirs as Europe was gearing up for war that 'My one big fear was that war would start before I got to sea. If war started before I got to sea, "how in the hell" could I ever catch up with the chaps just older, who were seagoing cadets, who might gain awards, and medals for bravery in action. This may sound far-fetched but really it was true.'[59]

In February 1915 the Southeast Cornwall Parliamentary Recruiting Committee revealed that recruiting had been 'steady' in that district, with most volunteers there joining the Navy.[60] Indeed, such was the rate of Cornishmen entering the Royal Navy that it was reckoned by some, including the *West Briton*, that Cornwall's contribution to the Navy was 'surpassing that of any other county in the United Kingdom in proportion to its population'.[61] The same view was adopted by G. Hay Morgans, who, writing to the *West Briton* from the House of Commons, had said that 'the Duchy provides a larger share of the Navy's personnel than any other similar portion of His Majesty's Dominions'.[62]

Whilst most Cornishmen preferred to serve in the Navy than the Army, thus accounting, to some extent, for the lack of Cornish volunteers for the Army, there is another aspect of Cornwall's contribution to Britain's initial war effort which is all too easily overlooked. This other contribution is the number of Cornishmen to be found in the armies of Britain's Dominions. It is estimated that during the course of the nineteenth century Cornwall had lost one-third of its population due to emigration, including the loss of 230,000 miners.[63] This emigration continued almost unabated until the start of the First World War. Though the diverse destinations to which Cornishmen emigrated have already been highlighted above, it was, however, confined mainly to South Africa, the United States, Canada, Australia and New Zealand. Thus, when these countries sent their forces to help Britain, they contained not only sons of earlier Cornish emigrants, but also many men who had been born and had lived in Cornwall but who were forced to emigrate. The *West Briton* reported in November 1914 that 'Cornishmen are in the contingents from our Colonies in very satisfying numbers'.[64] South Africa entered the war on 8 September and her Army contained a number of Cornishmen who would see service not only in South Africa's campaigns against Germany in German East Africa, but also on the Western Front. 'There were not a few South African Cornish', states Graham Dickason, 'at that piece of South Africa in France that will forever remain ours, Delville Wood.'[65] Winifred Hawkey of Redruth later recalled in her memoirs a cousin of hers who had emigrated to Australia shortly before the war and had joined the Australian Expeditionary Force. He was seriously wounded at Gallipoli and returned to Cornwall.[66] Other contingents of Cornishmen could be found in the New Zealand and Canadian armies. Later, in 1917, when the United States of America declared war on Germany her army included a number of Cornishmen. It has also been estimated that half of the surnames of American recruits from Grass Valley in California were Cornish.[67]

Aside from Cornwall's contribution to the Navy and to Britain's Dominion forces, attention must also be paid to the reaction of different classes in Cornwall. Cornish working men may have some-times been slow to answer the call of their country, but so were many middle-class businessmen. Many commentators, including Major Pike of the Duke of Cornwall's Light Infantry, considered the middle class to be shirking their duty. On the recruiting march discussed above, he had claimed that it was 'utterly distasteful to go into a shop and be served by great strapping young fellows who ought to be serving their country'.[68] The same, however, was not said of the well-to-do classes, who were never accused of lacking in devotion to the cause of their country. Any sense of a shared Cornish identity mattered little and Cornwall suffered the same class antagonisms as anywhere else in Britain. Members of the working class often believed that they were being used and exploited to fight a war from which they had little to gain and accused the upper classes of using them, whilst the well-to-do themselves viewed the workers as unpatriotic and lacking any sense of duty. Sons of the upper classes in Cornwall were quick to answer the call of their country. Some were already in the Army. Captain E.H.J. Boscawen and his brother Major The Hon. G.E. Boscawen, sons of Major-General the Viscount Falmouth, fought in the Coldstream Guards and the Royal Field Artillery respectively, the former being transferred later to the Royal Flying Corps on account of his aural vertigo. The Viscount's two other sons also served, one of them being the aide-de-camp to the Duke of Connaught in the Royal Horse Artillery. The Agar-Robartes family of Lanhydrock House near Bodmin also sent its sons to fight. Lieutenant C.E. Agar-Robartes served in the Rifle Brigade and the Tank Battalion, whilst his brother, Captain the Hon. T.C.R. Agar-Robartes (Liberal MP for Bodmin, 1906, and St Austell, 1908–15), served in the Royal Bucks Hussars and later transferred to the Coldstream Guards. Alfred Browning Lyne praised the response of Cornwall's aristocracy in comparison to some other groups: 'Have you not seen how the sons of the wealthiest families are going to the front? . . . Aristocracy is doing its bit . . . but some workers in Mid-Cornwall are not following the lead of their fellows in other industrial centres of the country.'[69]

Harry Tyack, though not a member of the aristocracy, was a member of a well-known and moneyed Cornish family that lived in Camborne. He volunteered immediately to serve his country and rapidly rose to the rank of captain. His father was a respected geologist and the family had travelled around the world and had only recently returned to Cornwall from Russia. A number of years later his niece recalled him volunteering as he believed that 'this was the war to end all wars and would make the world safe for her [his sister] and her children'.[70] Shortly before leaving for France he had told his sister that he was 'willing to give up his life if necessary and if this happened she was not to grieve on any account or to wear black, but to pray for his soul and the lives of his men'.[71] He was seriously wounded during the Allied summer offensive of 1918 and died a week before the Armistice from the shock of having his leg amputated.

CONCLUSION

The belief that the outbreak of the First World War led to an eruption of patriotic fervour among the people of Great Britain has been a long-held and unassailable feature of the war's historiography. Nevertheless, this view cannot be sustained. Clearly, some parts of the country did react with the kind of elation we have been led to believe, but not everywhere. Reflecting on the response in Cornwall to the war, Joseph Hocking commented in May 1915 that:

> The people instead of being easy to move are adamant. Young men laugh at appeals to the emotions, flights of oratory leave them cold. I have spoken to audiences all over Great Britain, and without exception, the Cornish are the most difficult to move. They are not stolid; they are stony.

They will listen keenly, intelligently, critically, and show no sign . . . They regard it as a kind of weakness to manifest anything in the nature of enthusiasm, and they act accordingly'.[72]

This article has sought to highlight how, in many respects, Cornwall's reaction to the outbreak of war in 1914 differed from the supposed response elsewhere in Britain. There were no nationalistic throngs of people greeting news of the war in Cornwall's main towns, and nor was there a rush to join the colours. Although the vast majority of the evidence indicates much early anti-war feeling and a supposed lack of patriotism, it may be that Cornwall was actually more patriotic than may be discerned from simply addressing issues such as recruitment rates. A glance at newspapers and diaries from that time reveals a real willingness among Cornish people to help the war effort in many other ways than volunteering to fight. Cornwall's patriotism was arguably of a more humanitarian variety than the simple crass jingoism of inebriated mobs cheering the news of war. Belgian refugees were taken in to be looked after, funds to raise money for the families of soldiers and sailors were set up and raised considerable sums of money, whilst women were often quick to form themselves into local committees to produce items of clothing for soldiers at the front.

Whilst Cornwall's initial reaction to the outbreak of the war may have been one of indifference or of latent hostility, this would not last for the duration of the war. With the mounting casualties produced by industrialized warfare on the Western Front, even the remotest of Cornish villages began to feel the impact of war and came to share in the war spirit so prevalent elsewhere in the country. Furthermore, any views among some in Cornwall at the start of the war that the Germans were not as evil as some made them out to be, proved ephemeral. The writer D.H. Lawrence and his German wife Frieda, who moved to Cornwall in 1916, were subjected to constant police monitoring and were eventually hounded out across the Tamar on trumped up charges of spying and provisioning German submarine crews on the Cornish coast. In September 1918, on holiday in Cornwall, Rudyard Kipling had written to Stanley Baldwin about the stoning of some Germans living in a nearby cottage.[73]

Nevertheless, the First World War never had the same effect, or aroused the same emotions, on Cornish people as the Boer War had done. Clearly this had much to do with the direct impact that the earlier conflict had had on Cornish mining interests in South Africa and the financial distress caused in the county by miners being unable to send money home to their families. It is instructive that, as late as

1950, the *Cornishman* could write: 'In 1939 the old men of St Just and Camborne had a clearer memory of Ladysmith and Spion Kop than of that long terrible struggle on the Somme'.[74]

The First World War, though causing much distress, never quite affected Cornwall as badly as had the South African War. Thus, when war came in 1914, the people of Cornwall already had first-hand knowledge of the misery and pain caused by war, knowledge not shared so keenly by the rest of the population, and did not want to live through it again. In combination with its remoteness and the distinct traditions of the industries that employed most men, Cornwall did not greet the coming of another war as something to celebrate. Coastal communities may indeed have reacted with excitement, but most sections of the population did not. Eventually, Cornwall would come to serve 'King and Country' and sacrifice its men with the same grim willingness as everywhere else in Britain, but that enthusiasm did not rage from the start of the war and needed to be constantly stoked to allow it to burn to its full patriotic intensity.

NOTES AND REFERENCES

1. Quoted in N. Ferguson, *The Pity of War*, London, 1998, p. 177.
2. Quoted in Ferguson, 1998, p. 177.
3. See C. Parry, 'Gwynedd and the Great War, 1914–1918', *Welsh History Review*, 14, 1988, pp. 86, 89.
4. *Cornish Guardian*, 7 August 1914.
5. *Cornish Telegraph*, 6 August 1914.
6. *West Briton*, 1 August 1914.
7. Cornwall Record Office (CRO), Truro, ST. 201, Elsie Stephens War Diary 1914–1916.
8. Of the 45,000 fishermen across England and Wales in 1914, half were called up as reservists at the outbreak of the war.
9. *St Ives Weekly Summary*, 7 August 1914.
10. Quoted in C. Scoble, *Fisherman's Friend: A Life of Stephen Reynolds*, Tiverton, 2000, p. 597.
11. A. Quiller-Couch, *Nicky-Nan Reservist*, 2nd edn, London, 1929, p. v.
12. The Reverend Joseph Hocking, brother of the Silas mentioned above, had made this claim. See *West Briton*, 20 May 1915.
13. *Cornish Guardian*, 7 August 1914.
14. *West Briton*, 27 August 1914.
15. *West Briton*, 27 August 1914.
16. *West Briton*, 2 October 1914.
17. Quoted in C. Appleby, 'Marching as to War: Cornish Methodists and the Great War', *Journal of the Cornish Methodist Historical Association*, 8, 1994, p. 102.
18. *Cornish Echo*, 7 August 1914.
19. *Cornish Guardian*, 2 April 1915.

20. *Royal Cornwall Gazette*, 8 April 1915.
21. See Appleby, 1994, pp. 131–2.
22. J. Fisher, *That Miss Hobhouse*, London, 1971, p. 16.
23. Fisher, 1971, p. 20.
24. M. Moore, *Winfred Burrows 1858–1929*, London, 1932, p. 107.
25. Quoted in H. Miles Brown, *A Century for Cornwall: The Diocese of Truro 1877–1977*, Truro, 1977, p. 72.
26. *Cornish Guardian*, 14 August 1914.
27. *West Briton*, 14 August 1914.
28. B. Walke, *Twenty Years at St Hilary*, London, 1935, p. 61.
29. *West Briton*, 17 August 1914.
30. Throughout the nineteenth century Cornish miners had, either through economic necessity or as part of some quest for riches and adventure, emigrated to virtually every major mining area of the world. It was often said that wherever there was a deep mine in the world there would be a Cornishman at the bottom of it. Destinations included the United States, Australia, New Zealand, Canada, South Africa, Jamaica, Cuba, Norway, Colombia, Mexico, Brazil, Bolivia and Chile.
31. These and following figures for the price of tin are taken from D.B. Barton, *A History of Tin Mining and Smelting in Cornwall*, Truro, 1967, pp. 246–7.
32. Figures from R.M. Barton, *A History of the Cornish China-Clay Industry*, Truro, 1966, p. 154.
33. Figures from Barton, 1966, p. 162.
34. *West Briton*, 28 January 1915.
35. Quoted in J. Hobhouse-Balme, *To Love One's Enemies: The Work and Life of Emily Hobhouse Compiled from Letters and Writings, Newspaper Cuttings and Official Documents*, Cobble Hill, 1994, p. 543.
36. Hobhouse-Balme, 1994, p. 545.
37. *West Briton*, 31 August 1914.
38. The Parliamentary Recruiting Committee held its first meeting on 27 August and was responsible for furthering recruitment. It produced all the popular recruiting posters that are still so well known today.
39. See, for example, *Cornish Guardian*, 13 November 1914 and *Royal Cornwall Gazette*, 25 March 1915.
40. *West Briton*, 29 March 1915. All local newspapers at this time contain details and reports of this march.
41. Figures from J. Winter, *The Great War and the British People*, London, n.d., p. 35.
42. Quoted in Winter, n.d., p. 35.
43. *Royal Cornwall Gazette*, 25 March 1915.
44. *Cornish Post and Mining News*, 23 December 1915.
45. *Cornish Guardian*, 2 October 1914.
46. *Cornish Guardian*, 2 October 1914.
47. *Cornish Guardian*, 14 November 1914.
48. *Cornish Guardian*, 2 October 1914.
49. Quiller-Couch, 1929, p. v.

50. *Cornish Guardian*, 22 January 1915.
51. *Royal Cornwall Gazette*, 10 December 1914.
52. *West Briton*, 20 May 1915.
53. *Royal Cornwall Gazette*, 10 September 1914.
54. See J.C.C. Probert, 'Recruiting for the 1914–1918 War and the Religious Census Etc.', *Journal of the Cornish Methodist Historical Association*, 9, 2000.
55. Figures and quotation in Appleby, 1994, p. 102.
56. *West Briton*, 23 March 1915.
57. Public Record Office, London, Admiralty Papers, ADM 1/8419/104, Admiralty memo on recruitment and training of seamen, 27 May 1915.
58. *West Briton*, 7 September 1914.
59. Imperial War Museum, 79/59/1, Memoir of Commander A.M. Williams CBE, DSC, DL, RN (1897–1985).
60. *Cornish Guardian*, 5 February 1915.
61. *West Briton*, 14 September 1914.
62. *West Briton*, 17 September 1914.
63. Fisher, 1971, p. 26.
64. *West Briton*, 16 November 1914.
65. G.B. Dickason, *Cornish Immigrants to South Africa: The Cousin Jacks' Contribution to the Development of Mining and Commerce, 1820–1920*, Cape Town, 1978, p. 71.
66. W. Hawkey, *Memoirs of a Redruth Childhood*, Redruth, 1987, p. 29.
67. See A.L. Rowse, *The Cornish in America*, London, 1969, pp. 262, 339, 364.
68. *Cornish Guardian*, 26 April 1915.
69. *Cornish Guardian*, 2 October 1914.
70. E. Flawn, *The Saga of a Cornish Family 1882–1975*, Penzance, 1996, p. 83.
71. Flawn, 1996, p. 83.
72. *West Briton*, 20 May 1915.
73. See C. Dakers, *The Countryside at War 1914–1918*, London, n.d., pp. 65–6, 72.
74. *Cornishman*, 5 January 1950.

SCREENING KERNOW: AUTHENTICITY, HERITAGE AND THE REPRESENTATION OF CORNWALL IN FILM AND TELEVISION, 1913–2003

Alan M. Kent

INTRODUCTION

One of the most popular comedies of the London stage of the past few years has been Marie Jones's play *Stones in His Pockets* (2000).[1] It is set in a village in County Kerry in Ireland, where a big-budget Hollywood 'Irish' movie is being shot. The play is a two-hander, where the actors play all fifteen characters on the film's location. It shows them trying to find a sense of reality in a world seemingly crazed by celebrities, all within the globalization of Irish culture ('Riverdance' *et al.*). Although set in Ireland, the play is actually profoundly relevant to the film culture of early twenty-first-century Cornwall. One of the pair of extras wishes to make his own 'realist' film of Ireland, but knows that the Hollywood vision and appropriation of the 'Emerald Isle' is the more likely project to gain funding and eventual success.

In exploring issues such as Anglo-Irish dialect coaching for the Hollywood actress, the poorly paid extras queuing up for extra portions of food at the catering van (a reflection of the poor rural economy), and the eventual suicide of an Irishman (placing 'stones in his pockets' so he will drown) after being rejected by the glitzy Hollywood *femme fatale*, for anyone aware of film culture in Cornwall the play will hit several chords. This is because although both independent ('national') and 'Hollywood' Irish film is better established than that of Cornwall, both territories face the same cultural interface: that which lies between what can legitimately be termed as Cornish and Irish film 'proper' and those films made in Cornwall or Ireland which make use of or even exploit the Cornish and Irish landscape and people, but which are not really reflective of Cornish or Irish history, politics or literature. Both territories have had to deal with issues of contested ownership, production money and production values, authenticity, development and distribution, not to mention the role of film within the manufacturing of 'national' identity and in tourism.

A good deal has already been written on the history and development of Irish cinema and television,[2] and much is also now beginning to be written on wider British and Welsh cinema,[3] in particular exploring the success of the so-called 'Brit Flicks' of the late twentieth century—*Trainspotting, Brassed Off, Four Weddings and a Funeral, A Life Less Ordinary, The Full Monty*[4] and the like—though we should ask where does Cornwall sit within this cinematic history of 'cool Britannia'? How is Cornwall affected by issues of national identity raised in film? Correspondingly, we need to ask where has Cornish cinema emerged from and what is its direction? What links do Cornish cinema and television have with other cultural and political events in Cornwall, for example with the recent campaign for a Cornish Assembly or with the so-called 'eighth wonder of the world'—the the huge glasshouses or biomes of the Eden Project near St Austell? How is it that Cornish cinema seems on an upward wave, yet the 'crossover' widely distributed 'Cornish' film has not yet been made? These are all issues which I attempt to address within this article.

As well as offering a much-needed critique of the commercial and critical success of Cornish films and of films made in Cornwall, I hope to provide some historical perspective to such films, as well as an exploration of the contemporary climate of film-making in Cornwall, by reference to the representation of marginalized communities like Cornish language speakers, changing attitudes to Cornish identity and the impact of heritage drama on tourism in Cornwall. Although the range of subject matter deemed appropriate for examination under the banner of Cornish Studies has increased markedly over the past decade,[5] academic enquiry into film has hitherto not been present, so this makes 'Cornish film' a highly suitable case for treatment. Given Cornwall's international reputation and growing status within the world of 'Celtic Studies', this is a more than appropriate time to take stock of the progress made and to offer an insight into new developments. Needless to say, this article will be indicative rather than exhaustive, and, as is the case with most Film Studies, most of the defined boundaries are artificial, whereas the reality of film 'on the ground' is much more fluid and organic.

The blend of more 'orthodox' Cornish Studies with the less

familiar world of Film Studies is therefore deliberate on my part, in order to map developments thus far. By working in this way, I hope I can offer an introductory account of 'screening Kernow' and begin to debate some of the central issues of authorship and agency, as well as genre, and specific film movements. Within this, issues of national and trans-national identity quickly become apparent—in particular in the minority film culture of Cornish 'Shorts'—as do constant questions of representation and how the films and television programmes under consideration construct images of the nation (both Cornish and British), class and cultural identity. Finally, by considering issues of heritage and tourism, and the Cornwall Film Fund, I shall deal with so-called 'enterprise culture' and regeneration, of which film often forms a crucial part. These metaphors of understanding should lead us to explore the major protagonists within the context of 'screening Kernow'. However, an important issue to consider, as Ashby and Higson note, is that 'the balance between historically-informed inter-pretations of films [and television programmes] and the present-day analyst is always therefore a precarious one'.[6] It is an issue we must keep in mind when negotiating our way through film and television representations of Cornwall and the Cornish.

THE FORUMS OF CORNISH FILM STUDIES

Critiques of Cornish film and film-making in Cornwall (I shall define these terms in more detail later) have thus far tended to have appeared only in the popular press in Cornwall. The main regional newspaper of south-west Britain (*The Western Morning News*) and the main Cornish newspapers (*The Cornishman, The Cornish Guardian* and *The West Briton* run regular film review columns and stories related to film production, the latter especially when it is linked to tourist benefits and increases in visitor numbers. Other Cornish-based magazines such as the magazine for the 'Cornish overseas' *Cornish World/Bys Kernowyon* and more specialized Cornish language magazines such as *An Gannas* carry the occasional article on films,[7] but this is couched in terms of 'news' rather than any serious analysis of film-making, direction or comparison to developments elsewhere in Britain, Europe or the USA. Of late, however, some writers and scholars have begun to look more seriously at film in Cornwall. Though hardly academic, in that it relies mainly on anecdote and location, Sue Craig and David FitzGerald's book *Filmed in Cornwall* (1999) was a step in the right direction in terms of cataloguing the filmatic ex-perience in twentieth-century Cornwall.[8] Craig, at the time of writing, was the Film Liaison Officer at the South West Film Commission,[9] and FitzGerald was a local television presenter, so they provide good knowledge of many productions around Cornwall, helpfully giving an initial chronology of film work at the end of their book.

The best work so far, however, in terms of applying film and tourist theory to Cornwall has come from Nickianne Moody in her article 'Poldark Country and National Culture' and Harold Birks's 'Jamaica Inn: The Creation of Meanings on a Tourist Site', both in Ella Westland's influential 1996 volume *Cornwall: The Cultural Construction of Place*.[10] Here 'space and place' theories of cultural geography are applied to the Cornish context with reference to Winston Graham's epic *Poldark* series and the cultural ramifications of Daphne du Maurier's novel *Jamaica Inn* and its various film and television productions. In the same volume I also completed a small analysis of the influential china-clay area film *Stocker's Copper* (1971), which remains a benchmark of 'realist' film about industrial Cornwall, and of *A Different Drummer* (1981), the bio-pic of the Anglo-Cornish blind and deaf poet Jack Clemo.[11] Elsewhere, I have also made brief commentaries on films about Cornwall, but these have generally either been made under the remit of literary studies—therefore referring to screenplays alone—or under the wing of contemporary Celtic Studies.[12] There have also been separate studies of significant programmes, but these tend to be more celebratory than academic.[13]

Critiques have come from other sources, however: Jon Guyver Cole's mid-1990s alternative magazine *Well Weird Cornwall* offered a 'Film Special' on 'Well-Weird Films';[14] while John Angarrack's controversial nationalist polemics have studied the media's 'manipulation' of Cornwall and the Cornish, and therefore, by implication, of all media processes, including the representation of the Cornish on film and in television.[15] Deacon, George and Perry in *Cornwall at the Crossroads*, and Clarke in his 1995 paper 'Broadcasting for One and All', all suggest that Cornwall should have its own media mechanisms.[16] The groundbreaking Cornish cinematographer John Bartlett gives occasional lectures on film-making in Cornwall, thus providing a forum for debate and discussion, as does Cornwall Media Resource, the recently evolved Cornwall Film Festival/Goel Fylm Kernow, and the now well-established international Celtic Film and Television Festival, which rotates around the Celtic territories.[17]

The specific problem with the later forum is that the festival tends to be dominated by the larger territories of Wales, Scotland and Ireland. It is only of late that Cornwall and Brittany have been submitting material; and the forums within tend to reflect the cultural needs of the larger places. Cornwall's issues are often sidelined within the festival, even (ironically) when it is held in Cornwall. In the recent Cornwall Film Festival, however, there was an event titled 'A

Proper Job: The Future of Filmmaking in Cornwall', so a critical forum is starting to develop. An additional issue is how Cornish film progresses to the larger cinemas of Cornwall. At the moment, much is shown exclusively at Arts Centres, such as that in Falmouth and the Acorn Theatre in Penzance. Given the need for 'town' cinemas in places like St Austell, Wadebridge, Truro, Penzance and Bude to survive, the screening of exclusively Cornish films seems unlikely unless they are packaged under other 'Arts' activities. The nearest multiplex cinema—the so-called Warner Village in Plymouth—seems even less likely to cater for the kinds of needs of cinema-goes from East Cornwall. The various annual or bi-annual Cornish Gatherings in countries such as Australia and the USA have, however, been places where Cornish film has been shown and debated.

CORNWALL IN FILM AND TELEVISION HISTORY
There has, historically, been more film-making in Cornwall than there have been Cornish films. I define the former as films using locations, people and crew in Cornwall, but which do not necessarily have Cornish themes or topic matter and are generally only using Cornwall as a 'backdrop'. But that is not to say that they have negligible impact on Cornwall, since many are now considered part of the heritage of Cornwall, or are noted for scenes shot here that have been transformed cinematically into somewhere else. Cornish films, by way of contrast, are films which generally have explicitly Cornish subject matter. These may be divided into three categories: those films which are exclusively made in Cornwall (such as the feature-length Cornish language film *Hwerow Hweg/Bitter Sweet*[18]); those which come with a Cornish-based writing and directing team, but which are often funded outside Cornwall, either in London or the USA (*Blue Juice* or *Saving Grace*[19]); or those films which have little or no explicit Cornish input in terms of their production, yet feature Cornish material (for example, Channel Four's *Merlin*, John Boorman's *Excalibur*[20]).

Before commencing a brief history of drama productions within Cornish film and television history, we might take a few steps back and consider various prior imagining of the territory and its people in a 'cinematic' sense. This comes in the main from literary and artistic sources, which over time have tried to capture for both internal and external reception images (in the broad sense) of Cornwall. The literary and cultural history of Cornwall has now begun to establish itself as a defined field,[21] though a more established area of study is that of the various travellers and artists who have come to Cornwall in order to paint and draw it. Such images of Cornwall have been defined by the various artistic developments, initially in Newlyn and Lamorna around the late nineteenth and early twentieth century, but also in St Ives in the post-war period.[22] Early photography has also been significant in documenting (in the ways that films do) the social, political, economic and cultural changes that have affected Cornwall.[23] Photography is important here, since it is from its development that early cinematography was itself developed, though we have since moved forward again to digital photography and cinematography.

There has not been much written about film and television history in Cornwall, and I am indebted to the work of Craig and FitzGerald,[24] and Cole, for recording what is known. There is reference to an early silent movie filmed at Talland Bay in 1913, but at present this is all that is known about it. A *c.*1920 film made at Readymoney Cove at Fowey was believe to have been called *Contraband* (it is perhaps appropriate that one of the earliest films made in Cornwall should be about such a topic). The first film proper came in 1929: the Pola Negri vehicle *Street of Abandoned Children*, which used the twin locations of Mevagissey and St Ives.[25] In the same year, there is also mention of *The Manxman*, the story of a fisherman, believed drowned, who eventually returns to his village only to find that his girlfriend is now pregnant from a liaison with his best friend. The 1930s saw *The Phantom Light* being made in Port Isaac and *Forever England*, starring John Mills, being made at Falmouth. By 1938, one of the most significant early Cornish films was being made at Sennen Cove and St Levan Church. This was an adaptation of Eden Philpotts's *Yellow Sands*. Other films of this early period included *The Thief of Baghdad* (1940), part of which was filmed at Gunwalloe, *Ghost Train* (1941) at Liskeard and *Next of Kin* (1942) made at Mevagissey.

As Marcia Landy has shown, one of the core production companies in Britain during the middle of the twentieth century was Gainsborough films,[26] and this organization made several films in Cornwall—among them *Love Story* (1944), shot partly at the Minack Theatre. It is a Second World War drama set in Cornwall and is concerned with a half-blind airman who falls for a pianist with a weak heart. The film starred Margaret Lockwood, Stewart Granger, Patricia Roc and Tom Wallis. *Miranda* (1947), starring Glynis Johns, was also shot in Cornwall. *Johnny Frenchman* (date unknown) came from the same period and involved a Frenchman (actually a Breton) arriving in Cornwall who falls in love with a Cornish girl played by Patricia Roc (clearly Roc was building an association with the territory; she was later to appear in 1951's *Circle of Danger*).[27] The film plays much on the links between Celtic Cornwall and Brittany, even including a wrastlin' match featuring the famous Chapman brothers. The 1940s concluded with the filming of Walt Disney's *Treasure Island* (1949) at

Carrick Roads and on the Helford Estuary, famously starring Robert Newton. Of course, there are many Cornish elements in Robert Louis Stevenson's novel—such as Squire Trelawney—and Stevenson had been connected to the territory in other ways,[28] so perhaps an attempt at maritime authenticity was being made by producers at Disney.

As we can see, relatively few of these productions may legitimately be termed films *about* Cornish subject matter. Most early film-makers were only interested in using Cornwall for location shots. This trend continued throughout much of the post-war period. *Knights of the Round Table* (1953), though filmed at Tintagel, was hardly an authentic imagining of the Arthur of the Cornish—not least for those Cornish Revivalists of the pre and post-war era, for whom the spirit of Arthur encompassed the whole ideology of the cultural recovery of Cornwall.[29] The production of *Dangerous Exile* came to Cornwall in 1957, though the subject matter again was not particularly Cornish, while in 1963 *Crooks in Cloisters*, filmed around Portloe, starred Barbara Windsor and Bernard Cribbins.[30]

It was the next decade which really began to alter public perception of Cornwall, when the territory seemed to crop up in more macabre and sinister dramas—ranging from science-fiction work such as *Doomwatch* and the BBC's *Dr Who* and *Blakes 7* (1970s), to *Crucible of Terror* (1971) and *Dracula* (1979).[31] In Dr Who, it was the china clay landscape of mid-Cornwall which doubled as alien planets, and reinforced still further that area's embodiment as a 'moonscape'. However, significantly, it was the 1970s which established the nature of Cornwall and the Cornish on film and in television. *The Onedin Line* continued to be filmed around Cornwall, and the series carried on until the late 1970s, but its successor was effectively *Poldark* (1975).[32] Poldark not only precipitated a range of historical romantic literature but also paved the way for the transition of Susan Howatch's Cornish epic *Penmarric* (1979) onto television.[33] The cultural impact of these two series has been massive and leads us into the modern era of film and television in Cornwall. It may seem an obvious point, but at that time no one had yet made any kind of drama in the Cornish language. Indeed, given the cost of such a venture, this would have to wait some fifteen more years until portable and inexpensive equipment and video became available.

WHEN HOLLYWOOD MET KERNOW: ISSUES OF OWNERSHIP AND AUTHENTICITY FROM *STRAW DOGS* TO *SAVING GRACE*

In general, in just the same way as say Bristol's HTV meets Cornwall in the shape of the adaptation of W.J. Burley's Cornish detective

Wycliffe,[34] there are, when Hollywood meets Kernow, similar difficult issues of representation, ownership, agency and authenticity. These issues, as we have seen above, have been present since the early days of filming Cornwall. Before we progress to Hollywood, though, let us examine *Wycliffe* as a case study. Although HTV's *Wycliffe* was a very successful series, for many Cornish viewers its results came across as mixed. The series successfully adapted the detective and many of the original stories, but was deemed very unrealistic by Cornish audiences since several of the actors' accents sounded inauthentic, some of the stories stretched reality (for example, the episode titled 'The Scapegoat' saw some white-clad Cornish druids enact an ancient ceremony involving the throwing of a burning wheel off a cliff) and the inherent geography of many of the episodes seemed illogical. As an agency of representation, *Wycliffe*'s problem was that it failed the authenticity test and left many Cornish feeling that they did not own the series. This was despite the fact that the programme-makers saw it having the same kind of appeal as other successful regional detective series, such as *Inspector Morse* (Oxfordshire), *Bergerac* (The Channel Islands) and *Taggart* (Glasgow).

Therefore, one of the problems facing both film-makers and tele-vision producers who have 'outside' money to invest in explicitly Cornish subject matter is how to balance the Cornish elements with the demands and expectations of a wide audience. Several instant problems come to mind. Because there is presently a lack of both professional theatre and uniquely Cornish media developing drama, there is a paucity of Cornish actors who can readily step into a large-scale production. With no disrespect to many of the larger Cornish touring companies—such as *Kneehigh, Miracle* and *Bedlam* (who have all provided first-rate actors for film and television)—there is not the perceived career development as, say, there could be in agencies in Wales or Scotland. This can mainly be put down to infra-structure, institutions and size.

The second issue is accent. Cornish actors might readily be able to handle authentic Cornu-English or even Cornish lines, but will they be intelligible to those watching the film or show in Manchester, or even further afield in Los Angeles? Intelligibility, as well as authenticity, is therefore important to bear in mind. Even the perceived Glaswegian accents of *Trainspotting* were modified from the original context of Irvine Welsh's novel.

The third issue is providing the kind of stories which have intimately Cornish subject matter but at the same time are able to transcend national borders and be truly international. There is no reason why the 'trans-national' Cornish cannot do this. In fact, there is good evidence that Cornish narrative travelled all over Europe well into the Renaissance,[35] and there is the fact that the mere mention of Cornwall globally conjures up a certain set of images.

This paradigm has certain advantages: an audience expects certain things in a film about Cornwall; various agencies throughout the history of film and television have negotiated this. However, for some Cornish screen-writers, film-makers and producers (and Cornish writers of novels and drama) the weight of past perception hangs heavily around the neck: the stereotypes, the locations, the historical romance is such a monolith to climb, how does one begin to assert new imaginings of Cornwall? Yet put simply, the craft of the film-maker is to tell a good yarn, rather than show 'how badly treated the Cornish have been by the English', which sometimes seems, as we shall see, the concerns of the indigenous and nationalist film-makers of Cornish 'Shorts'. That said, it is strange why certain narratives of the Cornish experience have not made it onto the big screen when they are of national British or international importance. We might have expected to see films depicting the 1497 Rebellion, making heroes of the Cornish 'bravehearts' Michael Joseph 'An Gof' and Thomas Flamank, or the story of Richard Trevithick, potentially a film or television serial which could be a superb and detailed portrait of the industrial revolution. These are 'national' British narratives, which in a territory with a larger filmatic or media infrastructure, along with appropriate agencies, would surely have been made, to help us understand ourselves and our past. Interestingly, it is at this point that the promoters of Cornwall's claim to devolution and those who see Cornwall as an essentially English county collide and collude, since such works in all probability celebrate a wider British identity, albeit framed from a Cornish perspective.

Much of this may be put down to economic and political issues. The British film industry itself, although successful, is clearly working on limited budgets and finance.[36] Given that most of this industry is focused in and around London and Glasgow, the main focus of its films is not (in the immediate future at least) going to reflect Cornish concerns. The same may be said of much television production in Britain as well. Related to this, although the Celtic card can neatly be played in Hollywood by the Irish and the Scottish, due to their seemingly more overt contribution to the development of the USA (see *Titanic, Road to Perdition* and *Braveheart*[37]), the historical in-visibility of the Cornish as 'English' has hitherto prevented their stories from being told on this 'blockbuster' scale. One notable exception is perhaps *Legends of the Fall*,[38] which is concerned with the lives of a second-generation Cornish family in the USA, and stars Brad Pitt (his character is named Tristan), Aidan Quinn and Anthony Hopkins.

Not only is live-action film development limited, but there have not been many animated visions of Cornwall either. Perhaps the most direct link is with Walt Disney's *The Sword in the Stone*,[39] which gave treatment to T.H. White's Arthurian novel. Far from setting it in Cornwall, however, as in most Disney productions the focus is on 'olde England'. A better attempt was made by animators at Warner Bothers in 1998 with the release of another Arthurian-themed feature, *The Magic Sword: The Quest for Camelot*,[40] which features a blind hero named Garrett, his girlfriend Kayley and a blue and red, two-headed dragon named Devon and Cornwall. While Warner Brothers were clearly making territorial connections, the dragon received much criticism in Cornwall, since while the Devon head of the dragon is tall and speaks in a refined English accent, Cornwall is stumpy, fat and unsophisticated, and given a Bronx-style accent. The film was released while local government boundaries were being debated with a potential combined 'Devonwall' region once again in the frame,[41] though had those who criticized the film looked close enough they would have seen that the dragon actually showed that such a body does not work—thus reaffirming the 'Cornish position' on the Devonwall issue. It is a pity that this film was viewed negatively since it is possibly the finest animated vision of Arthurian Cornwall that exists, perhaps even rivalling Disney's Welsh-based *The Magic Cauldron* (a film that for several years in the late 1980s was used by the Welsh tourist authority to promote the territory).[42]

The above conditions of cultural production outline the core issues which face film development 'when Hollywood meets Kernow'. But this interaction has had its successes, and I now turn my attention to three films, and their agencies of production, which appear to have helped define the populist cinematic vision of Cornwall in the late twentieth century.

Often quoted by incomers to Cornwall as an example of Cornish opposition to outsiders ('When I stepped into the pub, they all look at me. It was like something out of *Straw Dogs*!') is Sam Peckinpath's brutal 1971 film *Straw Dogs*.[43] The setting is Cornwall (the work was filmed in the 'isolated' West Cornwall village of St Buryan), where mild-mannered American academic David Sumner (Dustin Hoffman) has bought a house with his young wife Amy (Susan George) in the village where she grew up. David is mocked by the locals (one of whom is Amy's ex-boyfriend) and treated with growing contempt by his frustrated wife, but when his house comes under violent siege he finds unexpected reserves of resourcefulness and aggression. As the critic Philip Kemp notes, the film was much influenced by Robert Ardrey's macho-anthropological tract, *The Territorial Imperative*. Its take on Cornish village life is fairly bizarre—this is a Western in all but name—and many critics balked at the transposition of Peckinpah's trademark blood-and-guts to the supposed peace of the British countryside. A scene where Amy is raped caused particular outrage, not least since it's hinted she consents to it. Not for the first time in Peckinpah's movies there are disquieting elements of misogyny, and it doesn't help that the chemistry between Hoffman and George is non-existent. But taken as a vision of irrational violence irrupting into a civilised way of life *Straw Dogs* is powerful and unsettling, and the action sequences are executed with all Peckinpah's unfailing flair and venom. Oh, and that title? A quote from Chinese sage Lao-Tze, it seems, 'The wise man is ruthless and treats the people as straw dogs'.[44]

For over three decades, the film was withheld from home viewing on video and DVD by British censors (it was originally pulled from the shelves for the controversial usage of sexual violence which breached the 1984 Video Recordings Act), but a 2002 release presented it complete and uncut. The rape scene in the film is shocking, and there has been considerable debate over its recent release. However, *Straw Dogs is* like most films that have experienced censorship, where over time they are generally seen as misunderstood masterpieces (Stanley Kubrick's vision of Anthony Burgess's novel *A Clockwork Orange* has had a similar fate[45]). In this respect, *Straw Dogs* has become something of a 'cult' film, the thirty years of its cycle of reception coming full circle, with its presentation as the main feature of the 2002 Cornwall Film Festival at Falmouth Arts Centre.[46]

Cornish viewers, however, might be less concerned with the film's original censorship and rather more with the manner in which the inhabitants of the village are presented by Peckinpah as in-bred Cornish 'scum'. The film repeatedly asserts a vision of an ethnic 'heart of darkness' amongst the Cornish, and there is a supposition that life on Britain's fringe of civilization has affected their mentality. Not only this but they have an innate 'Celtic aggression' and a tendency towards violence. And yet, Peckinpah was doing nothing new, for the Cornish have often been treated as such by apparently civilized visitors and observers, such as W.H. Hudson and John Beddoe,[47] and also by writers such as the 'indigenous' H.D. Lowry and 'visitor' C.A. Dawson Scott in *Wheal Darkness* and by the 'visiting' but 'adopted' Daphne du Maurier in *Jamaica Inn*.[48] That said, it is the very 'uncivilization' of the periphery that draws the character Sumner towards Cornwall, a fascinating emplotment since the film was being made at a time when the arrival of mass tourism and mass in-migration had already begun to alter fundamentally the cultural geography of the imagined community that Peckinpah sought to present. In its way, this tension reflected that expressed in the wider growth of pan-Celtic nationalism across the Atlantic archipelago, which aimed to provide resistance against such cultural and economic shifts. In Cornwall specifically, the rise of Cornish national sentiment and the formation of the Cornish nationalist party, Mebyon Kernow, was evidence of indigenous resistance to the threat of overwhelming change.[49] Peckinpah's film was made in 1971, and the 1970s have since been regarded as the 'golden age' of Cornish nationalism. The film can thus be read against the grain, and seen as a touchstone of that cultural conflict which was to dominate Cornish cultural and political life toward the end of the twentieth century.

The power of 'cult' films, too, should not be underestimated in the pantheon of British cinema. Upon its release to video and DVD, *Straw Dogs* prompted a new round of publicity for the film and for Cornwall. Although the film-makers' presentation of the indigenous Cornish was by no means flattering, it reflected similar unsavoury depictions of indigenous people elsewhere—for example, the equally unflattering view of Scotland in films such as the pagan-themed *The Wicker Man* (in which, incidentally, there is a version of Padstow's 'Obby 'Oss).[50] Yet, paradoxically, such films reinforce both the 'coolness' of particular locations (West Cornwall fits this precisely, with its stone monuments, folklore and even Cornish language) and the attraction of the 'other', for the Cornish are 'different' ethnically. Therefore, although the presentation is unflattering, the film has both heightened and high-lighted the Cornish problem, alighting upon issues of cultural, social and economic change.

It was to be over two decades (and through the iconoclastic period of television's *Poldark* and *Penmarric*) before any large-scale films captured Cornish culture on screen. Carl Prechezer's *Blue Juice* (1995), funded by Channel Four and Pandora Cinema, is the story of a Cornish surfing hero, J.C. (played by Sean Pertwee), who has to decide whether he can continue to opt into the 'forever young culture' of surfing or realize his responsibilities to his girlfriend Chloe (Catherine Zeta Jones).[51] It is also a typical example of how Channel Four, acting as a development agency and distributor, sponsors and develops cinema in Britain. As I have argued elsewhere,[52] the Cornish surfing community presented is an attempt by the film-makers to achieve Cornish social realism and present aspects of mid-1990s rave culture. New Age-ism in the form of Heathcote Williams (playing a neo-Pagan Celtic surfing shaman) and biker/outlaw culture are blended to offer insight into the immediacy of late twentieth-century youth culture in Cornwall. The film manages to imagine Cornwall by using its village location (Chloe's 'Aqua Shack' cafe was constructed on the car park harbour area of Mousehole) as the setting for a series of clashes between a number of sub-cultural groups.[53] Against this, Cornwall is given a positive image. The raves take place in a post-industrial landscape of old copper mines and tin streaming works (filmed at places like Chapel Porth and the Blue Hills Valley), and the Cornish youth are given positive identities—enjoying a vibrant life, while living on the periphery. The text, considering its need for reception in a global context, is a reasonably authentic vision of the conflicting communities at work in Cornwall in the mid-1990s. It does not offer any nationalist vision of the territory, but it does give voice to Cornwall's youth culture.

In contrast, as we shall see, to *Saving Grace*, it is the 'London group' who are enticed to the periphery by the promise of adventure, despite Cornwall being described by the internal characters as 'this godforsaken, disease-ridden dump'. For the London characters, Cornwall is a utopian community where freedom rules: it is a place where the London couch potato Terry can dress up as the 'silver surfer' and where the problems of urban Britain can be escaped, actually the same mind-space offered by historical romance. The inauthentic aspects of *Blue Juice* come from other areas: for example, a Cornish village hosting a 'soul' club night is highly unlikely.

One interesting section of the film concerns a well-observed merging of established media in Cornwall. The film's 'Smuggler FM' ties the independent *Pirate FM* to *BBC Radio Cornwall* using the device of two local radio disc-jockeys, clearly filmatic versions of favourites Chris Blount and Ted Gundry, a veteran radio pairing which had long documented Cornwall's day-to-day life. Although the 'ooh-aarh' accents are easy to criticize, the film's positioning of the radio presenters makes interesting viewing since it is they who seem to encapsulate for the Cornish-based surfers the inherent peripherality of Cornwall, notably the lack of alternative, more appropriate music radio stations, such as would be available in urban Britain.

Some observers criticized *Blue Juice* for its depiction of the poser 'warm-weather' mentality within the surfing world, as well as the inauthenticity of the treacherous stretch of surging water known as the 'Boneyard' (from footage actually shot in the Canary Islands), and it has not really risen to the cult status of other Brit-Flick films of its era. However, as with all cinema, films and stars are interconnected, and *Blue Juice*'s status has started to shift as its stars have progressed in their careers. Catherine Zeta Jones (whose eroticism is celebrated both in the film and on the video box), at that time tentatively exploring a career in cinema, has since gone on to win a Best Supporting Actress Oscar in 2003 and has married into Hollywood through Michael Douglas. Ewan McGregor is without doubt one of the most important British actors of his generation, and a Brit-Flick favourite. However, although *Blue Juice* authenticity succeeds on several levels, for many viewers it fails since the representation of Cornwall is too rose-tinted, especially when it is compared to the other Brit-Flick films of the same era. The happy ending (J.C. and Chloe's marriage) of *Blue Juice* seems to tie too directly with the 'romance of the periphery' established by the costume dramas. It seems a 'gritty' Cornwall can rarely be authentically presented on film, an issue which, as we shall see later, seems to drive the producers of Cornish 'Shorts'.

The third film I wish to deal with is *Saving Grace* (1999).[54] This is an interesting example of how a larger-scale production can produce a legitimate and populist cinematic vision of Cornwall, which does not patronize the Cornish, yet demonstrates their cultural difference at the turn of the twenty-first century. It is also a film which, though it uses the Cornish landscape in powerful and dramatic ways (as in the opening sequence, when a coffin is carried across the cliff-tops), does not seek to romanticize it. In effect, it shows that the Cornish work and live in this environment. It may be picturesque but there is an economic awareness in the film, which actually promotes the film's overall theme—surviving on Britain's periphery. Its controversial plot, involving a widow (played by Brit-Flick actress Brenda Blethyn) who tries to clear her debts by cultivating marijuana plants, which reinforces the exoticism and freedom of 'relaxed' and hippy Cornwall and yet shows (for instance) that the Atlantic Archipelago's drug culture is not restricted to urban areas. It is Grace's gardener Matthew (played by Craig Ferguson) who first encourages her to grow the crop, and she soon turns her greenhouse into a hydroponics laboratory. To sell the crop, Grace travels to Notting Hill in London (another important location for Brit-Flick films) and the slice of 'reality' film which is made there (where Blethyn goes up to real people, i.e. not actors or extras] offering the drug] makes for a highly believable sequence. All this, however, is neatly tied around the North Cornwall fishing village of Port Isaac, where the village doctor is played by Martin Clunes. One reviewer of the film on *amazon.co.uk*, who comes from Cornwall, offers testament to the film's correct vision: 'Living in the same area as this film was portrayed, I would like to tell you how realistic this film is, from the story line, the people, and its fun elements. This is real life in the country. Who says country life is boring?'[55]

Not only do these elements of the film 'work', but so (importantly) does the soundtrack, a method of marketing which seemed to be elusive for the producers of *Blue Juice*. Often ignored in film criticism, the soundtrack is often an important component, and *Saving Grace* has some interesting choices. The main theme music, the acoustic guitar-driven 'Take a Picture', is provided by the American 'industrial rock' group Filter,[56] which at this time had a hit album in the USA, so although the film is very local, it is supported by a global phenomenon, perhaps part of the reason for its success at the Sundance Film Festival. In this way, we witness the significant marshalling of mainstream, global music with a tiny Cornish village, where of course anyone there can also listen to Filter's music. Put another way, it demonstrates that, through the music of Filter, the generation and global community that watches and is aware of MTV and VH1 is also associating the cultural geography of Cornwall with a hit single and video. Thus *Saving Grace* enters an entirely different sphere of engagement with the popular media. It is this kind of union of agencies which film-makers in Cornwall need to complete in the future, in the sense that increasingly film production is related to a whole number of other genres and merchandise: the internet, mobile phones, toys and action figures, soundtrack albums, cereal boxes, fast-food outlets, fashion and clothing. Such 'product' and 'placement' determines the sponsorship and co-promotion of the film, which in turn are necessary to guarantee success in a global context. The producers of *Saving Grace* realized this and gained a crucial distribution deal with 20th Century Fox Searchlight, which means that now one can walk into the local *Londis* store in Cornwall and hire *Saving Grace* on video or DVD.

CORNISH SHORTS: THE SUCCESSES AND THE SHORTCOMINGS

As we have seen, although the occasional multinational film with explicitly Cornish subject matter does appear, it is not common. Films known as 'Shorts' currently provide the mainstay of Cornish cinema. Though in development since the 1980s, the real revolution came in the 1990s, when technology and an initial 'low-budget' media infra-structure (centred around the Cornwall Video Resource in Redruth, the West Cornwall Film Fund [Penwith District Council] and the South West Media Development Agency) facilitated a series of writers, directors and production companies to try their hand at films with highly Cornish concepts and themes. On reflection, some might argue that the themes were *too* Cornish: the makers had wanted to tell 'real' and 'gritty' Cornwall on film in ways which other agencies were not.

The other infrastructural opportunities were brought about by funding arising from partnership grants, which, for instance, meant that some films had to be made connecting the 'Atlantic Arc', as in the case of *The Saffron Threads* (1995),[57] which tells a story involving the transnational trade of saffron between Galicia and Cornwall. Wild West films, in particular, and director Bill Scott, should be acknowledged as a pioneer of this early Cornish cinema in short films such as *The Last Words of Dolly Pentreath/An Dewetha Geryow a Dolly Pentreath* (1994)[58] and *Splatt dhe Wertha/Plot for Sale* (1997). The former explored the Late Cornish speaker and 'noble savage' fishjowster Dolly Pentreath, who finds herself transported to a contemporary Cornwall in which she seeks the Cornish language amongst an altered and confusing landscape of surfers, wind-farms and tourists. For the most part Dolly is bewildered but when she finds Cornish speakers she feels more at home.

In the avant-garde *Splatt dhe Wertha*, written by Andrew Lanyon (son of the St Ives School painter Peter Lanyon), 'three heroines from a nineteenth-century romantic Westcountry novel escape their author's imagination and, after visiting modern Cornwall, become inspired themselves to create'.[59] The ideology of both of these productions is founded along traditional 'Cornish nationalist' ethics and the feel, like many 'Shorts' from other cultures, is 'surrealistic'—a trend that has continued in the genre in Cornwall. In the case of *Splatt dhe Wertha*, this is clearly part of Lanyon's agenda, his reputation as a writer, illustrator and artist being strongly connected to a sense of the 'avant-garde' and the 'absurd'.[60] There is also a sense that such work is being conducted in the realm of contemporary 'art' or 'quality' progressive non-mainstream cinema. While perhaps appealing to those 'in the know' in Cornwall, both films' success outside these circles would seem limited, since the subject matter is still too 'Revivalist' and political, and not truly populist, and (as I have argued elsewhere) with regard to Cornish literature, it is this which inevitably restricts its cultural impact,[61] not only in Cornwall but elsewhere. If film is to have an impact, then it must transcend borders and the politics of identity. Such shorts, though highly innovative, are also too concerned with 'lamenting loss'.[62] A truly contemporary or historical Cornwall was much less visible in these early films.

Shorts, therefore, offer both advantages and disadvantages. While being able to offer new, young film-makers the opportunity to make films, their reception and distribution is limited. It is the latter that is the real issue with this cinema. Much has been made of the various films in the Cornish language which began to be produced in the late 1990s, though given that the 'Short' film audience is already limited, the 'ghettoization' of the resultant films often reinforced the peripherality of the language, in ways which were actually very similar to some of the rudimentary 'rusty staple' post-war publications of the Cornish language movement. There was a sense that it was now possible to make films solely in the Cornish language, but the real cultural impact was inevitably limited since the films were, for the most part, only circulated and sold as videos within the traditional Cornish language circles, such as the annual Lowender Perran Celtic Festival at Perranporth or the annual Cornish language weekends. There were signs, however, that at least indigenous Cornish film-makers were able to make their voice heard, even if that voice was expressing only one, rather narrow aspect of contemporary Cornish identity. Elsewhere, factual productions achieved greater penetration, such has West-country Carlton's *Kernopalooza!* (1998), which was a networked regional half-an-hour programme in the Cornish language, and with subtitles.[63] The programme was progressive and innovative in that it linked the language with surfing, skating and dance culture. But was far from perfect, since (for instance) it continued to use Revivalist iconography (Celtic knotwork and 'folksy' music), though it was aiming to place Cornish language before a mainstream audience.

A Short that was less restricted in its production values and was truly attempting to appeal to a mass audience was Three S Films' children's story *How Madge Figgey Got Her Pig* (1997).[64] The story, an adaptation of the famous folk-narrative of West Cornwall, recorded by Robert Hunt,[65] used unusual filmatic techniques. The production began in an animated form using the theme 'Tales from the Land's End' and the Cornish drollteller to set the narrative running. The picture then swapped to a combination of puppets in real locations. Though the inaccurate Cornu-English of the production left much to be desired, the production used comedy and puppetry to great effect, earning it the Young People's Award Torc at the 1998 Celtic Film and Television Festival at Tralee in Ireland. Considering the wealth of 'fairy' and 'folk' narrative that has survived in Cornwall, this might be one place where writers, directors and producers may be able to develop professional quality film and programmes. Such a technique has worked very well in Wales, although the mainstream breakthrough for Cornwall is yet to happen.

However, the role and place of 'Shorts' is beginning to change. Antal Kovac's *Hwerow Hweg/Bitter Sweet* (2002) made much of the fact that it was 'the first feature film ever made in Cornish'.[66] The West Coast Productions' film is a contemporary love story set in West Cornwall, and it is a significant achievement in Cornish-language film. However, its production methods relied more or less on the low-budget infrastructure established with the 'Shorts'—effectively film-making on 'a wing and a prayer'. The film was exhibited at the Montreal Film Festival, presumably as an 'art-house' foreign language film completed in a language in which there is actually a very small number of fluent speakers, but perhaps this only emphasized its exoticism and 'Celticity'. *Hwerow Hweg/Bitter Sweet* was a central plank of the 2002 Cornwall Film Festival, but a look through the programme shows a limited amount of progression in subject matter from the early films of the mid-1990s: for instance, Andrew Lanyon's *A Wood Near Madrid* takes as its theme 'how Alfred Wallis was not a mariner but a First World War Fighter pilot shot down over Madrid'.[67] The more progressive films with populist appeal appear to be Morag C. Smith's *Dying for One* ('a hard-hitting drama charting the effect of violence in the traveller community') and Vic Strike's *The Price to Pay* ('a tale of wreckers, a doomed French schooner and an avenging militia set in the Cornwall of 1800'),[68] the latter perhaps 'trad' Cornish material but told in a new way. Steve Tanner and Michael Wiese's *Field of Fish* is a more inventive piece based on the sailing of one Mr Joliff, with an eye on contemporary cinematography and design.[69]

Not surprisingly, the subject matter of other Cornish films in the 'documentary' section of the festival relied heavily on Cornish nationalism (Nick Darke's *Breaking the Chains*, an interview with John Angrarrack; and Paul Farmer's *Naw Kans Baner* about the march to Exeter held in July 1999 to commemorate the Prayer Book Rebellion)[70] or Celticity (Barbara Santi's *The Passion* and Tod Grimwade's *Christ and the Celts*).[71] For some observers this is not a problem, but it does illustrate in both drama and documentary the limits of film-making interest in Cornwall. Issues of sexuality, domesticity, class or growing up are rarely given voice. That said, given the lack of airtime on 'real' media such as Westcountry Carlton or the BBC, perhaps this voice is legitimate. Equally, given the fact that it is supremely difficult to manufacture a Cornish-themed drama for prime-time viewing, this alternative media is one way for the Cornish to offer expression. However, as I have suggested above, actual social realism seems a long way off and it comes with its own limitations of consumption and production values, far removed from what is offered in say *Blue Juice* or *Saving Grace*.

FILM AND HERITAGE: NEVER MIND THE CORNISH, HERE'S THE LOCATION

Both Nickianne Moody, in her analysis of the impact of 'Poldark culture' on Britain in general and Cornwall in particular,[72] and Amy Sargeant in her study of the use of film and television versions of Jane Austen novels,[73] have shown how the relationship between film,

heritage and tourism has increasingly become a process of 'making and
selling heritage' and that a certain 'style and authenticity' have a
particular appeal within the heritage tourist market. This we may
locate within the realm of historical period drama, mainly from before
the Second World War and best placed in eighteenth- or nineteenth-
century Britain (though actually mainly England). Certainly, the
'branding of Britain' has been concerned with bridging the gap
between classic works of fiction and the popular public, and the
marketing of middle- and upper-class British society. On a broad scale
Merchant Ivory's long success at providing cinematic images of
the British Empire and Edwardian Britain is matched by the BBC's
Sunday night serialization of classic texts, although ITV has also
attempted to rival this genre in recent productions. In Cornwall, this
'culture of heritage' and re-branding has manifested itself in a number
of ways, so much so that the territory now stands as a world leader in
this kind of market.

The first manifestation is economic and is driven by those who
wish to encourage film-makers and television companies to shoot their
material in Cornwall. For example, one of the 'Bibles' of the film
and television-making world, the *Crew and Services Directory* of the
South-West Film Commission, markets Cornwall in the following
way. Notice how it begins with the modern icon of Cornwall—surfing
(as depicted in *Blue Juice*)—but then returns to the traditionally
romantic. The Cornish 'locals' should not be feared, and it seems that
just being in Cornwall will cause any director or producer to make
good work:

> You'll find the best surfing beaches in Europe . . . magnificent
> river estuaries . . . elegant country houses . . . remote villages,
> farmhouses and cottages . . . wild and romantic moorland . . .
> spectacular headland hotels . . . and if harbour, cove and slip
> figure in your designs: the Cornish list is an all star cast in
> itself: Falmouth, Polperro, Charlestown, Boscastle, Mullion,
> Cadgwith, Mousehole . . . Anyone working in this atmosphere
> is bound to be inspired. You just have to get used to this in
> inspirational Cornwall. It's easy to work here too. There's a
> support crew as long as the uncut *War and Peace* (1967) as
> well as sympathetic and enthusiastic locals.[74]

Charlestown, listed here, is a case study example of the film/
heritage industry in Cornwall. It is promoted as one of the key
locations. *The Eagle has Landed* (1976), *The Three Musketeers* (1993),
Rebecca (1996), *Moll Flanders* (1996), *A Respectable Trade* (1997),

Frenchman's Creek (1998), *Mansfield Park* (1998), and *Wives and Daughters* (1999) were all shot there.[75] Meanwhile, press coverage of such productions tends to take the view that Cornwall should be uncritically grateful for such film and television programmes being filmed there, despite the fact that such films alter the cultural geography of the port itself, by putting up the prices of properties, and through the frequency of filming there changing the very way the Cornish conceive the place. Charlestown is, therefore, no longer a 'living' Cornish china clay port, but an epi-centre of imagining past maritime scenes for British and international film-makers. This in itself is perhaps a natural progression for a place that can no longer rely on real economic benefits from shipping, but nevertheless it re-defines its positioning in the Cornish landscape.[76]

The tourist authorities have also carefully drawn upon Jenny Agutter's impeccable credentials as an actress who lives in Cornwall to promote this kind of heritage. In her 'Film and TV Trail' she writes: 'Cornwall is a most beautiful county and it is a delight when its dramatic landscapes appear on the big and small screen all over the world'.[77] She also notes two other very significant 'heritage'-related productions in Cornwall. The first comes from a very high-profile source, whose name and work is as permanently linked to the Cornish landscape as that of Winston Graham and *Poldark*. Daphne du Maurier's work has long since been adapted for both the 'big' and 'small' screen and has had an enormous impact on how the world has 'imagined Cornwall' for much of the second half of the twentieth century.[78] Du Maurier's status as a writer continues to grow with academics, particularly those of a feminist persuasion. Instead of being perceived as a 'popular historical novelist' she is being re-marshalled as part of the traditional canon of 'English' literature,[79] and her name and literary heritage have also been used to promote a range of tourist and heritage activities within Cornwall, ranging from the direct linkage of the mid-Cornwall area to 'du Maurier country' to the now well-established Daphne du Maurier Festival of Literature and the Arts at Fowey.[80] All this seems rather a paradox considering that du Maurier realized that the success of her early fiction was partly responsible for the changing nature of Cornwall, prompting her to become an associate member of Mebyon Kernow in an effort to protect the 'authentic' Cornwall[81]—a fact which is rarely discussed by those controlling the heritage processes in Cornwall, such as the County Council, Restormel Borough Council and the Cornwall Tourist Authority.

Interestingly, when Alfred Hitchcock first shot his Oscar-winning version of *Rebecca* in 1940 it was filmed entirely in California, and Carlton Television's 1996 version only used one Cornish location:

Charlestown. HTV's 1982 version of *Jamaica Inn* did not use the original site at Bolventor (as Birks argues, it had been much altered, shaped by the tourism industry[82]) but re-built the notorious inn in Gloucester. However, despite the 'inauthenticity' of the film-making process, du Maurier's established Cornish credentials ensured appropriate representation. Here, perhaps only on an scale equalled in *Poldark*, heritage and film and television walk closely together as a cultural agency. This close linkage was enhanced further by the 1998 production of *Frenchman's Creek*, filmed at Helston, Padstow, St Clement and Charlestown.[83]

The second manifestation of the 'culture of heritage' comes from a transnational link. The works of the Lelant-born Anglo-Cornish 'romantic' novelist Rosamunde Pilcher are not only appreciated in the USA and Britain, but also in Germany, where she is the vision of Cornwall with which most German people associate. As Craig and FitzGerald record, 'her popularity there is evident from the major broadcaster ZDF's viewing figures: 7–8 million for every television adaptation of her stories'.[84] Central Television's 1989 version of Pilcher's most famous autobiographical novel, *The Shell-Seekers*, began the link.[85] It cast the actress Angela Lansbury as the novel's main character, Penelope Keeling, the recovering victim of a heart attack, who reflects on her life experiences, and when a dubbed version was broadcast in Germany it became an instant success. The German production company Frankfurter Filmproduktion then came to Cornwall for three consecutive years from 1994 to 1996 to shoot several Pilcher stories. So successful has Pilcher's image of Cornwall been, that Cornwall's Tourist Board has accompanied her to press conferences in Hamburg and Frankfurt to promote Cornwall as a holiday destination.[86] The climax of Pilcher fever came in 1997 with the Portman Productions and Tele-München co-production of her novel *Coming Home*,[87] which was directed by Giles Foster and included a cast of British television and film veterans: Joanna Lumley, Peter O'Toole, Emily Mortimer, Penelope Keith and David McCullum. Lelant, Lamorna Cove, Porthgwarra, Marazion, Penzance, Prideaux Place and Golden Manor, near Probus, have all been used in constructing the imaginary world of Pilcher's fiction on screen.

While accentuating still further the connection between Cornwall and Graham's epic, a more recent adaptation of the fifth *Poldark* novel *The Stranger from the Sea*[88] drew much controversy from organizations such as the Poldark Appeciation Society because it did not select the original actors from the 1970s series—Robin Ellis and Angharad Rees —to play the older Ross Poldark and Demelza. Instead, John Bowe and Mel Martin were chosen. Such was the 'heritage value' of *Poldark* and so ingrained in the public conscious were the original actors, that the success of this production (despite the involvement of other actors such as Ioan Gruffudd) and the greater realism of this production (using locations such as Wheal Prosper at Rinsey Cove) was doomed before it began. Heritage has not only shaped the world's interpretation of Cornwall, but that heritage was now having an impact on how outside agencies filmed that vision: an interesting twist.

Famously of course, the Poldark Mine at Wendron near Helston (an attraction originally marketing itself as 'Wendron Forge') has made much of its connection to the 1970s television series.[89] King Arthur's Castle Hotel at Tintagel promotes its filmatic heritage, ranging from the bedrooms being marketed as the place where Donald Pleasance once stayed[90] to its connections to several films, such as *Knights of the Round Table* (1953) and the BBC's *Dracula* (1979).[91] Meanwhile, the Headland Hotel at Newquay has promoted its link with *The Beatles' Magical Mystery Tour* film (1967)—a case of 'pop' heritage. Other properties and locations, however, are also undergoing a re-positioning with the heritage industry. One of the most famous developments of heritage marketing in Cornwall during the 1990s was the filming of Trevor Nunn's interpretation of William Shakespeare's *Twelfth Night* (1995) at several historical properties in Cornwall—Cotehele, Prideaux Place, St Michael's Mount and Mount Edgcumbe—and most significantly at Lanhydrock in mid-Cornwall.[92] The film, which contained a gallery of British stars (Helena Bonham Carter, Imogen Stubbs, Nigel Hawthorne, Imelda Staunton, Mel Smith, Richard E. Grant, Ben Kingsley and Toby Stephens), made good use of these Cornish locations, and Nunn's vision is highly developed and sophisticated.

Perhaps what makes the film successful is that Shakespeare creates a sense of 'otherness' in his conceptualization of Illyria, an otherness that is noticeable in the Cornish landscape. Like Charlestown, all of these properties now make a good deal of their involvement with this film and its cast because it makes important connections to icons of Britishness (Shakespeare, Nunn as an established director, Bonham-Carter's credentials in period drama) which are seen as desirable attributes. A linkage is even made between the typography used in the title sequence of the film and the properties in Cornwall. The National Trust in Cornwall obviously benefits financially from such productions, not only in terms of fees from the film-makers, but also because of the increase in visitor numbers generated by the film. The Cornish tourism bodies believe that such linkage does bear discernible economic benefits, though there are, as Sargeant notes, critics of this apparent 'vulgarization' of National Trust properties. As Stevenson observes: 'Escapism is one thing, but losing sight of the reality of our historical and literary inheritance is another. Instead of protecting this inheritance, the National Trust is in effect creating theme parks: surely a task better left to Disney?'[93]

It seems, then, that the specific histories of such properties and their place in the telling of Cornwall are becoming marginalized by their incorporation into cinematic visions. History is being re-written. It no longer matters that places such as Lanhydrock once exploited many of the local working-class Cornish as 'servants' and 'gardeners' because in its re-telling the property is 'owned by all of us'. It is a clever marshalling of culture and one which adeptly suits the purposes of the National Trust. This clever marshalling of culture brings us to another kind of film and place tie-in. The 2002 James Bond film *Die Another Day* has several sequences which were filmed in Cornwall.[94] Prior to the film's release, in the winter of that year, continual publicity emerged from the Eden Project at St Austell about the use of one of the biomes in the film as the villain's lair (actually imagined to be an 'ice palace' in Iceland), as well as the use of Holywell Bay doubling up as the coast of North Korea. In addition, the traditional pre-title sequence also used black, wetsuited 'spy' surfers, making an irrevocable link in the public's eye between Cornwall and Bond. Obviously, for Cornwall to be used in the filming of such a large-scale and established brand was not only important for the local economy—as the South West Film Commission would argue—but also for the wider Cornish tourism industry.

Several other interconnecting factors enhanced the image of 'cool' screen Kernow at this point. For example, the lead actress of the Bond film was Halle Berry, in 2002 the first black actresses to be awarded an Oscar for the film *Monster's Ball*, and at this point in time, a Hollywood A-list star. The film's soundtrack song was completed by Madonna, married to the British director Guy Ritchie of *Lock, Stock and Two Smoking Barrels* and *Snatch* fame. There was also the fact that the Eden Project had been one of the successes of Britain's Millennial celebrations, gaining international acclaim from most observers. It is not surprising, then, that in the 'Film and TV Trail' of the *For One and All* tourism brochure *Die Another Day* is its lead film, even though (paradoxically) the Cornishness of the film is non-existent.[95] Nevertheless, just like *Poldark*, du Maurier and *Twelfth Night*, it has been incorporated into the brief of the Cornish heritage psyche. It should be noted, however, that Cornwall is not the only place were such 'Film and TV Trails' are to be found (there are similar opportunities in London and Bath [where dozens of films have been made] and Sheffield ['The Full Monty Tour'], as well as the other

Celtic territorities such as Scotland and Ireland), but it does appear to
be leading the way.

CORNISH LONGS: THE NEXT STEP

Clearly, what Cornish film and television writers, directors, actors and
producers are seeking is a between-platform between the Cornish
'Shorts', which have come a long way in their ten-year history, and the
kind of films and television dramas that have been most successful
either in a national or international context, whether 'heritage' or other
types of film. As Clarke contends, the infrastructural problem remains
for Cornwall. While Wales, Ireland, Northern Ireland, and Scotland
have the media infrastructure and autonomy to produce their own
drama and film, Cornwall does not. Neither does it have a regional
television structure which will facilitate drama production: the BBC
and Carlton Westcountry in Plymouth do not make drama or co-
produce with other companies.

The establishment of a Cornwall Film Fund at Pydar House,
Truro, through Objective One Funding in 2000 appeared to offer hope
to a new generation of film-makers operating in Cornwall. The project
was financed by the European Union and a partnership of Cornwall
County Council, Cornwall Enterprise and South West Screen. The
Cornwall Film Fund's original mission included the six objectives,
which were to:

1. Raise the quality of work produced by Cornish production
   companies and writers, so that they can compete effectively in
   national and international markets.
2. Enable the production of major film and television projects set
   in Cornwall and which promote Cornwall to national and international audiences.
3. Develop the skills base of the film and television production
   sector in Cornwall and create a skilled, confident workforce.
4. Create improved employment or self-employment opportunities for Cornish people in the film and television
   production sector.
5. Ensure that the Cornish economy derives maximum benefit
   from film and television production.
6. Increase the prosperity of media businesses in Cornwall and the
   economic benefit of TV and film production to the county's
   [*sic*] ancillary and service sectors.[96]

Three target areas were also noted:

1. The Development of feature films and major television
   projects: 'We will advance up to £50,000 or 45% of the total
   development budget [whichever is less], as repayable aid
   [repayable on the first day of principal photography]. At the
   time of repayment a premium equivalent to 50% of the sum
   advanced will also be payable.'
2. The production of short films: 'We will advance up to £50,000
   of 45% of total production budget [whichever is less] for
   individual short film [defined as up to 15 minutes in length].
   This will be in the form of a recoupable advance but these sums
   are only repayable if, as and when the film makes a profit.'
3. The development of new scripts: 'We will make grants [in the
   form of repayable aid] of up to £10,000 for the writing of new
   fiction scripts for feature films or major television dramas/
   drama series [but not short films] up to 3rd draft stage. No
   match funding is required for this part of the Fund.')[97]

So far, however, certainly amongst the film-makers, writers and
producers I know, and who wish to develop the genre, the Cornwall
Film Fund has not met all of these expectations. Frustratingly, although
there has been interest in working with the Cornwall Film Fund
expressed by larger-scale production companies outside of Cornwall
(who have the necessary infrastructure and technical expertise, for
example in Plymouth or Bristol), the fund is presently bound by
geographical limitations based unrealistically on the River Tamar and
strict economic entry requirements (for example, 'the applicant will
provide evidence of employment figures before and after funding
request'[98]) and is not always able to fund this kind of work, even if it
restricts the development of the kind of stories of Cornish social
realism that are needed.

Although the Cornwall Film Fund has been able to fund the
Cornish Film Festival, there seems to be a sense of frustration amongst
many screenwriters that their work has not being considered by the
fund, and that much of the funding has gone to the traditional 'outside'
London-based film producers who simply want to use Cornwall as a
location, or to those making initial steps into making that now very
Cornish film—the 'Short'. Against the background of the arguments
presented in this chapter, neither is good enough. Some impression of
the frustrations of the Cornwall Film Fund come in an open letter
dated 27 March 2003 from its then director Colin Rogers:

As many of you know, I feel bitterly frustrated that after two
years work getting Phase 2 through the EC minefield, we have

now been told by Government Office [of the South West] that no Objective One money has been kept aside to fund it and all the money for measure 1.2. (under which the Fund falls) has already been allocated. This is an unforgivable waste of many people's time, energy and above all, their hopes . . . For the people who hoped to bring their projects to fruition with our help, it is more than just a disappointment—it is a disgrace.[99]

CONCLUSION

Rogers' gloomy assessment seems to herald the probable dissolution of the Cornwall Film Fund, a great shame bearing in mind the steps necessary to produce the kind of film and television drama appropriate to Cornwall's needs. We may also despair as to whether the representation of the Cornish people on screen has really altered since *Straw Dogs*. Though incorporating Cornish language speakers and showing them on prime-time television throughout the United Kingdom, the Dawn French situation comedy vehicle *Wild West* (2002) attracted much criticism from within Cornwall. It showed 'the Cornish as inbred fools, thieves with limited exposure and brain power', wrote one disgruntled viewer on the BBC Radio Cornwall website.[100] In the series, French plays the lesbian Mary Trewednack, who lives in the village of St Gweep (the series is filmed in Portloe). Simon Nye, the creator of *Men Behaving Badly*, was the scriptwriter. He admitted that he knew little about Cornwall, saying: 'I didn't do research, although I did read the odd book. I was fairly neutral about Cornwall but I never thought of setting it anywhere else. I needed a small community where they asphyxiated each other.'[101] Although Cornwall may not have the media control over the stories it wishes to tell, it was at the start of the twenty-first century much more prepared to question inauthentic or pejorative representations and the large agencies (like the BBC) who were still resorting to stereotypes.

However, there are some positive moves in other quarters. A former theme park in St Agnes is now being converted into film studios, and we need to remember the extremely poor state that Cornish film and television drama were in as little as ten years ago. In contrast, today's situation seems more promising. Carlton Westcounty now runs a trust fund set up by the Cornish television executive and co-founder of Westcountry Television, Frank Copplestone (who died in 1996), to provide support and financial assistance to Cornish or Cornish-based people embarking on careers in film and television.[102] Mick Catmull, a documentary film-maker who has his own production company (A38 Film) and works (amongst other things) as a producer for BBC South West, has in the past produced investigations into Cornwall's Celtic heritage. More recently, he has produced a documentary on *Dewhelans The Cornish Homecoming*,[103] and has publically outlined his plans to set up Kernow Television. It may be that deregulation of the media, as well as the possibilities offered by cable, satellite and 'box' technology, will provide Cornwall with more of its own media forums.

I suspect that there will continue to be many films which are shot in Cornwall and yet which provide little social, economic or political benefit for the Cornish, just like Marie Jones's community in County Kerry.[104] No doubt many will continue to be 'inauthentic' in the manner described above and will contribute further to the heritage industry of Cornwall and Britain. Elsewhere, though, I believe there is now a 'head of steam' of indigenous film talent in Cornwall that did not exist ten years ago. That group must pick a carefully conceived project to put 'Cornish film and television' on the map, should the opportunity for development come internally. It is important that the project should address the 'nationalist' issues in Cornwall from a new angle, one that leaves the tired post-war devolutionary politics in the past. In terms of film and television drama, the story must be resolutely Cornish but resolutely international at the same time. We are used to gazing with envy at Hollywood and India, but one should look, for example, at how film-makers in a territory like Germany have imagined their country in, say, *Goodbye Lenin* (2003),[105] a film which explores an East Berlin woman's experiences after waking up from a coma. She is in the coma during the fall of the Berlin Wall. Coca-Cola signs and satellite dishes are hidden from her by her son as she wishes to carry on the ways of the old East Germany. Eventually, however, the charade fails and she realizes that she must now wave goodbye to the old life. The film is not typical Hollywood material, but has an international enough narrative to make impact elsewhere. Similarly, *Solino* (2002) explores the experience of an immigrant Italian family stuck in a coal-mining town in the post-war period, only to find success in opening the first pizzeria in Germany.[106] These are the kinds of stories the Cornish might be able to tell, and maybe Cornwall should look at the ways in which other continental European territories (often small countries) fund and develop their cinema.

Additionally, given the fact that more outside agencies (political, social, literary, historical) in Britain, Europe and America are beginning to understand better the separate experience of the Cornish (thanks to those concerned with telling its authentic story),[107] there now seems no reason why the familiar icons of 20th Century Fox, Universal, Miramax or Dreamworks could not open a film with a resolutely Cornish theme. When it does happen, I shall have my bag of popcorn and be in the front-row at the St Austell Filmcentre, waiting for the Pearl and Dean advertising.[108]

ACKNOWLEDGEMENTS
I am indebted to the National Film and Television Archive, British Film Institute, London, the Cornwall Film Fund, Truro, and the South West Film and Television Archive, Plymouth, for their assistance in the writing of this chapter.

NOTES AND REFERENCES
1. M. Jones, *Stones in His Pockets*, New York, 2000. London production directed by Ian McElhinney.
2. A. Slide, *The Cinema and Ireland*, Jefferson, NC, 1988; T. Byrne, *Power in the Eye: An Introduction to Contemporary Irish Film*, Lanham, MD, 1997; M. McLoone, *Irish Film: The Emergence of Contemporary Irish Cinema*, London, 2000.
3. D. Berry, *Wales and the Cinema: The First Hundred Years*, Cardiff, 1996; J. Richards, *Films and British National Identity: From Dickens to 'Dad's Army'*, Manchester, 1997; R, Murphy (ed.), *British Cinema of the 90s*, London, 1997; J. Ashby and A. Higson (eds), *British Cinema: Past and Present*, London and New York, 2000; M. Hjort and S. Mackenzie (eds), *Cinema and Nation*, London and New York, 2000.
4. D. Boyle (dir.), *Trainspotting*, Film Four, 1995; M. Herman (dir.), *Brassed Off*, Film Four, 1996; M. Newell (dir.), *Four Weddings and a Funeral*, MGM, 1993; D. Boyle (dir.), *A Life Less Ordinary*, Film Four, 1997; P. Cattaneo (dir.), *The Full Monty*, 20th Century Fox, 1997.
5. For a useful overview of developments, see the contributors to P. Payton (ed.), *Cornish Studies: Ten*, Exeter, 2002.
6. Ashby and Higson, 2000, p. 13.
7. See *Cornish World/Bys Kernowyon*, 9, 1996, p. 3; 18, 1998, p. 13; *An Gannas*, 309, 2002, p. 4.
8. S. Craig and D. FitzGerald, *Filmed in Cornwall*, Launceston, 1999. Another useful publication is D. Clarke, *Location Cornwall*, St Teath, 1990.
9. South West Film Commission (ed.), *Crew and Services Directory 1998/99*, Saltash, 1998.
10. N. Moody, 'Poldark Country and National Culture' and H. Birks 'Jamaica Inn: The Creation of Meanings on a Tourist Site', in E. Westland (ed.), *Cornwall: The Cultural Construction of Place*, Penzance, 1997, pp. 129–36 and 137–41.
11. A.M. Kent, 'The Cornish Alps: Resisting Romance in the Clay Country', in ibid., pp. 53–67. The former follows events during the Cornish Clay Strike of 1913.
12. A.M. Kent, *The Literature of Cornwall: Continuity, Identity, Difference 1000–2000*, Bristol, 2000, pp. 266–7 and 'Celtic Nirvanas: Constructions of

Celtic in Contemporary British Youth Culture' in D.C. Harvey, R. Jones, N. McInroy and C. Milligan (eds), *Celtic Geographies: Old Culture, New Times*, London and New York, 2002, pp. 208–26.

13. See W. Graham, *Poldark's Cornwall*, London, 1994 [1983]; G. Tibballs, *The Wycliffe File: The Story of the ITV Detective Series*, London, 1995.

14. Jon Guyver Cole (ed.), *Well-Weird Cornwall*, No. 2, 1995, p. 8.

15. J. Angarrack, *Breaking the Chains: Propaganda, Censorship, Deception and the Manipulation of Public Opinion in Cornwall*, Camborne, 1999 and *Our Future is History: Identity, Law and the Cornish Question*, Cornwall, 2002.

16. B. Deacon, A. George and R. Perry, *Cornwall at the Crossroads: Living Communities or Leisure Zone?* Redruth, 1988; R. Clarke, 'Broadcasting for One and All', paper read at the Identities without Borders Conference, Liege, 7–9 July, 1995.

17. Cornwall Media Resource, *An Evening of Contemporary Cornish Films at the Acorn Theatre, Friday 18th April 2003*, Cornwall, 2003, p. 1; Goel Fylm Kernow, *Cornwall Film Festival Guide: Falmouth Arts Centre October 25—27*, Cornwall, 2002; 20mh Fèis Film is Telebhisein sna Dùthchanan Ceilteach 1999, *Festival Programme,* Scotland, 1999; 22nd Celtic Film and Television Festival/22a Goel Fylm ha Pellwolok Geltek, *Festival Programme/Towlenn an Goel*, Cornwall, 2001.

18. A. Kovacs (dir.), *Hwerow Hweg/Bitter Sweet*, West Coast Productions, 2000.

19. C. Prechezer (dir.), *Blue Juice*, Channel Four Films and Pandora Cinema, 1995; N. Cole (dir.), *Saving Grace*, 20th Century Fox Searchlight, 1999.

20. J. Boorman (dir.), *Excalibur*, Warner Bros, 1981; Steve Barron (dir.), *Merlin,* Film Four, 1998.

21. Kent, 2000; S. Trezise, *The West Country as a Literary Invention: Putting Fiction in its Place*, Exeter, 2000.

22. See T. Cross, *The Shining Sands: Artists in Newlyn and St Ives 1880–1930*, Tiverton, 1994; M. Whybrow, *St Ives 1883–1993: A Portrait of an Art Colony*, Woodbridge, 1994; A. Oldham, *Everyone was Working: Writers and Artists in Postwar St Ives*, St Ives, 2002. An interesting documentary film related to this field is N. Levine (dir.), *A Writer's View of his Town: Norman Levine's St Ives*, Three S Films, 2000 [1972].

23. See James Whetter, 'Lewis Harding 1807–93: Pioneer Photographer', *An Baner Kernewek/The Cornish Banner*, 105, 2001, pp. 22–3.

24. Craig and FitzGerald, 1999, pp. 6–7.

25. Craig and FitzGerald, 1999, p. 8. See also Clarke, 1990, pp. 62–5. Pola Negri was a silent film star of Polish descent. She felt the native Cornish were very suspicious of her.

26. M. Landy, 'The Other Side of Paradise: British Cinema from an American Perspective', in Ashby and Higson, 2000, pp. 63–79.

27. Craig and FitzGerald, 1999, pp. 8–9.

28. See Robert Louis Stevenson, *Treasure Island*, London, 1994 [1883], p. 1; A.L. Rowse (ed.), *A Cornish Anthology*, Penzance, 1988 [1968], p. 7.

29. R. Thorpe (dir.), *Knights of the Round Table*, MGM, 1953. For comment

on Cornish imaginings of King Arthur, see A. Hale, A.M. Kent and T. Saunders (eds), *Inside Merlin's Cave: A Cornish Arthurian Reader 1000–2000*, London, 2000.

30. Craig and FitzGerald, 1999, p. 10.
31. Ibid., p. 93.
32. See Winston Graham, *The Poldark Omnibus*, London, 1991 [1945, 1946, 1953, 1953]; C. Berry (dir.), *Poldark 1: Part One*, BBC, 1975; K. Ives (dir.) *Poldark 1: Part Three*, BBC, 1975; P. Dudley (dir.), *Poldark 2: Part One*, BBC, 1977, *Poldark 2: Part Two*, BBC, 1977; P. Dudley and R. Jenkins (dirs.), *Poldark 2: Part Three*, BBC, 1977, *Poldark 2: Part Four*, BBC, 1977.
33. See Susan Howatch, *Penmarric*, London, 1971; T. Wakerell (dir.), *Penmarric: Part One*, BBC, 1979; T. Wakerell and D. Martinus (dirs.), *Penmarric: Part Two, Part Three and Part Four*, BBC Video 1994 [1979].
34. See Tibballs, 1995; F, Fairfax, M. Friend and A.J. Quinn (dirs.), *Wycliffe*, HTV, 1995.
35. Kent, 2000, pp. 22–69.
36. See P. Corbin, 'From *The Third Man* to *Shakespeare in Love*: Fifty Years of British Success on Continental Screens', in Ashby and Higson, 2000, pp. 80–91.
37. J. Cameron (dir.), *Titanic*, 20th Century Fox, 1997; Sam Mendes (dir.), *Road to Perdition*, Dreamworks, 2002; M. Gibson (dir.), *Braveheart*, 20th Century Fox, 1995.
38. E. Zwick (dir.), *Legends of the Fall*, Tristar, 1994. The film was based on the novella by Jim Harrison.
39. W. Reitherman (dir.), *The Sword in the Stone*, Walt Disney, 1963.
40. F. Du Chau (dir.), *The Magic Sword: Quest for Camelot*, Warner Bros, 1998.
41. See 'Camelot' in *Cornish World/Bys Kernowyon*, 1998, p. 13.
42. R. Rich and T. Berman (dirs.), *The Black Cauldron*, Walt Disney, 1985. The story is based on elements of the *Mabinogion*.
43. S. Peckinpath (dir.), *Straw Dogs*, Freemantle, 1971.
44. www.amazon.co.uk/reviews. According to critic Pauline Kael, *Straw Dogs* was 'the first American film that is a fascist work of art'.
45. S. Kubrick (dir.), *A Clockwork Orange*, Warner Bros, 1971. The film was banned for over thirty years, but finally given a theatrical and video release in 2000.
46. Goel Fylm Kernow, 2002, p. 5.
47. W.H. Hudson, *The Land's End: A Natualist's Impressions in West Cornwall*, London 1981 [1908], pp. 95-6; J. Beddoes, *The Races of Britain*, London, 1885. Beddoes provides an index of nigrescence for Britain and Ireland. Cornwall has the highest index. For comment on this, see J. Vernon, 'Border Crossings: Cornwall and the English (Imagi)nation' in G. Cubitt (ed.), *Imagining Nations*, Manchester, 1995, pp. 153–72. For a wider critique, see G. Carruthers and A. Rawes (eds), *English Romanticism and the Celtic World*, Cambridge, 2003.

48. H.D. Lowry and C.A. Dawson Scott, *Wheal Darkness*, n.d.; D. du Maurier, *Jamaica Inn*, London, 1978 [1936], p. 18.
49. P.B. Ellis, *The Celtic Dawn: A History of Pan Celticism*, London, 1993; P. Payton, *Cornwall*, Fowey, 1996, pp. 290–2.
50. R. Hardy (dir.), *The Wicker Man*, British Lion, 1973. Several different versions of the film exist.
51. Prechezer, 1995.
52. Kent, 2000; Kent, 2002.
53. For background, see Craig and FitzGerald 1999, pp. 58–9.
54. Cole, 1999.
55. www.amazon.co.uk/reviews.
56. Filter, *Title of Record*, Reprise Recordings, 1999.
57. B. Scott (dir.), *The Saffron Threads*, Wild West Films, 1995.
58. B. Scott (dir.), *The Last Words of Dolly Pentreath/An Dewetha Geryow a Dolly Pentreath*, Wild West Films, 1994.
59. B. Scott (dir.), *Splatt dhe Wertha/Plot for Sale*, Wild West Films, 1997, rear cover of video box.
60. See A. Lanyon, *Roundabout West Cornwall*, St Ives, n.d. The book is 'in memory of Cornwall, shot on location'.
61. Kent, 2000, pp. 278–84.
62. See A.M. Kent, 'Lamenting Loss in Contemporary Cornish Literature', in P. Payton (ed.), *Cornish Studies: Six*, Exeter, 1998, pp. 183–6.
63. H. Foster (dir.), *Kernopalooza!*, Carlton Westcountry, 1998.
64. Alison de Vere, Ben Weschke, Julia McLean and John Adams (dirs.), *How Madge Figgey Got Her Pig*, Three S Films, 1997.
65. R. Hunt (ed.), *Romances of the West of England: The Drolls, Traditions, and Superstitions of Old Cornwall (Second Series)*, London, 1865, pp. 332–4.
66. Kovacs, 2000. For background to minority languages in Europe, see European Charter for Regional or Minority Languages, *From Theory to Practice: The European Charter for Regional or Minority Languages*, Strasbourg, 2002.
67. Goel Fylm Kernow, 2002, p. 22.
68. Ibid., p. 25.
69. Ibid., p. 26.
70. Ibid., pp. 9 and 10.
71. Ibid., pp. 14 and 15. One significant exception to this trend is Mick Catmull (dir.), *Joan*, A.38 Films, 1998.
72. Moody, 1997.
73. A. Sargeant, 'Making and selling Heritage Culture: Style and Authenticity in Historical Fictions on Film and Television', in Ashby and Higson, 2000, pp. 301–15.
74. South West Film Commission, 1998, p. 12.
75. See Craig and FitzGerald, 1999, pp. 29–34; J. Agutter, 'Film and TV Trail', in *For One and All: Cornwall 2003*, Redruth, 2003, pp. 13–14.
76. For historical images of Charlestown, see J. Wilson, *Around St Austell Bay*, St Teath, 1986, pp. 82–5.

77. Agutter, 2003, p. 14.
78. See J. Cook, *Daphne: A Portrait of Daphne du Maurier*, London, 1991.
79. See, for example, Alison Light, *Forever England: Femininity, Literature and Conservatism between the Wars*, London and New York, 1991, pp. 156–207.
80. See G. Busby and Z. Hambly, 'Literary Tourism and the Daphne du Maurier Festival', in P. Payton (ed.), *Cornish Studies: Eight*, Exeter, 2000, pp. 197–212.
81. See Kent, 2000, pp. 178–87.
82. Birks, 1997.
83. F. Fairfax (dir.), *Frenchman's Creek*, Carlton, 1998.
84. Craig and FitzGerald, 1999, p. 24.
85. Rosemunde Pilcher, *The Shell Seekers*, London, 1987.
86. See Craig and FitzGerald, 1999, p. 26.
87. Rosemunde Pilcher, *Coming Home*, London, 1996.
88. R. Laxton, (dir.) *Poldark 3*, HTV and First Independent, 1996.
89. See N. Kennedy and N. Kingcome, 'Disneyfication of Cornwall—Developing a Poldark Heritage Complex', *International Journal of Heritage Studies*, 4.1, 1998, pp. 45–59.
90. King Arthur's Castle Hotel leaflet.
91. Craig and FitzGerald, 1999, p. 63.
92. T. Nunn (dir.), *Twelfth Night*, Renaissance, 1995.
93. Quoted in Sargeant, 2000, p. 308. Original letter by K. Stevenson in *The Times*, 25 January 1996, p. 19.
94. Lee Tamahori (dir.), *Die Another Day*, MGM, 2002.
95. Agutter, 2003, p. 13.
96. Cornwall Film, *The Cornwall Film Fund: What We Can Do For You and How To Apply*, Truro, n.d., p. 3.
97. Ibid., pp. 4–5.
98. Ibid., p. 7.
99. Letter from Colin Rogers, Cornwall Film, 27 March 2003, p. 1.
100. Quoted from the BBC Radio Cornwall website on www.chortle.co.uk under the heading 'Wildly Offensive: Cornwall Blasts Dawn French Sitcom'.
101. Ibid.
102. See www.tv.carlton.com/westcountry.
103. Conversation with Catmull, January 2003. See also Goel Fylm Kernow, 2002, p. 9.
104. Jones, 2000.
105. W. Becker (dir.), *Goodbye Lenin*, Warner Bros, 2003.
106. F. Akin (dir.), *Solino*, Wüste Filmproducktion, 2003.
107. Payton, 2002.
108. See Brian Hornsey, 'Ninety Years of Cinema in St Austell', *An Baner Kernewek/The Cornish Banner*, 2001, pp. 20–1. A study of the development of cinema in Cornwall is needed.

CORNWALL'S VISUAL CULTURES IN PERSPECTIVE

Patrick Laviolette

Here every corner was a picture and . . . the people seemed to fall naturally into their places and to harmonise with the surroundings. (Stanhope Alexander Forbes 1913[1])

INTRODUCTION

From the tourism industry to the legacy of art colonies, the visual realm has had a profound relationship with the Cornish peninsula. This article explores some of the visual modes for communicating what this place is all about. It offers various materialist and ethnographic interpretations of the meaning behind certain images and depictions of Cornwall. By investigating the landscape representations of familiar settings and items of popular culture, this paper looks at how spaces (such as the home, gardens and public murals) and visual artefacts (such as tourist brochures, postcards and the Cornish tartans) shape and are shaped by a diversity of Cornish identities. I intend this piece as an ethnographic follow-up to the more art-historical and literary analysis of landscape iconography that appeared in *Cornish Studies: Seven*.[2] In illustrating the means by which residents and visitors produce and consume some of this peninsula's visuality, this article is generally concerned with the appropriation of environmental images west of the Tamar.

Visual culture is a burgeoning field in the social sciences and humanities. With the launch of several new journals as well as the writing of countless books and research projects, it is clear that the subject has been expanding considerably over the past two decades.[3] Although some studies in this growing field have analysed the ways in which visual forces influence artists, a dearth of information still exists concerning the social relations of artistic circles.[4] Despite some advances, we are also some way from constructing a comprehensive theory of artistic taste.[5] In his attempt to amend these situations, Halle argues that we need 'an understanding of art and cultural items in the audience's own terrain, namely the social life, architecture, and surroundings of the house and neighbourhood'.[6] Investigating the meaning of landscape art in everyday settings is especially pertinent because both the home and the landscape genre are imbued with many European ideals and ideologies. Looking at the interplay between artistic meaning and the visual context of representation requires a novel approach to studying the mode of dwelling— one that concentrates on the materiality of everyday settings.

In this respect a focus on popular objects is equally essential. Edwards reveals that the artefacts linked with holiday-makers 'are an important facet in the ongoing consideration of the politics of representation'.[7] Further, according to Dann,[8] social analysts are showing a growing interest in the representations of identity that occur in promotional and other tourist-related memorabilia. He stresses the importance for semiotic ethnographies of media-construed images of the travel market. Brown and Turley[9] amplify this call by suggesting that scholars should consider the materiality of travel in its everyday settings. They warn that Baudrillardian views of hyper-reality—where simulacra or reproduction take precedence over authentic images— often do not do justice to the diversity of real life holiday experiences.

My examination of art in familiar places in Cornwall provides a deconstruction of representative environmental scenes (e.g. paintings, pictures and prominent views) in typical domestic and public spheres. The objective is not as ambitious as constructing a theory of taste or artistic social relations, but I do hope to illustrate the material conditions in which residents and visitors encode visual messages of Cornwall into their everyday lives. Hence, the idea is to go beyond traditional models of artistic appropriation.

RESEARCH SETTING
Opinions differ as to whether the Cornish peninsula exists as a land apart or as a quintessentially British periphery. Overall, my research in Cornwall has uncovered a diversity of social identities that promote such contesting views. My fieldwork, from May 1998 to October 1999, has taken place within the context of multi-sited ethnography.[10] Methodologically, this consisted of living and working in a variety of places in the area so as to participate in the lifeworlds of disparate groups of informants. Generally it was amateur footballers, artists,

farmers, fisherfolk, immigrants, landscape gardeners, scholars and tourists that were the best groups of informants. My research methods also included extensive interviews, walks and focus sessions with such persons. By actively participating in the everyday life of these different groups of insiders, outsiders and those in between, I have sought to investigate the relationships between landscape as an artefact of material culture and the creation of a diversity of social identities. This has demanded that I question the character of environmental experiences and representations: a questioning that explores how diverse social identities both shape and are shaped by the Duchy's cultural landscapes.

My general line of investigation has addressed the diversity of cultural meanings attributed to the Cornish countryside and coastline through phenomenological as well as visual theories and practices of social anthropology, cultural geography and material culture studies. The present paper therefore stems from a particular concern with the way in which people appropriate Cornwall's visual cultures. It focuses on how certain visual phenomena intertwine with this region's everyday lifeworld.

STUDIOS AND THE FAMILIAR

Home Imagery
Based on a sample of around 105 homes throughout Cornwall, part of my research has sought to discover whether residents display local landscape representations (i.e. paintings or photographs) in their homes. A simple typology of four groups summarizes the situation: i) people who do not have landscape images on their walls; ii) people who do have landscape images but not of Cornwall (these are usually though not exclusively reproductions of famous international artists, e.g. Constable, Monet); iii) people who largely own originals, or to a lesser extent reproductions, of regionally well-known artists (e.g. Richard Tuff, Kurt Jackson, Ben Nicholson); iv) people who have some pieces by more obscure local artists (those in this group are often directly or indirectly linked with local/regional art scenes; they are either hanging samples of their own work or the work of friends and colleagues, hence demonstrating their commitment to the scene and an empathy with local artists).

The first group of this typology is particularly interesting because it is the most obviously related to a person's class or vocation, whereby the visual abstraction of what is intimately known is minimal due to their significant levels of environmental experiences and embodiment.[11] It is in physically imposing themselves upon the outside world that this group of people lay claim to their familiar settings. In so doing, they generate a more confident self-image, one in which the exterior realm with which they are most acquainted seems to fall under their control and mastery. They are no longer confined to an indoor space of calculation and deliberation but instead become an integral part of the outside world—a world that they embrace with gesture and do not try to filter with an array of objects. It is perhaps also this physical sense of outdoor familiarity that explains why the people in this group rarely hang environmental representations in their homes. They have little need to simulate what is intimately known.

For people like Mr Durgan (aged 68), the land is more than a way of life. It is where he weighs his life. He has little time for any abstractions of the countryside like his wife's landscape photographs that dominate the 'domestic' spaces of their house such as the kitchen, bathroom and utility rooms. This reminds us of the need to be attentive to the issues of gender that have been nicely illustrated in *Cornish Studies: Eight*,[12] for clearly the world of landscape representation is a contested arena in which different roles and stereotypes are played out. As an active farmer from the parish of Lanivet who—like generations before him—has lived in Cornwall all his life, Mr Durgan has a daily contact with his extensive fields. While crossing his land, he moves purposefully because every time he strolls over his terrain he is working. Every movement is an opportunity to examine the well-being of his animals and to watch over the progress of his crops. His surveying means their survival. Consequently, he does not use the same paths twice in the same day. Instead, he attempts to cover as much ground as possible whilst minimizing the amount of energy that he expends while moving. He walks quickly and in front of me, blazing the way forward.

One can see from his gestures, conversation and surveillance techniques that his fields, cattle, sheep, farmstead and family are extensions of himself. He allows himself to stop walking only when talking about such intimate things. He then taps himself in the chest with his hands clasped together before extending them to the objects, animals or people that he his speaking about. In doing so he asserts that these reference points are part of his extended personality. His identity and heritage are wrapped up in them. They are indeed part of his responsibility to look after but also one of his greatest joys in life. Though his land is his burden, he reaps its fullest benefits. Such rewards are intimately tied to a rich and involved knowledge of every corner of this place.

A sense of inhibition indoors helps to explain why it is most often miners, farmers and fishermen that rarely put up pictures of the landscape in their homes. Given their concrete, physical and recurrent relationship with the Cornish environment, they do not even consider this as an option. They generally have a low or sporadic income and live in dwellings that they see as temporary, or transitional. So on the one hand they think of such pictures as a luxury beyond their means and on the other as an inappropriate gesture of permanence. Those who live in traditional houses also find it out of keeping to hang what are predominantly avant-garde images of the environment in their homes. They tend to prefer old portrait photographs and seafaring, mining or war paraphernalia with some historical significance. The presence of these tangible objects from the past informs their vision of the present landscape more satisfactorily than any abstract image could.

Landscape artists and photographers fit into a similar lifestyle model as miners, farmers and fishermen, since many also have an erratic income and frequently search for engaged environmental experiences (such as working *en plein air*). They differ, however, in that they are usually less nostalgic for material artefacts from the region's past. Instead they graphically illustrate elements of Cornwall's natural world in their homes by depicting their own work or the work of acquaintances in the art community. They are therefore abstracting their familiar space with personalized visions of outdoor environments. Such expressions are about conforming to or resisting convention regarding the Duchy's visual representation. That is, they can be individualistic or socio-political illustrations—visual narratives—about whether or not to conform to the conventions of particular artistic genres or schools. As Rachel, an artist from a small village near Launceston, says:

> Why do people make art, or landscape art? Some artists will make it purely to sell. Others will be making a much more personal statement, and the thought of it selling is nowhere uppermost in their mind at this time.

Perhaps expectedly, those class-groups of less modest means or of a higher social standing are the ones that financially support the various local art scenes. Retirees, middle-class immigrants, scholars and local white-collar workers make up the bulk of those residents who frequently display purchased images of Cornwall from photographers of repute and renowned painters. They leave the kitsch down-market works to others who have less cultural and/or financial capital invested in the art world. It is likely that in this case the presence of landscape images in the home is related to social class distinctions. In many public and private spaces, people try to invoke familiar scenes related to their past or their cause. By portraying places that range from the earliest periods of Cornish (pre) history to places linked with contemporary political events, residents who do have Cornish landscape representations fall into one of two further categories: a) those that are constructing more heretical discourses about belonging, marginality and self-reliance (often with nationalistic undertones); and b) those that construe discourses about homeland, diaspora and aesthetics. To illustrate these two categories I will use the examples of Rachel and Pete.

Rachel is an example of someone whose convictions about her art and socio-political views are strong. In her words she describes the link between artistic success, social standing and local gentrification:

> Artists often unintentionally 'promote' an area, draw attention to it, indicate the beauty in it which hitherto was (by others) unrecognized. Or even dismissed. Artists can unintentionally 'ruin' an area by changing its character through drawing the attention to it of those who couldn't see the beauty for themselves. The fact that they then have to move away is due to the increase in real estate prices as well as the change in character. The wealthy who move in might or might not buy work of that immediate area by very local artists, they might just as easily bring work in from artists from elsewhere. Whether or not they buy the art is for me irrelevant, it is that they SEE it—in galleries here, in galleries upcountry, or in people's houses upcountry—which brings them here. It is an unintentional promotion of the exact area painted. If the artists had made the same paintings but without disclosing the location, how different life would be!

For those outsiders of the middle classes, local acceptance is not guaranteed simply by supporting local artists. Sometimes it is even hindered. Their choice to buy and display a considerable proportion of distinguished landscape art might be an attempt to lay claim to local authority. It might even reduce the animosity of those who act as the local producers of images, tastes or trends. But as a class-based appropriation, a means of portraying cultural capital, it only communicates a will to belong to like-minded people, while maintaining a social distance with many insiders of different social standings.

This instance shares significant similarities with Bourdieu's look at the cultural production of art and taste in France. In this synthesis of his ideas about the acquisition, distribution and struggle of cultural capital, he suggests that the sites of cultural production define their own audiences who arbitrate the quality of the consumed product. This is so because parities exist between the fields of production and consumption, which certify or discount a person's cultural currency. In this sense, the control and manipulation of artistic classificatory schemes acts as a signpost for good or bad taste. In Bourdieu's own words:

> As is seen more clearly in avant-garde painting than anywhere else, a practical mastery of these markers, a sort of sense of social direction, is indispensable in order to be able to navigate in a hierarchically structured space in which movement is always fraught with the danger of losing class, in which 'places'—galleries, theatres, publishing houses—make all the difference.[13]

The example of Pete from Falmouth (aged 29) illustrates another angle, one more to do with aesthetics and longing. He has many paintings by local artists in his home and has been interested in Cornish art for many years. After graduating from university he even tried to set up his own art business to promote local artists. This was not a successful undertaking and so he has recently moved to London to find work. Despite this, he has kept his house in Falmouth and lets it out. The view from the window of his room in London intentionally mimics the one from his Falmouth house. The print he has brought with him was chosen because it reminds him of home. He has also brought an enlarged photo of Kynance Cove. These scenes are crucial in allowing him to adjust to life in London, especially since he claims that 'every aspect of life is so incredibly different in the city'. He has even duplicated the layout of the furniture in his room in London to mimic his home setting in Falmouth. To a degree, then, he finds a security in this familiar set-up. This allows him a constant contact with home. The importance of this is made even greater because his ideal of letting out the basement of his Falmouth house as a separate self-contained flat has not worked out yet. Since he has instead rented out the main part of the house to a friend, he must himself use the basement as his space when he returns. His room in London is therefore what Mitra[14] might call a kind of surrogate space for what he has temporarily lost in his house. These arrangements and images thus act as surrogates of belonging. They substitute one's loss of personal everyday contact with home. Rather than being *aide-mémoires*, such images have become material memories in their own right.

Murals

Painted murals abound in Cornwall. These form a meaningful part of this region's cultural landscape, with numerous striking examples occurring in Callington, Falmouth, Launceston, Penzance, St Agnes, St Austell and Tintagel. The mural trail in Callington is undoubtedly an important source of local pride. This on-going 'art in the community' endeavour comprises fifteen murals from both professional and amateur artists alike, with plans for new ones in the works (Figure 1). This project is a form of gentrification that is simultaneously meant to support local artists and traditions. The main theme for the images is Cornwall old and new, real and imagined. The scenes depict: a Viking longship and Sir Bedevere's army; an underwater scene of aquatic life; a Celtic mirror framing a view of Kit Hill; a group of fisherman and their catch; the mythical setting of the Secret Pasty Factory; the wildlife of the Tamar Valley; an image of contemporary life; the mythological

1. Mural Trail, The Secret Pasty Factory (Callington Murals Project, July 1999, photo by author).

return of King Arthur; a Celtic knot; a historical scene of a farrier's shop; a vintage car garage; an iconically illustrated map of Cornwall; a view of Kit Hill and Callington in spring bloom; a historic montage of Callington; and finally the most recent addition, a traditional steam engine.

While I was taking photographs of the various murals on Gala Day in August, not ten minutes passed before I was approached by one the project's founders. He had seen me and was obviously keen to find out if I was a journalist ready to publicize the artworks. Enthusiastically, he recounted the rationale for the town's creative undertaking. He told me about Callington's historical decline into a decrepit state, its bored youths, its unemployment and countless other related problems. Believing that the large-scale paintings would help curb this situation, he claimed that 'the murals are meant to give the area a new image, rejuvenate the place, put some new blood back in'.

Nor was this a unique feeling or an unusual encounter. In fact, several residents stopped me in the street to ask me about my interest in the paintings and to share their own anecdotes about them. What comes across from speaking to them is that essentially these murals feed on a regional artistic reputation (which is hardly as renowned in this area as it is in West Penwith because of its internationally famous art schools) to alleviate Callington's recent socio-economic plight. In attempting to do so, they effectively turn the town into an open-air studio or gallery. The mural trail is thus effectively acting to conceal the town's dereliction. It functions as a way of exhibiting art, difference and identity—a way of recreating a local pride of place as well as reclaiming both the real and mythical pasts.

Again Rachel, the local artist from the Launceston area introduced above, recounts her own encounters with the Callington murals:

> It's not often I have to go to Callington . . . maybe to the bank if passing that way, or to the excellent hardware store for frame-stain. Like Camelford before 1996 (pre art centre and the subsequent town regeneration), you wouldn't really have reason to go there, it was 'just a town'. I used to bypass it if travelling to Plymouth, over the edge of Kit Hill. Now I choose to drive through, looking for new murals, and if I have time park up and go and look. The murals exert a positive and confident feel in the town.

In relation to identity, she also sees the murals as having a strong symbolic emphasis:

It is typical Cornish attitude—this is what we have so let's make the most of it, in one-and-all fashion, sharing, in a multitude of ways, just get on and do it. It's beyond just direct socio-economic activity, it's a statement about 'we have art and we are proud of our artists'. It is about collective self-pride before tourism lure. It's about being bold and not being coy about making a statement—which some dismiss or ridicule.

Yet she does not disregard the influence of socio-economic factors. Despite the presence of several highly talented and recognized artists in the East (although many do not paint murals), she feels that this area has been peripheral in a Truro-dominated scene that has tended to promote the West of Cornwall first. This, she suggests, is partly why she feels that the region's cultural capital is not evenly spread, though it is beginning to change. From an artist's point of view, however, she believes the most positive aspect to come from them is the subject matter's openness. Artists who do public work usually have creative restraints, regarding the subject matter, style, goal or direction of the piece. Here the Mural Committee remains open to all suggestions, giving the painter complete artistic freedom. She suggests this is the reason why the murals are seen as successful and affirms 'no one can predict the next mural's location, subject matter or style. What a recipe for success! Respect for artist's ability, not control.' The artists have had a chance to express their feelings, aspirations and ideals or their perceptions of the town's past, present and future, its cultural history. Any pre-conceived prescriptions have been largely removed.

With reference to the pair of murals in Launceston, one of which is pretty aged and needs redoing, Rachel says the following:

Generally you forget they are there, then suddenly you walk past, see one and think something about it or because of it. They are a kind of visual story telling, where you are given/ receive/interpret a personal version of a publicly shared story.

The first of these murals is a small (1 x 1.5m) eye-level depiction of a historical scene. This mural illustrates an important time in the town's history, when the castle was built and the town moved from the low ground of Lanstefan to where it is now at the top of the hill. The second mural, on the side of a building that houses an interior design business on the town's outskirts, features a local landscape.

For Rachel, these murals are more to do with belonging at a local scale than at a regional one, although she admits to not really thinking about murals as being significant to Cornish identity before. Being less familiar with murals in locations other than Callington and Launceston, she'd assumed their local importance. She nonetheless concedes that they may be a part of Cornish identity too, an open sharing from one end to the other. Again in her words: 'I imagine they are also a statement to "outsiders"—a public sharing and education (of history, culture, humour, landscape, wildlife, changes etc.) before whatever it is gets dismissed by incomers'.

Interestingly, Launceston and Callington are not particularly well off towns and their residents do not display an abundance of landscape art in their homes. In this sense, the presence of the murals might seem to counter the social-class issues explained above. By mobilizing shared resources in the towns such as wall space, local creativity and promotional funds, this form of social marker depicts a determination to assert difference even in difficult circumstances. If local people cannot or do not portray as much landscape art in their homes, they find other means of representation that are often more socially poignant of their situation. This artistic expression thus acts as a social surrogate for the visual communication of a common regional hardship. These are therefore public displays of landscape that preserve a certain degree of socio-economic activity. In doing so, they counteract the more privileged position of private representation that comes across as less politically pro-active and more aesthetically inclined.

Gardens
If murals are features that are significant in the Cornish town-scapes, then large-scale landscaped gardens are a ubiquitous part of the countryside. Those at Antony House, Cotehele House, the Eden Project, Glendurgan, Heligan, Lanhydrock, Penjerrick, Trebah, Tregothnan, Trelissick, Trengwainton and Trewithen are amongst the best known examples. Gardens are visually interesting in a Cornish context for several reasons. Firstly, they are part of a popular concep-tion about the peninsula's favourable climatic conditions. This has fed a self-perpetuating view of the Duchy as exotic, Mediterranean, semi-tropical and thus as strangely other. Regardless, this 'othering' is kept in a realm of familiarity due to the emphasis on the particular Englishness of these countryside features.

In his own way, Richard (aged 43), a landscape gardener from Bodmin, emphasizes these perceptions. He claims that Cornwall's gardens give this region credibility as a tourist destination. By pro-viding alternatives to theme parks or the bucket and spade beach visit, gardens dilute the kitsch nature of holiday-making in the peninsula.

They are part of what allows Cornwall to act as an escape space for visitors. In his words:

> There's dozen of places [in Britain] for tourists ta go ta if they fancy beaches, carnivals, moors or camping sites. I think Cornwall works best for people when they feel they've gotten away from all that, that's why it's those that come in winter that like it best. What we can offer that's outta the usual is our mild climate which means we've gotta different ecology and can grow different plants. People come here and see palm trees and these massive semi-tropical gardens and for a minute they've forgotten where they are. Gives them the feeling they're on one of those Spanish Islands or somethin'.

Gardens are also significant in Cornwall because they relate to the region's artistic legacy. This is so because they act as environmental art works in themselves (providing a media with which to work and as a source of creativity for artists) or because they provide a setting to work in as well as a realm for exhibiting. These categories are far from mutually exclusive. The presence of garden galleries such as the Tate's Barbara Hepworth exhibition in St Ives illustrates the point. This practitioner of sculpture and earth art had associated herself, both practically and theoretically, with the art of landscape gardening. She designed her installations and artworks so that people could experience them within the context of a crafted, nurtured and burgeoning environment. As such, her work deliberately blurs the distinctions between gardening and the arts. Here, landscape gardening is intersected with sculpture as well as with the active modelling of a Cornish identity concerned with the issues of regional inspiration.

Another reason for the visual significance of gardens in Cornwall is their role as oases against the area's extensively scarred industrial landscape. According to many interviewees and informants, the culture of Cornish horticulture is a means of reclaiming and healing the environment. For instance, many residents like conservationists or members of the local intelligentsia see the mining industry as pretty un-sustainable. They claim that its scarring of the landscape is akin to the act of killing the countryside. Such people are happy to see the clay mining 'blights' on the land disappear. Recent plans for habitat reclamation have thus come to the fore. English China Clay's Carloggas Downs heathland restoration project is one example. Another is the development of heritage sites such as the Wheal Martyn China Clay Museum in Carthew (near St Austell).

Often, these endeavours become part of a righteous dialogue that parallels the Christian discourse about resuscitation and resurrection. Indeed, certain policy planners and environmentalists appropriate the vestiges of the Methodist and Catholic past in order to play on the religious sensibilities of long-term inhabitants. The past comes to appease the ecological worries for the future. The very name 'The Eden Project' (a tropical bio-dome facility in the St Austell china clay area that opened during the holiday period of Easter 2001) supports the notion that a public preoccupation with the salvation of nature is currently taking shape. Basically, it hovers around the message voiced here by Brian from Liskeard that 'if the Cornish people are to prosper, our history needs to be redeemed and our land needs to be saved'. This anxiety with socio-ecological deliverance reveals a flagrant contradiction—a local love/hate attitude towards these white mountains, a paradox that is complicated because such issues are never very far away from those concerning employment, identity and place.

In a similar line to what Morris[15] says of British war cemeteries abroad, the management of horticultural projects of this type has more recently come across as forms of land restoration that can both add and remove significance and identity to local derelict lands. They designate enclosed settings that acquire historical importance as emblems of the victory over post-industrialization. Consequently, landscape gardening and habitat reclamation become part of a wider concern with rural environmental salvation, or as some have called it, 'ecological redemption'. Part of why gardens are so important in Cornwall has to do with the relationship that they have with fecundity and the need to be hopeful for a better future. In this sense, this peninsula desperately searches for a sustainable economic regeneration. The nationalist position is often that this region needs a revival in political autonomy. Many members of the local intelligentsia share the view expressed by a local academic that 'the Duchy needs a rehabilitation of identity and cultural distinction'. Stretching these views further, then, the significance of gardens and horticulture partially relates to how Cornwall is made to be closer to an exotic otherworld. Its population has generally suffered and this subsumes the idea that it is the archetype of a meek body politic—a group that deserves better and will one day re-seed itself.

In this respect, it is interesting to question whether this has been a deliberate strategy for social reorientation, designed not only to guide an awareness for people's relationship with nature or place but also to camouflage the full environmental impacts of the region's industrial activities. If this is the case, then these green spaces have been part of a strategy to prescribe recommended viewpoints for tourists and the outside world. In this vein, Bhatti and Church have recently put forth that 'the uses and meanings of gardens will, to some degree, reflect differences in cultural and national identities'.[16] Hence the importance of gardens for Cornwall's economy and in the establishment of its personified landscape. Perhaps, then, landscape gardens specifically and horticulture more generally are spatial platforms for marking identity in the Cornish peninsula.[17]

A WORLD OF IMAGES

In tandem with the increasing perception in many quarters that modern tourism threatens the very fabric of Cornish identity, we are witnessing a rise in the use of emblems meant to mitigate the contradictions in promoting Cornishness.[18] But it is nevertheless a point of contention, at least within Cornish Studies, as to whether what outlines the 'Duchyesque' locally and to the outside world is becoming increasingly colourful and complex or more simplistic—more black and white as it were. Such a debate is of course healthy if it problematizes perceptions of Cornwall. It should not, however, reach a point where it becomes obsessed with the controversy regarding who should contribute to, or have control over, the (re)-production of indicators of belonging, for some authors have warned us of the problems of this slippery slope.[19]

Cornish Tartans

The Cornish national tartan is a particularly good example of the role of materiality in the study of visual culture. It is a tradition of the modern world, (re)-invented in 1948 and popularized in the 1950s and 1960s. As an objectified depiction of the environment, the pattern of this cloth encompasses an internally coherent topographic representation of the region in its weave. As several informants have explained to me, the motif itself is made up of five main colours: black, white, blue, red and golden yellow, as well as three washed tones of yellowish grey, bluish grey and a blurred blue yellow. The central feature consists of a white cross on a black square. This represents Cornwall's national flag of St Piran. The surrounding strips of golden yellow stand for the prominence of flowering gorse that covers the moors and heaths in sheets of mustard ochre from April until June. Similarly, the blue weave is an environmental analogy. It depicts the sea and the River Tamar which surround the region's borders and almost cut it off completely from the mainland. Finally, the thin red stripes are meant to commemorate the blood shed by the Cornish during the rebellions of 1497 and 1549, although another interpretation insists that they reflect the red legs of the Cornish chough and thus the reincarnation of King Arthur. More generally, the use of red symbolizes the Duchy's reputation as a nation that has repeatedly fought against its oppression.

In addition to the national tartan, Cornwall also boasts a regional hunting tartan. These two motifs and the Cornish kilt with which they are associated are especially interesting if we place them in a broader historical context. Let me, therefore, make a few cross-cultural comparisons with the precursory use of Scottish tartans that are also part of a reinvented tradition. According to Stewart,[20] clan chiefs in the mid-nineteenth century seem to have been rather uninformed as to the origins of the tartan sets that they and their forebears had been wearing. Nonetheless, these were fast becoming integral to the popular imagination of the Scots as well as the newly developing Victorian tourist trade. Many books seeking to justify and validate the use of tartans thus appeared in that time period. Despite this, little academic work had focused on the meaning of these symbols.

A recent exemption is Scarlett,[21] who considers three factors of highland tartans: first their role as material anti-Union protest statements, then as symbols of Jacobite sympathies and finally as trademark Scottish icons. Scarlett argues that tartan has always been an art form. Weavers have repeatedly attempted to assert either the great antiquity or relative modernity of plaid. Tartan (*tertane*) originally referred to a type of cloth and gradually came to mean a colourful type of chequered pattern. Scarlett suggests that tartan might have attained some symbolic significance as an emblem of identity at the onset of the eighteenth century, though he doubts that that there had yet formed any systematic understanding of district tartans. More probably, some basic regional motifs prevailed that local weavers altered to suit circumstances, preferences and techniques.

Local patterns of this kind came to identify the people of a locality, who were often of one predominant clan or family group. When the notion that clan tartans had been worn for time immemorial established itself, these patterns became clan tartans. By around 1815, tartans began to require a family surname to authenticate them and this process quickly confirmed their synonymous status. The 'cult of the tartan' gained support and the symbol came to represent Scottishness. By Victorian times, along with the presence of mass tourism and the influence of romantic pastoral writers in northern Britain, clans and their tartans became a public symbol. A type of heraldic tartan myth established itself in the minds of outsiders and within the family histories of clansfolk. This prompted unprecedented genealogical name searches to create clan associations and identification.

The same type of affiliation with kinship and clans in Scotland does not exist as such in Cornwall. Rather, residents of the latter area fall into an extended kinship system that encompasses a Celto-Cornish essence of belonging. The Cornish tartans are an attempt to capture some of the success of this symbol. By strengthening the links between Cornish and Scottish Celticity, marginality and sovereignty, these designs might be considered as agents for emancipating Cornishness by association. In the words of Tom, a proud wearer of the Cornish kilt, 'the Cornish tartans are indispensable local images, powerful symbols of the homeland for many nationalists and Celtic enthusiasts'. Further, they are akin to maps as a type of icon filled with visual metaphor. They are themselves products derived from mapping identity onto and into regional dress. The national tartan is a consciously designed microcosmic emblem. It voices the significance of identification through the material world. In this case it communicates the message: countryside onto costume, custom onto countryside. By mediating between an invoked mythical past and a comparatively concrete engagement with the geographical world, the national tartan creates a symbolic nexus of ties with the present by invoking both a Celtic genealogy and a historically weighted environmental ideology. Cornish tartans thus share with Scottish tartans what Shanks and Tilley[22] would call an 'obviousness' that is socially validated through the combination of tradition with visual imagery and material culture.

À La Post-Carte
In Britain, picture postcards began to appear during the middle to late 1890s. Their popularity was at its highest just before the First World War. Post Office records reveal that the number of postcards sent in 1898 was 313 million and rose to 926 million by 1914.[23] This rise inextricably connects with what has been termed the 'democratisation of travel', what many authors consider to be the development of the modern tourist industry. People generally ascribe postcards to the realm of popular culture, belittling their significance as transient artefacts. More recently, however, their fleeting elements have helped them pass the threshold into the realm of credibility as signifiers of culture. Consequently, these items of material culture have succeeded in gaining the attention of certain influential post-structuralists and post-modernists.[24]

Indeed, some scholars are attempting to fashion a strong link between postcards and post-modernism. The factor that they play on is the fundamentally figurative or metaphorical persona that these items bear, especially inasmuch as they highlight the illusive 'wish you were here' discontinuity which such authors advocate in their discourses. According to Brown and Turley, for example, post-modern theorists

are especially fond of examining the medium of the postcard and its
fickle postal metaphors. In their words:

> Postcards in general and those from the edge in particular
> offer an excellent metaphor to motivate concrete illustrations
> about how the creative centre of consumption and the most
> penetrating insights from research often lie at the boundary
> —the brink—the verge, the liminal region, the littoral zone—
> where one realm of experience meets another. The special
> nature and profound power of moments spent at the margin
> between one world and another.[25]

Mandy (aged 27), from Falmouth, works for her dad's marine
engineering firm. Her opinion about postcards is that they have
changed in recent times—the older picture postcards of ten years ago
reflecting Cornwall more accurately than they do at the moment. As
she states, 'they showed places as they were—straightforward, honest
depictions', whereas now she believes they have been glossed up in
an attempt to sway people to visit. She adds: 'in fact, they've become
more like tourist brochures than anything else'. Postcards either reflect
an idyllic nostalgia or exaggerate the picturesque. This informant
also feels that they are becoming more crass, accommodating the
infiltration of English humour onto local Cornish scenes (e.g. beach
bums: scenes of posteriors in the sand; Beast of Bodmin: a Neanderthal
waving a bone; St Michael's eclipse: picture of Mount's Bay where a
pasty eclipses the sun). She explains 'these are very obvious, slapstick
type jokes . . . first level stuff, no subtlety or sarcasm. They revert
towards titillation not sophistication. Perfect for the type of tourists we
generally get.' In this sense, postcards no longer record information for
oneself or others such as 'this is where we were' or 'this is what we did'
but instead boast more exclusively visual messages such as 'look where
you should be' or 'see what you've missed out on'.

Another person who also knows a thing or two about postcards
is photographer Frank Gibson. As John Le Carré explains in his
introduction to Cowan's *A Century of Images*, the Gibson family has a
long lineage of photography in the Isles of Scilly and they have had a
shop in Hugh Town for three generations.[26] In this business one needs
to pay attention to what images customers like and dislike. Mr Gibson
has thus developed an acute knowledge about what makes good postcard imagery and more importantly about what sells. He remarks that
the choices of postcards by visitors to Brittany, Cornwall's counterpart
in France, are more artistically inclined. Cornwall's tourists by comparison are not so visually liberal and do not quite appreciate 'arty'.

I have also found this to be the case when speaking to photographers of Padstow's May Day. Several have commented that they love black and white images but have resigned to taking colour photos because tourists and magazines would not be interested otherwise. They have equally suggested that tourists want everything to be included in one scene, hence the popularity of montage postcards. As one of them claims:

> It's tricky 'cause they want it all really: the sea, the cliffs, the boats, the harbours and even the blasted churches, engine houses and standing stones if you can get 'em in there. God forbid you'd include people unless it was something like this event and don't forget the colour please. May Day is actually a good opportunity for me to explore the medium of taking action shots of people.

By comparing such comments with a sample of postcards that I collected during my fieldwork, one can indeed substantiate these claims. For example, of the 132 postcards, 82 per cent are in colour, with at least one or more of the features just described (i.e. water, cliffs, moors, architectural structure and so forth). Roughly 71 per cent of the depicted scenes would be described as landscape, while 21 percent are of a panoramic, bird's eye outlook. Additionally, 23 per cent of the postcards include a collage of several scenes.

A postcard anecdote worth recounting comes from Andrew (aged 45), an ardent Cornish nationalist and pig farmer in Crantock on the outskirts of Newquay. He spoke to me about taking a walking excursion around the coast of West Penwith some twenty years ago. During his trek he sent four postcards to his own house from various places (namely St Ives, Land's End, the Lizard and Falmouth). Indeed, he specified how the first one from St Ives arrived several days after he had returned home. His explanation for this is particularly reflexive. He believes that it is because postcards from Cornwall typically leave the Duchy. There is no expectation that they might be used for local purposes and thus the card would have been lost in the system for several days before being redirected to the proper destination. Something that Andrew does not immediately comment on but is equally interesting is his motivation for sending these messages home. This action reveals that his journey was a form of holiday for him and that this was a telling way of recording or even objectifying his adventure. At first he comments that it was simply to let everyone know he was all right since 'there could 'ave been a few dangers'. His reaction to the reply that he could have simply phoned enforces my point though: 'ya, guess I could 'ave but it would 'ave been like a chore, making sure to ring at the right times, etc.'. When asked about his itinerary, he adds that his hike arose from the fact that he had never actually seen most of the places along that stretch of coast before (other than the towns of St Ives and Falmouth). He eventually suggested that his excursion must have been somehow inspired by the desire to overcome a lacunae of knowledge about his 'own backyard' as he put it.

Surely the destinations from which he sent the cards are telling as well. Interestingly, he assured me that this had to do with choosing places that were fairly equidistant from each other and his point of departure. Such a justification is itself indicative of a practice of spatial mapping. Further, it reveals a certain rationale about appropriating tourism because there are hundreds of small places from which he could have sent these cards yet he nonetheless decided to send them from the main towns and tourist sites. Once pushed on this, he admitted that there was a slight degree of irony involved in sending home postcards of home. Sending cards from the most obvious places seemed to make them even more local again by undermining the exotic value that holiday-makers ascribed to them. This raises as a point of interest the actual images he sent: the harbour of St Ives, the First and Last, the cliffs of Lizard Point and Pendennis Castle. In this sense, Andrew's action is at once a nostalgic expression of belonging, a modernist statement about appropriation and a post-modernist mocking of tourist behaviour *inter alia*. Sending postcards to oneself like this is more than a way of mapping one's itinerary. As I have tried to suggest, it is simultaneously a way of mapping one's own identity and the identity of place. Indeed, the links between maps, mapping and the formulation of Cornish identities are profound and I explore such issues in more depth elsewhere.[27]

Tourist Brochures

In *Mythologies* Barthes analyses the role that world holiday guides play in France by examining Hachette's series of global 'blue guides'.[28] Overall, he argued against the idea that these items were essentially products destined to enhance one's appreciation of landscape. Nor, he claimed, did they act as educational devices in the service of increasing one's cultural capital in terms of perception and geographical aware-ness. Instead, Barthes's alternative was to claim that travel guides are blinding agents, directing the user's attention away from the everyday. They mask what is 'real' in the mundane history of human experience. Consequently, by this profusion of sensationalism, these guides advance an ideology of individualism that considers the ethos of travel to be 'effort and solitude'. Through introducing the concept of sight-seeing, such guides have come to allow for the purchase of effort and it is in this indirect sense that they are able to serve the bourgeoisie. Duncan and Duncan thus suggest that these travel guides form part of an ideological strategy of leisure:

> originating in a nineteenth-century 'Helvetico-Protestant morality' that promotes the aesthetic appreciation of uneven ground, mountains, gorges, torrents, and defiles. This ideology is described as a 'hybrid compound of the cult of nature and of puritanism' which espouses 'regeneration through clean air, moral ideas at the sight of mountain tops, summit climbing as civic virtue, etc.'.[29]

In recognizing the blue guide's likening of such notions as scenery and the picturesque, Barthes has uncovered the leading, although not altogether uncontested, ideological process that underscores the bourgeois gaze. He concludes that these guides mystify socio-political realities via an almost totalizing interest in monuments. Further, for all intents and purposes, their imagery depopulates the landscape. These factors contribute to a sickness or even a 'disease' of thinking in essentialist terms—a populist and extravagandist order that he argues governs the bourgeois gaze and lies behind its mythologies.

Parallels with this scenario exist in the use of tourist brochures in Cornwall, especially regarding the glossy marketable ones that are part of the tourism machine. Nevertheless an interesting paradox remains in that generally this area is hardly perceived as an exclusively bourgeois tourist destination. Cornish tourist brochures target British holidaymakers because Cornwall is predominantly an English tourist destination. The perception is that one cannot fully appreciate Cornwall's appeal unless one is accustomed to perceiving landscapes from a British point of view. My interview data suggests that even non-nationals realize this, with a majority of over 80 per cent of non-UK visitors stating as much. As a repository for traditional values, Cornwall is an advertisement for the implementation of colonial or imperial policies at home, for what Bunce calls 'the countryside ideal'.[30]

Frank (aged 28), a key informant from Redruth, reflexively articulates how many local people intuitively feel about the way tourist brochures represent Cornwall. He told me about a time when he worked in the Poldark mine in the summer and was able to observe visitors interacting with brochures. His opinion about this form of tourist adverting is that:

> Such accessible and disposable items only expose tourists to
> the theme park activities and unfortunately conceal from
> them what is really important to see, what Cornwall is really
> about. Also, the industry promotes things like Cornish Pearl,
> Cornish Goldsmiths or the American Western Theme Park.
> Again, how do any of these have anything to do with
> Cornwall?

In this sense, brochures invite holiday-makers to visit the region but
only to go to specific places. He equally feels that they 'discourage
tourists from staying very long. How can we expect to develop
a sustainable tourist trade then?' Frank adds that it is okay when
'emmets' are herded about, rarely given the opportunity to establish
firm connections with the area or a genuine bond with local people.
'However, the return guest who respects Cornwall is what we need and
we shouldn't be putting them off with images that make the place seem
like it's only suitable for aggressive short-term pleasure seekers.'

Most brochures thus channel the traveller's attention towards a
restricted realm of possibilities. In their overemphasis on the natural
and legendary, brochures act to depoliticize Cornwall and administer
a simplified view of cultural complexity into its leisure industry.
According to Mr Pascoe (aged 71) from St Day 'this produces a
Disneyfication of the area. The symbols they deploy have little to do
with the historical reality or the manner in which most people, except
maybe young families, experience our diverse region.' The brochures
thus engender a structured set of meanings for consumption by
illustratively steering tourists away from everyday experiences. They
reinforce the modern Western search for the exotic, the esoteric and
the enigmatic. Consequently, the concern is that this creates a need for
an escape from the everyday and concurrently generates the illusion of
cultural simplicity.

In my sample of 229 brochures and pamphlets of various sorts,
8 per cent advertised non-commercial groups or activities. Even including those produced by special interest groups, there is a distinct
lack of 'nationalist' signifiers like St Piran's flag or slogans in the
Cornish language in the brochures. At a more general level, overall
references to Cornishness or the existence of a distinct Cornish identity
are markedly absent. This is interesting because the tourist industry
often tries to sell various aspects of Cornish 'difference', such as its
mythical and legendary past, while in this case simultaneously divorc-
ing itself from a specific association with issues of sovereignty or even
cultural dissimilarity. Taken together, then, most tourist brochures
allow such images as the Beast of Bodmin, King Arthur or theme parks

to become identifiable with being a tourist but they do not necessarily target the issues of being an outsider.

As a result, similarities with the work of Barthes or Dann[31] are clear. The later has also suggested that many tourist brochures focus mainly upon the relationship between the central attributes of tourists and the peripheral characteristics of local residents. His findings are loaded with implications about the politics of power and dependence given that the photographic and linguistic elements of brochures provide tourists with an unambiguous position of control over the local populace of many destinations. Consequently, brochures are myths that transform images of destinations into texts with ideologically potent meanings for tourists. Dann notes, however, that brochures also communicate a locally self-generated self-image to the outside world. In this sense, these bits of tourism paraphernalia form part of a discourse on freedom. But according to him the language of freedom in brochures reproduces—by its own enunciation—a situation of greater peripheral marginalization and socio-political dependence.

The problem is that authors such as Dann usually consider tourist brochures and their visual meaning as texts and discourses. Once we seek to understand their visual essence outside of this discursive semiotic field, however, we are exposed to a material plane of significance that is much more complex and open to alternative inter-pretations. Indeed, there is an important paradox regarding brochures in Cornwall in that they sometimes give an agency to the local that does not simply reinforce the region's dependence on some external entity. Hence when Ken Pennell (aged 37) says 'the tourist brochures here are a visual dumbing down of culture for outsiders who have no culture of their own', we are confronted with the possibility that these images are also part of a local aversion to tourists and the tourist industry. It is not Cornwall's culture that is dumbed down through these images but the culture of holiday-making. The presence of a more rare locally produced type of tourist brochure that addresses regional issues equally illustrates this. These are interesting because they are visually simple and thus challenge the overemphasis on appearance. Their existence reveals that some political identities of resistance do indeed become mapped-out on brochure representations.

Furthermore, by emphasizing local stereotypes about mysticism, parochiality or quaintness, tourist brochures in Cornwall are also re-gional commodities that inadvertently foster claims of cultural distinction. They isolate and describe specific icons that justify claims of locality and belonging. Their kitschness helps maintain the region in a classless realm of tourism instead of one that is essentially bourgeois. If brochures have become items of pop-culture that are now taken for granted,[32] then their taken for grantedness mean that Cornwall's representation as different becomes so as well.

CONCLUSION

This article has explored how Cornwall's landscapes figuratively convey meanings that are both visually and materially significant. The idea has been to respond to Marcus Banks's recent call in visual anthropology about considering the materiality of visual forms.[33] In Cornwall, ephemeral relationships with landscape are often captured in such visual realms as painting, photography, horticulture, postcards, theatre, tourist brochures and so forth. These are noteworthy in making up a list of things that are available for those who advance the project of defining Cornwall's unique sense of place or delimiting its awareness of cultural distinction. Consequently, material expressions of visual cultures outline powerful networks for the formulation of social identities. They form spatial records that partly serve to anchor the ambiguities of difference. Indeed, the artworks and items of popular material culture that I have considered here relate visual narratives about how this region is communicated to its own population and to others.

For instance, as promotional devices, postcards and brochures often focus on major icons rather than abstractions. They act as advertisements for this place as an exotic but accessible destination. The Cornish tartans and landscape imagery in the home are generally more abstract and conceptual. They are also more frequently used in transforming experiences into material mementoes. Gardens and murals for their part are more outward-looking. They are physical representations of the *plein air* tradition that has been so important in the construction of Cornishness through the art world. Taken together, these elements of Cornwall's visual cultures stand for conviviality, heritage and sociality. They are symbolic forms of complexifying sight and situating it in a public sphere, in the domain of wider social memories and cultural identities.

In the same Geertzian[34] way that certain events contradict prevailing social norms, the visual spaces and artefacts that I have examined in this article are paradoxical. By stating that idiomatic events do not necessarily arrange the values of culture in any logical or consistent way but rather simply depict and articulate them, Geertz claims that specific events are often metaphors, instead of mirror images, of a broader cultural context. Hence, in attempting to resolve certain socio-cultural paradoxes, he presents us with a framework with which to consider many of Cornwall's enigmas or contradictions.

Tilley[35] extends this conceptual framework of the metaphorical so as to take into account the materiality of metaphor. He demonstrates that in considering 'solid metaphors' we take an important step away from the logic systems of structuralism and semiotics. Instead, we move in the direction of a new vantage point upon which it is possible to discover the importance of material culture studies as residing in a metaphorical logic of things or places and not being reducible to linguistic analogies. If we are to achieve any real progress in understanding the signifying power of the object world's tangibility, we have to go beyond the popular comparisons with language that dominate the social sciences. In other words, he suggests that social theorists should be moving towards objectified, embedded and embodied knowledges.

Even though not everyone is directly drawn to the Cornish peninsula because of its artistic associations, a kind of visual metaphor for the expression of cultural distinction nevertheless exists. By doing so, they appreciate and appropriate the landscape as well as contextualise their own lifeworld. If the creation of identity through art and images orients itself towards the issues that surround class, belonging and local knowledges, then one can understand the pictorial representations of environmental perception such as those described above as a way of manipulating Cornish agencies. In this instance, a rationale for cultural distinction makes itself seen in gardens and murals. It can also be found in the books, postcards, tourist brochures and magazines about this peninsula as well as on and between the walls of its habitual places. The production, consumption and awareness of visual cultures are therefore important facets in the formulation of the social identities that take place in Cornwall.

ACKNOWLEDGEMENTS

I should like to thank Professors Barbara Bender and Chris Tilley for their comments on earlier drafts of this paper, as well as an anonymous referee. For their friendship, hospitality and introductions to 'proper' Cornwall, I am especially grateful to Phil Matthews, Robin Paris, Nick Pavitt, Spencer and Pat Pawson, Paul Syrett, Mark Burgoyne and the Wells family. I would also like to acknowledge the assistance of the Québec Ministry of Education for post-graduate research funding as well as the University of London Central Research Fund for financial support in the latter stages of my fieldwork.

NOTES AND REFERENCE

1. Stanhope Alexander Forbes, quoted in C. Fox, *Stanhope Forbes and the Newlyn School*. Newton Abbot, 1993.
2. P. Laviolette, 'An Iconography of Landscape Images in Cornish Art and

Prose', in Philip Payton (ed.), *Cornish Studies: Seven*, Exeter, 1999, pp. 107–29.

3. M. Banks and H. Morphy (eds), *Rethinking Visual Anthropology*, New Haven, 1997.

4. A. Gell, *Art and Agency: An Anthropological Theory*, Oxford, 1998.

5. P. Bourdieu, *Distinction: A Social Critique of the Judgement of Taste*, trans. R. Nice, Cambridge, 1984.

6. D. Halle, *Inside Culture: Art and Class in the American Home*, Chicago, 1993, p. 3.

7. E. Edwards, 'Postcards—Greetings from Another World', in T. Selwyn (ed.), *The Tourist Image: Myth and Myth Making in Tourism*, London, 1996, p. 216.

8. G. Dann, 'The People of Tourist Brochures', in Selwyn, 1996.

9. S. Brown and D. Turley, 'Travelling in Trope: Postcards from the Edge of Consumer Research', in S. Brown and D. Turley (eds), *Consumer Research: Postcards from the Edge*, London, 1997.

10. G.E. Marcus, 'Ethnography in/of the World System: The Emergence of Multi-sited Ethnography', *Annual Review of Anthropology*, 24, 1995, pp. 95–117.

11. P. Laviolette, 'The Awareness of Whereness: Landscape, Embodiment and Contrasting Cornish Identities', in C. Tilley (ed.), *Material Culture and Social Identity*, forthcoming.

12. See especially L. Abrams; K. Bradley; T. Crago; R. Perry; and S. Schwartz in Philip Payton (ed.), *Cornish Studies: Eight*, Exeter, 2000.

13. P. Bourdieu, *The Field of Cultural Production: Essays on Art and Literature*, ed. and intro. R. Johnson, Cambridge, 1993, p. 95.

14. A. Mitra, 'Virtual Vommonality: Looking for India on the Internet', in S.G. Jones (ed.), *Virtual Culture: Identity and Communication in Cyberspace*, London, 1997.

15. M.S. Morris, 'Gardens "for ever England": Landscape, Identity and the First World War British Cemeteries on the Western Front', *Ecumene: A Journal of Environment, Culture, Meaning*, 4. 4, 1997, pp. 410–34.

16. M. Bhatti and A. Church, 'Cultivating Natures: Homes and Gardens in Late Modernity', *Sociology*, 35.2, 2001, p. 367.

17. P. Laviolette, 'Landscaping Death: Resting Places for Cornish Identity', *Journal of Material Culture*, forthcoming.

18. R. Burton, 'A Passion to Exist: Cultural Hegemony and the Roots of Cornish Identity', in Philip Payton (ed.), *Cornish Studies: Five*, Exeter, 1997, pp. 151–63; B. Deacon and P. Payton, 'Re-inventing Cornwall: Culture Change on the European Periphery', in Philip Payton (ed.), *Cornish Studies: One,* Exeter, 1993, pp. 62–79.

19. For a parallel discussion about the politics of control in Aboriginal art see N. Thomas, *Possessions: Indigenous Art/Colonial Culture*, London, 1999.

20. D.C. Stewart, *The Setts of the Scottish Tartans*, Edinburgh, 1950.

21. J.D. Scarlett, *Tartan: The Highland Textile*, London, 1990.

22. M. Shanks and C. Tilley, *Re-constructing Archaeology: Theory and Practice*, London, 1987.

23. A. Briggs, *Victorian Things*, London, 1988.
24. J. Derrida, *La Carte Postale: de Socrate à Freud et au-delà*, Paris, 1980; Edwards, 1996; A. Briggs and D. Snowman (eds), *Fins de Siècle: How Centuries End 1400–2000*, New Haven, 1996.
25. Brown and Turley, 1997, p. 17.
26. J. Le Carré, 'Introduction' to R. Cowan, *A Century of Images: Photographs by the Gibson Family*, London, 1997.
27. P. Laviolette, 'Contours of Cornishness: "Anthropography", The Mapping of Belonging', unpub. paper presented at the annual meeting of the American Anthropological Association, New Orleans, LA, November 2002.
28. R. Barthes, *Mythologies*, Paris, 1957.
29. J. Duncan and N. Duncan, 'Ideology and Bliss: Roland Barthes and the Secret Histories of Landscape', in T.J. Barnes and J.S. Duncan (eds), *Writing Worlds: Discourse, Text and Metaphor in the Representation of Landscape*, London, 1992, p. 20.
30. M. Bunce, *The Countryside Ideal: Anglo-American Images of Landscape*, London, 1994.
31. Dann, 1996.
32. A. Byatt, *Collecting Picture Postcards: An Introduction*, Malvern, 1982.
33. M. Banks, *Visual Methods in Social Research*, London, 2001.
34. C. Geertz, *Works and Lives: The Anthropologist as Author*, Cambridge, 1988.
35. C. Tilley, *Metaphor and Material Culture*, Oxford, 1999.

'A TRUE CORNISH TREASURE': GUNWALLOE AND THE CORNISH CHURCH AS VISITOR ATTRACTION

Graham Busby

INTRODUCTION

Many Cornish churches occupy positions in areas of great land-scape value: consider St Just in Roseland, St Anthony in Meneage, St Winnow, St Enodoc, Tintagel and St Gennys, to name but a few, renowned for the quality of their settings. Gunwalloe is one such church, located just off the northern side of the beach, surrounded by National Trust land, on the western coast of the Lizard peninsula. Whilst published visitor numbers and other data exist for English cathedrals,[1] much less is known about those visiting parish churches, the repositories of so much religious, cultural and social history as well as genealogical connections and architectural interest.

This article reviews the definitions of visitor attractions in order to justify the use of the term for an ecclesiastical property and discusses the particular concept of churches as heritage attractions. A brief review of the English church heritage data is presented in order to provide a comparative background for the Cornish perspective. This, in turn, leads to an examination of the entries in the Gunwalloe visitors' book for the year 2000 in order to identify particular themes of importance to visitors. The quotation in the article title is an extract from one of these entries and is shown in full below.

VISITOR ATTRACTION DEFINITIONS

The 'attractions' at a destination can be the primary motivation for both tourists and excursionists (day-trippers).[2] They are frequently

1. Gunwalloe Church.

used to market the destination area and when they are of international significance they become icons of promotion for certain tourist market segments (for example, Niagara Falls and honey-mooners).[3] The terms *tourist attraction* and *visitor attraction* are used interchangeably to describe these locations, although, strictly speaking, the former would be receiving only those individuals who have travelled away from home for more than twenty-four hours. The term visitor attraction permits the inclusion of day-trippers or excursionists and is, therefore, more appropriate to this study.

One frequently cited definition in the tourism research literature is that of the Scottish Tourist Board; a visitor attraction is thus:

A permanently established excursion destination, a primary purpose of which is to allow public access for entertainment, interest or education, rather than being principally a retail outlet or a venue for sporting, theatrical or film performances. It must be open to the public without prior booking, for published periods each year, and should be capable of attracting tourists or day visitors as well as local residents.[4]

A critique of this definition would focus on, firstly, the requirement of permanence. Many sports and cultural events, such as festivals, are not permanently established—some occur infrequently whilst others change locations annually.[5] Secondly, this definition excludes the growing number of tourist shopping villages, often referred to as TSVs.[6] These are purpose-built developments of designer outlets, such as those of Clark's at Street (Somerset), Gretna and Bicester; out-of-town complexes, such as those at Thurrock and Blue Water, also require consideration. Finally, the issue of being open without prior booking is pertinent to Cornish churches—the vast majority are open throughout the year.

A distinction between attractions and destinations has been made by Swarbrooke on the basis that 'attractions are generally single units, individual sites or very small, easily delimited geographical areas based on a single key feature. Destinations are larger areas that include a number of individual attractions together with the support services required by tourists.'[7] However, some attractions are on such a scale, providing serviced accommodation on site, that they could be considered a destination according to this definition, a classic case being Disney World at Orlando, Florida,[8] and perhaps even Land's End.[9] To further confuse matters of definition, Urry suggests categorization according to three dichotomies: whether the attraction is 'an object of the romantic or collective tourist gaze'; whether it is 'historical or modern'; and whether it is 'authentic or inauthentic' (though admitting that the latter raises a number of difficulties).[10] However, for visitors to churches, this apparent complexity could in fact be a useful set of distinctions: the possibility being that they (the visitors) are proponents of the romantic gaze, viewing historical attractions that are, undoubtedly, *authentic*. Also useful are Swarbrooke's visitor attraction typologies, shown in Table 1, a straightforward assessment of an attraction's origins.[11]

Table 1 Swarbrooke's typology of tourist attractions

Natural	*Man-made* but not originally designed primarily to attract visitors	*Man-made* and purpose-built to attract tourists	*Special events*

It is worth noting too that, for statistical purposes, the English Tourism Council uses the following categories of attractions: historic properties; museums and galleries; leisure parks; wildlife sites; gardens; farms; country parks; visitor centres; workplaces; steam railways; and 'other'.[12]

HERITAGE VISITOR ATTRACTIONS

Having outlined the diversity of definition and categorization of 'visitor attractions', it is useful to focus more specifically on what might be encompassed by the term 'heritage visitor attraction'. It is legitimate to consider churches as visitor attractions, falling neatly as they do into Swarbrooke's category of man-made but not originally designed to attract visitors.[13] At first glance, it also seems obvious that they must be heritage attractions. But what are the defining features of heritage attractions? According to Millar, it is the attitude of the public that 'turns a tract of land, monument, park, historic house or coastline into a heritage attraction'.[14] What should be added to this is that there is also a temporal dimension; for example, visitors to battlefield sites in the years after 1945 tended to be former combatants but with the passage of time the motivation has 'less to do with remembrance and more to do with a day-trip excursion, less of a memorial and more of a tourist attraction'.[15]

One of the first typologies of heritage attractions was that created by Prentice. His twenty-three categories (Table 2) are comprehensive because of their very inclusiveness, although, as Prentice recognizes, some elements might sit uncomfortably in such broad company, such as genocide (for example, Auschwitz and Holocaust memorials) or, more prosaically, field sports.[16] In Prentice's view, religious attractions are multi-denominational and comprise cathedrals, churches, mosques, temples, synagogues, shrines, wells, and similar sites. Incidentally, it has been argued elsewhere that most of the visitor attractions in Cornwall which make an admission charge can be further categorized as 'heritage attractions'.[17]

Table 2   Prentice's heritage attraction categories

Natural history attractions: nature reserves, nature trails, rare breeds centres, wildlife parks, zoos, butterfly parks, geological sites including caves, cliffs and waterfalls

Science-based attractions: science museums, technology centres, 'hands-on' science centres

Attractions concerned with primary production: agricultural attractions, farms, vineyards, fishing, mining, water impounding reservoirs

Craft centres and craft workshops: water and wind-mills, potters, woodcarvers, glass-makers

Attractions concerned with manufacturing industry: the mass production of goods including pottery, porcelain, breweries, distilleries, economic history museums

Transport attractions: including transport museums, preserved railways, canals

Socio-cultural attractions: prehistoric and historic sites and displays including domestic houses, social history museums, costume museums, toy museums

Attractions associated with historic persons: including sites and areas associated with writers and painters

Performing arts attractions: including theatres, street-based performing arts, circuses

Pleasure gardens: including period gardens, arboreta, model villages

Theme parks: including 'historic' adventure parks but excluding amusement parks (where the principal attractions are exciting rides and the like)

Galleries: principally art galleries

Festivals and pageants: including historic fairs and countryside festivals

Fieldsports: fishing, hunting, shooting

Stately and ancestral homes: palaces, manor houses

Religious attractions: cathedrals, churches, mosques, shrines, wells

Military attractions: castles, battlefields, naval dockyards, military museums

Genocide monuments: sites associated with the extermination of other races

Towns and townscape: principally historic townscape

Villages and hamlets: principally 'rural' settlements, usually of pre-twentieth-century architecture

Countryside and treasured landscape: including national parks

Seaside resorts and 'seascapes': principally seaside towns of past eras and marine 'landscapes'

Regions: including pays lande, counties, or other historic areas identified as distinctive by their residents or visitors (for example, Thomas Hardy Country in Wessex)

To summarize thus far, not only does the English church typify Swarbrooke's visitor attraction type defined as 'man-made but not originally designed primarily to attract visitors',[18] it is also clearly part of the 'national heritage'—and would have been considered so even before the expansion over the last couple of decades of the term to include what are, essentially, cultural features of British society and working life.

THE ENGLISH CHURCH HERITAGE AND VISITORS

In England, over 11,000 of the 16,800 Anglican churches are Department of Environment-listed 'as being of architectural or historic interest [and] at least 3,000 are of Grade A or equivalent status'.[19] Many are in rural areas; in fact, 61 per cent of those listed Grade 1 are in the West Country, East Midlands and East of England, regions which together account for just 26 per cent of the populace.[20] Perhaps it is not surprising, given this plethora of quality heritage, that the English Tourism Council (ETC) considers churches and cathedrals to be 'the most popular type of historic building accounting for over 40% of the 69 million annual visits to historic properties'.[21] The International Council on Monuments and Sites (ICOMOS) refers to approximately 31 million visits to cathedrals and churches in the UK in 1999, of which 'about 12 million visits are made to parish churches . . . with the remaining 19 million visits being to cathedrals and greater churches'.[22] No definition is provided for greater church, although Westminster Abbey is cited as an example; it seems unlikely that any of the Cornish churches, even Bodmin or St Germans, would qualify for this designation.

However, given Davies's concerns over the calculation of visitor numbers for English museums and galleries,[23] it is possible that an attraction such as a church may receive rather more visits than those estimated. Publications such as *Nicholson's Guide to English Churches*,[24] Richard Brier's *English Country Churches*,[25] Durant's *Good Church Guide*[26] and Simon Jenkins's *England's Thousand Best Churches*[27] have only helped to increase these visitor numbers, it is suggested. For example, an entry in the Gunwalloe visitors' book for 19 April 2000 states: 'Just as Simon Jenkins describes on this foul day'. Another for 2 October, reads: 'One of England's 1000 best churches'. Several books, widely available, specifically address the Cornish church heritage: amongst those currently in print are Hilary Lees's *Cornwall's Churchyard Heritage*[28] and Joan Rendell's *Cornish Churches*.[29]

Visitor book data may be of value in calculating annual numbers, but the single greatest constraint is uncertainty over how many people actually make an entry: Yale refers to un-sourced surveys at Selborne, Hampshire and Bolton Abbey, Yorkshire, which indicated ratios of one in four and one in fifteen, respectively,[30] whereas Hanna considers it 'unlikely that more than one in four visitors' sign their name.[31] The ETC's Heritage Monitor lists 28 parish churches in England attracting more than 50,000 visitors and for 19 of these it provides the number recorded in their respective visitors' books.[32] The ratios for these nineteen have been calculated and are presented in Table 3.

Table 3 Visitors' book ratios, in 1998, for those English parish churches attracting in excess of 50,000

	Estimated numbers of visitors	Numbers recorded in visitors' book	Ratio	
Beverley Minster	71,580	5,742	1:12	(12.46)
Bolton Abbey	178,620	17,862	1:10	
Bosham	50,000	10,000	1:5	
Burford	86,837	10,499	1:8	(8.27)
Cambridge, Round Church	75,000	7,500	1:10	
Cartmel Priory	70,000	7,346	1:10	(9.52)
Chilham	50,000	5,145	1:10	(9.71)
Dedham	50,000	5,203	1:10	(9.60)
Dover, St Mary in the Castle	270,000	20,528	1:13	(13.15)
Eyam, St Lawrence	80,000	30,000	1:3	(2.66)
Godshill	86,000	17,200	1:5	
Holy Island	132,020	11,001	1:12	
Malmesbury Abbey	55,000	6,900	1:8	(7.97)
Ranworth	96,800	10,000	1:10	(9.68)
Rye, St Mary	160,000	9,773	1:16	(16.37)
St Just in Roseland	67,400	13,491	1:5	(4.99)
Shrewsbury Abbey	61,200	10,886	1:6	(5.62)
Waltham Abbey	75,000	2,939	1:26	(25.50)
Wimborne Minster	100,000	5,214	1:19	(19.17)

Source: adapted from ETC, *The Heritage Monitor*, 1999.

It was on behalf of the former English Tourist Board (ETB) that Hanna undertook a survey of Anglican incumbents in 1982 and achieved responses from 2,626. This revealed that visitors were most interested in 'the monuments followed (in order) by the architecture, stained glass, towers, fonts, associations with people and brasses . . . [although] as many as 155 different types of feature' were recognized.[33] However, it is argued that a flaw in this survey was the apparent failure to discriminate between tangible and intangible features, the former being potentially easier to measure.

Two further points to note are, firstly, that whereas visits to heritage attractions tend to be for 'general, rather than specific interests . . . [churches] may be exceptions to this general rule'[34] and, secondly, there is 'currently no published research information on the profile of visitors to churches', according to Keeling.[35] Rather simplistically, he suggests that, based on anecdotal evidence, there are two categories, namely general interest visitors and special interest visitors. This can be supplemented by the Reverend Evans, chairman of the National Churches Tourism Group, who observes that church visitors actually 'come for so many reasons'.[36] In Cornwall, examples which come to mind include St Juliot and the Thomas Hardy connection, and St Winnow with its *Poldark* filming, although of course there are difficulties in measuring this form of tourism.[37]

Before considering Cornish church heritage specifically, mention must be made of the nature of the church heritage *experience*. It is unsophisticated, in the main, and a matter of individual interpretation. This contrasts strongly with Richards's assessment of the development of attractions such as shops and malls where an ever-greater level of product awareness and experience is demanded.[38] More than this, some attractions even use the term: *The White Cliffs Experience, The Tower Bridge Experience*, and those that imply a 'story' around which the attraction is constructed.[39] Consider *The Oxford Story, A Day at the Wells, The Canterbury Tales*. This infers the existence of visitor types satisfied by short-term consumption as opposed to those with rather more discerning critical faculties. Ironically, Ritzer refers to experiences in malls, department stores and such like settings as 'cathedrals of consumption . . . [possessing] sometimes even sacred, religious character for many people'.[40]

THE CORNISH CHURCH HERITAGE AND VISITORS
In reviewing the number of Anglican establishments in Cornwall, Hamilton Jenkin[41] identified 220 parish churches, to which should be added various minor buildings such as chapels of ease. For visitors, Cornish churches are classic examples of what Kennedy and Kingcome term 'serious heritage'.[42] In terms of the proportion of Grade I and II* properties to the total for Cornwall, the current estimate, based on the Truro Diocesan Directory, suggests that there are 224 churches of which 130 are listed Grade I and 66 are Grade II*, representing 58 and 29 per cent of the total respectively.[43] Two points should be noted: firstly, typographical errors might somewhat affect the listing details in the directory, and secondly, some of the locations are arguably chapels rather than churches. However, visitors are unlikely to discriminate; Tregaminion is a chapel of ease, built for the Rashleighs of Menabilly, and attracts visitors because of the du Maurier connection—for

which reason it is also featured in the annual festival (see Busby and Hambly[44]). The number listed as Grade I appears to have been reviewed since December 1993 when 77 were identified.[45]

The richness of the Cornish church heritage can only be understood by considering its chronological development from earliest times, although, according to Crew and Sims, 'there is no ideal spot on the temporal continuum that inherently deserves emphasis . . . in elevating or admiring one piece of the past we tend to ignore and devalue others'.[46] Significantly, Canon Miles Brown noted that visitors might be puzzled by the characteristics of Cornish churches and the names of the saints to which they are dedicated and, in many cases, after which parishes are also named. He also imagined that visitors would ask themselves why Cornish churches are 'different-looking from those of other counties'.[47] Indeed, it can be argued that the church in Cornwall both symbolizes Cornish culture, historically, and (to some extent) reproduces it for today and tomorrow. As David Everett shows elsewhere in this volume, Anglicans in Cornwall (such as the celebrated Canon Doble, chronicler of Cornish saints) played a major role in the Celtic Revival of the late nineteenth and early twentieth centuries, creating the 'Celtic' diocese of Truro and investing the church with a range of 'Celtic' attributes—from the ancient 'Celtic Church' of which it was ostensibly an inheritor to Celtic saint dedications, Cornish crosses and holy wells, and even architectural styles and 'Celtic' aspects of Anglo-Catholic practice, liturgy and theology. All this made for a heady mix which both contributed to the iconography of the Celtic Revival in Cornwall and added to the 'tourist gaze', persuading visitors from across the Tamar that the church in Cornwall was 'Celtic' not 'English', and perhaps even that Cornwall (with its own diocese) should be considered a distinct component of the Anglican Communion (as indeed Wales was).

Scholars outside the Celtic Revival have also pointed to the distinctive characteristics of the church in Cornwall. Paul Cockerham, for example, has reviewed this cultural distinctiveness in the form of slate memorializations in the early modern period, suggesting that they are icons of ethnic difference and reflect the Cornish character and independence.[48] Such conclusions add to the repertoire of Cornish 'difference' from which today's tourist entrepreneurs may draw, and Cornish religious *resources* may well become more important with the further development of heritage tourism, just as Boissevain has demonstrated in the case of Malta.[49] The expansion of the world wide web may also have some influence in this: the site Cornish Light (www.cornishlight.freeserve.co.uk) depicts a number of examples of churches, whilst some parishes have created web-sites for their own church. St Just in Roseland, one of the top two visited churches in Cornwall, has an extensive range of views of the property (www.stjustinroseland.btinternet.co.uk) and the diocesan web-site (www.truro.anglican.org) features a 'Parish of the Month' link. Virtual tours of some of these properties are complemented by virtual visitors' books.

Data on visitor numbers for Anglican sites is presented by the University of Exeter's Tourism Research Group, the ETC (formerly ETB) and ICOMOS. The Tourism Research Group note that, in 1999, 19.9 per cent of all survey respondents (n = 3,331) visited Truro Cathedral[50] and the ETC's *Sightseeing in the UK* reports an estimated 500,000 visitors to the cathedral in 1998 with just two churches attracting in excess of 30,000 visitors, these being the church of St Winwalloe at Gunwalloe and St Just in Roseland.[51] The ETC's *Heritage Monitor* shows a rather more precise figure for St Just in Roseland, for 1998, of 67,400 and Gunwalloe at an estimated 50,000-plus visits. *The Heritage Monitor* also lists churches receiving between 10,000 and 50,000 visitors in 1998; included here is another Cornish property—Padstow with 16,000.[52]

Returning to the ETB's (1995) *English Heritage Monitor* produces interesting results, for whilst St Just in Roseland is estimated to have received over 50,000 visits in 1994, Gunwalloe is estimated at 100,000—based on 50,000 recorded in the visitors' book.[53] Is this a reporting error? Padstow is shown as receiving an estimated 14,000—the only other Cornish church for that year. The possible inconsistency for Gunwalloe is highlighted by consulting the *English Heritage Monitor* (1994) when the total estimated for the year 1993 was also 100,000—but based on 30,000 entries in the visitors' book. St Just is, again, recorded as over 50,000 and Padstow as 10,000.[54]

Stepping back one more year, to 1992, reveals Gunwalloe still with 100,000 visitors but based on just 2,000 visitors' book entries![55] In 1992, St Just in Roseland was estimated at 132,942, based on 22,157 entries. Padstow, at 10,000, was joined by Tintagel also with 10,000.[56] Whilst the same properties appear year after year in the table detailing those attracting more than 50,000 visitors (with slight changes in position), only Eyam comes anywhere near to Gunwalloe for the fluctuation in reported visitors' book numbers—24,444 in 1992, 17,939 in 1993, 43,000 in 1994, and 30,000 in 1998. This still does not compare with the range of 2,000 to 50,000 for Gunwalloe visitors' book entries over the same years.

Moving on from the ETB/ETC publications, data is also available from a different source entirely: ICOMOS reports 500,000 visitors to Truro Cathedral for 1999 or earlier. The only Cornish church respondent to their survey was Bodmin (St Petroc) and, perhaps surprisingly, this is estimated at 2,000—the lowest figure reported from the 97 cathedrals and churches in the UK.[57]

Ease of access, in terms of the church being open, clearly has an influence on visitor numbers and Cornwall in this respect differs from many areas of England: in 1982, 93 per cent of those in Cornwall were open compared to as few as 20 per cent in Merseyside'.[58] Hanna has described churches as the 'Cinderella' of tourism, based on the significant difference between their intrinsic interest for visitors and the scarcity of finance for promotion.[59] In Cornwall, the creation of joint diocesan/heritage coast service church trail packs, covering the entire territory, has brought promotion of churches into the limelight, although it is argued that they are being purchased by certain types of visitor: not simply dilettantes or enthusiasts but the wider spectrum of those wishing to pursue historic, cultural and similar tastes at an introductory level.

GUNWALLOE: VISITORS' BOOK DATA

Content Analysis
Data from visitors' books is of some value in attempting to chart the numbers, views and interests of visitors to Cornish churches. Before considering this source, some of the theoretical and procedural background to the use of such material is presented. Scott proposes a twelve cell typology for documents which leads to four important questions in terms of evaluation: their authenticity (original and genuine?), their credibility (whether they are accurate), their representativeness (whether they are representative of the totality of documents in their class) and their meaning (what they state).[60]

Having spent many hours with the Gunwalloe data, I would argue strongly that the site has authenticity, is credible to the extent that it is accurate for those who sign, and probably conveys the meaning that the experience has for many visitors. Unlike observation and interviewing, visitors' book analysis has the benefit of 'reducing to zero the respondent contamination' and yet few researchers appear to utilize such material.[61] According to Punch, such documentary evidence is ignored because other data collection methods have 'become more fashionable'.[62]

Whilst entry authors are likely to be stating their genuine, personal thoughts, the issue of representativeness needs to be considered, that is, are the authors representative of visitors to the church? Where the estimated ratio for writers to visitors is low, the answer is more likely to be positive. Clearly, entries are representative of visitors who write comments; whether the same views and opinions are held by non-signers is difficult to measure without triangulation. From another perspective, Macdonald[63] emphasizes the importance of testing whether documents are genuine, complete and reliable: the manifold styles of hand-writing, alone, would suggest that the visitors' book entries are authentic, although it is impossible to identify whether a few names are fictional.

Despite Berg's[64] observation that content analysis may be used effectively in qualitative analysis with counts of textual elements merely providing a means for identifying, organizing, indexing and retrieving data, many researchers consider it an essentially quantitative process. The more interpretative or qualitative analysis of text is termed hermeneutics.[65] Content analysis, then, involves the classification of contents in such a way as to bring out their basic structure. The objective analysis of messages conveyed in a given set of data is accomplished by means of explicit rules of selection, which must be established before the process begins.[66] These should reflect all relevant aspects of the messages, be sufficiently exhaustive to account for each variation of message content and must be rigidly and consistently applied so that other researchers or readers, looking at the same messages, would obtain the same or comparable results.[67]

With content analysis, *reliability* is, therefore, of key significance, i.e. would another researcher come to the same conclusions?[68] The

Table 4   Components of content analysis

Instrumental	A sense of achievement
	Cognitive satisfaction
	Economic value
Expressive	Self-expression
	Meeting affiliative needs
	Showing concern for others
	Defining purpose—the religious-philosophical needs
Other aspects	Individualistic
	Physiological
	Political
	Miscellaneous

Source: White, 1951, cited in Ryan, 1995.

Gunwalloe data was checked by asking a colleague, anthropologist Dr Steven Butts, to identify categories and themes without any prior discussion of the research in any way: the same themes were identified. Many of the individual words are taken to have similar meanings: for example, *beautiful* and *pretty*. Words sharing a similar connotation permit the grouping of synonyms by category and can emphasize particular themes or concepts.[69] At this point, Ryan's comments on classification are relevant: drawing on White (1951), he classifies the components as shown in Table 4.[70]

Ryan fully recognizes that 'the distinction between the instrumental and the expressive is itself difficult to maintain in practice within the holiday context' because the tourist activity is an expression which becomes instrumental once carried out.[71] Nonetheless, the visitors' book comments demonstrate a range of these components, as will become apparent.

The Findings and Discussion

Table 5 presents data on visitor nationality by month, from the 177 pages of A4 visitors' book entries for Gunwalloe church in the year 2000. It is worth noting that although some nationalities could be represented by just one group visiting, there are clearly different names during the month for just one or two individuals. In many cases, the address or just town is given, but where none has been provided, the visitor has been classified as UK—the surnames appear to be 'British' in most cases. The figures presented in Table 4 are conservative; for example, where an entry reads the Jones Family, this has been interpreted as three, and where only one name is entered, this has been taken to be a single individual despite the likely possibility of there being at least two visitors.

Finnegan[72] raises the issue of *audience*: for whom is the visitors' book comment intended? Whilst most of the Gunwalloe entries are neutral, a number imply that it is the church-wardens/parochial church council who will see that a visitor has appreciated the building being kept open; in this context, the comments are 'unconscious decisions'.[73] The first theme to mention, then, is that of access: 62 entries refer to the church being open—the associated feature of trust is also mentioned occasionally. Gunwalloe church certainly conforms to the Scottish Tourist Board definitional requirement of being open to the public without prior booking!

The theme of returning to one's roots is evident from many of the entries—not surprising really. The Cornish diaspora of the nineteenth century, when many thousands emigrated to Australia, New Zealand, the USA, Canada and South Africa, might account for a large

Table 5 Visitors' book data for Gunwalloe, Cornwall, for the year 2000 (numbers by stated nationality)

	Jan	Feb	Mar	Apr	May	Jun	Jul	Aug	Sep	Oct	Nov	Dec	Total
UK	144	169	245	429	497	604	677	852	554	471	107	133	4,882
USA		1	8	9	17	22	19	17	7	1	1	1	103
Germany				8	5	6	28	19	20	16			102
Canada	1		6	8	11	14	8		7	3		1	59
Australia	2	3	3		4	11	5	1	11	6	3	1	50
Holland			2		4	14	6	7	8	2			43
New Zealand				4	2	9	7	3					25
France		2		2		1	9	1	2	3			20
Switzerland					4	7	3		1	4			19
S. Africa		1				6	2		6				15
Norway							12		2				14
Belgium				4		2	2						8
Austria				2			1	3		1			7
Sweden				3		1	3						7
Ireland	1						1	3					5
Italy		2	1					1					4
Indonesia							3						3
Colombia						2							2
Seychelles	1												1
Turkey		1											1
British Virgin Islands		1											1
Argentina				1									1
S. Korea				1									1
Japan					1								1
Trinidad and Tobago					1								1
Finland					1								1
Poland						1							1
Antigua						1							1
Andorra								1					1
Zimbabwe									1				1
Greece									1				1
Hong Kong											1		1
Total	149	178	266	472	546	700	788	908	620	507	112	136	5,382

proportion of visitors from these nations today. The figures put forward are substantial: citing Deacon's research, Payton suggests that 'at least 240,000 Cornish had gone overseas in the years 1840–1900' and that in 1900 an estimated '25 per cent of white miners on the Rand were Cousin Jacks'.[74] Rowse appositely states that many of the Cornish overseas are still 'geared' to thinking of 'back home'; a Harvard

Cornishman told him 'that, of all the British stocks in the United States, the Cornish were the most addicted to going back to their native heath, if only on visits'.[75]

Numerous entries in the Gunwalloe visitors' book allude to such connections. For example: 'We have ancestors buried here—a special moment' (written on 22 April 2000 by a New Zealander) and 'Have been on a visit to this church where my ancestors are buried' (from an Australian, 12 October). It is tempting to perceive such visitors as conforming to Cohen's tourist in *existential mode*, those who desire 'to find one's spiritual roots. The visit takes on the quality of a home-coming to a historical home.'[76] This typifies Ryan's observations that the activity can be both expressive and instrumental: self-expression and affiliative needs combine with religious-philosophical ones to produce a sense of achievement once the site is reached.[77] Another feature of the data is that visitors from the two Commonwealth countries of Australia and Canada are spread fairly evenly through the year, statistically insignificant but worthy of further research for tourist board purposes.

Many visitors are drawn back again and again. A typical entry is that for 4 April: 'Third time back. Just as lovely everytime.' This is also a good example of the need to review all entries carefully; simply undertaking a word count for *visit* fails to reveal the proportion of repeat visitors. There are many entries which make statements such as 'here again' and 'Thanks, just as beautiful as 4 years ago'. In total, there are 228 entries which state or clearly imply a repeat visit is being made. Reflecting on the various comments concerning return visits, it appears as though there are at least two categories. There are those who have not been for many years and sometimes refer to child-hood holiday memories (or, in one case, to active service: 'Recalling memories from RAF Predannack 1943', (11 September) and those who visit either yearly or at least every few years. Content analysis indicates that these are expressive components: self-expressive for all, it would seem, otherwise why refer to the fact that it is a repeat visit?

As an adjunct, Darnell and Johnson emphasize not just the im-portance of repeat visiting but also its trickle-down effect, whereby opinions influence others to visit for the first time—such effects have not been considered by researchers.[78] Two examples illustrate this point at Gunwalloe: 'Called in 5 years after Alan and Caroline who recommended this place' (visitors from Cambridge, 23 February) and 'We had heard all about it—now we see for ourselves. Lovely!' (from Birmingham, 26 October).

Not surprisingly, there are in Gunwalloe visitors' books comments on the natural environment—the sea might be spectacular or protection is offered from the wind and rain. The words *sea*, *waves* and *wind* are referred to in 44, 8 and 19 entries, respectively, whereas landscape appreciation is expressed in terms such as *beautiful setting, surroundings* or *location*; these occur 6, 14 and 3 times. The juxtaposition of this church in such a setting would appear to improve the experience, one that it is up to each individual visitor to interpret. A number of comments appear to justify the church as being the object of the romantic, historic gaze[79] for many visitors: 'A glorious sight. Windows are lovely and ceiling beams the best we've seen. Well carved' (22 April); 'First visit here, wildly romantic' (23 April); 'Jane xxxxxxx—a lover of old churches' (4 May); 'What a glorious heritage we have' (12 September); and from a German visitor, 'First time here and I'm surprised to see a church in this unusual rough and windy spot. I think in former times 11th/12th century when life was difficult for these poor people here, they were in urgent need of a church and the help of a mighty power—perhaps God?' (15 September).

The overall impression gained from many of the entries conforms to Tresidder's observation that 'sacred spaces act as a means of reference, their association with nostalgia, heritage, community or the natural, allow us to find roots in a rootless world'.[80] Whilst many visitors are deliberately seeking to recapture these associations, for others the church is an unexpected find: 'Such a lovely place, didn't know places like this existed' (2 July, from Manchester) and 'What a beautiful church you have! It is nice to stumble upon a true Cornish treasure. It is a place of true beauty and thank you for keeping the doors open so that we could come in and share it!' (18 March).

A number of comments indicate that this church acts as a point of reference for those visitors seeking guidance; the following quote is taken from a Somerset visitor, writing on 8 October: 'A big thank you to the people who keep this wonderful place open—at a very difficult time in my life, when everything appears to be disrupted and not right, even though I am not at all religious I know that I could come here this afternoon and just shut my self away for half an hour and have some peace'. Such comments must surely justify leaving the church unlocked.

As Prentice[81] has stated, visitors may have 'specific interests', and this is nowhere better illustrated than by quoting one of the visitors' book entries for 11 August 2000:

Rita and Bob xxxxxxxxx came here following in the footsteps of George Kemp who was G. Marconi's right hand man. Kemp visited this church most Sundays whilst he was supervising the errection [*sic*] of Marconi's aerial and transmitter for the Atlantic leap by wireless telegraph. Marconi received

the letter 'S' (three dots) at Signal Hill, Newfoundland on Dec
12 1901 which was transmitted from the site adjacent to the
Poldhu Hotel on the furthest side of next bay. God helped
him with this work which provided the foundation for todays
[*sic*] communications.

Historic connections clearly appeal to those individuals who
have undertaken some sort of study of the particular topic. As Ryan
puts it, 'curiosity was the motive for the visit, the satisfaction of
curiosity is an addition to knowledge. How that knowledge is put to use
becomes another instrumental process.'[82] This is further illustrated by
one reference in the year 2000 entries to Father Sandys Wason,[83] the
'High' (Anglo-Catholic) Anglican incumbent of Cury with Gunwalloe
from 1905 to 1920: 'Keeps the faith which Fr. Sandy [*sic*] Wason taught
here—bless his soul, rest in peace' (5 September). Incidentally, the
novelist Compton Mackenzie was living in Gunwalloe at the turn of
the twentieth century and wrote an introduction to Wason's novel
Palafox; unlike other literary tourism sites in Cornwall, Wason's work
at Gunwalloe has been forgotten.

With regard to the church dedication, to St Winwaloe, Orme[84]
suggests the earliest documented reference dates to 1433. Perhaps
surprisingly, only four entries in the visitor books make any reference
to this particular Celtic saint. This may be explained by the fact that by
the time visitors reach Gunwalloe, they have seen ample evidence—in
the form of road signs—of the range of such names in Cornwall and
assume Celtic dedications to be commonplace, the norm, no longer
worthy of special comment.

Only a small number of entries refer to the actual church fabric or
fixtures. For example, there are only three comments concerning the
woodwork—'Incredible to find remains of original rood screen in a
Cornish church' (27 March). There are seven references to the ceiling:
'What lovely painted panels and carved ceiling and old font—is it used
still??' (23 August), and one to the stained glass: 'is the stained glass by
Kemp, or perhaps his pupil??' (4 October).

This raises the question as to how educated, in architectural
or artistic matters, most visitors are. It is suggested that most are
not concerned with how authentic various features are, i.e. does any
Victorian 'restoration' affect the authenticity of a particular church?
The 'restorers' have altered what might be a genuine medieval building
—but it is genuine Victorian 'pastiche', reflecting their interpretation
of the colour and brilliance of what existed before the Reformation
and the iconoclasm of the Civil War and Commonwealth. Blisland
church, for example, 'restored' by Eden, is commended to the visitor

by Davidson.[85] The floor plans of the churches at Tremaine, Tintagel and St Breward[86] illustrate the extent of genuine Norman content but also how successive generations have altered the original structure. What does authenticity mean in this context and are the majority of visitors concerned? They are likely to be more interested in how the alterations reflect changes in the local and national culture over time.

Featherstone believes that many visitors 'have no time for authenticity'[87] and, in any event, 'what may be interpreted by one visitor as authentic may not be so interpreted by another'.[88] Richards is more emphatic, asserting that 'experiences are personal and, therefore, no two individuals can have the same experience'.[89] Perhaps the distinction of *authenticity of self* and *authenticity of experience*, made by Tresidder, is of critical value here: 'together identified as the search for individual and collective meaning'.[90] Many of the Gunwalloe visitor comments indicate that a period of reflection has been undertaken by individuals during their visit—they have experienced authenticity of self.

Expressions such as 'queer little church by the sea' (3 January) and 'we don't get churches like this at home' (1 February, visitor from Melbourne, Australia) imply that the church might be 'different-looking from those of other counties,' as Canon Miles Brown believed visitors may think.[91] Added to this is the fact that 68 entries refer to it being a *little* church; clearly, these visitors are used to rather larger properties. Only four entries refer to St Winwaloe—another of the aspects that Brown considers might puzzle visitors. Orme's research[92] concerning these Cornish *saints* is for the serious student of Cornish Studies rather than the average visitor. One of the themes to emerge from a study of these *saints* is their harmony with the environment and a lack of grandeur. This has a relationship with words and comments concerning the simplicity of the place, in a busy modern world: a resonance with John Lowerson's comment that 'Cornwall has come almost to represent a British Tibet; distant, valued by outsiders and threatened by an occupying power'.[93]

Finally, in reviewing entries by nationality, a clear feature is that overseas visitors seldom provide any comments. In fact, there are only 68 for the year. However, one of the entries, made by a visitor from Andorra, is of particular interest: 'My father told me that the origin of our family came from Gunwalloe. There were Gabriels living in Gunwalloe in the XV [century]. I'm spending my holidays in Devon and have come especially to visit this church as apparently the Gabriels have given a donation a few years ago to restaure [sic] the church.' To conclude this section, two comments are cited which typify the experience: from a visitor from Texas, 'Very Cornish with the sound of the sea' (23 October), and from a British Columbia, Canada visitor, 'Enjoy the peace and solitude of this church. Was here in August last year and had to come back both to this quaint, beautiful country and this lovely old church' (30 June).

Cornish Inter-Church Comparisons
To avoid giving the impression that Gunwalloe visitors' book comments are distinct from those found in other churches, two comparative examples are provided. Visitor comments at St Gennys, a church which also occupies a position of great landscape value, are broadly similar, as indeed are those at St Juliot. However, the latter receives fewer comments concerning the Thomas Hardy connection than might be expected: there are only five between 24 July and 28 September 2001. Before leaving the issue of comparisons, another point needs to be made. Having mentioned Padstow and Tintagel and implied that they occupy third and fourth place in terms of visitor numbers to Cornish churches, based on the published figures, it is now suggested that applying a visitors' book commentator/visitor ratio of 1:10 to St Gennys and St Juliot puts them in a comparable position—at something like 14,000 and 13,000 visitors, respectively, in the year 2000.

Of course, this raises a number of further questions. For example, how many other Cornish churches attract more visitors than previously

Table 6   Church visitor loyalty—survey conducted between March and August 2002

	Gunwalloe	St Just in Roseland	Lanteglos by Fowey
First visit to church	134	124	83
Repeat visit	76	85	33
Last visit: 2002	8	8	4
Last visit: 2001	23	22	12
Last visit: 2000	10	10	1
Last visit: 1990–1999	18	25	7
Last visit: 1980–1989	10	8	1
Last visit: 1970–1979	2	6	0
Last visit: 1960–1969	1	3	0
Last visit: pre-1960	3	2	0
Cannot remember year	1	1	8

Source: Busby, 2002.

thought? What has been the effect of the Diocesan Church Trail packs? If we accept that the Church should be providing a ministry to the visitor, should individual properties not be more actively promoted? Over the last few years, a number of highway authority road signs have appeared identifying specific churches in Cornwall— not the white on brown tourist signs but rather the conventional black and white road signs. As Moffat has observed, in the Land of the Saints many road signs stimulate the imagination of the visitor.[94]

In terms of repeat visits, a survey undertaken in 2002 produced the results shown in Table 6, confirming how visitors are drawn back time and again. Gunwalloe is compared with St Just in Roseland and Lanteglos by Fowey, with interviews occurring between March and 31 August.[95]

CONCLUSION

Churches in Cornwall are very much part of the Cornish heritage, commemorating names of Celtic holy men and women even if the extant buildings were constructed six hundred or so years later than their supposed lives. Many, indeed it may be the majority, are kept unlocked, thereby providing an important resource for both the casual and serious visitor besides those in need. It would appear that only Gunwalloe and St Just in Roseland attract significant numbers of visitors. According to the published literature, Bodmin has received 2,000 per annum in recent years and Tintagel and Padstow between 10,000 and 14,000 each. However, with church visitors' books reviewed to date, there is almost always a sizeable proportion of overseas visitors; it may even be that the number of non-English speakers is greater than thought as their language (and, perhaps, culture) preclude any entry.

This links back to Table 3 where the ratios have been calculated from the estimates and visitor book numbers (provided by the English Tourism Council) by this author. The range is from 1:3, at Eyam, to 1:26, at Waltham Abbey, although the norm would appear to be 1:10. It is argued, therefore, that churches such as St Gennys and St Juliot are almost certainly attracting in excess of 10,000 visitors per annum. The range of ratios does beg the question of what the external influencing factors are.

Gunwalloe is but one of many Cornish churches of great appeal and yet it is one of only two that receive in excess of 40,000 visitors per annum. This suggests that properties such as St Winnow, Launcells or Minster require active searching whereas Gunwalloe has a captive audience in the form of both beach visitors and coastal path walkers, aided by the proximity of well-publicized National Trust property, including a substantial car park. It is hoped that ongoing research at several Cornish churches might shed light on the propensity—or otherwise—of visitors to provide a written entry.

The visitors' book review suggests the following themes: a search for roots which might, more precisely, be a genealogical interest or the desire to find that at least one place remains unchanging, over the years, providing reassurance through its very continuity. Allied to this sense of continuity is that of 'atmosphere', which could help to explain the large number of return visitors. There is also substantial evidence to confirm Prentice's view that churches as heritage attractions are likely to attract visitors for specific reasons besides those of a more general nature.[96] The Marconi example illustrates the wider Cornish heritage besides that of the church, as does that of the Cornish-descended visitors from overseas. Finally, the point needs to be made that Gunwalloe Church provides for a small weekly congregation and yet also manages to be a successful heritage visitor attraction providing somewhere for reflection, curiosity and even shelter from the weather. As many visitors request: long may it remain unlocked.

NOTES AND REFERENCES

1. M. Shackley, 'Space, Sanctity and Service: The English Cathedral as Heterotopia', *International Journal of Tourism Research*, 4.5, 2002, pp. 345–52.
2. G. Busby, 'The Cornish Church Heritage as Destination Component', *Tourism*, 50.4, 2002, pp. 371–81.
3. J. Urry, *The Tourist Gaze*, London, 1990.
4. Scottish Tourist Board, *Visitor Attractions: A Development Guide*, Edinburgh, 1991.
5. A. Brierley and G. Busby, 'Festivals and Seasonality: A Panacea for the Quiet Times?', www.tourism-2002.com. Online conference paper, 25 November–6 December 2002.
6. D. Getz, 'Tourist Shopping Villages: Development and Planning Strategies', in C. Ryan and S.J. Page (eds), *Tourism Management: Towards the New Millennium*, Oxford, 2000, pp. 211–26.
7. J. Swarbrooke, *The Development and Management of Visitor Attractions*, Oxford, 1995, p. 7.
8. S. Page, P. Brunt, G. Busby and J. Connell, *Tourism: A Modern Synthesis*, London, 2001.
9. Busby, 2002.
10. J. Urry, 'Gazing on History', in D. Boswell and J. Evans (eds), *Representing the Nation: A Reader—Histories, Heritage and Museums*, London, 1999, pp. 208–32.
11. Swarbrooke, 1995.
12. English Tourism Council, Statistics on tourism and research web-site, displayed at www.staruk.org.uk on 22 November 2001.

13. Swarbrooke, 1995.
14. S. Millar, 'An Overview of the Sector', in A. Leask and I. Yeoman (eds), *Heritage Visitor Attractions: An Operations Management Perspective*, London, 1999, pp. 1–21.
15. D. Uzzell, 'Interpreting Our Heritage: A Theoretical Interpretation', in D. Uzzell and R. Ballantyne (eds), *Contemporary Issues in Heritage and Environmental Interpretation: Problems and Prospects*, London, 1998, pp. 11–25.
16. R. Prentice, *Tourism and Heritage Attractions*, London, 1993.
17. Busby, 2002.
18. Swarbrooke, 1995.
19. M. Hanna, *English Churches and Visitors*, London, 1984, p. 5.
20. English Tourism Council, *The Heritage Monitor*, London, 1999a; A. Keeling, 'Church Tourism—Providing a Ministry of Welcome to Visitors', *Insights*, 2000, pp. A13–A22.
21. English Tourism Council, *Heritage Monitor*—quoted on ETC web-site, 13 November 2000.
22. ICOMOS (International Council on Monuments and Sites), *To be a Pilgrim—Meeting the Needs of Visitors to Cathedrals and Churches in the United Kingdom: A Survey Undertaken in 2000*, London, 2001, p. 8.
23. S. Davies, 'Attendance Records', *Leisure Management*, 15.2, 1995, pp. 40–4.
24. S. Vayne, *Nicholson's Guide to English Churches*, London, 1984.
25. R. Briers, *English Country Churches*, London, 1989.
26. D.N. Durant, *The Good Church Guide*, London, 1995.
27. S. Jenkins, *England's Thousand Best Churches*, London, 1999.
28. H. Lees, *Cornwall's Churchyard Heritage*, Truro, 1996.
29. J. Rendell, *Cornish Churches*, St Teath, 1982.
30. P. Yale, *From Tourist Attractions to Heritage Tourism*, King's Ripton, 1991.
31. Hanna, 1984, p. 20.
32. English Tourism Council, 1999a.
33. Hanna, 1984, p. 5.
34. Prentice, 1993, p. 79.
35. Keeling, 2000, p. A15.
36. G. Evans, 'Glyn Evans New NCTG Chairman', *Faith in Tourism*, 2001, Spring, p. 4.
37. G. Busby and J. Klug, 'Movie-Induced Tourism: The Challenge of Measurement and Other Issues, *Journal of Vacation Marketing*, 7.4, 2001, pp. 316–32.
38. G. Richards, 'The Experience Industry and the Creation of Attractions', in G. Richards (ed.), *Cultural Attractions and European Tourism*, Wallingford, 2001, pp. 55–69.
39. Richards, 2001, p. 57.
40. G. Ritzer, *Enchanting a Disenchanted World: Revolutionizing the Means of Consumption*, Thousand Oaks, CA, 1999, cited in Richards, 2001, p. 58.
41. A.K.H. Jenkin, *The Story of Cornwall*, London, 1934.

190   *Cornish Studies: Eleven*

42. N. Kennedy and N. Kingcome, 'Disneyfication of Cornwall—Developing a Poldark Heritage Complex', *International Journal of Heritage Studies*, 4.1, 1998, pp. 45–59.
43. Diocese of Truro, *Truro Diocesan Directory*, Truro, 2001.
44. G. Busby and Z. Hambly, 'Literary Tourism and the Daphne du Maurier Festival', in P. Payton (ed.), *Cornish Studies: Eight*, Exeter, 2000, pp. 197–212.
45. English Tourist Board, *English Heritage Monitor*, London, 1995.
46. S. Crew and J. Sims, 'Locating Authenticity: Fragments of a Dialogue', in I. Karp and S. Lawine (eds), *Exhibiting Cultures: The Poetics and Politics of a Museum Display*, Washington DC, 1991, cited in F. Schouten, 'Heritage as Historical Reality', in D.T. Herbert (ed.), *Heritage, Tourism and Society*, London, 1995, pp. 21–31.
47. H.M. Brown, *What to Look For in Cornish churches*, Newton Abbot, 1973, p. 9.
48. P. Cockerham, '"On my grave a marble stone"': Early Modern Cornish Memorialization', in Payton, 2000, pp. 9–39.
49. J. Boissevain, 'Ritual, Tourism and Cultural Commoditization in Malta: Culture by the Pound', in T. Selwyn (ed.), *The Tourist Image: Myths and Myth Making in Tourism*, Chichester, 1996, pp. 105–20.
50. Tourism Research Group, *Cornwall Holiday Survey*, Exeter, 1999.
51. English Tourism Council, *Sightseeing in the UK 1998*, London, 1999b.
52. English Tourism Council, 1999a.
53. English Tourist Board, 1995.
54. English Tourist Board, *English Heritage Monitor*, London, 1994.
55. English Tourist Board, *English Heritage Monitor*, London, 1993.
56. English Tourist Board, 1993.
57. ICOMOS, 2001.
58. Hanna, 1984, p. 5.
59. Hanna, 1984.
60. J. Scott, *A Matter of Record: Documentary Sources in Social Research*, Cambridge, 1990.
61. G. Dann, D. Nash and P. Pearce, 'Methodology in Tourism Research', *Annals of Tourism Research*, 15.1, 1988, pp. 1–28.
62. K.F. Punch, *Introduction to Social Research. Quantitative and Qualitative Approaches*, London, 1998, p. 190.
63. K. Macdonald, 'Using Documents', in N. Gilbert (ed.), *Researching Social Life*, 2nd edition, London, 2001, pp. 194–210.
64. B.L. Berg, *Qualitative Research Methods for the Social Sciences*, 3rd edition, Needham Heights, 1998.
65. A.J. Veal, *Research Methods for Leisure and Tourism*, 2nd edition, Harlow, 1997.
66. C. Frankfort-Nachmias and D. Nachmias, *Research Methods in the Social Sciences*, 5th Edition, London, 1996.
67. Berg, 1998; K. Krippendorff, *Content Analysis: An Introduction to its Methodology*, London, 1980.
68. D. Silverman, *Interpreting Qualitative Data*, London, 1993.

69. R.P. Weber, *Basic Content Analysis*, 2nd edition, London, 1990.
70. R. White, *Value-Analysis: The Nature and Use of the Method*, New York, 1951, cited in C. Ryan, *Researching Tourist Satisfaction: Issues, Concepts, Problems*, London, 1995.
71. Ryan, 1995, p. 110.
72. R. Finnegan, 'Using Documents', in R. Sapsford and V. Jupp (eds), *Data Collection and Analysis*, London, 1996, pp. 138–51.
73. Finnegan, 1996, p. 144.
74. P. Payton, *The Cornish Overseas*, Fowey, 1999, pp. 42, 28.
75. A.L. Rowse, *The Little Land of Cornwall*, Gloucester, 1986, p. 5.
76. E. Cohen, 'A Phenomenology of Tourist Experience', *Sociology*, 13, 1979, pp. 179–201.
77. Ryan, 1995.
78. A.C. Darnell and P.S. Johnson, 'Repeat Visits to Attractions: A Preliminary Economic Analysis', *Tourism Management*, 2001, pp. 119–26.
79. Urry, 1999.
80. R. Tresidder, 'Tourism and Sacred Landscapes', in D. Crouch (ed.), *Leisure/Tourism Geographies: Practices and Geographical Knowledge*, London, 1999, pp. 137–48.
81. Prentice, 1993, p. 79.
82. Ryan, 1995, p. 108.
83. C.C. Hordern, 'Introduction to S. Wason', *Corpus Domini and Other Poems*, York, n.d.
84. N. Orme, *English Church Dedications with a Survey of Cornwall and Devon*, Exeter, 1996.
85. R. Davidson, *Cornwall*, London, 1978.
86. C. Holdsworth, 'From 1050 to 1307', in N. Orme (ed.), *Unity and Variety: A History of the Church in Devon and Cornwall*, Exeter, 1991, p. 23–52.
87. M. Featherstone, *Consumer Culture and Postmodernism*, London, 1991, p. 60.
88. G. Shaw, S. Agarwal and P. Bull, 'Tourism Consumption and Tourist Behaviour: A British Perspective', *Tourism Geographies*, 2. 3, 2000, pp. 264–89.
89. Richards, 2001, p. 56.
90. Tresidder, 1999, p. 144.
91. Brown, 1973, p. 9.
92. Orme, 1996; N. Orme, *The Saints of Cornwall*, Oxford, 2000.
93. J. Lowerson, 'Celtic Tourism—Some Recent Magnets', in P. Payton (ed.), *Cornish Studies: Two*, Exeter, 1994, pp. 128–37.
94. A. Moffat, *Kernow: Part Seen, Part Imagined*, Episode 2, Carlton Television, 20 April 2001.
95. Busby, 2002.
96. Prentice, 1993.

CELTIC REVIVAL AND THE ANGLICAN CHURCH IN CORNWALL, 1870–1930

David Everett

INTRODUCTION

In recent years the Celtic Revival in late nineteenth- and early twentieth-century Cornwall has attracted considerable attention, with scholars seeking to illuminate the process and offer explanations for the phenomenon. Intimations of links both ideological and practical between this new Celticism and Anglican renewal in Cornwall abound but there has not yet been a sustained attempt to explore this relationship.[1] This article seeks to address this gap in Cornish scholarship by offering a preliminary discussion of the symbiotic connections between the Celtic Revival and the Anglican Church in Cornwall during the critical period 1870 to 1930, surveying those decades that witnessed the rise of both Celtic and Anglican Revivalism. Specifically, the aim is to tell the story of the Celtic Revival in Cornwall and to consider the part played by the Anglican Church in this process by examining the activities of some of its leaders, both clergy and laymen. Significantly, the period 1870 to 1930 matches almost exactly the adult life of Henry Jenner, son of an Anglican clergyman, who was the pivotal figure of this Revival. Jenner was involved intimately in the study and revival of the Cornish language, but this article also looks beyond the linguistic component of the Celtic Revival to see how the Anglican Church in Cornwall reflected the Celtic heritage of Cornwall through its institutions and structures, its calendar and services.

Cornwall was, of course, the first Celtic territory to 'lose' its historic language in the modern period. When Edward Lluyd, Keeper of the Ashmolean Museum in Oxford, came to Cornwall in 1700 he and his companions found enough Cornish, in manuscript and spoken form, to keep them busy for nearly four months. His interest was essentially antiquarian, and he tended to favour the use of manuscripts rather than Cornish speakers for his research.[2] One hundred years later, the Cornish language had 'died'.[3] Moreover, with the development of mining for copper and tin, Cornwall became caught up in the British industrial revolution, producing a culture that was assertively 'Cornish' but based now on contemporary industrial and technological prowess rather than 'Celtic' attributes. Its dominant religion became Methodism, itself a central plank of this reformulated Cornish identity. As the nineteenth century progressed, many Cornish men and their families emigrated to other mining areas around the world, especially North America, South Africa and Australia, taking with them their assertive industrial culture and proclaiming everywhere the identity of 'Cousin Jack'.[4]

And yet, paradoxically, by 1900 the Celtic heritage of Cornwall was being 'rediscovered' and reasserted. Indeed, by 2000 the Celtic identity of Cornwall was in 'better shape' than at any time during the last two hundred years, the result of more than a century's sustained effort by a committed band of enthusiasts determined to 'rediscover' or 'reinvent' Cornwall as a 'Celtic nation'. During the nineteenth and twentieth centuries each of the Celtic lands had experienced linguistic decline, prompting the emergence of political and cultural nationalists determined to combat cultural marginalization and restore vigour to their languages.[5] But Cornwall's experience was 'different'. It was the only Celtic land to have undergone a complete loss and rebirth of its historic language. It was also different because, unlike any other Celtic land, it was ostensibly an 'English county', governed for all practical purposes as an integral part of England. It was encompassed, there-fore, within the Established Church of England, despite the fact that numerically the strongest church in Cornwall over the last two hundred years has been the Methodist Church. Cornwall, therefore, while being an exemplar of a wider Celtic experience also exhibits its own distinctive features and merits study in its own right. In this article, four aspects are considered—the language, the Cornish Gorsedd, the saints, the stones, and the Diocese and Cathedral—with a view to identifying the Anglican personalities, imperatives and initiatives that often lay behind them.

THE LANGUAGE

It is generally agreed that the Cornish language ceased to be used in public about 1800.[6] Some Cornish words were still used by a handful of individuals and families and some occupational groups (such as fishermen), and the language survived in the form of place names, personal surnames and occasional dialect words and usages. However, for all practical purposes Cornish had died out in the late eighteenth century, or even earlier. Writing of his research in 1874 into the then present state of another Celtic language, Manx, Henry Jenner (then working at the Manuscript Department at the British Museum) commented: 'It [the Manx language] is now almost exactly in the same state that Cornish was in at the time at which Edward Lluyd wrote his *Archaeologia Britannica* (1709), and though that survived in a sort of way for another century, for all purposes of conversation it was dead in less than half that time'.[7]

This is not the place to consider who the last person was to speak Cornish as their native language, whether it was Dolly Pentreath of Mousehole, near Penzance, who died in 1777, or John Davey (junior), born at St Just in 1812, who died at Boswednack, near St Ives, in 1891. Our interest here is in what motivated the people who wanted to preserve the remnants of a language that was dead (but not buried), and the steps by which the Cornish language came to be spoken again as a 'living' language. As the Cornish language became increasingly a distant memory during the nineteenth century, so the desire to preserve it grew. It was seen now as being as much a part of a valued Cornish heritage as the saints and stone crosses (which we shall consider later), and the work of antiquarians went hand in hand with that of the philologists. It was not their intention to preserve the Cornish language as a spoken language, as it had already ceased to be used for that purpose, and at first there was certainly no thought of reviving it. Instead, they desired to understand how the Cornish language, which had once existed and had been preserved in documents and manuscripts, fitted into the overall picture, structure and meaning of the Celtic languages. This was essentially an academic project.[8]

At first much of the work on the Cornish language was done by non-Cornish scholars. Edwin Norris produced *The Cornish Drama, with a Sketch of Cornish Grammar* in 1859 and Revd Dr Robert Williams, a Welshman, published his *Lexicon Cornu-Britannicum* in 1865. These were to remain standard works on the Cornish language throughout this period from 1870 to 1930. In 1869 the medieval drama *Bewnans Meriasek* (The Life of Meriasek) was discovered among the Hengwrt manuscripts in Wales. It was published in 1872, with notes and translation, and it 'proved an epoch-making event in the history of the revival of the study of the ancient Cornish language', according to Canon Gilbert Doble, writing over sixty years later.[9] The drama had been originally published in the early years of the sixteenth century and emanated from Glasney College, Penryn, the main intellectual centre in West Cornwall. It tells the story of Meriasek, who came to Cornwall from Brittany in the sixth century and settled in the area of Camborne. We shall consider this Cornish drama in more detail later in this article.

One of the first men in Cornwall to take a serious interest in the preservation of the Cornish language was Revd Dr John Bannister of Trinity College, Dublin. He was a Yorkshireman by birth and did not come to Cornwall till 1857, when he was appointed to the then Perpetual Curacy of St Day, a mining village near Redruth, best known for its St Day Carol. His *Glossary of Cornish Names* was printed in 1871 and contained 20,000 words. Bannister had planned to follow his *Glossary* with a companion volume to Dr Williams's *Lexicon Cornu-Britannicum* in which the English words would come first. Unfortunately he died in 1873, in his 58th year, leaving his work unfinished. His widow presented to the Royal Institution of Cornwall Bannister's interleaved copy of Dr Williams's *Lexicon* in which he had made notes for the proposed companion volume.[10]

Revd Wadislas Somerville Lach-Szyrma was another early pioneer to take a strong interest in the preservation of the Cornish language. He became vicar of St Peter's, Newlyn, in 1874. Like Revd Dr John Bannister he was from outside Cornwall, being born at Devonport, Plymouth, in 1841, the son of Polish parents who had left Poland in 1820. He read Classics at Brasenose College, Oxford, graduating in 1859. After travelling in Europe for several years and visiting Polish émigré communities he was ordained in 1865, becoming, first, curate of St Ive, Liskeard, followed by a curacy at St Paul's, Truro, in 1869, then in 1871 vicar of Carnmenellis, a parish near Redruth. He had hopes of a chaplaincy appointment in Paris the following year, but this move was blocked by opposition in Europe, and he returned to England as tutor at St Augustine's College, Canterbury, and for a brief period as curate at St Faith's, Stoke Newington, in north London. His move to Newlyn in 1874 marked the start of a seventeen-year period in this fishing village near Penzance, apart from a break of sixteen months between 1886 and 1888 when he did an exchange with a parish in Liverpool. He moved to Barkingside, Essex, in 1891.[11]

During his time at St Peter's, Newlyn, Revd W.S. Lach-Szyrma threw himself energetically into the task of discovering and interpreting Cornish antiquities in and around his area of Newlyn, Penzance and West Penwith. He played an important part in the social and intellectual life of the Penzance area. He was President of the Penzance Natural History Society in 1884–5 and again in 1889–90. In 1875 Lach-Szyrma was accompanied by Henry Jenner, from the British Museum, on a visit to Newlyn and Mousehole to collect and record fragments of the Cornish language still being spoken by local Cornish people. Jenner went on to describe the results of their investigation, which he divided into three categories: the numerals, detached words, and complete sentences. He listed the numerals up to twenty from two informants, assuming that this sequence of numbers survived in Cornish because it was used for counting fish in the pilchard trade in Mounts Bay.[12] He then listed twenty detached words in Cornish, some with Welsh and Breton equivalents, and three sentences, two of which derived from fishing. He concluded the report of his visit to Cornwall for the Philological Society with three recommendations:

1. That 'several proverbs, songs, and sentences of late Cornish' should be printed and annotated.
2. That 'a supplement should be made to the excellent Cornish *Lexicon* of the Rev. Robert Williams' which should contain words or parts of words not included in this work.
3. That 'Lastly, perhaps a grammar should be made, based upon Dr Norris's *Sketch of Cornish Grammar*, and that in Lhwyd's [*sic*] *Archaeologia Britannica*, only bringing in *every* period of the language'.[13]

Although he did not realize it at the time, Jenner was to fulfil this last recommendation himself nearly thirty years later when his *Handbook of the Cornish Language* was published in 1904.

In the meantime, the work of the antiquaries continued. One of Lach-Szyrma's earliest books was *A Short History of Penzance, S. Michael's Mount, S. Ives, and the Land's End District*, published in 1878. The book was dedicated to the Lord Bishop of Truro, Rt. Rev. Edward White Benson, and contained a chapter on 'The Old Cornish Language'[14] in which Lach-Szyrma stated:

An explanation of our local names is the most practical and useful illustration of the old Cornish language, i.e. the modernized tongue of the ancient Britains [*sic*] of the South-West. A good deal has been done on this subject of late by the Revd. Dr. Bannister and others, so that one is not without a guide in the enquiry.[15]

Lach-Szyrma admitted the limitations of his book. However, he made reference to some of the Cornish words which he had heard spoken in his parish of Newlyn, including the Lord's Prayer, the numerals, and a few 'Cornu-British' words still in use among the fishing and mining folk of West Penwith. After a list of 24 such words 'still in use', he concluded this chapter by arguing in favour of a comparative dictionary of recent Cornish that would also cover the Cornish words embedded in the modern dialect.

About this time Lach-Szyrma floated various ideas to Jenner about awakening and cultivating interest in the Cornish language. In a letter to Jenner he suggested a Cornish examination and prizes, and stressed the need for 'a plain sort of school manual of Cornish illustrating existing words and terms and giving the main principles of the old language'. In this letter, Lach-Szyrma included a revealing comment about the attitude of the Methodists to the study of old Cornish. They think it 'carnal: and wicked (which does not affect our old-fashioned church people) and that "it does not pay"'.[16] From Lach-Szyrma's perspective, Methodist theology and Methodist utilitarianism were fundamentally opposed to the Cornish language, prejudices from which Anglicans ('our old-fashioned church people') were spared.

The person who did most to revive interest in the Celtic language was Henry Jenner. He was born in 1848 at St Columb Major, near Newquay, the son of Revd Henry Lascelles Jenner, Anglican curate of the parish. After moving as a child to Kent, he was educated at St Mary's College, Harlow, Essex. One of the books he used at school when he was 12 or 13 was Latham's smaller *English Grammar*. He recounts how he started to learn Cornish: 'Latham did not mind very much what he put into his books, and he included, besides a lot of miscellaneous information about English, specimens of the Celtic languages, and among them specimens of Cornish. At once I said, "I must learn this", and I learnt it all.'[17] Henry Jenner senior was made Bishop of Dunedin in New Zealand but his son remained in England, doing some short-term school-mastering and for 18 months worked as a clerk in the Principal Registry of H.M. Court of Probate.[18] When the younger Jenner became 21 in 1869:

> the first thing I did was to apply for a reading ticket for the British Museum. When I went there for the first time a very civil attendant asked me what books I wanted to consult, and I said I wanted any books I could have on the Cornish language. These were the first books I ever used in the British Museum. The attendant brought me Norris's *Cornish Drama*, and I read his *Cornish Grammar* for the rest of the afternoon.[19]

After sampling the Cornish remains in the British Museum, Jenner then started work there in July 1870 as an assistant in the Manuscript

Department, having been appointed there on the nomination of Arch-bishop Tait. He transferred to the Department of Printed Books, where he remained until his retirement in 1909, after completion of forty years service. He was a frequent visitor to Cornwall, and in 1877 married Katharine Lee Rawlings of Hayle. It was not until he was over 60 years of age that he returned to live at Hayle and to remain in Cornwall for the rest of his life. He died in 1934. His life, therefore, spans the whole of the period of this survey, and he is indeed the central figure.

While he lived and worked in London, Jenner attended various meetings of learned societies. He went to meetings of the Philological Society, to which he read in 1875 a paper on the 'Grammar, Literature, and Present State of the Manx Language'. The Philological Society, it should be noted, was a very prestigious assembly. It was the body which took upon itself in 1879 the production of the *New English Dictionary on Historical Principles*,[20] better known as *The Oxford English Dictionary*. Another august body which Jenner attended was the British Archaeological Association. In 1877 Jenner gave a lecture on 'The History and Literature of the Ancient Cornish' Language' to the Congress of the British Archaeological Association, starting with these words: 'Though most people know of the former existence of the Cornish language, it is very curious what a vague and confused notion prevails, even in Cornwall, as to what it was or when it ceased to exist'.[21] Cornish, Jenner emphasized, was a subject of antiquarian interest, a language of the past which had died out in the last hundred years. He gave a brief summary of the evidence for the Cornish language, starting with the Cornish names in the Bodmin Gospels[22] and the Cornish vocabulary in the Cottonian document of the latter part of the twelfth century, where 'the earliest mention of the Cornish language that I have yet discovered' occurs in a Latin life of St Cadoc.[23] He ended his survey of the Cornish language and literature with a letter he came across in the British Museum 'addressed to Sir Joseph Banks, dated 1791, in which the writer mentions his own father as the only living man who could speak it'.[24]

> Then, as a spoken language, Cornish died out entirely, and there only remained various traditions thereof in the shape of words, sentences, etc., handed down among the inhabitants of the districts where it was last current. Even these have very much diminished of late years, and, though there are many people still living who have heard such things as the Creed, Lord's Prayer, etc., repeated in Cornish by the old folk many years ago. When I made some investigations last year at

Newlyn and Mousehole, I only found that a few people of great age could repeat the numerals as far as twenty, and one or two knew a few detached words and two short sentences.[25]

Lach-Szyrma had hinted at Anglican sympathy (or at least neutrality) towards the Cornish language. But here Jenner (the son of an Anglican priest), in his assertion that some people in the far west had only recently heard the Creed and Lord's Prayer in Cornish, was suggesting that the Church, even if unwittingly, had contributed to the survival of the Cornish language because of its generally conservative attitude towards its official formularies and rituals. Whether these forms really had survived in church usage is open to debate and requires further research but it is Jenner's assumption of Anglican continuity and sympathy that is telling. Given that Jenner was at the heart of the Cornish language movement as it emerged, this assumption acquired its own significance and was to influence later Revivalists who sought to wed Celtic Revivalism in Cornwall to the efforts of the Anglican Church.

Certainly, Jenner's reputation developed apace. In 1877 he had discovered at the British Museum a fragment in Cornish on the back of a fourteenth-century charter endorsement, probably the earliest surviving piece of Cornish literature. It consisted of 42 lines of verse. Jenner's visits to Cornwall were sporadic during the latter decades of the nineteenth century. He started writing poems in Cornish to his wife and verses in Cornish for his Christmas cards. These compositions in Cornish were for private use and consumption. Jenner's interest in the Cornish language did have a topical and useful application for his own times, even though the revival of the Cornish language as a spoken language was probably far from his mind. He wanted to see some accuracy and consistency in the spelling of Cornish names. He complained about the lack of method in deciding how to spell Cornish place names in the last Ordnance Survey map.

Here Jenner had touched upon the heart of the problem: how is a language that has ceased to be a living and a spoken language to be preserved? If it is going to be preserved as a written language, upon what principles is it going to be reconstructed? How much is going to be borrowed from related languages? He advocated the establishment of a committee to 'decide on all questions relating to Cornish spelling' and offered his service to such a body. The task of this committee would be to decide on the spelling of Cornish words 'on principles consistent with the present sound, the derivation, and the meaning'. He declared that such a system should 'be based upon modern English, avoiding all scientific affectations . . . and all use of accents'.[26]

Jenner's long-awaited *Handbook of the Cornish Language* was
published in 1904. It was subtitled *chiefly in its latest stages with some
account of its history and literature*. The need for such a publication had
been evident for some considerable time. Jenner traced its genesis to
a request by the Secretary of the Celtic-Cornish Society (Cowethas
Celto-Kernuak) to produce a Cornish grammar. Rather disarmingly,
Jenner admitted that the request came after he had dropped his
Cornish studies for more than twenty years, presumably during most of
the 1880s and 1890s, and had had to start again almost from scratch![27]
Before the *Handbook* appeared, he had clearly become fluent again. In
1903 he made a speech in Cornish at a Celtic Congress in Finisterre,
Brittany, 'perhaps the first that had been made for two hundred years
and rather to his astonishment he was fairly well understood by the
Bretons'.[28]

It is important to note that the book published in 1904 was not
called a *Grammar*, still less a *Glossary* or *Dictionary*. Its main concern
was with the language when it was last used, i.e. in the seventeenth and
early eighteenth centuries. This was important, because when it came
to reviving Cornish as both a written and a spoken language, Jenner
was to advocate the period ('Late' or 'Modern' Cornish) when it was
last used widely, not the earlier medieval period of the fourteenth and
fifteen centuries which had left a larger body of literature, consisting
mainly of religious drama and verse.

On the title page of his book, in small print, Jenner described
himself as a member of the Gorsedd of the Bards of Brittany and as a
Fellow of the Society of Antiquaries. He had become a member of the
Breton Gorsedd in 1903 and he obviously felt the importance of this
title. Earlier, in 1883, he had become a Fellow of the Society of
Antiquaries. Also on the title page there was a quote, with a line
of Cornish, from a seventeenth-century play, containing a clear
reference to contemporary spoken Cornish: 'Never credit me but I will
spowt some Cornish at him. *Pedn bras, vidne whee bis cregas.* (The
Northern Lass, by Rich. Brome, 1632.)'. In the opening sentence of the
Preface to the *Handbook*, Jenner stated the purpose of the book.
There was the hint or the hope of Cornish becoming again a spoken
language: 'This book is principally intended for those persons of
Cornish nationality who wish to acquire some knowledge of their
ancient tongue, and to read, write, and perhaps even to speak it'.[29]
Indeed, the book was intended, not for the specialist or the philologist,
but for the general Cornish public.

Jenner appealed to Cornish patriotism as the main reason why
the people of Cornwall should learn their language. Being an ardent
royalist and Tory (as well as an opponent of Celtic political

nationalism), he insisted that this Cornish patriotism was not at odds with patriotism towards England or Britain but was in addition to it. In a footnote, as if recognizing that patriotism towards England was too hard for some Cornish people to swallow, he referred to the Bretons of his day who habitually spoke of Brittany as 'notre petite patrie' and France as 'notre grande patrie'. But if patriotism was not enough, then 'sentiment' would do:

> Why should Cornishmen learn Cornish? There is no money in it, it serves no practical purpose, and the literature is scanty and of no great originality or value. The question is a fair one, the answer is simple. Because they are Cornishmen . . . The reason why a Cornishman should learn Cornish, the outward and audible sign of his separate nationality, is sentimental, and not the least practical, and if everything sentimental were banished from it, the world would not be as pleasant a place as it is.[30]

Although he was discreet enough not to make it plain, Jenner was in his appeal to the 'sentimental', and in his admission that learning Cornish was 'not the least practical', echoing Lach-Szyrma's earlier criticism of Methodist utilitarianism and its negative attitude towards Cornish.

Jenner also paid tribute to the other scholars of the second half of the nineteenth century who had worked in this field and made the *Handbook* possible: Mr Edwin Norris, Canon Robert Williams, Dr F. Jago, Dr Whitley Stokes and Prof. Joseph Loth of Rennes University, particularly the two last named. Jenner was certainly familiar with the best authorities on the Cornish language, and he was optimistic that this *Handbook* would achieve what was intended. He certainly saw the Celtic Revival in Cornwall, of which the *Handbook* was a part, as part of a wider movement among the Celtic nations: 'Whether anything will come of the Cornish part of the Celtic movement remains to be seen, but it is not without good omen that this book is published at "The Sign of the Phoenix"', the address of his publisher David Nutt of Long Acre, London.[31] As an indication of what he meant, Jenner added that 'The composition of twentieth century Cornish verse has already begun', giving some examples.[32] He concluded by noting the preparation of subsequent publications, to include 'some reading lessons, exercises, and vocabularies', though he had no idea as to when these would be available.[33]

Jenner retired from the British Museum and moved to Cornwall in 1909, living at Hayle, the home town of his wife. He threw himself energetically into the work of the Royal Institution of Cornwall and the Royal Cornwall Polytechnic Society. There flowed a constant stream of papers and articles, talks and resolutions. He held various posts with these organizations as a member of the Council, Secretary, Editor of the Journal, and President. He had by now become the leading authority on the Cornish language. There were still enormous difficulties ahead and, after the initial optimism generated by the appearance of the *Handbook*, his move to Cornwall seems to have produced a renewed mood of scepticism about the possibility of Cornish ever becoming a spoken language. A few months after he retired and settled at Hayle, he told the Royal Institution of Cornwall at their Annual Meeting on 9 December 1909: 'As no living person has ever heard Cornish spoken, our ideas of its pronunciation must be largely conjectural. Exact phonetics are not attainable, and no doubt Cornish philologists differ on many details.'[34] Over the years, Jenner had become very critical of Dr Bannister's *Glossary of Cornish Names*. In his opinion, 'Dr Bannister's book is worse than useless, it is misleading. It is a monument of immensely hard work, marvellously misapplied.' According to Jenner, 'Dr Bannister had a very large vocabulary of separate Cornish words, but he was no philologist and had no idea of how to put them together'.[35] Jenner conceded that 'a large number of easy and obvious derivations are correctly given, but even the easy ones are often wrong'.[36]

Jenner drew upon his knowledge of Breton and Welsh to point the way forward. He affirmed that Cornwall, though in his opinion now legally and administratively part of England, differed from all other counties. In addition to a distinctive constitutional history, 'It once had a Celtic language of its own, not a mere dialect, but a real separate language'. He then placed the Cornish language in its relation to its neighbouring languages, Welsh and Breton: 'It is too far off from Welsh to be a dialect of that, as some people have held; and as for the much nearer allied Breton, if there is any question of dialects, I would say that Breton is a dialect of Cornish, rather than Cornish a dialect of Breton'.[37] Jenner's paper read at the Annual Meeting of December 1909 started with an important resolution: 'That it is desirable that the Royal Institution of Cornwall should take some steps towards promoting a systematic general survey and collection of Cornish place and family names, with a view to their correct interpretation'.[38] To achieve this survey and collection, Jenner proposed a method similar to his survey of the Manx language in 1874, together with the rather grander method used by the Philological Society in compiling the *New English Dictionary on Historical Principles*—the setting up of a committee of experts. The members of the committee would each take a district of

Cornwall, and each district would be sub-divided into different areas to collect and record names, and a final revision committee would work out the result. He also suggested using the services of 'foreigners' to help in this task: Sir John Rhys, Principal of Jesus College, Oxford (a Welshman), and Professor Joseph Loth of the Rennes University (a Breton).[39] The council of the Royal Institution of Cornwall indicated their approval of this suggestion and the resolution was not formally proposed and seconded.

A further development in reviving the Cornish language came four years later. At the Annual Meeting of the Royal Institution of Cornwall in December 1913, the President, Mr Thurston Peter, submitted a resolution urging that there be a production of the ancient Cornish miracle play *The Life of St Meriasek* at Perran Round, Perranporth. Mr Jenner, then Secretary of the Royal Institution of Cornwall, seconded the resolution and said he would offer advice and assistance to those who would produce and perform the drama. However, he regretted that the performance could not be done in Cornish. He admitted that he was probably the only person who wished to see it in Cornish, though he hoped it might have one scene in the language. The aim would be to show Cornish people what their ancestors' plays were like, making the performance as historically exact as possible. By the time of the Royal Institution of Cornwall's resolution, the translation and adaptation of the play were well advanced. It was intended to include some medieval music taken from ancient manuscripts of Miracle Plays, such as those of York, and also from pageants about the lives of saints in Brittany.

The resolution was carried unanimously. It was hoped to produce the drama in the summer of 1915 but the First World War intervened and the resolution lapsed. It was to be eleven years before the resolution was fulfilled, with the first performance of *Beunans Meriasek* in June 1924, not at Perran Round, but at St Andrews Church, Redruth.[40] However, the 1913 resolution was the first indication that Jenner had moved beyond an antiquarian, private or poetic interest in the Cornish language, to one where it could be used in a spoken form to address the Cornish people about their culture and heritage. Moreover, despite his earlier focus on Late or Modern Cornish, Jenner had by now fully embraced the earlier medieval 'Middle Cornish' of the miracle plays, in the process no doubt dwelling upon the religious characteristics of this pre-Reformation drama, characteristics that appealed increasingly to Anglicans in Cornwall, especially those of Anglo-Catholic persuasion. It was no accident that the 1924 performance of *Beunans Meriasek* was in an Anglican Church, nor was it a coincidence that the play's translator was an Anglican priest, the Anglo-Catholic and Celtic Revivalist enthusiast Gilbert Doble.

Jenner became President of the Royal Cornwall Polytechnic Society in 1916 and President of the Royal Institution of Cornwall in 1922, having been Secretary of the latter body for ten years. When he was elected as President in 1921, he signalled the continuing importance of the Cornish language to his own studies and to the life of the Royal Institution of Cornwall. He told members:

> In order to talk a language you must have somebody to talk to, and the difficulty in this case is to find somebody. I think I shall arrive at that after a bit, because there is a member of the Royal Institution of Cornwall (Mr. R. Morton Nance) who writes me beautiful postcards in Cornish, and I think before long we shall be able to talk to each other.[41]

When he actually became President in 1922, Jenner's presidential address was on the subject of *The Bodmin Gospels*.[42] In this talk he gave ample evidence of his wide-ranging knowledge of ecclesiastical and liturgical matters, further reinforcing Revivalist assumptions about the relationship between the language and religion. He drew the attention of the members of the Institution to 'four very long articles of my own in the New York *Catholic Encyclopaedia*' which he had written about the Ambrosian, Celtic, Gallican and Mozarabic Rites.[43] He had been introduced as the new President of the Institution by the retiring President, Canon Henry Holroyd Mills, yet another Anglican antiquarian enthusiast, in glowing terms which could not help juxtaposing the philological and the ecclesiastical: 'Mr Jenner is a man of many parts, as his numerous scholarly articles on philological, ecclesiastical and antiquarian subjects testify. He is a great authority on all matters concerning the Celtic peoples and the greatest living authority on the Ancient Cornish Language.'[44] With the benefit of hindsight we can add that Jenner's toils had also had the effect of reinforcing the link, already insinuated by Lach-Szyrma and others, between Celtic Revivalism and the Anglican Church in Cornwall.

THE CORNISH GORSEDD

Jenner had became a bard in 1903, not of the Cornish Gorsedd, but of the Breton Gorsedd which had been founded in 1900. Thereafter, the development of the Cornish language and the formation of the Cornish Gorsedd went hand-in-hand, and Jenner was the driving force behind both these movements. But he could not revive a language and start its cultural expression all on his own. Ralph Morton Nance was his colleague both in the language revival and in the formation of the Old Cornwall Societies. The first such local society was formed in St Ives in the Spring of 1920 with Henry Jenner as the President. As Morton Nance was to write later, 'It was a performance of *Duffy* at St Ives that led to the formation there in 1920 of the first Old Cornwall Society—and so in time to the Federation of Old Cornwall Societies and to the Cornish Gorsedd'.[45]

After the destruction and loss of the Great War, there was a general desire on the part of many of the Cornish population to salvage remains from the past before all was lost. In the first half of the 1920s, eight local Old Cornwall Societies were founded in West Cornwall, with a Federation of Old Cornwall Societies starting in 1924. In the next few years, more local groups were formed in the rest of Cornwall. With its journal *Old Cornwall*, which started in 1925 and appeared at six-monthly intervals, the Old Cornwall movement could claim to represent the whole of Cornwall. The aim was reflected in the motto of the movement, a verse taken from the miracle of the Feeding of the Five Thousand: '*Kyntelleugh an brewyon es gesys, na vo kellys travyth*' ('Gather ye the fragments that are left, that nothing be lost').[46]

Anglican clergy and lay members were involved in the Old Cornwall movement from the start, further evidence of the relationship between the Celtic Revival and the Anglican Church. Ideological sympathy may have underpinned this relationship but what is notable from an even cursory glance is the sheer predominance of Anglican leaders within the Old Cornwall movement. Henry Jenner was President of the St Ives and the Hayle Old Cornwall Societies. He was also the first President of the Federation of Old Cornwall Societies. The first Vice-President was the Revd J. Sims-Carah, vicar of Penponds, near Camborne. He was also Chairman of the Camborne Old Cornwall Society. The Vice-President of the Madron Old Cornwall Society was the Revd Canon Jennings. One of the members of the Redruth Old Cornwall Society, Revd Gilbert Doble, wrote the play based on the life of St Meriasek which was performed in English at St Andrew's, Redruth, in June 1924. Thus, eleven years after it was first agreed by the Royal Institution of Cornwall, the production of the Life of St Meriasek took place, thanks to the enthusiasm of an Anglican clergyman.

Henry Jenner felt that the priorities of the Old Cornwall movement should focus on cultural and literary activity, rather than on political objectives. In this way the movement would serve the ideal of 'fostering Cornish National Sentiment',[47] and the Cornish would be able to take their rightful place among the Celtic nations, but without the (in his view) undesirable prospect of being ensnared by the likes of

Irish republicanism or Breton separatism. A big step towards the
fulfilment of this ambition took place in 1924. A delegation consisting
of three men, the Anglicans Canon Gilbert Doble and Mr Charles
Henderson, and Mr R. Morton Nance (intriguingly, a Methodist) from
the Royal Institution of Cornwall, attended the Celtic Congress in
Quimper, Brittany. Morton Nance made a short speech in Cornish to
the Congress and read a long letter in Cornish by Henry Jenner who
was in Spain at the time The result was that the Celtic Congress was
held in Cornwall two years later in July 1926, followed by Cornish
participation in the Inter-Celtic Festival in Brittany in 1927. The scene
was set for the holding of a Cornish Gorsedd in Cornwall in September
1928, something which Jenner had long wanted to take place.

The Cornish Gorsedd was built on the rite and ceremony of the
Welsh and Breton Gorseddau, but only bards took part. There were no
druids and ovates. Jenner was not keen on the pagan or political
connotations of the word druid. The Gorsedd of 1928 brought together
many of the leading Anglicans, and if echoes of pagan allusion could
still be detected within the ceremony, there was also more than a hint
of Anglican Christianity. Henry Jenner was elected the first Grand
Bard. Revd James Sims-Carah, vicar of Penponds, Camborne, became
a bard. He had been a curate of St Peter's Newlyn and shared
with Revd W.S. Lach-Szyrma a strong interest in antiquarian matters.
The list of early bards included the names of Gilbert Doble, Charles
Henderson and Thomas Taylor, Anglicans who were all initiated in
recognition of their services to Celtic Revivalism in Cornwall.

THE SAINTS

The Cornish Language may have been extinct for most of the nineteenth century. The Cornish saints were almost as obscure. Many
names of saints existed as place-names, but very little was known about
them. It was thanks to a handful of leading Anglican scholars that the
Cornish saints emerged from their obscurity and to a large extent
became recognizable individuals. Of course, the figure of the antiquarian clergyman taking a keen interest in local history was a familiar
one throughout nineteenth-century England and Wales, but in
Cornwall the activity acquired a Celtic Revivalist dimension, not least
amongst the High Churchmen and Anglo-Catholic Anglicans who saw
in their hagiographic study a means of asserting a particular cultural-
religious identity as well as constructing links with other Celtic
territories, especially Brittany.

Amongst the first to shed some glimmer of light on the saints was
the celebrated Revd Robert Stephen Hawker. He was particularly
interested in the patronal saint of his own parish, Morwenstow, in

North Cornwall. The first chapter of his book *Footprints of Former Men in far Cornwall*, published in 1870 and containing articles written in the previous ten years, states his case plainly: 'There cannot be a scene more graphic in itself, or more illustrative in its history, of the gradual growth and striking development of the Church in Keltic and Western England than the parish of St Morwenna'.[48] According to Hawker, Morwenna was a daughter of the Keltic [sic] king Breachan [sic] of Wales, who lived in the ninth century at the time of the Saxon occupation of England. Hawker even put her in one of his poems and stated with due scholarly authority, 'I am not disposed to assign a later origin than from A.D.875 to A.D.1000'.[49] But Hawker was a better parish priest and poet than a historian. His imagination was fuelled by his cell, built of driftwood, on the Cornish cliffs near his parish church. Here he composed poetry about his local landscape and local people. His poems were often in the form of ballads, and contained perhaps more of a medieval and 'Arthurian' flavour than a Celtic one, although at certain levels all three became inextricably entwined, not least in the minds of many Celtic Revialists. Be that as it may, it was left to Revd Sabine Baring-Gould to try to correct Hawker's faulty chronology. Writing in 1876, the year after Hawker's death, Baring-Gould stated that Brychan of Brecknock in Wales, an Irish invader, died in 450 AD and that Morwenna was apparently his grand-daughter. She was, therefore, located in the late fifth century or early sixth century, not the ninth or tenth.

Revd John Adams was both an antiquarian and a geologist, and another key Anglican scholar in Cornwall in this period. He was born at Morwenstow in 1822 and would have known 'Parson' Hawker after the latter became incumbent there in 1834. Adams went to Oxford and became curate of Tregony, followed by Grampound. Finally he moved to Berkshire and became incumbent of Starcross in 1857. Before he left Cornwall, he started writing articles on the saints of Cornwall for the *Journal of the Royal Institution of Cornwall*. His series of articles, called 'Chronicles of the Cornish Saints', appeared between 1867 and 1875 in eight parts. The series included articles on St Cuby, St Petroc, St Constantine, St Samson, St David, St Buryan, St Crantock and St Gunwallo [Winwaloe]. These articles started life as talks given to various meetings of the Institution, later appearing in print. The list of saints would undoubtedly have been longer had it not been for his untimely death in a fire at the Southern Hotel in St Louis, USA in 1876. Mr. W.Copeland Borlase paid tribute to Revd John Adams in his presidential address to the Royal Institution of Cornwall: 'It is to the memory of . . . the late Mr Adams that we owe the heaviest debt of gratitude for the most persevering attempt yet made to reduce into form the scattered fragments of Cornish Hagiology [*sic*]'.[50]

Borlase's presidential address to the Royal Institution of Cornwall, called 'The Age of theSaints', was printed as a book with this title in 1878. It was regarded as the standard work on the Cornish saints until replaced by that of Revd Sabine Baring-Gould. Baring-Gould became President of the Royal Institution of Cornwall in 1897. Although not a Cornishman, he had became vicar of Lewtrenchard, just across the border in Devon, in 1881 and was to play a major role in the Celtic Revival in Cornwall. *His* presidential address was called 'The Early History of Cornwall' and this was followed a year later with a second presidential address on 'The Celtic Saints'. What Baring-Gould did was to interrogate Irish, Welsh and Breton authorities and to locate the Cornish saints firmly amongst the 'Celtic nation', an explicitly Revivalist project which both confirmed the Celtic credentials of the Cornish saints and placed Celtic saints generally within a yet more ancient Celtic tradition. They were the successors, he argued, of the bards and druids. Between 1899 and 1907, Baring-Gould produced a series of articles, which he called 'A Catalogue of Saints connected with Cornwall'. Much of his work on the Cornish saints was published as Volume 16 of *Lives of the Saints*.

Baring-Gould spent eighteen months in Brittany collecting its traditions and consulting its records. In Brittany, he said, the antiquaries worked on their own local materials without relating them to evidence in Wales, Cornwall and Ireland, thus not only failing to construct a comparative picture but missing inter-Celtic connections and similarities: 'What was needed was the fusing together of the traditions found in Wales, Ireland, Cornwall, and Brittany'.[51] For his series of articles, Baring-Gould was awarded the Henwood Medal by the Royal Institution of Cornwall in 1902.

In 1914 Revd Thomas Taylor also became a winner of the Henwood Medal. He was also not a Cornishman by birth but had become vicar of St Just in Penwith in 1900. In 1916 his work *The Celtic Christianity of Cornwall* was published and dedicated to the Breton scholar M. Joseph Loth. Taylor's other main work was *The Life of St Samson of Dol*, which included a lengthy introduction and English translation, and was published in 1925. He also wrote a book about St Michael's Mount and various articles on ecclesiastical matters for the *Journal of the Royal Institution of Cornwall*. Like others before him, he expressed in his work, implicitly and sometimes explicitly, an uncritical assumption of a direct link between the 'Celtic Christianity' in the distant past that he had identified and the Anglican Church in contemporary Cornwall in which he was active. To that extent Taylor, and others like him, actually lived the Celtic Revival in Cornwall, so that Celticism was gradually becoming ingrained in the cultural fabric of the Anglican Church.

But the person who has become most associated with the lives of the Cornish saints is Canon Gilbert Doble. He was born in Penzance in 1880, went to Exeter College, Oxford, and was ordained deacon in 1904. He joined the staff of the parish of Redruth in 1920 and in 1925 was appointed vicar of Wendron, near Helston, where he remained until his death in 1945. He was made a canon in 1931 and for his work on the Cornish saints he was awarded the Oxford Doctorate of Divinity in 1943. Doble's interest in the Cornish saints started in the early 1920s with the publication in 1923 of a booklet called *Saint Mawes*. This was reprinted in 1938 as No. 1 in what was to become the impressive and extensive Cornish Saints series, some volumes of which remain in print today. He collaborated with the historian Charles Henderson, who was one of his closest friends and colleagues. Doble wrote about a particular saint, while Henderson wrote about the church building and the parish bearing the name of the saint. It proved to be a most fruitful partnership until Henderson's untimely death in 1933.

A particular dimension to Doble's work, in addition to his thorough library and documentary research, was the visits he made to locations in Brittany and France: 'Always churches, castles, holy wells, had to be visited, rare manuscripts examined in obscure libraries'.[52] Here he was following in the footsteps of Baring-Gould and the other Anglican clergymen who had written on the Cornish saints. Revd Adams produced his *Chronicles* of Cornish saints, Revd Baring-Gould wrote his *Catalogues* of Cornish saints, but the standard work for the rest of the twentieth century was to be Canon Doble's *Series*. Each writer had built on the work of his predecessor but the most accurate, scholarly and lasting work was that done by Canon Doble: 'In the realm of scholarship Doble is significant, not merely for the quantity of his output, but for rigorous application of critical methods to hagiography, his favourite subject. He made it historically respectable, beyond the dream of earlier students in this country.'[53]

THE STONES

Cornwall may be lacking in old documents, ancient manuscripts and hagiographical material, but it is rich in inscribed stones and crosses. In 1913, the government of the day passed an *Ancient Monument and Consolidation Amendment Act* which made provision for the establishment of a County Committee to deal with ancient monuments. The first chairman of the county committee in Cornwall was Henry Jenner, who by now was Honorary Secretary of the Royal

Institution of Cornwall and a Vice-President of the Royal Cornwall
Polytechnic Society. Although he was more at home with manuscripts
than with monuments, his experience at the British Museum made him
eminently suitable for this role. And so Cornwall's ancient stone monuments became co-opted by the Celtic Revivalist establishment in
Cornwall. The Cowethas Celto-Kernuak had already claimed them as
part of Cornwall's Celtic heritage while the many wayside and churchyard crosses, with their characteristic 'wheel' heads, were routinely
proclaimed as evidence of 'Celtic Christianity'.

In his remarks on the 1913 Act, Jenner explained to the Royal
Institution of Cornwall that 'We have more prehistoric antiquities to
the square mile in Cornwall than in any other county, except, perhaps,
some parts of Wiltshire. We must set the best possible example to the
country in our care of them.'[54] The first task was to compile an
inventory of the ancient Cornish monuments. A provisional list was
drawn up and adopted by the County Committee in July 1913. It
was then published in the pages of the *Journal of the Royal Institution
of Cornwall*.[55] It contained the names and locations of twenty-nine
disused ecclesiastical buildings, headed by St Piran's Oratory at
Perranporth, and details of stone-castles, cliff-castles, earth-works,
stone-circles, longstones, quoits, underground chambers, huts and hut
circles, barrows, and over eighty ancient and holy wells. This inventory
did not include the names of Cornish crosses but instead referred
people to over three hundred stone crosses in Arthur G. Langdon's
book *Old Cornish Crosses* and to the monuments in *Inscribed Stones*
by the same author.[56]

The task of discovering, interpreting, guarding and preserving
ancient stones was ideally suited to the Anglican clergy in Cornwall,
many of whom, as we have seen, were already devotees of the Celtic
Revival. Many of the stones and monuments were located in churches
or churchyards, and it was natural for clergy in Cornwall as elsewhere
to take an interest in such durable relics from the past. One such
Anglican clergyman was the antiquarian Revd William Iago, of
Westheath, Bodmin, 'one of the most zealous of Cornish antiquaries'
as he was described.[57] He frequently reported to the Royal Institution
of Cornwall on the discovery of inscribed stones and crosses, including
those disguised as gateposts or as part of stone walls. For example, he
reported in 1870 on the discovery and erection of the stone cross at
Mylor near Falmouth. It is the tallest stone cross in Cornwall and was
previously upside down, being used as a buttress against the south
wall of the church, with its head in the ground. Iago became President
of the Royal Institution of Cornwall from 1885 to 1887, having served
on its council for many years. A few years later, the *Journal of the*

Royal Institution of Cornwall reported on another of his spectacular finds:

> The Rev. W. Iago B.A. has recently discovered the oldest Inscribed Stone known in the county. It is a Roman Military Stone and forms the lich-stone in the eastern grill of Tintagel Churchyard . . . It dates from the early part of the fourth century and is prior to the St Hilary stone, the only Roman Military Stone in Cornwall, hitherto known.[58]

Iago was also responsible for bringing to the attention of the public the discovery of Ogham stones at Lewannick, a definite indication of immigrants from Ireland settling in Cornwall. He had joined with Parson Hawker of Morwenstow, Professor Rhys and other anti-quaries in searching for Ogham stones, and together they had been successful in discovering stones with such writing from the fifth and sixth centuries. Such was his expertise and interest in these matters that he was appointed the Local Secretary for Cornwall by the Society of Antiquaries, London, and was issued with the Society's diploma. He was also the first winner of the Henwood Medal in 1890 for his article on 'Recent Archaeological Discoveries in Cornwall', published in the *Journal of the Royal Institution of Cornwall*. This article, with his own illustrations, was one of many such articles written by Revd William Iago for the *Journal* over a period of some twenty years. He died in 1918 and was given a glowing obituary in the *Journal* that he had supported so loyally:

> During his long term of membership he contributed a very large numberof papers and notes to the Journal. In the General Index down to 1906 there are no less than forty-three separate entries under his name, and probably these might be brought up to fifty by the addition of subsequent years. He was a skilled antiquary and an accomplished artist, with an immense power of work, and his services to Cornish archaeology cannot be over-estimated.[59]

Revd W. Iago was indeed an accomplished illustrator. His work was continued by the photographic work of Canon Henry Holroyd Mills, another of that band of Anglican enthusiasts. The year before Iago died, Canon Mills presented to the Royal Institution of Cornwall in 1917 a complete collection of photographs of Cornish crosses, taken by himself and containing over 350 examples. He had started this collection before the First World War and had almost completed it by

1914, with the proposed resultant book intended as a companion to the work of Arthur G. Langdon. Canon Mills had been a member of the Royal Institution of Cornwall since 1902 and was President from 1919 to 1921. He was elected by the Institution as one of the Trustees of St Piran's Oratory in 1917. As this structure was top of the list of ancient monuments cared for by the county committee, it is not surprising that it attracted the attention of Henry Jenner. In 1911, the members of the Royal Institution of Cornwall went to see for themselves the work of encasing the ruin which had emerged from the sands in the nineteenth century and to hear a paper read by Henry Jenner on 'Christian Worship in St Piran's Oratory in the Sixth and Seventh Centuries'. Jenner thought he could reconstruct the form of worship originally used at St Piran's Oratory, based on manuscripts surviving elsewhere, both in Ireland and on continental Europe.

THE DIOCESE AND THE CATHEDRAL
Although Cornwall had enjoyed a brief period as an independent see as part of Athelstan's tenth-century settlement, what was to become the Diocese of Truro was originally part of the Diocese of Exeter, in the nineteenth century the largest in 'England'. The distance from one end of the diocese in Cornwall to the cathedral city was 140 miles. Interest and support for a separate Diocese of Truro had been gathering pace during the nineteenth century. Advocates ranged from Revd John Wallis, Anglican vicar of Bodmin, who in 1847 wrote with almost nationalist vehemence that the creation of a Cornish bishopric would be 'an act of tardy justice. For 800 years we have been deprived of our ancient See', to those who wished to launch an Anglican Revival to claw Cornwall back from the Methodists and saw the establishment of a Cornish diocese as the means of achieving this. Wallis insisted that 'Cornwall should be treated as an Island. *One and All* is our motto', while Anglo-Catholics and Celtic Revivalists amongst those planning Anglican Revival saw in the prospect of a separate diocese the means of creating explicitly Celtic expressions and forms. Various attempts failed, until a window of opportunity occurred with the death of Bishop Philpotts of Exeter in 1869. Before he died, Bishop Philpotts had been in favour of dividing his diocese into two parts and had even offered to give up part of his revenues for a Cornish bishopric.[60]

One of the principal advocates of a new diocese for Cornwall was, not surprisingly, Revd W.S. Lach-Szyrma. He sent an open letter to the Prime Minister, W.E. Gladstone, setting out seven reasons in favour of the restoration of the 'Ancient See of Cornwall'. Echoing the earlier views of Wallis, he concluded that 'In other words, from a geographical, an historical, an ethnological, a practical and an economical point of view, the friends of the division [into two separate dioceses] urge their claims'.[61] Even Methodist adherents were swept along by such sentiment, and as the movement to establish a Cornish diocese gathered momentum it unleashed what A.L. Rowse called 'an astonishing stream of Cornish patriotism'.[62] In the end the pressure was irresistible, and during the episcopacy of Rt Revd Frederick Temple, the last bishop of the undivided diocese, the legislation for the creation of the new Diocese of Truro passed through Parliament. The first Bishop of Truro was Edward White Benson, Chancellor and Canon of Lincoln Cathedral, and he was enthroned on 1 May 1877. From the beginning this new Anglican diocese was seen as being somehow 'Celtic', and to help Benson on his way:

> Before he left Lincoln, the students and tutors of the *Scholae Cancellarii* presented him with a handsome pastoral staff of Celtic design, which he used for nearly twenty years in his dioceses of Truro and Canterbury, and which now occupies a niche in the southern or 'Benson' transcept of Truro Cathedral.[63]

One of the first meetings he attended after his enthronement was the Spring meeting of the Royal Institution of Cornwall on 11 May 1877. He was to become a regular attender of the Institution's meetings and became President in November 1879. In his presidential address, Bishop Benson put forward a suggestion that the Institution make a little effort 'to obtain a more accurate chronicling of the details of the whole of our Cornish churches from St Levan to Morwenstow'. He added, 'It seems to me that there must be history of some remarkable kind underlying the aspect of our churches. I have visited a very large number of them.'[64] Although he was not a Cornishman, Bishop Benson soon came to love the country of his adoption and its people. A few months after his enthronement, he wrote to a friend enthusing about Cornwall's sense of difference: 'This Cornubia is a land of wonderment —historical, physical, spiritual. I'm not sure that it is part of the created universe.'[65] As Canon H. Scott Holland was to write of Benson after his death, he was smitten by the idea of Cornwall as a mysterious land apart:

> His warmth of feeling responded to the imaginative emotion of the Cornish. Strange memories, archaic visions hovered mistily over uplands and hollows: the past, in its fascinating shadowiness, in its weird oddities, met him at every turn of

the road, in the quaint form of suggested aloofness which most appealed to his swift curiosity.[66]

Part of Bishop Benson's lasting legacy to his diocese was the name of his residence, to which he gave the Cornish-language title of Lis Escop, instead of the more prosaic English Bishop's Court.[67] The name persists to this day, although the residence has changed several times. But Benson's vision for a 'chronicling of the details of the whole of our Cornish churches' was not to be realized for another forty years until the work of Charles Henderson in the 1920s. Henderson was born in Jamaica in 1900, then came to live in Okehampton, Devon, then in Falmouth and Hayle. At the age of twelve years he started to write about the parochial churches in the various deaneries of Cornwall. He developed a strong interest in the history embodied in these buildings and began to study parish registers and details of ecclesiastical visitations. He then moved on to collecting private deeds, titles and legal records.

In Hayle where he lived he made the acquaintance of Henry Jenner, who had retired there in 1909. His education at Wellington, where Benson had been headmaster, was interrupted at the age of fifteen and he returned home to receive private tuition. While at home he took his interests and problems to Henry Jenner, and also to Canon Thomas Taylor, vicar of St Just-in-Penwith. Both men had a profound influence upon the young Henderson, moulding his interest in Celtic and medieval Cornwall and in Cornish parochial and ecclesiastical history. After obtaining a first class degree in Modern History, he returned to south-west Britain. He started work in 1924 as a lecturer for the University College of the South-West, the forerunner of today's University of Exeter. He had a roving brief around his native Cornwall and started to write his parochial histories of Cornish churches. In 1925 his *Cornish Church Guide* was published. In this guide, Henderson listed each of the 254 parishes in the Diocese of Truro, comprising 212 ancient parishes and 42 new ones since 1800. He identified 174 as 'evidently Celtic', of which 98 seem to have been 'important and monastic'.[68] For these Celtic foundations, he gave the dedication and the Celtic name. Henderson admitted, 'The only existing list of dedications was completed by Dr. Oliver so long ago as 1846'[69] and there had been much research done since then. His aim was eventually to write a comprehensive *Parochial History of Cornwall*, but this was never finished. He died prematurely of pleurisy in Rome in 1933. Many of his articles and lectures were published posthumously as *Essays in Cornish History* in 1935.

Henderson's scholarship had been inspired, at least in part, by the

Celtic Revivalist-Anglican relationship and his work had done much to popularize and perpetuate it. A few years earlier, in 1924, Bishop Walter Frere, similarly inspired, had begun his attempts to include 'Celtic' observances in the Anglican life of Cornwall. For example, he 'revived' the ancient pilgrimage to St Piran's Oratory at Perranporth. According to one local newspaper:

> For the first time since the ancient place of worship was restored, a service was held at St Piran's Oratory, on the sand dunes about two miles from Perranporth yesterday. The Oratory is the oldest place of Christian worship in England of which part of the four walls are standing . . . There was a very large attendance of people from the utmost limits of the county—from Kilkhampton and Penzance. The Bishop of Truro took part in the service.[70]

The jubilee of the new Anglican Diocese of Truro took place in 1927, and by now the assumption that the see was 'Celtic' was explicit. At a meeting of the Synod of Clergy that year, Canon Gilbert Doble proposed that a 'complete kalendar containing the names of all the saints honoured in Cornwall' be drawn up. This resolution was carried by an overwhelming majority and endorsed by the Bishop of Truro. A committee was established consisting of: Canon Thomas Taylor, Canon Gilbert Doble, Mr Charles Henderson, and Mr Percival Rogers. The committee consulted a variety of ancient sources, including the Exeter Martyrology of the twelfth century, the Cornish kalendars seen by William of Worcester in 1478, the notes written by Nicholas Roscarrock in the sixteenth century, the liturgical books of the dioceses of Brittany, and other documents. They also drew on the 'Celtic Calendar' which had been included for many years in the Truro Diocesan Kalendar. The committee presented is report to Bishop Walter Frere in June 1933. Tellingly, it referred to 'several well-known Celtic saints whose names we have added, such as St Patrick; as we feel they should be honoured in a Celtic diocese'.[71] Pre-eminence was given to 'five chief Saints which may be commemorated by a celebration of Holy Communion year by year on their day, throughout the diocese'. Not surprisingly, each of these was 'Celtic'. They were:

April 28. St. Winwaloe, Abbot
May 23. St. Petroc, Abbot
July 28. St. Samson, Missionary
Oct. 10. St. Paul, Aurelian, Missionary
Nov. 18. St. Piran, Missionary[72]

Earlier, in 1929, as part of this drive to emphasize the diocese's ancient 'Celticity' (and its Anglo-Catholic credentials), Bishop Frere had rehabilitated the Collegiate Church of St Endellion, which was 'part-way between a clergy-house and religious order.'[73] St Endellion was, like St Morwenna, one of the 'daughters' of Brychan, who was said to have migrated from Wales to Cornwall during the fifth or sixth centuries.[74] Her work was continued in Cornwall by a colony of priests, which was still there in the thirteenth century. The four prebendaries survived through the centuries and perhaps lay patronage of these appointments saved the collegiate church from suppression during the sixteenth century. The creation of the new Diocese of Truro provided an opportunity to give this ancient Celtic foundation a new lease of life. Bishop Frere grasped this opportunity and issued new statutes for the collegiate body.[75]

A new diocese needed a new cathedral. Truro Cathedral was the first cathedral to be built 'in England' since St Paul's Cathedral was rebuilt after the Great Fire of London. The person chosen for this task was J.A. Pearson, an architect in the Gothic and Anglo-Catholic tradition. He was also the architect of St Augustine's, Kilburn, so his style was well known. The foundation stone was laid in May 1880. The south aisle of St Mary's, Truro, was retained and incorporated into the new cathedral. Cornish materials were used wherever possible and the new structure made extensive use of granite, serpentine and copper. Although built in the Gothic style, Bishop Benson's influence was seen in various features of the new cathedral. In particular, the stalls of the honorary canons were named after the Cornish saints, and this made the cathedral different from Anglican cathedrals in England. The first eight titles of Honorary Canons were created in 1878 and by 1890 the list of Honorary Canons required two dozen stalls at the Cathedral. With the exception of St Aldhelm of Sherborne, all the names were of saints associated with Cornwall.

The 'Celtic past' of the diocese was also acknowledged in the statues and windows of the cathedral. For example, there was one window in which St Piran, St Germans and St Petroc were depicted in the 'Alleluia' victory, recorded in Constantius' *Life of St Germanus*.[76] Some artistic licence had been taken, because St Piran and St Petroc were not born at the time of St Germanus' visit to Britain in the early fifth century. However, as a group, the saints were taken as representative of 'the days of Celtic Christianity'[77] of the fifth and sixth centuries. The construction of the cathedral was completed in 1910. Although Gothic in design and construction, the cathedral added tangible and visual reminders of the diocese's Celtic heritage.

CONCLUSION

The completion of Truro Cathedral represented the triumph of Anglican renewal in Cornwall, a movement that had successfully articulated Cornwall's Celtic identity as part of its drive to create a separate Cornish diocese and had claimed common cause with the Celtic Revival in reclaiming and celebrating the Celtic past. Cornwall's High Church tradition stretched back to at least the days of Parson Hawker, and the Anglo-Catholic sympathies of much of the Anglican clergy (with their enthusiasm for Breton and Irish comparisons and their consciousness of an earlier 'Celtic Christianity') had done much to encourage the relationship between the Celtic Revival and the Anglican Church. And yet, by the early 1930s the Anglican leadership of the Celtic Revival in Cornwall was already waning. Charles Henderson died in 1933, ironically the year of the first church service in Cornish at Towednack, near St Ives. Henry Jenner died the following year and on his gravestone in the burial ground of St Uny, Lelant, near St Ives, the words of a hymn were inscribed in Cornish. Bishop Frere, who had been ill for some time, died in 1935; his successor as Bishop of Truro was the Low Church and former Methodist Joseph Hunkin. But the foundation these Anglican leaders had laid was strong enough to survive and was built upon by others, so that even today the Anglican strand of the Celtic Revival is readily apparent in Cornwall.

NOTES AND REFERENCES

1. Philip Payton, 'Paralysis and Revival: The Reconstruction of Celtic-Catholic Cornwall 1890–1945', in Ella Westland (ed.), *Cornwall: The Cultural Construction of Place*, Penzance, 1997, pp. 25–39'; Amy Hale, 'Rethinking Celtic Cornwall: An Ethnographic Approach' and 'Genesis of the Celto-Cornish Revival? L.C. Duncombe-Jewell and the Cowethas Kelto-Kernuak', in Philip Payton (ed.), *Cornish Studies: Five*, Exeter, 1997, pp. 85–99 and 100–111.
2. D.R. Williams, *Prying into Every Hole and Corner: Edward Lluyd in Cornwall in 1700*, Redruth, 1993.
3. P.A.S. Pool, *The Death of Cornish*, Cornwall, 1982.
4. P. Payton, *The Cornish Overseas*, Fowey, 1999.
5. V.E. Durkacz, *The Decline of the Celtic Languages*, Edinburgh, 1993.
6. P. Berresford, *The Cornish Language and its Literature*, London and Boston, 1974, p. 124.
7. H. Jenner, 'The Manx Language—Its Grammar, Literature, and Present State', paper read before the Philological Society, London, 18 June 1875, p. 27.
8. I.C. Zeuss, *Grammatica Celtica*, 1853.
9. G.H. Doble, *The Saints of Cornwall*, Truro, 1960, Part 1, p. 111.
10. *Journal of the Royal Institution of Cornwall (JRIC)*, 5.16–19, 1874–7, p. 15.

11. Margaret Perry, 'Revd W.S. Lach-Szyrma, Eminent Westcountryman, Honorary Cornishman', *JRIC*, New Series, 2.3–4, 2000, p. 154–67.
12. There is still a Pilchards Works in Newlyn.
13. H. Jenner, 'Traditional Relics of the Cornish Language in Mounts Bay in 1875', *Transactions of the Philiological Society*, 1876, p. 540.
14. W.S. Lach-Szyrma, *A Short History of Penzance, S. Michael's Mount, S. Ives, and the Land's End District*, London, 1878, Part 1, ch. 1.
15. Lach-Szyrma, 1878, p. 31.
16. A.M. Kent and T. Saunders, *Looking at the Mermaid: A Reader in Cornish Literature 900–1900*, London, 2000, p. 322.
17. *JRIC*, 21.69–72, 1922–5, p. 29.
18. *Journal of the Royal Cornwall Polytechnic Society [JRCPS]*, 83rd Annual Report, New Series, 3.2, 1916, p. 165.
19. *JRIC*, 1922–5, p. 29.
20. S. Winchester, *The Surgeon of Crowthorne*, London, 1999, p. 99.
21. H. Jenner, 'The History and Literature of the Ancient Cornish Language', *Journal of the British Archaeological Association*, June 1877, p. 137.
22. Jenner, June 1877, p. 139.
23. Jenner, June 1877, p. 139.
24. Jenner, June 1877, p. 145.
25. Jenner, June 1877, p. 145.
26. Jenner, June 1877, pp. 145f.
27. H. Jenner, *A Handbook of the Cornish Language*, London, 1904, Preface p. xiii.
28. Jenner, 1904, p. 7.
29. Jenner, 1904, p. ix.
30. Jenner, 1904, p. xi.
31. Jenner, 1904, p. xii.
32. Jenner, 1904, p. xv.
33. Jenner, 1904, p. xvi.
34. *JRIC*, 18.56–7, 1910–11, p. 141.
35. *JRIC*, 1910–11, p. 142.
36. *JRIC*, 1910–11, p. 143.
37. *JRIC*, 1910–11, p. 140.
38. *JRIC*, 1910–11, p. 140.
39. *JRIC*, 1910–11, p. 145.
40. Doble, 1960, Part 1, p. 112.
41. *JRIC*, 1922–5, p. 29.
42. *JRIC*, 1922–5, p. 113–45.
43. *JRIC*, 1922–5, p. 123.
44. *JRIC*, 1922–5, p. 23f.
45. R. Morton Nance, *The Cledry Plays*, Penzance, 1956, Preface (no page number).
46. *Old Cornwall*, April 1925, p. 6.
47. *Old Cornwall*, April 1926, p. 42.
48. R.S Hawker, *Footprints of Former Men in Far Cornwall*, 1870, repub. London, 1948, p. 1.

49. Hawker, 1870 and 1948, p. 6.
50. *JRIC*, 6.20–3, 1878–81 pp. 16, 18.
51. *JRIC*, 15.48–9, 1902–3, p. 257
52. R.M. Catling and J.P. Rodgers, *G.H. Doble: A Memoir and A Bibliography*, Exeter, c.1950, p. 2.
53. Catling and Rogers, c.1950, p. 4.
54. *JRIC*, 19.58–61, 1912–14, p. 445.
55. *JRIC*, 1912–14, pp. 446–55.
56. See A. Langdon's article on 'Inscribed Stones' in 'Early Christian Monuments' in *A History of Cornwall in Four Volumes* (in The *Victoria History of the Counties of England—Cornwall*), London, 1906, pp. 407–9.
57. *JRIC*, 4.13–15, 1871–3, p. xciv.
58. *JRIC*, 9.32–5, 1886–9, p. 502.
59. *JRIC*, 20.62–8, 1915–21, p. 386.
60. W.S. Lach-Szyrma, *Letter to Right Hon. W.E. Gladstone M.P.*, 1869, p. 8.
61. Lach-Szyrma, 1869, p. 20.
62. A.L. Rowse, *The Little Land of Cornwall*, Gloucester, 1986, p. 278.
63. A.B. Donaldson, *The Bishopric of Truro: The First Twenty-five Years*, London, 1902, p. 51.
64. *JRIC*, 1878–81, p. 370.
65. A.C. Benson, *The Life of Edward White Benson*, 2 vols, London, 1899, Vol. 1, p. 428.
66. Donaldson, 1902, p. 190, citing the *Journal of Theological Studies*, 2.5, October 1900, p. 34.
67. Benson, 1899, Vol. 1, p. 425.
68. C. Henderson, *Cornish Church Guide*, Truro, 1925, p. 18.
69. Henderson, 1925, p. 18.
70. *Royal Cornwall Gazette*, 13 August 1924.
71. *Cornish Church Kalendar*, 1933, no page number.
72. *Cornish Church Kalendar*, Preface, no page number.
73. E. Stark, *Saint Endellion*, Redruth, 1983, p. 29.
74. C. Thomas, *And Shall These Mute Stones Speak?*, Cardiff, 1994, p. 151.
75. Stark, 1983, p. 31.
76. F.R. Hoare, *The Western Fathers*, London, 1954, p. 96.
77. Donaldson, 1902, p. 392.

TRURO: DIOCESE AND CITY

John Beckett and David Windsor

INTRODUCTION

The founding in 1877 of the Diocese of Truro brought to an end a long campaign to establish a separate identity for Cornwall in Anglican ecclesiastical matters. It also affected the status of the new see town. While the diocese was intended to be the territory of Cornwall, the cathedral was placed in Truro. In August 1877, by letters patent issued in the name of Queen Victoria, Truro became a city. The background to these events lay in a particular conjunction of circumstances in mid-Victorian England, of which Truro was a major beneficiary.

The Church of England had its roots firmly in rural England, and it was not until the 1830s and the formation of the Ecclesiastical Commission that it began the long process of catching up with a rapidly urbanizing and industrializing society. One of the questions it had to tackle was the matter of diocesan provision, and the process of re-drawing the geography of 'Anglican England' began with the foundation of the dioceses of Ripon and Manchester in 1836 and 1847 respectively. From these beginnings came a great deal of discussion about other new dioceses, and in south-west Britain the debate was couched in terms which reflected the prevailing thinking of the time. Cornwall, it was argued from the 1840s, should be a separate diocese, not simply because of its population and size, but also because it had been a separate diocese in the past, and because, it was argued, the Cornish were ethnically, culturally, socially and occupationally different from the people of Devon with whom they were currently in the same diocese. The debate was initiated by Bishop Henry Phillpotts of Exeter, who called in 1842 for the division of his massive diocese, which covered the Isles of Scilly in addition to Devon and Cornwall.

From the mid-1850s Cornwall's case was developed in historical, ethnic, cultural and geographical terms. The historical claim was that the see of St Germans, which had been lost in 1050 when the dioceses of Crediton and St Germans were amalgamated to form the diocese of Exeter, should be re-established. The ethnic and cultural arguments stressed that Cornwall was 'different'. The differences included the 'Celticity' of the Cornish, by contrast with the supposed Saxon stock east of the River Tamar. This distinctiveness was regarded as justification in its own right of the need for Cornwall to have its own bishop.[1]

TOWARDS A CORNISH SEE

A second issue debated during the 1850s and 1860s was the location of the see: should it be in Bodmin, Newquay, St Austell, St Germans, or Truro, all of which were suggested at one time or another. Among the front runners, Bodmin had the more impressive church, Truro had the land on which to build a cathedral and was on the main railway line, and St Germans could argue its case on the grounds that it was the see of the historic diocese. Newquay had the advantage that in 1854 Dr Samuel Edward Walker, who was incumbent of nearby St Columb Major and owned the advowson, offered his church, rectory and endowment for the new bishopric.[2]

The idea of a new diocese was taken up in a practical form in C.J. Frewen's unsuccessful private members bill in 1846, and more seriously in 1861 when Lord Lyttleton introduced the first of several unsuccessful bills aimed at promoting an increase in the episcopate. Lyttleton's abortive 1867 bill for expanding the episcopate specifically named Truro along with St Albans and Southwell as potential new sees,[3] but it was not successful and Bishop Phillpotts died in 1869 with nothing achieved. His successor, Frederick Temple, was just as enthusiastic about the idea of dividing the diocese, but it was only with the return of a sympathetic Conservative government in 1874 that Anglican diocesan sub-division became a practical, as opposed to a theoretical issue. After decades of arid debate it was a welcome boost to the Church of England when R.A. Cross, the Home Secretary, expressed his willingness to accept a limited expansion of the episcopate. Once this news reached the South-West, a meeting was called in Plymouth to press for the division of the diocese, and a deputation went to Downing Street on 28 May 1875. The government assured the delegates that it would sponsor legislation, but it stressed that funding of the see would have to be raised locally. Consequently, the Diocesan Conference in November 1875 was told of the financial needs, and a committee was appointed to raise subscriptions. It met for the first time early in 1876, when Lady Rolle of Exmouth, a Cornish-woman, reputedly offered £40,000 towards the endowment. Bishop Temple began raising funds among the clergy of the diocese, and the Additional Home Bishoprics Fund, founded in February 1876, offered grants totalling £3,000.[4]

In 1875 and 1876 Home Secretary Cross sponsored two bills for the promotion of new dioceses. These were to be centred on St Albans and Truro. In the Truro bill St Mary's, the parish church of Truro, was named as the cathedral.[5] The bill received the Royal Assent on 11 August 1876. With the funding already safely in place Truro caught up with St Albans, where money was more of a problem. The Order in Council naming Truro as the see of the new diocese was made on 15 December 1876, and both dioceses came into being in 1877. Dr Edward White Benson, nominated to be the first Bishop of Truro, was enthroned in May 1878.

TRURO A CITY?

The new diocese, and the subsequent campaign to fund a suitable cathedral, came to symbolize a new and assertive Cornish identity which was little less than a renewal of Cornish patriotism.[6] It also had significant implications for Truro itself; indeed, it was assumed in Cornwall that diocesan status meant that Truro would now be a city, and that the Order in Council establishing the diocese 'virtually created Truro a City, ecclesiastical and historical evidence are alike in favour of this deduction'.[7] The town clerk of Truro actually referred at a meeting of the corporation to the 'City of Truro', but Alderman Heard admitted to being so uncertain as to whether Truro really was a city that 'he had taken some little trouble to look into the matter, and he found that Manchester was not made a city until six years after the See was created, and then by a special order in Council; and that at the present time Ripon, although a See, was only a borough town'.[8] In fact Ripon was already a city.

No one actually knew, and the issue was discussed in the town through the winter of 1876–7. Some thought Truro was now a city merely through the appointment of a bishop and the nomination of a cathedral. Others believed a separate Order in Council would be needed. Legal opinion seemed to suggest that simply by having a bishopric Truro was a city, but the town clerk thought it needed something more tangible.[9] Nor was this uncertainty surprising. City status in England was generally considered to be linked to the posses-sion of an Anglican cathedral, and many thought that this should, therefore, apply to Cornwall and Truro too. However, since most Anglican dioceses had been formed either before 1133 or in the 1540s there was little recent experience to suggest whether city and cathedral were always linked. Ripon, the first 'modern', i.e. nineteenth-century diocese, assumed it was a city but eventually had to confirm the appellation through the 1865 City of Ripon Act. Manchester, created a new diocese in 1847, finally achieved the coveted city status in 1853. There were no other precedents. Was city status automatic on the creation of the see, or did it have to be applied for and, if the latter, what was the procedure? No one really knew.

Truro's town clerk approached Colonel Sir J. McGarell Hogg, one of the borough's MPs, who wrote to the Home Office on 5 March 1877 asking what steps needed to be taken 'so that Truro may be designated a City?'. Hogg reflected the uncertainty in Truro. 'Some think that the Bishop being appointed, the name of City follows as a matter of course, but the precedent of the City of Manchester shows that a petition must be presented. Will you kindly let me know what is to be done.' The Home Office informed Hogg that the town council needed to petition the Queen.[10] Hogg passed the information to the town clerk, and on 3 April the mayor read out a letter at a meeting of the corporation 'relative to the conversion of Truro into a City'. Nothing further was done immediately, because the corporation now became concerned about the likely cost. The town clerk was commissioned to find out via the borough MPs what the potential outlay would be, and the mayor wrote to his opposite number in Manchester.[11]

While this research was in progress, Benson was consecrated Bishop of Truro in St Paul's Cathedral on 25 April, and enthroned in St Mary's Cathedral on 1 May 1877. The town council debated the city status issue at length when it met again on 8 May. The town clerk and mayor between them projected an outlay of £150, and the town clerk reported Hogg's findings about procedures. The general view prevailed that they should proceed. Alderman Smith argued that although Truro 'might practically be a City now, he really thought they ought to do whatever might be necessary to have the town erected into a City, and he should be very happy to move that an Order in Council be applied for'. He did not believe the corporation would consider the cost excessive, and consequently he moved that 'such steps as were necessary should be taken to make Truro a City', and that a committee should be appointed to raise the required £150. The motion was seconded by Alderman Clyma, who thought that 'if the Corporation were to neglect this opportunity of making Truro a City, they would become the laughing-stock of the whole county'. The motion was passed unanimously, and Alderman Smith joined the mayor (J.G. Chilcott), two other aldermen and four councillors, on the committee.

Their brief was to take 'the necessary steps' in order have Truro made a city.[12]

The committee now received some unexpected support when Mr S. Tucker, a Cornishman who was Rouge Croix Pursuivant at the Herald's Office, offered to undertake the legal work required free of charge and so reduce the costs. Consequently, the corporation now went ahead and drew up a petition, and when it next met on 20 June the deputy town clerk read aloud the petition to the meeting. Alderman Chirgwin moved that the mayor should sign it on behalf of himself and the burgesses.[13] The memorial was submitted by Tucker to the Home Office on 22 June.[14]

When Tucker had received no response by 21 July he wrote again to the Home Office. He was, he commented, 'anticipating from the precedent of Manchester, a favourable answer to that petition', and consequently the authorities in Truro were making preparations and would, not surprisingly, like an early decision on their petition. Queen Victoria approved grants of city status to Truro (and to St Albans) on 6 August 1877, and letters patent were dated 28 August.[15] When the council met on 19 September 'the mayor placed on the table the Letters Patent constituting this Borough a City'. Although in his view 'outside Truro it would be said that this was not of much importance. . . . He certainly thought it was a matter on which they ought greatly to congratulate themselves.' As the letters patent had cost only £90, rather than the anticipated £150—largely because Tucker had given his professional assistance free of charge—the committee felt able to recommend that this sum should be paid out of corporation funds. A large majority supported the Chairman of the City Committee who made this proposal, although one curmudgeonly councillor complained that it was a waste of money and 'it would be better if they renewed their subscriptions which had been withdrawn from the Royal Cornwall Infirmary and Truro Dispensary'.[16]

However, the person who really felt put out was the town clerk, Mr Cock. He clearly thought it was his job to undertake the work of obtaining letters patent, and the fact that the corporation had seized on the offer from Mr Tucker—who also offered his services to St Albans and was turned down—seemed to be a vote of no confidence in his abilities. Indeed, he considered it 'an insult', especially as St Albans had paid no more for their letters patent than Truro. 'Had the Corporation lost confidence in their town clerk?', asked Mr Cock, 'If so the sooner they got someone else to fill the office the better.' And for good measure he added that 'He considered it a slur on him as Town Clerk that he, as a man, could not obtain that which the Town Clerk of St Alban's had'. This outburst put something of a dampener on proceedings, but the mayor assured his town clerk that there had been 'no intention whatever to offend Mr Cock', and the matter was then dropped.[17]

When the corporation met again on 9 November the minutes referred to the City Council of Truro rather than the Borough Council. The outgoing mayor, Mr Chilcott, told the corporation of his efforts since September to have a new coat of arms for the town prepared, and his satisfaction in having received the relevant letters patent on the previous evening. Mr Tucker of the Herald's Office had again been consulted, although apparently this time without offending the town clerk, and the bishop had suggested an appropriate motto. The costs, £56, were met by the two MPs for Truro, and after Chilcott was thanked for his hard work, the town clerk was commissioned 'to obtain a proper seal of the new City'.[18] This in turn was used for the first time beneath the mayor's signature at the council meeting on 16 January 1878.

CLOSING THE LOOPHOLE

The events of 1877 were remarkable in other ways. Truro was the first new Victorian diocese in which the cathedral was not regarded as a key issue. Ripon and Manchester had been selected because they had collegiate churches. As a writer in the *Church Quarterly Review* noted in the 1870s, 'we may generally say that the schemes of some twenty or thirty years back were rather more solicitous as to a sufficient cathedral than more modern reforms', adding that when Ripon and Manchester were formed 'the choice no doubt was determined by the presence of the two collegiate churches, with their surviving chapters; though in the case of Manchester, the place itself had irresistible claims'.[19] St Albans was uncontentious because its abbey church of Norman origin was the obvious cathedral. Truro was the first diocese to be created which lacked what was considered to be an adequate cathedral. The same problem occurred three years later with the formation of the new diocese of Liverpool. Truro and Liverpool adopted a similar approach to the issue by building a cathedral. The Prince of Wales, Duke of Cornwall, laid the foundation stone of the new Truro Cathedral in May 1880, although it took another thirty years to build at a total cost of £120,000. Considering that it had so recently been necessary to raise £70,000 for the endowment of the see, this was a remarkable achievement, at least partly inspired by the Celtic Revival and the idea that the new cathedral, with its Breton ambience, represented a statement of Cornwall's patriotic zeal.

In raising Truro and St Albans to city status on becoming the sees of new dioceses, the Home Office began to have doubts about a 'policy' of, in effect, automatic promotion, but the issue was defused when the next two new dioceses, Liverpool and Newcastle, were created in 1880 and 1882 since neither caused it real problems. Southwell (1884) did not apply, and Wakefield was granted city status in 1888, but thereafter the door was closed. In the twentieth century no town, on becoming a diocesan see, has automatically been raised to city status, although in a few cases this has followed in time. But Blackburn, Chelmsford and Guildford are among modern diocesan sees which are not cities. Truro was a precedent because no one really knew what, if any, policy there was, but by automatically giving city status to towns such as Truro and St Albans the Home Office grew concerned that new industrial towns such as Birmingham, Sheffield and Leeds were being unfairly discriminated against simply because they did not have an Anglican cathedral. It closed this particular loophole almost before it was fully open.

CONCLUSION

Celtic Revivalism gave the Cornwall diocesan question a head of steam in the middle decades of the nineteenth century, which was largely about self-determination in local government. Truro was the passive beneficiary of this movement because simply by being named as the see, despite (at the time) its perceived lack of an appropriate cathedral, it was able to claim and then retain the status of city. Slightly bizarrely, city status was almost removed from Truro less than a century after the town had been promoted. Local government reorganization in 1974 would have led to city status being lost but for the fact that an application was made for the title to be reconferred as of 1 April. On 25 July that year, Princess Anne visited Truro and handed over the new letters patent.[20]

NOTES AND REFERENCES

1. P.S. Morrish, 'History, Celticism and Propaganda in the Formation of the Diocese of Truro', *Southern History*, 5, 1983, pp. 238–66; A. Burns, *The Diocesan Revival in the Church of England, c.1800–1870*, Oxford, 1999, p. 201.
2. Philip Payton, *Cornwall*, Fowey, 1996, p. 223.
3. O. Chadwick, *The Victorian Church*, Part 2, London, 1970, p. 344.
4. M. Brown, '*A Century for Cornwall*': The Diocese of Truro 1877–1977, Truro, 1976, pp. 18–20; H.M. Brown, *The Story of Truro Cathedral*, Redruth, 1977.
5. Brown, 1976, p. 20.
6. Philip Payton, *The Making of Modern Cornwall: Historical Experience and the Persistence of 'Difference'*, Redruth, 1992.
7. *Royal Cornwall Gazette*, 16 December 1876, 23 December 1876.

8. *Royal Cornwall Gazette*, 23 December 1876.
9. *Royal Cornwall Gazette*, 9 February 1877.
10. Public Record Office, (PRO), HO 45/9432/62565.
11. Cornwall Record Office (CRO), B/TRU/99/3, Corporation of Truro Minute Book, 1862–1878.
12. *Royal Cornwall Gazette*, 11 May 1877.
13. CRO B/TRU/99/3, Corporation of Truro Minute Book, 1862–1878; *Royal Cornwall Gazette*, 22 June 1877.
14. PRO HO 45/9432/62565.
15. PRO HO 45/9432/62565.
16. *Royal Cornwall Gazette*, 21 September 1877.
17. *Royal Cornwall Gazette*, 21 September 1877.
18. *Royal Cornwall Gazette*, 16 November 1877; CRO B/TRU/99/3, Corporation of Truro Minute Book, 1862–1878
19. *Church Quarterly Review*, October 1876, p. 210.
20. W.J. Burley, *City of Truro 1877–1977*, Truro, 1977, p. 63.

WHERE CORNISH WAS
SPOKEN AND WHEN:
A PROVISIONAL SYNTHESIS

Matthew Spriggs

*I may seem too conjectural to those who will make no
allowance for the deficiencies of History, nor be satisfied with
anything but evident Truths; but, where there is no Certainty to
be obtained, Probabilities must suffice; and Conjectures are no
faults, but when they are either advanced as real Truths, or too
copiously pursued, or peremptorily insisted upon as decisive.*
(William Borlase[1])

INTRODUCTION

Roman colonial rule in much of Britain from the mid-first century
AD represented language contact as well as major changes to material
culture and many other aspects of life. Latin, however, did not replace
the Brittonic Celtic language of the Romanized area, although borrowings did occur. In contrast, Anglo-Saxon colonialism represented a
massive and rapid case of language shift over much of England during
the fifth to seventh centuries to what became Old English. Some would
argue that Norman colonialism nearly represented another language
shift to Norman French, but even though that did not in the end
happen, Norman influence did cause significant contact-induced
language change in English. One must not forget Viking settlement in
the ninth and tenth centuries as another historical process having
linguistic effects. This was much more localized, however, although
certainly significant in affected areas.[2]

It is interesting that only one of these colonial episodes led to complete language replacement, the language shift from a Brittonic Celtic language to Old English.[3] This took place extremely rapidly over much of what is now England, with very few Brittonic words entering Old English at all. Although in local areas there may have been the slaughter sometimes boasted about in the *Anglo-Saxon Chronicle*, most authors now discount this as a general explanation of the situation.[4]

The importance of the completeness of this shift from Brittonic to Old English has perhaps not been fully appreciated. It fits well, however, within the evidence of conformism seen in other aspects of Anglo-Saxon culture.[5] Hines discusses how the use of material culture to symbolize group identity spread from its Saxon source on the continent to other Germanic-speaking areas such as those of the Angles and Jutes in about the mid-fifth century. While all these separate group identities were then carried over into Britain at that time, he also points out that there is some evidence of hybridization with aspects of sub-Roman British material culture during the earliest period of migration, telling us something about relationships between natives and colonists.[6] This aside, what differences there were between the colonizing groups soon came to be much less clearly marked in material symbolism. As Hines puts it, 'England by now existed structurally, even if conceptually its time were yet to come'. In material culture there was a 'marked shift towards uniformity around the late sixth century, particularly in art and dress styles where regional diversity had formerly prevailed'.[7] The different Germanic languages of these groups also began to reconverge at a surprisingly early period to form Old English.

Hines suggests that a stronger sub-Roman British ethnic identity arose in resistance to this new 'English' ethnic identity. This was transmitted both through symbolically powerful material culture items and perhaps through the medium of heroic poetry. He asks 'how justified we might be in proposing that where material culture was a primary medium for the expression of identity in the Germanic world, language and discourse served that function in the Celtic British one?'.[8]

Language and poetry clearly served as a primary medium for expressing identity in the English world as well, however. This, to me, is the significance of the 'purity' of Old English, with virtually no borrowing from the native British tongue. The defining criterion of being English was linguistic: speaking Old English (or dialects of it) without any trace of a British substrate. Such total language replacement in a short period of time could well have to do with a deliberate colonial policy of conformity which would have encouraged or forced people to shift language.

We know from the laws of Ine of the late seventh century that

British subjects of Anglo-Saxon kings were treated in a discriminatory manner compared with English ones.[9] But by that time who were the British? The definition must surely have been essentially linguistic. Language shift in this case represented a shift in ethnicity. The British were not genocidally dispersed; by language shift they too became English.

THE CASE OF CORNWALL

When we leave England, however, and cross the River Tamar, that most long-standing of European political borders, to Cornwall, we find a different situation. Here, in contrast, the Brittonic language continued to be spoken for nearly a thousand years after becoming subject to the Anglo-Saxon kingdom of Wessex. This contrast is interesting in itself. Cornwall was conquered later than most of what is now called England, apart from Cumbria[10] and the Welsh Marches where the language also survived for a period after conquest. By then the migration period was over, its end marked by fundamental social as well as material culture changes in the late sixth century.[11] The more fluidly organized migrant elites of earlier periods were at that time coalescing into the groupings that became the formal leadership of the Anglo-Saxon kingdoms.

The subjection of Cornwall occurred initially in the ninth century and more decisively in the tenth century, with Athelstan's expulsion of the Cornish from Exeter and his fixing of the boundary between the Britons and English at the Tamar perhaps in 936 AD. To describe this event as 'ethnic cleansing' might seem exaggerated, and the report of it could just be another example of the common Anglo-Saxon hyperbole about how they dealt with the Britons they met.[12] If the early twelfth-century chronicler William of Malmesbury, who provides our only surviving account of this event presumably based on now lost sources, is to be trusted, however, then this local solution to the British problem was indeed a radical one: 'Urbem igitur illam quam contaminatae gentis repurgio defaecaverat . . .' (Having cleansed the city of its defilement by wiping out that filthy race . . .).[13]

We can only be thankful that Athelstan chose not to attempt this tactic beyond the Tamar, but instead used more conventional colonial administrative procedures. He, if Finberg's interpretation echoed by Padel is to be accepted, even restored the ancient boundary of the Tamar to the Cornish, although Anglo-Saxon colonization had already proceeded some way beyond it.[14] Archaeological evidence suggests that the Tamar was indeed the long-standing boundary of a distinctly Cornish identity going back to Roman times or even earlier.[15] The late conquest of Cornwall—whether complete or initially leaving a client state still ruled by local leaders is debated—doubtless has much to do with the survival of the language until the modern period.[16]

Anglo-Saxon domination of England was secure by the ninth century against an indigenous population who had overwhelmingly by then become Anglo-Saxon in speech and ethnicity. The threat in the tenth century was not really a few Cornish speaking an alien language but the Vikings who spoke a much more closely related one. And so, once subdued decisively and no longer a potential Viking bridgehead, the Cornish were largely left alone linguistically and, some would argue, administratively as well.[17]

THE DECLINE OF THE CORNISH LANGUAGE

In the end, of course, the language did decline and die out. Why? It is hard to go past the ten to seventeen reasons given by William Scawen in various manuscript versions of his great work on the decline of the language, *Antiquities Cornu-Britannick; Or Observations on an Ancient Manuscript written in the Cornish Language*, written between 1678 and 1689.[18] Scawen noted factors of varying weight, among them:

1. Loss of contact between Cornwall and Brittany with the Reformation in Britain in the sixteenth century. These languages are very close indeed and contact across the Channel was common until that time.
2. The cessation of miracle plays in the Cornish language, performances probably being suppressed between about 1575 and 1600 as in the rest of the country when Puritanism began to take hold.[19] Stagings of these religious dramas were clearly events that brought together people united by a common language and tradition. As Scawen put it: 'This was a great means to keep in use the tongue with delight and admiration, and it continued also friendship and good correspondency of the people'.[20] They were thus key performances of Cornish culture by actors and spectators alike.[21]
3. The Cornish gentry abandoned the language and became Anglicized. This seems to have occurred particularly in Tudor times, perhaps paralleling processes in Wales at the same time. The language then became stigmatized as low class.
4. To quote Scawen:
   > The coming in of strangers of all sorts upon us, artificers, traders, home born and foreigners, whom our great commodities of tin (more profitable to others than ourselves) and fishing, have invited to us to converse with, and often to stay with us; these all, as they could not easily learn our tongue, for

which they could not find any guide or direction . . . and such, for the novelty sake thereof, people were more ready to receive than to communicate ours to any improvement to them.[22]

More recently, Halliday put this point nicely:

The discovery of the New World led to the discovery of Cornwall by the London merchants, by the adventurers, and all those interested in the exploitation of the Indies, as the struggle for the New World and the consequent war with Spain led to the development of the magnificent natural harbours along the southern coast of the county. From being an almost forgotten extremity of the island, Cornwall found itself at the very centre of mercantile, maritime and military activities, and the slumbering centuries of isolation were at an end.[23]

5. The failure to translate the Bible into Cornish at the Reformation is another factor often cited. It is one always invoked in relation to the preservation of the Welsh language.[24] The lack of much other literature in Cornish as the world entered the age of printing is also clearly important.

Scawen also mentioned further causes such as the loss of the Duchy of Cornwall records, in his estimation presumably containing a wealth of Cornish language material, during the Civil War, a general malaise or apathy among the population ('A general stupidity may be observed to be in the whole county'),[25] a lack of interest in the language among the learned, the spread of English church and place-names, the proximity of English-speaking Devon, and 'foreign marriages' among the gentry, that is marriages outside of Cornwall.[26] Other causes which can be adduced include the rapid spread of English-language schooling around 1500 AD. As Orme has noted: 'Schools have played important roles in the decline of small indigenous languages in Post-Medieval Europe'.[27]

WHERE CORNISH WAS SPOKEN AND WHEN

There are quite different views current as to where Cornish was spoken at any particular time. Earlier scholars looking at the issue include the early revivalists Henry Jenner and Robert Morton Nance. Jenner believed that 'until at least the 15th century the Tamar was the general boundary of English and Cornish' and elsewhere noted that in East Cornwall 'the language has been dead for three centuries'.[28] In 1939 Nance opined that Old Cornish had been spoken over the whole of Cornwall at one time, Middle Cornish of the fourteenth and fifteenth centuries had been spoken over about half of Cornwall, with Late Cornish of the sixteenth century onwards being limited to only a quarter of Cornwall at best. All this was based on place-name evidence.[29] Elsewhere he is quoted as saying that in north-east Cornwall the language 'could hardly have been spoken there much later than 1000 AD'.[30] Henderson's opinion was that: 'It is convenient for philological purposes, to divide Cornwall by a line from Padstow through Bodmin to Fowey'.[31]

The first detailed consideration of the issue, however, was by Wakelin.[32] He saw an early and rapid decline of the language back to the Fowey–Padstow line by about 1100 AD and beyond Truro by 1500 AD. His evidence was based to some extent on spot references attesting to Cornish speech, but mainly on sound changes in place-names that can be tracked as occurring at particular times. The examples he uses are *-nt* to *-ns* (e.g. Trewent, 1086 > Trewens, 1300) and *-d* to *-s* (often *-d* is *-t* in place-names: Renti, 1086 > Rensy, 1387) occurring (he believed) soon after 1100 AD, and *-n* to *-dn* (Tewynnak, 1523 > Towidnacke, 1659) which usually occurred in place-names from around 1575.[33] In support of his 1100 AD boundary he quoted the opinion of Henderson cited above. Henderson had ventured no date, however, for when this formed a language boundary.[34]

In contrast and quoted often is a 1986 map by George, based in large part on an unpublished conference paper by Holmes and reproduced here (Figure 1). Holmes gave evidence from his own studies which backs up the map's 'isobars', particularly for eastern Cornwall. This is mainly based on the same sound changes in place-names showing *-nt* to *-ns* and *-d* to *-s* used by Wakelin and thought to have occurred about 1100–1200 AD according to Holmes. The difference is that he found many examples of the changes to the east of the Padstow–Fowey line examples cited by Wakelin.[35] Thus Wakelin's 1100 AD line becomes the Holmes–George 1500 AD line and his 1500 AD line becomes their 1650 AD line. The published paper by George in which the adjusted map occurs is more focused on how many people spoke Cornish at any particular time, and thus the actual evidence on which the map was produced has never been aired in published form. George, while broadly accepting Holmes's conclusions, does note that the arguments concerning the implications of the 1100–1200 AD sound changes for where Cornish was generally spoken have not received 'general acceptance'.[36] What appears to be an updated version of the same map appears in a 1989 French publication by Abalain.[37]

More recently, Williams has suggested that instead of the slow but steady retreat of Cornish represented by the Holmes–George map, there was an early decline in late Saxon times but then a resurgence in the twelfth and thirteenth centuries with the arrival of Normans and Bretons in Cornwall. In the eastern part there would then have been a

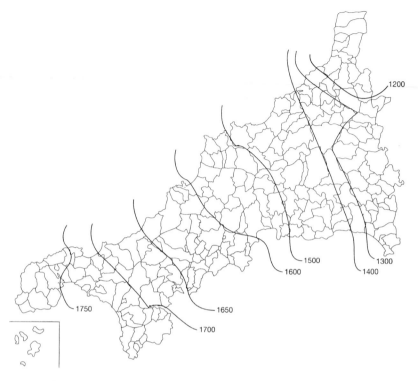

1. *The Holmes–George 1986 map of Cornish language retreat.*

language shift back to Cornish from English. He concludes that 'Cornish was spoken by a proportion of the population at least as far as the Tamar until the fifteenth century, if not until the Reformation'. It would then have suffered a catastrophic decline in less than a hundred years except in the far west beyond Truro.[38] His argument is based on a different interpretation of both when the sound changes occurred and a theory of dialectal variation between West and East Cornwall. Thus *-n* to *-dn* never happened in East Cornwall because it occurred only in the western dialect of Cornish, rather than because Cornish was not spoken there at the time that this sound change occurred. He dates this sound change 'not very much later' than 1250, rather than the usual date of around 1550–1600 based on place-names and other evidence.[39]

Williams has been roundly criticized for his interpretations by Dunbar and George, who dispute almost every one of the ideas he presents. No additional published support for Williams's ideas on language distribution has come from any other linguist as far as I am aware.[40] Along the way Dunbar and George produce a new map indicative of where Cornish may have been spoken at particular periods, based this time on the structure of place-names in particular areas. This produces a tripartite division of Cornwall with two early English-speaking enclaves in the east.[41] Padel suggested that these areas became English-speaking in the eighth and/or ninth centuries and represent a pre-Athelstan English migration across the Tamar.[42] The second major division with initial Cornish settlement names and English names of the separate parts of the settlement stretches nearly to the Fowey–Padstow line. In fact it probably represents a better approximation of the long-standing language boundary than earlier characterizations do, such as Henderson (quoted above) and the Holmes–George 1500 AD boundary. Cornish primary and secondary names predominate to the west of that boundary. The boundary seems so sharp that it must represent a significant still-stand in language shift to English, one perhaps lasting some hundreds of years. The names they discuss were those recorded between 1250 and 1550, although the primary evidence is not presented.[43]

SOURCES FOR A LINGUISTIC GEOGRAPHY OF CORNISH

Linguistic and historical evidence for constructing such maps can come from:

1. Linguistic innovations reflected in place-name changes. Where the linguistic innovation has occurred, say a change from an -*nt* ending to -*ns*, then the language is thought to have been still spoken in that area at the time the innovation took place. The problem here is a seeming lack of such innovations in the period between about 1200 and 1500 AD.[44] In addition, there is as yet no definitive survey available of where such changes occurred. One has to use what are at present only partial and potentially misleading data.

2. Attestations of Cornish speech in historical records. I have been looking at these for the period up to 1800 (see Appendix 1). These are in the form of pleas by priests who say they want to give up their benefices as they cannot understand their Cornish-speaking parishioners, travellers' reports from the 1530s onwards on stating where Cornish was still heard, Consistory Court evidence that someone called someone in church 'whore bitch in English and not in Cornowok' (thus suggesting Cornish as a still-living tongue used for less heated speech), or lists of parishes where Cornish was still spoken during its final decline. Although 1800 AD is conventionally given here—following Nance—as the date by which use of Cornish as community language had died out, Lyon has recently collated a significant body of evidence to suggest the

possibility that the language was still in use in pockets until about 1850 or slightly later.[45]

3. Surname evidence, such as the practice of people taking their father's Christian name as their surname, Cornish language descriptive and occupation surnames, and two-part surnames made up of two Christian names.[46] These latter names may have particular significance for the survival of Cornish language and other distinctly Celtic cultural practices. Padel had earlier discussed the distribution of personal names containing the Cornish word *plu* 'parish'. These are found from about 1450 to 1550 to the west of Padstow. The concentration of such names in documents from St Columb Major allowed him to suggest that Cornish was still spoken there in the mid-sixteenth century.[47] In addition, surnames too may show the sound shifts found in placenames. Thus the surname usually recorded as Chegwin or Chigwen is recorded as Chigwin and Chegwidden in 1641 in Sithney, and somewhat felicitously Pengwyn or Pengwen becomes Pengwidden in Gwennap in 1664.[48]

4. Records of borrowings into recent Cornish dialects of English of Cornish language words, indicating that the language was spoken later in those areas.[49]

Any map is going to represent a simplification of the real linguistic situation. The 'isobars' produced do not mean that no one spoke Cornish at that time to the east of them, or that no one spoke English to the west of them. They are generalizations showing areas where Cornish-speaking could be generally found. By about 1700 at the latest there would have been no monolingual Cornish speakers, and even in the westernmost peninsula of Penwith many could have been found who spoke no Cornish at all. Some have suggested that the towns were largely English-speaking from an early date,[50] but the late retention of alternative Cornish names for several of the more important centres such as Bodmin (Bosvenna), Padstow (Lodenek), Fowey (Couwhath—perhaps a misprint for Fouwhath?) and Helston (Hellas) suggests that enough Cornish-speakers had reason to go to those centres that such names were retained in memory.[51]

It may be that fishermen moving from port to port kept Cornish going longer in coastal areas after it had died out in the more inland districts along the main road route to the west, via Launceston, Bodmin, Truro, Camborne, Redruth, St Erth and on to Penzance in Madron parish.[52] Perhaps the relatively late attestation of Cornish in Minster parish in the east, incorporating the fishing port of Boscastle, in 1349 and 1355[53] was because of regular contact by sea with Cornish-speaking ports further west such as Lodenek?

Before presenting a provisional synthesis of the current evidence for where Cornish was spoken and when, there are two perennially popular linguistic issues which need to be addressed. The first is the suggestion that Cornish was spoken during the medieval period in parts of South Devon, and the second concerns the claim that John Moreman, the vicar of Menheniot in the east of Cornwall, was ministering to a Cornish-speaking flock at the time of the Reformation in the 1530s.

WAS CORNISH SPOKEN IN DEVON?

The answer to this baldly stated question is clearly a qualified yes, in that prior to the Anglo-Saxon conquest of eastern Dumnonia during the seventh and eighth centuries, the language of Devon would have been a form of Brittonic similar to that from which historical Cornish subsequently derived. But how long did British speech survive in Devon? On the evidence of place-names, not long enough to be recorded. For instance, there are something like 1,300 place-names of the form *tre-* in Cornwall, but only 3 in Devon.[54] Other Celtic place-names are rare. The Cornish expelled by Athelstan from Exeter would have been identifiable by their language (see above), but whether any other British communities survived in Devon by that late date is unknown. Todd notes of Celtic place-names in the fertile South Hams area of south-west Devon that 'there are virtually none'.[55]

Despite this, there has been an oft-repeated claim that Cornish survived in the South Hams area between the Plym and the Dart until the fourteenth or sixteenth centuries. Polwhele wrote in 1806 that 'The Cornish language was current in a part of the South-hams, (which I have called East-Cornwall) in the time of Edward the First; and long after, in all the vicinities of the Tamar. In Cornwall, it was universally spoken.' He had earlier opined that although English had become fashionable among the Devonian upper classes, 'the inferior classes adhered firmly to their old vernacular tongue. Not that the Cornu-British was abandoned by every Devonian of rank or education: It was certainly spoken in Devonshire by persons of distinction, long after the present [Saxon] period.'[56]

There was some discussion of the issue of Cornish speech in Devon in the pages of *The Western Antiquary* during 1882, when E.S. Radford asked for corroboration of the assertion by one 'G.A.' (possibly Grant Allen) in *Cornhill Magazine* of November 1881 'that Welsh was spoken in remote parts of Devonshire as late as the reign of Elizabeth'. W.S. Lach-Szyrma also asked for clarification of the South Hams statement, but nothing was forthcoming in response to either of these questions which extended the trail back past Polwhele.[57] The source of G.A.'s statement is almost certainly Isaac Taylor's 1865 *Words and Places*, where he states: 'In remote parts of Devon the ancient Cymric speech feebly lingered on till the reign of Elizabeth'.[58] He does not reference Polwhele in this work, although some later Cornish publications are quoted which might provide an indirect source, but one has to wonder whether Elizabeth was simply a slip for Edward here?

The matter is complicated by a further reference to Cornish being spoken in Elizabethan Devon. The culprit here is Nicholas Boson (1624–1708), who in *Nebbaz Gerriau dro tho Carnoack (A few words about Cornish)* wrote concerning the Cornish motto of the family of Harris of Hayne found on a coat of arms engraved on silver 'of above a hundred year's [sic] old'. Hayne itself is at Stowford in Devon, although the family seat was near Penzance, and the Devon connection led Boson to conclude that 'so late (it seems) Cornish was in use in that County, & now it is almost disus'd in this'.[59] Stowford, however, is a bit far north to be considered part of the South Hams.

The source of Polwhele's statement remains obscure, but as *Nebbaz Gerriau* was first published in 1879 the Boson statement may have influenced Jenner and others who further repeated references to Elizabethan-age Cornish in Devon.[60] Obscure or not, however, there is no good evidence of British speech surviving to the fourteenth century anywhere in Devon.[61] The fertile South Hams district abuts an area of Cornwall which shows overwhelming and early English settlement, probably by the ninth century (see below). Cornish was only spoken on the Cornish side close to the Tamar into the medieval period in the vicinity of Launceston on place-name evidence, and by Elizabeth's reign it had retreated far to the west.

WHAT LANGUAGE DID JOHN MOREMAN SAY HIS PRAYERS IN?

As ever popular as the claim of Cornish speakers in the South Hams is that of a Cornish-speaking enclave in the parish of Menheniot in East Cornwall lasting until the Reformation. The claim is that the vicar of Menheniot in eastern Cornwall near Liskeard, from 1529 to 1554, Dr John Moreman, was the first to teach the Lord's Prayer, Creed and Ten Commandments in English, with the implication being taken that prior to that date they would have been taught in Cornish. Most recently this has been strenuously championed by Williams,[62] but it has a much longer history among Cornish language scholars.

The myth appears to have arisen from two sources. First, it may have begun from a too-literal reading of a passage in Carew's 1602 *Survey of Cornwall* that 'the Lord's Prayer, the Apostles' Creed, and the Ten Commandments have been used in Cornish beyond all remembrance',[63] which may possibly have been true in the west of Cornwall at this time but was most unlikely to have been the case for easternmost Cornwall on the evidence of Appendix 1. Secondly, and informed by the first reading, it stems from a misinterpretation of Hooker's account of Moreman which may have first been made by that most inaccurate of Cornish historians, William Hals (1655–1737), and then repeated endlessly by others.[64]

As quoted by Prince, Hooker wrote: 'and (what is very remarkable) that he was the first, in those Days, that taught his Parishioners and People to say the Lord's Prayer, the Belief, and the Commandments, in the English Tongue, and did Teach and Catechize them therein'.[65] Defoe, whose source is presumably Prince, states the matter plainly: 'Dr John Moreman of Southold, famous for being the first Clergyman in England, who ventured to teach his Parishioners the Lord's Prayer, Creed and Ten Commandments in the English Tongue'.[66] As Nance pointed out, and as would have been clear to readers at the time, these would have previously been given in Latin throughout England.[67] Indeed, in one of the government's responses to the petitions of the 1549 Prayer Book rebels, the previous language of the prayers is explicitly noted: 'And where ye saie certein Cornish men be offended because they have not their service in Cornish for so much as thei understand no English, whie shulde they nowe be offended more when they understand it not in English, then when they had it in Laten, and understood it not?'.[68]

A REVISED VIEW

In the set of maps map presented here (Figures 2–6) I have tried to summarize the evidence available to me of the above kinds for a series of time slices from about 1200 to 1800 AD. Figure 7 synthesizes the information contained therein and in Appendix 1. The Williams scenario of Cornish being spoken up to the Tamar border until the 1500s, followed by a catastrophic decline to the west, does not seem at all likely. On the other hand Wakelin's 1975 judgement seems far too harsh in the other direction, given the evidence available. Figure 7 is generally comparable to the 1986 Holmes–George map, not surprisingly perhaps as it is based very much on the same lines of evidence. It is even closer to the Abalain map.[69] It has been adjusted, however, to take account of the very sharp place-name evidence boundary identified by Dunbar and George in 1997 from near Tintagel to Fowey, which I take to represent a potentially long-standing linguistic boundary, perhaps from about 1300 to 1500 or even slightly later.

I also take into account the early English-speaking enclaves

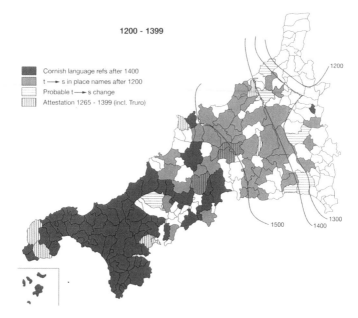

2. *Evidence for the Cornish language 1200–1399. The isobars for 1200 to 1500 are from the Holmes–George map of 1986.*

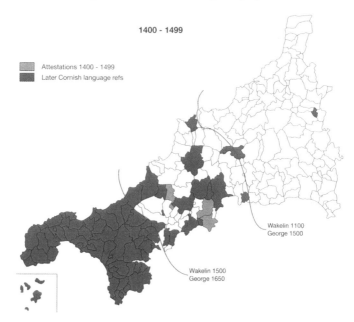

3. *Evidence for the Cornish language 1400–1499. Isobars from Wakelin and the Holmes–George map.*

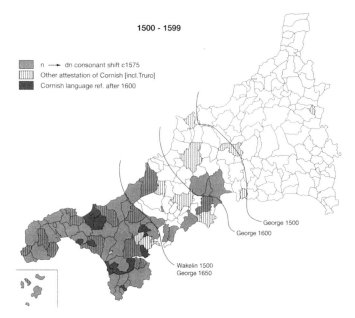

4. *Evidence for the Cornish language 1500–1599. Isobars from Wakelin and the Holmes–George map.*

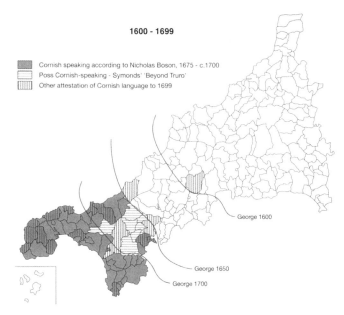

5. *Evidence for the Cornish language 1600–1699. Isobars from the Holmes–George map.*

6. *Evidence for the Cornish language 1700–1799.*
    Isobars from the Holmes–George map.

7. *A revised map of where Cornish was spoken and when.*

identified by the Dunbar and George map and by earlier researchers, which I see as the boundary at about 1000 AD. The south-eastern enclave was not indicated in the Holmes–George map of 1986, but was alluded to by Holmes in his earlier paper.[70] But for the area in between the enclaves and the proposed 1300–1500 AD boundary I find the evidence difficult to interpret. I can only refer the reader to Holmes's detailed treatment of the issues involved (see his contribution in this volume). There are clearly post-1300 Cornish-speaking outliers, such as Minster mentioned above, but it is possible that the area where Cornish was spoken retreated significantly soon after the sound shifts of about 1100–1200 AD. I have thus chosen not to give 1100 or 1200 'isobars' of Cornish language speech.[71]

West of the adjusted 'Padstow–Fowey' line as indicated by Dunbar and George my view largely parallels that of the 1986 Holmes–George map, but with some significant differences. For instance, Figure 7 diverges from their 1600 AD line by taking into account factors such as loans from Cornish language into the English dialects recently spoken in areas such as St Austell and St Dennis as well as evidence for the -*n* to -*dn* change.[72] I know of no evidence for Cornish-speaking in places such as Cubert and Crantock at this time which fall to the west of the Holmes–George 1600 AD boundary, and the association of Newlyn East with John Tregear, the translator of Bonner's Homilies, seems less likely than an association with St Allen.[73] I follow Thomas in seeing the Scillies as Cornish-speaking until about 1600.[74] My 1650 line includes St Agnes and Feock, the former because of a Cornish song and other fragments recorded there in 1698 and the latter because of new evidence that Cornish was spoken there after the date of 1640 usually quoted.[75] On the north coast it is thus to the east of the Holmes–George line. Thomas suggested a 1650 line including an additional five parishes to the north-east but the basis for this is not given in his paper.[76] My 1700 line seems to me better to reflect the evidence given by Lhuyd that the language survived longest in these coastal areas. It agrees with the 1700 line presented by Thomas on the map already alluded to. Finally, my 1750 line is essentially the same as the Holmes–George line, but theirs seems to exclude Penzance as still Cornish-speaking, whereas it seems to me likely that the language could still have been heard in the town then—at least if Dolly Pentreath had come to market that day—among fishermen in the port.[77]

Some information cited by others as evidence of Cornish speech has not been included. This is either because I have not been able to trace or check the source, or because the evidence does not seem convincing and is open to other interpretation. Jenner refers to a general reference to Cornish speech in Spanish State Papers of Elizabeth I's reign which I have not yet seen, and also records: 'Some years ago the present writer came upon a letter in the British Museum addressed to Sir Joseph Banks, and dated 1791, the author of which mentions his own father as the only living man who could speak Cornish. Unluckily the reference to the letter has been lost, and there is so much Banks correspondence in the British Museum that it is almost impossible to find it again.'[78] Julyan Holmes's paper (this volume) refers to the value of documents listing field-names such as those abstracted by Henderson for Veryan in 1698 and St Enoder in 1713, as showing when Cornish was still spoken. He suggests that Cornish field-names will not generally survive the demise of the language in an area for more than a generation. Clearly there is a rich source of information here which I have not been able to address beyond published sources.

At the end of Appendix 2 I list 'Wheal Whiddon' names which include the *-n* to *-dn* ending that occurred in place-names after about 1550–1600.[79] Although these would seem to help fill in the information on post-1600 Cornish-speaking in the area immediately west and north of Truro, which is one of two concentrations of such names, they are generally much later there than in the other concentration in West Penwith. Holmes (this volume) would exclude such simple mine names from consideration as they could be used to share by association the success of tin mines further west, where the names were first coined. This is even more certainly the case with the examples from Ashburton in Devon!

Some of the information given in Appendix 1 is clearly open to varying interpretations and not all accounts have been given equal weight in constructing Figure 7. Thus the Cornish rhymes recorded in St Agnes in 1698 and 1704 are not taken as evidence of Cornish-speaking there at that time, but rather as solitary remembered pieces in an area where Cornish had not been a living language for perhaps a generation or more.

CONCLUSION

I have called this paper 'a provisional synthesis' because the project described is always going to be one 'under construction'. Some of the evidence we do have is ambiguous and open to other interpretations. New evidence will emerge from further study of manuscript material that may well clarify or refine our knowledge. Further analyses of place-name and surname evidence are clearly needed too. Padel's published work on place-name elements is a precondition for a study of place-name distribution relevant to questions of linguistic geography, but it is not itself that study. As noted earlier, drawing lines on maps is a somewhat misleading way to summarize the evidence—although it is not at present clear to me how we can better represent the situation. One can only echo the words of the great eighteenth-century Cornish antiquary William Borlase which began this exposition. There are indeed 'deficiencies of history' involved in our quest, and there are no evident truths here to compensate for them. In such circumstances probabilities must suffice, and conjectures—duly hedged about with all necessary qualifications—are indeed no faults.

ACKNOWLEDGEMENTS

I would particularly like to thank Julyan Holmes, who has been most generous in sharing data from his earlier studies on language distribution. I also thank Richard Gendall, Chris Gosden, Andrew Hawke, John Hines, Neil Kennedy, Rod Lyon, Joanna Mattingly, Oliver Padel and Philip Payton for discussion and/or additional information useful in the preparation of this paper, and Oliver Padel for commenting on an earlier draft. None of the above should be charged with any of the errors in it, however. Ian Heyward of the Cartography Unit, Research School of Pacific and Asian Studies, Australian National University, prepared the figures. The research on which it is based was largely carried out while on study leave from the Australian National University, during a visiting scholarship at St John's College, Cambridge. During that time I also enjoyed being a visitor at the McDonald Institute and at the Department of Archaeology of the University of Cambridge. These institutions are heartily thanked for their support. An earlier version of some parts of this paper was first given in the McDonald Institute seminar series in February 2002, and later in the month at the University of Wales Centre for Advanced Welsh and Celtic Studies in Aberystwyth, and in March at the University of York. The audiences are thanked for helpful comments and suggestions. As ever, Philip Payton is thanked for his Buddha-like patience in waiting for receipt of the manuscript.

APPENDIX 1: REFERENCES TO WHERE CORNISH WAS SPOKEN AT PARTICULAR TIMES

949, Egloshayle: 'the country folk of that district call [it] by the barbaric name Pendavey', 'amongst the Welsh at Pendavey' (quoted in Hooke 1994: 18–19).

*c.***1175–1200, general**: 'St Michael's Mount being "called in the idiom of that province" Dinsol (or the Mount of the Sun)' (Jenner 1904: 9, quoting Ms. Cotton Vespasian A, xiv, a Latin life of St Cadoc).

1193–4, general: 'In both Cornwall and Brittany they speak almost the same language as in Wales. It comes from the same root and is intelligible to the Welsh in many instances, and almost in all. It is rougher and less clearly pronounced, but probably closer to the original British speech, or so I think myself' (Gerald of Wales 1978: 231). Original Latin reads: 'Cornubia vero et Armorica Britannia lingua utuntur fere persimili, Cambris tamen propter originalem convenientiam in multis adhuc et fere cunctis intelligibili. Quae, quanto delicata minus et incomposita magis, tanto antiquo linguae Britanniae idiomati, ut arbitror, est appropriata' (quoted in Jenner 1904: 10).

1265, Budock: Founding of Glasney College and Cornish saying 'In Polsethow ywhylyr Anethow' (Glasney Cartulary, quoted in Peter 1903: 4; see also Nance 1951). Glasney is geographically within Budock although it is sometimes said to belong to St Gluvias.

1318, Budock: Master Adam Murymouthe exchanged his prebend at Glasney with Master John de Lancestone at Exeter Cathedral in part because he did not know Cornish ('propter Linguam Parcium Cornubie quam non nostis') (quoted in Peter 1903: 117).

1328–9, general: 'lingua eciam, in extremis Cornubie non Anglicis set Britonibus extat nota' [Furthermore the language known in the extremities of Cornwall is still not English, but British] (Grandisson in Hingeston-Randolph 1894–9 I: 97–8; translation in Orchard 1937). Oliver Padel suggests a better translation is 'There is a language current in the furthest parts of Cornwall, familiar not to the English but to the Britons'.

1330s, Warleggan, possibly Lanivet: Ralph de Tremur was a Cornish-speaking rector of Warleggan (Grandisson in Hingeston-Randolph 1894–9 II: 1180; see also Orchard 1937). He may have come from Tremeer in Lanivet.

1336, St Buryan, St Just in Penwith: Parishioners in St Buryan swore oaths in English, French and 'alii in Cornubico'; Master Henry Marsely, rector of St Just, interpreted and translated the sermon into Cornish for these monoglots (Grandisson in Hingeston-Randolph 1894–9: II: 820–1; see also Orchard 1937).

1339, St Merryn: J. Polmarke licensed to assist the vicar and 'expound the Word of God in the said church in the Cornish language' (Grandisson in Hingeston-Randolph 1894–9 II: 910; translation in Orchard 1937).

c.1340, St Stephen in Brannel: Cornish language 'Charter Fragment' on back of a deed of 1340 (BL Add. Charter 19,491; Nance 1932; Toorians 1991).

1346, Budock: Sir Adam de Carletone of Glasney sought an exchange with a rectory in Huntingdonshire, in part because he 'would find his speech better known' there. This is taken by Peter (1903: 116 footnote) to mean that he did not understand Cornish.

1349, Minster: Prior and brethren 'know not the English or the Cornish tongue' (Calendar of Patent Rolls 1909: 29, Edward III, pt II, m. 19; also quoted in Hingeston-Randolph 1894–9: III: lxix).

1354–5, Bodmin: Brother John, among others, appointed a confessor in Cornish and English (Grandisson in Hingeston-Randolph 1894–9 II: 1145–6; see also Orchard 1937).

1354–5, Truro: Roger Tyrela appointed confessor in Cornish (Grandisson in Hingeston-Randolph 1894–9: II: 1145–6; see also Orchard 1937).

1355, Minster: Prior and his fellow-monk 'know not the English or the Cornish tongue' (Calendar of Patent Rolls 1909, Edward III, Vol. 10: 247, 252, referring to 20 and 21 June).

1437, St Erme: Resignation '(in the person of Richard Penpons, literate, his Proctor) of Sir Walter Countersint' in part as he could not speak Cornish: 'atque Linguam vulgarem Cornubicum penitus ignorans' (Hingeston-Randolph 1909: 225).

1450, St Ewe: Vincent Clement resigned benefice 'eo quod ipse ideoma Cornubicum loqui et parochianos in idomate [sic] sui instruere et docere minime sit expertus' (Lacy 1967–9: 73–4), i.e. because he could neither speak Cornish nor keep personal residence.

1477, Gorran: Thomas Marbury resigned the living 'propter idoneatatis defectum et vulgaris lingue ignorantium' (Henderson 1956: 182), i.e. because he could not speak Cornish.

***c.*1500, Sancreed**: incident at 'Mirable Play', presumably play in Cornish (CRO X/50/5, quoted in Joyce and Newlyn 1999: 519–20).

1504, Camborne: Dominus Rad Ton writes/copies *Beunans Meriasek*, a play about the patron saint of Camborne. Thomas (1967: 23) notes Richard Ton as priest of Crowan in 1537, and Ric. Tone, priest, buried at Camborne in 1547, from the parish registers.

1506, Falmouth area: Cornish spoken 'in the midst of a most barbarous race, so different in language and customs from the Londoners and the rest of England that they are as unintelligible to these last as the Venetians' (Calendar of State Papers, Venetian, Vol. I: 1202–1519, p. 314: Vincenzo Quirini to the Signory, 1506).

1512, Gwennap: J. Busveall of 'Wennepp' hears Michael and Nicholas quarrelling at a place near Poldyth 'in lingua materna, hoc est in Cornysh' (information from Julyan Holmes, pers. comm.).

1522, Probus: John Tregian objected in a Star Chamber dispute that: 'There is no such place in Lambrobus as Martyn's Field. There is however a parcel of land called "Gwele Marteyn"' (Henderson Ms. EA, Vol. 2, p. 54, quoting Star Chamber, Henry VIII, XVII no. 209r VIII).

1528–31, general: 'The language of the English, Welch, and Cornishmen is so different, that they do not understand each other. The Welchman is sturdy, poor, adapted to war and sociable [*conversevole*], the Cornishman is poor, rough and boorish [*selvatico*], and the Englishman mercantile, rich, affable, and generous [*nobile*]' (Calendar of State Papers, Venetian, Vol. IV, 1527–1533, p. 294: Report of England, made to the [Venetian] Senate by Lodovico Falier, 1531).

1532, Breage: William Godolphin to Thomas Cromwell, 'I received your letter . . . to have two proper fellows for the feat of wrestling, and I have sent you two of my household servants who are reckoned the best for that feat . . . Their English is not perfect' (L & P, 1532: 1093).

1538, general: 'That all having cure of souls do every Sunday declare in English, or in Cornish where English is not used, all or part of the epistle or gospel of that day, or else the Pater Noster, Ave Maria, Creed, and Ten Commandments . . . All chantry priests, soul priests, and other stipendiaries to avoid idleness by teaching the children of their parishes their Pater Noster, Ave Maria, Creed, Ten Commandments with the seven works of mercy in English or Cornish' (Bishop John Voysey's instructions following his 1538 Visitation, given in L & P, 1538: 1106; cf. Blake 1914: 385).

1538, general: 'From the Thames the coast adjoins Picardy, Normandy, and Brittany as far as Brest, and is furnished with good ports, a great necessity for France; and it contains Wales and Cornwall, natural enemies of the rest of England, and speaking a language which is French; for it is "Breton Bretonnant"' (Castillon to Montmorency, L & P, 1538: 1162).

1538, Breage: Godolphin sent Samson and John Herry (mining experts) to Thomas Cromwell, with Herry to interpret 'because their English is very bad' (L & P, 1538: Addenda 1342; not 1324, as quoted by Ellis 1974: 59).

1538, Budock area, Fowey, Goonhilly, Helston, Launceston, Padstow, Paul, Scilly Isles ('Innischawe'), Sennen area: Leland gives names in English and Cornish (Leland 1538 in Smith 1907: 179, 189, 193, 199, 203, 316, 318, 320, 325).

1542, general: 'In Cornwall is two speches: the one is naughty Englyshe, and the other is Cornyshe. And there be many men and women the which cannot speake one worde of Englyshe, but all Cornyshe' (Andrew Boorde, *The Fyrst Boke of the Introduction of Knowledge*, published 1547; see Furnivall 1870: 120–5).

1545–9, Helston: Document translating Cornish field names into English (Henderson 1928a: 407).

1547, probably Gwennap: 'in Cornishe: deese meese te lader' (come forth thou thief), said to ? Tracy by John Richard during a dispute (Loth 1911: 445; Loth's information from Reverend Taylor, quoting from 'Star Chamber, Henri VIII, 8/171–5').

1549, general: Articles of the rebels, 1549, item 8: 'And so we the Cornyshe men (whereof certen of us understande no Englysh), utterly refuse thys new Englysh [service]' (quoted in Fletcher 1983: 115 from a manuscript in Lambeth Palace Library).

***c.*1550, St Columb Major**: Padel (1975a: 22) cites surname evidence suggesting that 'Cornish was in use in St Columb in the mid-sixteenth century'.

1555–83, St Allen: John Tregeare translated 'Bonner's Homilies' into Cornish. Evidence that he was vicar of St Allen at the time and died in 1583 when his will (now destroyed) was proved at Exeter. (C. Henderson, 'A History of the Parish of St Allen', RIC Henderson Mss. Collection).

***c.*1560, general**: 'Item that it may be lawfull for such Welch or Cornish children as can speake no English to learne the Praemisses in the Welch tongue or Cornish language' (BL Egerton Ms. 2350, f. 54r, quoted by Jenner 1904: 13).

1572, Lelant: William Hawyshe witnessed 'dew whallon gwa metton in eglos de Lalant' [i.e. upon All Saint's day in Lelant church] Agnes Davy was called 'Hore and Horebytche in Englysche and not in Cornowok' by Cycely

James (Consistory Court Proceedings, Henderson Ms. X: 124, quoted in Rowse 1941: 23; also in Hoblyn 1936).

1579, St Anthony in Meneage, Constantine, Manaccan: Court case brought by Lawrence Rescaden of Manaccan over land in Constantine, where a witness from Constantine talks of his father reading the contents of a deed 'bothe in Inglishe and Cornishe' to the complainant, and another reports John Tregosse of St Anthony as having 'saide unto him in Cornishe' (Henderson 1937: 82–5).

1583, Gorran: William Richards testimony in court case in 1587 that in the 1583 case 'the Complainant caused an interpreter to demande of certaine of the fishermen that could not well speake or understand English' (Whetter 1962: 69, quoting PRO E. 134 30 Eliz. Hil 2 or CRO MTD32/2).

1584, general: 'The Cornish people for the moste parte, are descended of the Britishe stocke, thowgh much entermixed since with the Saxon and Norman bloude: but untill of late yeares retayned, the British speache corrupted, as theirs is of Wales . . . But of the late the Cornishe men have muche conformed themselves to the use of the Englishe tounge, and their Englishe is equall to the beste, especially in the easterne partes; even from Truro eastwarde it is in manner wholy Englishe. In the weste parte of the Countrye, as in the hundreds of Penwith and Kerrier, the Cornishe tounge is moste in use amongste the inhabitantes, and yet (whiche is to be marveyled) thowgh the husband and wife, parentes and children, Master and Servantes, doe mutually communicate in their native language, yet ther is none of them in manner but is able to convers with a Straunger in the Englishe tounge, unless it be some obscure people, that seldome conferr with the better sorte: but it seemeth that in few yeares the Cornishe Language wilbe by litle and litle abandoned' (Norden 1728: 26–7 [1966: 21]; quoted in Price 1976).

1584, Bodmin, Gorran area, Helston, St Ives, Launceston, Mabe, St Michael Caerhayes, Paul, Perranzabuloe, Truro: Norden gives Cornish as well as English names (Norden 1728 [1966]: 27, 28, 34, 38, 40, 44, 47, 50, 66).

1592, Stithians: Death of Dr John Kenall or Kennall, Cornish language scholar (see quotation 1602 below), vicar of Gwennap 1550, rector of Mabyn 1559, of Mawgan 1559, and of St Columb Major 1560 (Venn and Venn 1922; Wakelin 1975: 90 fn), vicar of Wendron 1549 (Whitley 1882: 131). Family home was at Kennal in Stithians.

1595, St Ewe: Clare Gourden and Petronella John talking together both 'in Cornishe and Englishe' (Consistory Court Proceedings, Henderson Ms. X: 176, quoted in Rowse 1941: 23; also in Hoblyn 1936).

1601, Camborne: Statement of the parish bounds includes Cornish phrasing ('Eneeis Cusven', alongside Coswin) and hedge name ('a hedge called Keazek vres') suggestive of Cornish being spoken there at that time. By 1613 this phrasing has disappeared (Thomas 1967: 177).

1602 [probably written 1594], general: 'for the Lord's Prayer, the Apostles' Creed, and the Ten Commandments have been used in Cornish beyond all remembrance. But the principal love and knowledge of this language lived in Dr Kennall the civilian, and with him lieth buried, for the English speech doth still encroach upon it and hath driven the same into the uttermost skirts of the shire. Most of the inhabitants can speak no word of Cornish, but very few are ignorant of he English; and yet some so affect their own to a stranger they will not speak it, for if meeting them by chance you enquire the way or any such matter, your answer shall be Meea navidna cowzasawsneck, "I can speak no Saxonage"' [actually, I will speak no Saxonage!] (Carew 1602: 127; Halliday 1953: 125ff.).

1603, general: Of Elizabeth I, 'She possessed nine languages so thoroughly that each appeared to be her native tongue, five of these were the languages of peoples governed by her, English, Welsh, Cornish, Scottish, for that part of her possessions where they are still savage, and Irish. All of them are so different, that it is impossible for those who speak the one to understand any of the others' (Calendar of State Papers, Venetian, Vol. IX, 1592–1603, p. 565: Giovanni Carlo Scaramelli to the Doge and Senate, April 1603).

1609, St Ives: Agnes Hicks called Elizabeth Clerke a whore in English and Cornish (DRO Ms. cc3/112, witness statements to court case; information from Julyan Holmes, pers. comm.).

1611, Helston: William Jordan wrote or copied Cornish play 'Creacioun of the Worlde' in Helston. The family seat was at Trelill in Wendron (Gilbert 1820: II 770).

1613, Zennor: Parish bounds named in Cornish. First bound 'is named in the Cornish speech Meane-an-Toll' (Henderson 1928b and Pool 1997, quoting CRO ARD/TER/444).

1614, general: (Anon. 1966, quoting Brerewood 1614): Of languages 'Brittish in Wales, Cornewaile, and Britaine of Fraunce' (Chapter 3). In France 'there are two other, which have no affinity with the Roman or Latin; those are the Britan, which seemes not to differ much from our Cornish; & the Biscay' (Chapter 27).

1616, general: 'England is also divided into three great Provinces, or Countries, & every of them speaking a severall and different Language, as English, Welsh, and Cornish; and their language (which is strange) alters upon the sodaine, even as the provinces part: for in this Towne they speake English, and do not understand Welsh, or Cornish, and in the next Towne Cornish, not understading [sic] English or Welsh: but in many things the Welsh and Cornish something agree' (Hopton 1616: 197).

1622, Wendron: will of Francis John alias Trevallack; Grace Rillstone interpreted his last testament given in Cornish and some English (CRO ACP/W/J/288/3, referred to by Pool 1982: 9).

1630, general: 'They have a particular language, called Cornish (although now much worn out of use) differing but little from the Welsh, and the Language of the Britains in France; which argueth their Original to have been out of one nation' (Dodridge 1630: 77–8).

1636 or before, St Just in Penwith, Sennen: Parson Drake's certificate in Cornish, dating to some time between 1582 when the first William Drake became parson of St Just and 1636 when his son, also parson there, died (different versions in RIC Tonkin Ms. B; BL Add. Ms. 28,554; Nance 1925d).

*c.*1640, Feock: William Jackman preaching in Cornish: 'The Cornish tongue was so Retain'd in this psh by the old old inhabitants thereof 'till about the yeare 1640 that Mr Wm Jackman elder, Vicar thereof . . . Brother to John Jackman, Vicar of Kenwin and Key . . . was forced for Divers yeare to administer the Sacrament to the communicants in the Cornish tongue, because the aged people did not well understand the English as himselfe often told me' (BL Add. Ms 29,762, fo. 76r; cf. Hals *c.*1740–3: 133).

After 1640, Feock: 'John Jackman Vicar of this Parish, aged 63 years that dyed about 23 years (Son to John Jackman Vicar of Kenwin & Key) hath often declared to the Writer of these lines & many others, that for many years after his Induction into the Vicaridge, he was necessitated to administer the Sacrament in the Kernawish Tongue to the Aged People of the Parish, As his Predecessors had done, because they did not understand the moderne Teutonick or Mother Tongue to Us' (RIC Tonkin Ms. H). Information is from William Hals *c.*1702, and suggests death of John Jackman was *c.*1679. John Jackman in fact died April 1674 (Feock Parish Registers, CRO).

1644, general: 'The language is spoken altogeather at Goon-Hilly & about Pendennis. & at the Lands-End. they speake no english. All beyond Truro they speake the Cornish Language' (BL Add. Ms. 17,062, quoted in Price 1976; see also Symonds 1859).

*c.*1650, general: 'They have a speech perculiar to themselves, Somewhat agreeing with the Welsh, And that used in Little Brittany in France: And by the opinion of the learned, it is the relict of the language of the Ancient Brittons inhabiting this isle; Who, by sundry invasions were forced to withdraw themselves among the Mountaines of Wales, And hilly country of Cornwall. And some over into France, which part from them is called Brittany. But now that speech with us is much worne out, and English spoken overall: Which, by report, is as good as any in England, Especially At & near the Sea Ports' (Peter Mundy, transcribed by Thomas Tonkin, BL Add. Ms. 33,420, page 94 pen, 105 pencil; see also Mundy 1984: 80).

1656, Sennen: 'another said in Cornish that it was a holy cross and if it were good before it is good now': statement of John Ellis (CRO Ms. SF285/68,69; quoted in Stoyle 2002: 182).

1660, St Stephen in Brannel: 1660 tin bounds of the manor of Brannel give names in English and Cornish suggesting to Henderson that Cornish was still spoken at that time, but it could just be a copy of an earlier document. By 1671 and 1696 names conform much more to English usage (Henderson 1927). Hodge (1998: 3–4) paraphrases Henderson. Cornish probably was spoken here until *c.*1600 (see Figure 7).

1662, general: 'We met with none here but what could speak English; few of the children could speak Cornish; so that the language is like, in a short time, to be quite lost' (Ray 1760: 281; Ray 1846: 190).

1662, St Just in Penwith: Richard Angwin, Cornish language scholar, lived there: 'the only man we could hear of that can now write the Cornish language' (Ray 1760: 281; Ray 1846: 190; see also Henderson 1931). Angwin died in 1675.

1667, St Just in Penwith: John Ray visited 'Dickan Gwyn' (Richard Angwin) there: 'and had from him some Cornish words. He is esteemed the most skilful Man of any now living in the Cornish language; but being no good Grammarian, we found him very deficient. Another there is, Pendarvis by Name, who is said to be a Scholar, who doubtless must needs have better Skill in the Tongue' (Ray 1760: 279 footnote; Ray 1846: 189 footnote).

*c.*1669, **St Agnes**: St Agnes tin bounds of *c.*1669 named overwhelmingly in Cornish, with compound names such as Wheal-an-fugow Mengouse, said to mean 'The mine of the cave by the stone in the wood' (Jenkin 1928: 437).

1670 or before, Landewednack: Francis Robinson preached in Cornish (see 1678 Scawen quotation). Nance (1935) suggests that this took place in 1670 or earlier. Letter of 1674 claimed Robinson had been 'non-resident this four years and now turned from Minister to Maryner' (RIC Henderson Ms. Vol. XI, p. 102, quoted in Henderson 1958: 283).

1675–1708, general: 'being almost only spoken from the Lands-End to the Mount and towards St Ives and Redruth, and again from the Lizard to Helston, and towards Falmouth: and these parts in the narrowest two Necks of land, containing about twenty Miles in Length, and not quarter or half that Breadth, within which little Extent also there is more of English spoken than of Cornish, for here may be found some that can hardly speak or understand Cornish, but scarce any but both understand & speak English' (*Nebbaz Gerriau Dro Tho Carnoack*, 'A Few Words about Cornish', by Nicholas Boson, Ms copy by Rev. Henry Ustick, 1750, in RIC, quoted in Padel 1975b: 24).

1676, Gwithian: 'let not the old woman be forgotten, who died about two years since, who was 164 years old, of good memory, and healthful at that age, living in the parish of Gwithian, by the charity mostly of such as came purposely to see her, speaking to them (in default of English) by an interpreter, yet partly understanding it' (Scawen 1777; Gilbert 1838 IV: 216 fn). She was Chesten or Christian Marchant, born according to Tonkin in St Agnes (RIC Tonkin Ms. B, p. 133).

1678, general: 'some of our old folks also, for we have some among these few that do speak Cornish, who do not understand a word of English, as well as those in Wales, and those may be many in some of the western parts, to whom Mr. Francis Robinson, parson of Landewednack told me, he had preached a sermon not long since in the Cornish tongue, only well understood by his auditory' (Scawen 1777; Gilbert 1838 IV: 216).

1680, St Ives, St Hilary, Madron: 'Sermons in Cornish and English. Preached by Rev. Joseph Sherwood at St Ives, Marazion and Penzance 1680. Ms penes Jonathan Rashleigh' (Boase and Courtney 1882: 1335; Spriggs 1998).

1690s, Mylor: Thomas Tonkin records hearing Cornish song at Carclew, Mylor (RIC Tonkin Ms. B, p. 207).

*c.*1690s, **Sancreed or St Just**: William Rowe translated part of Matthew's Gospel into Cornish. He was born in 1660 or 1666 in St Buryan or St Just. His children were mainly baptised in St Just but he seems to have moved to Hendra in Sancreed in 1697–8 (St Buryan, St Just, Sancreed Parish Registers, CRO). Date of death not known. His writings are in BL Add. Ms. 28,554, fo. 97 on; Nance 1936/1937.

1695, general: 'The old Cornish is almost quite driven out of the Country, being spoken only by the vulgar in two or three Parishes at the Lands-end; and they too understand the English. In other parts, the inhabitants know little or nothing of it; so that in all likelihood a short time will destroy the small remains that are left of it. 'Tis a good while since, that only two men could write it, and one of them no Scholar or Grammarian, and then blind with age' (Gibson 1695: 146, quoted in Wakelin 1975: 92). From Bodleian Library Ms. Eng.b.2042, fo. 164r, the source of this information is John Ray (1628–1705), who wrote, probably early in 1694: 'As for ye Cornish (wch is nothing else but the ancient British, differing only in dialect from ye Welsh, as found by comparing many words) it is almost quite driven out of the Countrey, it being spoken only in two or three parishes at the Lands end, by the vulgar, who also can speak English: else-where the Cornish understand it not. So that in all likelyhood in a few generations more it will quite be lost there being then when we were in the Countrey only two men that could write it, that is Mr Pendarves, & one Dick en Gwyn as they called him; wch last was no scholar or Grammarian & then blind with age.' See also the entries for 1662 and 1667 in this Appendix.

1695, St Just in Penwith: Songs in Cornish by John Tonkin, a tailor of St Just, written according to Jenner (1904: 36) in 1695. They are in BL Add. Ms. 28,554, fo. 130r, 131r,v. See also Nance (1930a, b).

1698, St Agnes: Cornish rhyme collected by Thomas Tonkin from Captain Noel Cater of St Agnes (RIC, Tonkin Ms. B, p. 207; Nance 1925c).

1700, general: 'At our first coming we did not at all understand the people, but now I apprehend most they can say, it is spoaken not only in 2 parishes as in the Last Edition of Cambden, but there are some remains of it, all along the South Coast for nigh 30 miles in Length & I believe on the North Side about 20' (Edward Lhuyd letter to Dr Richardstone, *c.* 10 September, quoted in Campbell 1976: 38).

1700, general: 'The Cornish is much more corruptly spoken than the Armorican, as being confin'd to half a score parishes toward's the Land's End; whereas [Armorican is] the common language of a country almost as large as Wales' (Edward Lhuyd, letter to Henry Rowlands, 10 March 1700, quoted in Gunther 1945: 441).

1700, general: 'The places in Cornwal that at this day retain the Ancient language, are the parishes of St Just, St Paul, Burrian, Sunnin [Sennen], St Lavan, St Krad [Sancreed], Marva [Morvah], Maddern [Madron, including Penzance], Sunner [Zennor], Trewednok [Towednock], St Ives, Leigian [Ludgvan], Kynwal or (as now pronounced) Gyval [Gulval]; And all along the sea shoar from the Land's end to St Kevern's near the Lizard point.

But a great many of the Inhabitants of those Parishes, especially the Gentry, do not understand it; there being no necessity thereof, in regard ther's no Cornish Man but speaks good English' (Lhuyd 1707: 253). The 'sea shoar' referrred to would have included the additional parishes of St Hilary (including Marazion), Perranuthnoe, Breage, Sithney, the coastal portion of Wendron, Gunwalloe, Mullion, Landewednack, Grade, Ruan Minor and St Keverne. Jenner (1904: 18) would add Germoe and Ruan Major, although neither of these is actually coastal.

1700, Penzance (Madron Parish): 'in yt town ye Coman language is Cornish' (BL Add Ms. 51020, fos 60–1). Letter from someone associated with Edward Lhuyd's visit.

1700, St Just: 'The way that I took to get some knowledge of the Cornish Language, was, partly by writing some down from the mouths of the people in the West of Cornwall, in particular in the parish of St Just' (Lhuyd 1707: 222, translated by Tonkin and Gwavas from the Cornish in Pryce 1790: 12 [unpaginated]).

1702, Sennen: an area 'call'd in Cornish Pullen da' (Jones 1702).

1704, Paul: Dated Cornish inscription on a Paul hurling ball (Mayne 1943: 45).

1704, Penzance (Madron): Dolly Pentreath, baptised in Paul in 1692 (Paul Parish Registers, CRO): 'her father being a fisherman, she was sent with fish to Penzance at twelve years old, and sold them in the Cornish language, which the inhabitants in general (even the gentry) did then well understand' (Barrington 1776: 283).

1704, St Agnes: Cornish proverb and rhyme recorded from William Allen of St Agnes by Thomas Tonkin (RIC Tonkin Ms. B; BL Add. Ms. 28,554; Nance 1949).

1705, Paul: Thomas Boson composes inscription for William Gwavas's hurling ball (BL Add. Ms. 28,554, fo. 137; Nance 1925b: 37–8).

*c.***1706, St Ives**: John Hicks reported 'The language of the inhabitants was anciently Cornish, which is not very different from the Welsh . . . This language, within the last fifty years, is almost forgotten, being seldom used by any of the inhabitants, excepting fishermen and tinners' (Gilbert 1820 II: 710). Hicks's manuscript is now lost. Dating based on statement that he had carried the Passion Poem from William Scawen to John Keigwin to be translated 24 years earlier. Keigwin's translation is dated 1682 (Lambeth Palace Library, Ms. 806, Art. 17).

*c.***1708, Paul and St Just**: Borlase states in 1758 of Cornish that 'about fifty years since it was generally spoken in the parishes of Paul and St. Just, the fishermen and market-women in the former, and the tinners in the latter, conversing one with the other for the most part in the Cornish tongue' (Borlase 1758: 315–16).

1710, America: Letter from Gwavas to an unknown correspondent in America in Cornish (BL Add. Ms. 28,554; Nance 1925a: 37).

1710, Penzance (Madron): Gwavas records a folk rhyme: 'James Harry, of Ludgian [Ludgvan], a Mason, now of Penzance, aged abt. 65, told me this rime' (RIC Gwavas Commonplace Book, Gatley Ms. quoted by Nance 1929: 24).

1711, Paul: Letter in Cornish from Oliver Pender of Newlyn to William Gwavas (BL Add. Ms. 28,554; Nance 1926).

1711, Penzance (Madron): Death of James Jenkins 'our Cornish Bard' (see Nance 1948).

1711, St Ives: John Stevens deposition 'when the tenth baskett came to be delivered the fishermen called out Deka Deka' (quoted in Matthews 1892: 339–40, 401–5).

1734, St Just, Paul, Sennen: 'ye moderne Cornish yt is known according to pronunciation amongst us at Newlyn, Mousehole, St. Just, and the Land's End' (Bilbao Ms. fo. 16r, Letter of William Gwavas to Thomas Tonkin, Penzance, 26 February 1734).

1736, St Just, St Keverne, Paul, Sennen: 'ye familiar dialect now retained by tinners, and ye fishermen in our westerne parts only, which will be a great satisfaceon to them, as dwell in St Just, Paul, Lands End & St. Kevern' (Bilbao Ms. fo. 30r, Letter of William Gwavas to Thomas Tonkin, Newlyn, 1 December 1736; cf. draft or copy in BL Add. Ms 28,554, fo. 20r).

*c.***1746, Ludgvan**: Daines Barrington in 1777 told of John Nancarrow junior, who 'had learned the Cornish language from the country people during his youth, and can now converse in it' (Barrington 1779: 84). He was born in St Agnes in 1734 but brought up largely in West Cornwall, including in Ludgvan from 1746 for some years where he probably learned Cornish. He later settled in Marazion and married there in 1762. Nancarrow migrated to Philadelphia in America in 1774 and was still alive in the United States in 1804 (Jeffery 1984, 1985).

1756, West Cornwall: 'In some few parishes, indeed, near the Land's-end, there is a corrupt dialect of the Cornish tongue even still retained' (Anonymous 1756, quoted by Nance 1933).

1772, Towednack: 'The families of Stevens and Trewhella were among the last to keep up the Cornish language in the parish of Towednack. The late Dr Stevens of Saint Ives told the writer that his great-grandfather, Andrew Stevens of Trevegia, used to take his [Dr Stevens's] grandfather on his knee, and say . . . [Cornish follows]' (Matthews 1892: 404). Nance (1923: 146) states that Andrew Stevens died in 1772.

1776, Paul: William Bodinar wrote a letter in Cornish to Daines Barrington, seen as the last extended piece of Cornish prose (Letter in Society of Antiquaries, published by Pool and Padel 1975/6). Bodinar died in 1789 (Paul Parish Registers, CRO).

1777, Paul: Dolly Pentreath, last fluent native speaker, died (Jago 1882: 333–41; see also Barrington 1776, 1779).

1789, Truro: Polwhele meets engineer Tompson of Truro and considers him to be fluent in Cornish (Polwhele 1806 V: 43–4).

?1789, Paul: Of Mousehole villagers: 'They preserve some of the remains of the old Cornish language; and as they are frequently employed as pilots to Brittany, are understood by the natives there; but as they send their children to English schools the language wears out apace. Their tone of speaking approaches to singing or chanting' (Gough 1789 I: 13). Earlier he refers to Barrington (1776, 1779) and the information perhaps comes from there.

*c.*1789, **Paul**: 'yet my opinion would have been confirmed by what I have heard from a very old man now living at Moushole near Penzance, who, I believe, is, at this time, the only person capable of holding half an hour's conversation on common subjects in the Cornish tongue' (Pryce 1790: 4 [unpaginated]). It is generally believed that this refers to William Bodinar (see under 1776).

1799, St Levan and Newlyn (Paul): Whitaker told of an old man of St Levan and a woman in Newlyn who could speak Cornish (Whitaker 1804: 42).

1800, Newlyn (Paul): 'William Matthews, of Newlyn, near Penzance, who died there about thirty years ago [c.1786], also spoke the Cornish language later and much more fluently than Dolly Pentreath. His son, William Matthews, was also well acquainted with it; he died in the same village about the year 1800' (Gilbert 1817 I: 122).

APPENDIX 2: CONSONANT SHIFTS -N TO -DN, -M TO -BM

St Agnes (Williams 1995: 74): Chytodden; Codna-coos.

St Anthony in Meneage (Williams 1995: 74): Godna.

St Austell (Holmes p.c.): Pedniddon.

Breage (Williams 1995: 73): Chytodden; Pengwedna.

St Buryan (Williams 1995: 74): Codna Willy; Pridden.

Camborne (Williams 1995: 73): Chytodden; Pencobben.

Constantine (Williams 1995: 73): Chegwidden; Crack-an-Godna; Park-an-Gubman; Park-an-Todden; Park-Cabben; Park-Tobma; Pedn Billy; Penbothidnow; Polgwidden Cove.

Crowan (Williams 1995: 73): The Ladden.

St Enoder (Holmes p.c.): Pednacarne.

St Erth (Williams 1995: 74): Parke an Clibmier.

St Ewe (Williams 1995: 74): Park Todden.

Feock (Wakelin 1975: 77): Chegwidden 1841 (now Chywine); Pednapill Point 1597 (now Pill Point); Porthgwidden.

Gerrans (Wakelin 1975: 77): Pednvadan.

Gorran (Whetter 1998): Cotna; Luddengarth.

Grade (Williams 1995: 73): Ingewidden; Polgwidden.

Gulval (Williams 1995: 73): Carnaquidden.

Gwennap (Wakelin 1975: 77): Mennergwidden; (Williams 1995: 73): Cascadden.

St Hilary (Williams 1995: 74): Brevadnack; Tolvadden.

Illogan (Wakelin 1975: 77): Tolvadden.

St Ives (Williams 1995: 74): Pedn Olva; Porth Gwidden.

St Just in Penwith (Williams 1995: 74): Balleswidden; Cargodna; Cudna Reeth; Leswidden.

St Just in Roseland (Williams 1995: 74): Marcradden.

St Keverne (Williams 1995: 74): Chywednack; Frogabbin; Gull Gwidden; Laddenvean; Pednavounder; Pedn-myin; Pedn Tiere; Polpidnick.

Landewednack (Williams 1995: 73): Landewednack; Kilcobben Cove; Peddenporperre.

Lelant (Williams 1995: 73): The Gabmas; Pedndrea; Porth Kidney Sands.

St Levan (Williams 1995: 74): Pednvounder.

Ludgvan (Williams 1995: 73): Menwhidden.

Madron (Williams 1995: 73, 74): Nangidnall; Pednpons; Pedn Venton; Todne Rosemoddress; Trewidden; Street an Dudden (in Penzance).

Manaccan (Anon. 1961): Park Lobben.

St Mawgan in Meneage (Williams 1995: 74): Carlidna.

St Mewan (Henderson 1927, cf. Holmes p.c.): Peden Halvegan.

Morvah (Pool 1990: 62): Gunwidden.

Mullion (Williams 1995: 73): Lo Cabm; Pedn Crifton.

Mylor (Williams 1995: 73): Crockagodna.

Paul (Williams 1995: 73–4): Park Tuban; Pedn Bejuffin; Pedn Tenjack; Pedn y coanse; Todden Coath.

Perranarworthal (Wakelin 1975: 77): Trewedna; (Williams 1995: 74): Blankednick.

Perranzabuloe (Williams 1995: 74): Codnidne.

Redruth (Williams 1995: 74): Pedn-an-drea.

Ruan Major (Williams 1995: 74): Pednanvounder.

Sancreed (Williams 1995: 74): Chirgwidden; Codnagooth.

Scilly Isles (Holmes p.c.): Pedn an thes 1777; Pednbean 1744; (Williams 1995: 74): Cudedno.

Sennen (Williams 1995: 74): Enys Dodman; Pedden an wollas.

Sithney (Williams 1995: 74): Croc-an-codna; Cudno; Pednavounder; Prospidnack; Taban Denty; Ventonvedna.

St Stephen in Brannel (Henderson 1927): Crouse-widden 1660.

Stithians (Williams 1995: 74): Carnwidden.

Towednack (Williams 1995: 74): Towednack; Amalwhidden; Beagletodn; Chytodden; Park Gwidden; Skillywadden.

Truro (Williams 1995: 74): Street Eden.

Veryan (Wakelin 1975: 77): Carn Pednethan; (Holmes p.c.): Penavadan.

Wendron (Williams 1995: 75): Calvadnack; Crackagodna; Roselidden.

Zennor (Williams 1995: 75): Boswednack; Pedn Kei; (Henderson 1928b): Carrack Pedden Mellen 1613.

'Wheal Whidden' names (Brooke 2000). In W. Whidden or Widden forms unless indicated:

St Agnes 1724; 1842 (Wheal Widdon); 1874 (Wheal Withern).

Ashburton [Devon] 1755, 1795; 1724 (Wheal Whitten); 1806 (Wheal Widdon).

Chacewater 1820.

Gulval 1670, 1736.

Gwennap 1827.

St Just in Penwith 1786.

Kea 1836, 1847; 1817 (Wheal Widdin).

Kenwyn 1820.

Lelant 1811.

Madron 1685 (Wheal Whitta).
St Mewan 1824.
Morvah 1741, 1820.
Perranzabuloe 1838; 1733 (Wheal Wider).
Redruth 1746; 1817 (Wheal Widdin); 1841 (Wheal Wynn).
Scorrier [Gwennap?] 1778 (Wheal widn).
Wendron 1835.

BIBLIOGRAPHY FOR APPENDICES 1 AND 2

Manuscripts
Biblioteca de la Diputacion Foral de Bizkaia, Bilbao, Spain
Ms. Bnv-69 (The 'Bilbao Ms.' of Thomas Tonkin). See under 1734, 1736.

Bodleian Library, Oxford
Ms. Eng.b.2042 (William Gibson's materials for the 1695 edition of Camden).

British Library
BL Add. Charter 19,491. The 'Charter Endorsement' of *c*.1340.
BL Add. Ms. 17,062. Richard Symonds diary. See under 1644.
BL Add. Ms. 28,554. Papers of William Gwavas, compiled 1730s. See under 1636 to 1736 entries.
BL Add. Ms. 29,762. W. Hals, Manuscript of his History of Cornwall. See under *c*.1640.
BL Add. Ms. 33,420. A transcript of Peter Mundy's 'Acct of the County of Cornwall and Town of Penryn' by Thomas Tonkin. See under *c*.1650.
BL Add. Ms. 51,020, fos 60–61. Letter by an associate of Edward Lhuyd. See under 1700.
BL Egerton Ms. 2350. See under *c*.1560.
BL Ms. Cotton Vespasian A, xiv. See under 1175–1200.

Cornwall Record Office, Truro
CRO X/50/5. See under 1500.
CRO MTD32/2. See under 1583.
CRO ACP/W/J/283/3. See under 1622.
CRO SF285/68,69. Relation of John Ellis of Zemming [Sennen]. See under *c*.1656.
CRO ARD/TER/444. Zennor bounds. See under 1613.

Devon Record Office
DRO Ms. cc3/112. Witnesses statements, St Ives, 1609.

Lambeth Palace Library
Mount Calvary, translated by John Keigwin, 1682. Ms. 806, Art. 17.

Public Record Office, Kew
Exchequer Documents, E. 134 30 Eliz. Hil 2 (Gorran case of 1583).

Royal Institution of Cornwall, Truro
Boson, N. *Nebbaz Gerriau dro tho Carnoack* (copy by Ustick of a Nicholas Boson essay). See under 1675–1708.
Gwavas, W. Commonplace Book, 1710. Gatley Ms. See under 1710.
Henderson Mss. Collection. See under 1555–1558, 1572, 1595, 1670 or before.
Tonkin, T. Tonkin Manuscript B. See under 1636 to 1704 entries.
Tonkin, T. Tonkin Manuscript H. See under after *c*.1640.

Society of Antiquaries, London
Bodinar, W. 1776 letter.

Published Sources
Anonymous 1756. *Youth's Philosophical Entertainment, or the Natural Beauties of Cornwall, Devonshire, Dorsetshire and Somersetshire, with Additional Remarks by Various Hands*. London.
Anonymous 1961. 'Field and Coast Names in the Helford District'. *Old Cornwall*, 6.1, pp. 17–18.
Anonymous 1966. 'William Brerewood on the Cornish Language in 1614'. *Old Cornwall*, 6.10, pp. 472–3.
Barrington, D. 1776. 'On the Expiration of the Cornish Language'. *Archaeologia*, 3, pp. 279–84.
Barrington, D. 1779. 'Mr Barrington on some Additional Information relative to the Continuance of the Cornish Language'. *Archaeologia*, 5, pp. 81–6.
Blake, W.J. 1914. 'A History of Cornwall, 1529–1539'. *Journal of the Royal Institution of Cornwall*, 19.3, no. 61, pp. 360–94.
Boase, G.C. and W.P. Courtney 1882. *Bibliotheca Cornubiensis*, Vol. III. London.
Borlase, W. 1758. *The Natural History of Cornwall*. Oxford.
Brerewood, W. 1614. *Enquiries Touching the Diversity of Languages, and Religions, Through the Chiefe Parts of the World*. London.
Brooke, J. 2000. 'Open Workings'. *Old Cornwall*, 12.7, pp. 22–3.
Calendar of Patent Rolls 1909. *The Calendar of Patent Rolls Preserved in the Public Record Office: Edward III, vol. 10, A.D. 1354–1358*. London.
Calendar of State Papers, Venetian, Vol. I, (1202–1509), Vol. IV (1527–1533), Vol. IX (1592–1603). London.
Campbell, J.L. 1976. 'Unpublished Letters by Edward Lhuyd in the National Library of Scotland'. *Celtica*, 11, pp. 34–42.
Carew, R. 1602. *The Survey of Cornwall*. London.
Dodridge, J. 1630. *An Historical Account of the Ancient and Modern State of the Principality of Wales, Duchy of Cornwall and Earldom of Chester*. London.
Ellis, P.B. 1974. *The Cornish Language and its Literature*. London.
Fletcher, A. 1983. *Tudor Rebellions*. London.

Furnivall, F.J. (ed.) 1870. *The Fyrst Boke of the Introduction of Knowledge. Early English Text Society, Extra Series* 10.

Gerald of Wales (Geraldus Cambrensis) 1978. *The Journey through Wales/The Description of Wales* (translated by L. Thorpe). London.

Gibson, E. 1695. *Camden's Britannia, Newly Translated into English: with Large Additions and Improvements.* London.

Gilbert, C.S. 1817, 1820. *An Historical . . . Survey of the County of Cornwall, Vols I (1817) and II (1820).* Plymouth.

Gilbert, D. 1838. *The Parochial History of Cornwall.* 4 vols. London.

Gough, R. 1789. *Camden's Britannia (edited with additions by R. Gough).* 3 vols. London.

Gunther, R.T. 1945. *Early Science in Oxford, Vol. XIV: Life and Letters of Edward Lhwyd.* Oxford.

Halliday, F.E. (ed.) 1953. *Richard Carew of Antony: The Survey of Cornwall.* London.

Hals, W. *c.*1740–3. *The Compleat History of Cornwall.* Truro. Often erroneously given as published in 1750.

Henderson, C. 1927. 'Some Old Names on Black-More'. *Old Cornwall*, 1.6, pp. 1–5.

Henderson, C. 1928a. 'Records of St Johns Hospital, near Helston'. *Journal of the Royal Institution of Cornwall*, 22.3, no. 95, pp. 382–407.

Henderson, C. 1928b. 'The Bounds of Zennor'. *Old Cornwall*, 1.7, pp. 13–15.

Henderson, C. 1931. 'Nicholas Boson and Richard Angwyn'. *Old Cornwall*, 2.2, pp. 29–32.

Henderson, C. 1937. *A History of the Parish of Constantine in Cornwall*, ed. G.H. Doble. Long Compton.

Henderson, C. 1956. 'The Ecclesiastical Antiquities of the 109 Parishes of West Cornwall (part II)'. *Journal of the Royal Institution of Cornwall*, N.S. 2.4, pp. 105–210.

Hendersion, C. 1958. 'The Ecclesiastical Antiquities of the 109 Parishes of West Cornwall (part III)'. *Journal of the Royal Institution of Cornwall*, N.S. 3.2, pp. 211–382.

Hingeston-Randolph, F.C. (ed.) 1894–9. *The Register of John de Grandisson, Bishop of Exeter (A.D. 1327–1379)* 3 vols. London.

Hingeston-Randolph, F.C. (ed.) 1909. *The Register of Edmund Lacy, Bishop of Exeter, AD 1420–1455. Part I: Register of Institutions.* London.

Hoblyn, W.T. 1936. 'In English and Not in Cornowok'. *Old Cornwall* 2.11, p. 11.

Hodge, P. 1998. *The History of Cornish in the Parish of St Stephen In Brannel. Background to Cornish Series*, 8. Gwinear.

Hooke, D. 1994. *Pre-Conquest Charter-Bounds of Devon and Cornwall.* Woodbridge.

Hopton, A. 1616. *A Concordancy of Yeares . . .* London.

Jago, F.W.P. 1882. *The Ancient Language and the Dialect of Cornwall.* Truro.

Jeffery, C.C. 1984. 'The Nancarrows, a Forgotten Cornish Engineering Family. Part 1—John Nancarrow, Senior'. *Old Cornwall*, 9.10, pp. 493–6.

Jeffery, C.C. 1985. 'John Nancarrow Junior'. *Old Cornwall*, 10.1, pp. 31–5.

Jenkin, A.K.H. 1928. 'Cornish History in Mine Plans and Cost Books'. *Journal of the Royal Institution of Cornwall*, 22.3, no. 75, pp. 422–44.

Jenner, H. 1904. *A Handbook of the Cornish Language*. London.

Jones, H. 1702. *Reasons Humbly Offered for Building a Mould or Harbour in Whitsand-Bay at the Lands-End, in Cornwall*. No printing details given.

Joyce, S.L. and E.S. Newlyn (eds) 1999. *Cornwall (Records of Early English Drama)*. Toronto.

L & P. 1538. *Letters and Papers of the Reign of Henry VIII* (1532, 1538 volumes). London.

Lacy, E. 1967–9. *The Register of Edmund Lacy, Volume III*. Canterbury and York Society, Part CXXXIV. Torquay.

Lhuyd, E. 1707. *Archaeologia Britannica*. Oxford.

Loth, J. 1911. 'Une Phrase Inédite en Moyen Cornique et un Mot Rare'. *Revue Celtique*, 32, pp. 443–4.

Matthews, J.H. 1892. *A History of the Parishes of St Ives, Lelant, Towednack and Zennor*. London.

Mayne, W.B. 1943. 'Stray Notes on Paul Parish'. *Old Cornwall*, 4.2, pp. 45–54.

Mundy, P. 1984. *The Travels of Peter Mundy 1597–1667*, ed. J. Keast. Redruth.

Nance, R.M. 1923. 'John Davey of Boswednack, and his Cornish Rhyme'. *Journal of the Royal Institution of Cornwall*, 21.2, no. 70, pp. 146–53.

Nance, R.M. 1925a. 'The Cornish Language in America, 1710'. *Old Cornwall*, 1.1, p. 37.

Nance, R.M. 1925b. 'A Hurling-Ball Inscription of 1705 in Cornish'. *Old Cornwall*, 1.1, pp. 37–8.

Nance, R.M. 1925c. 'A Fisherman's Catch'. *Old Cornwall*, 1.2, p. 31.

Nance, R.M. 1925d. 'Parson Drake's Cornish Certificate'. *Old Cornwall*, 1.2, pp. 38–41.

Nance, R.M. 1926. 'A Cornish Letter, 1711'. *Old Cornwall*, 1.3, pp. 23–4.

Nance, R.M. 1929. 'Two Hitherto-Unnoticed Cornish Pieces'. *Old Cornwall*, 1.10, pp. 22–4.

Nance, R.M. 1930a. 'A Cornish Song, to the Tune of "The Modest Maid of Kent"'. *Old Cornwall*, 1.11, pp. 26–9.

Nance, R.M. 1930b. 'Kanna Kernuak'. *Old Cornwall*, 1.12, pp. 41–2.

Nance, R.M. 1932. 'The Charter Endorsement in Cornish'. *Old Cornwall*, 2.4, pp. 34–6.

Nance, R.M. 1933. 'Cornish in 1756'. *Old Cornwall*, 2.5, p. 44.

Nance, R.M. 1935. 'The Proposed Landewednack Tablet'. *Old Cornwall*, 2.10, p. 44.

Nance, R.M. 1936/1937. 'The Cornish of William Rowe'. *Old Cornwall*, 2.11, pp. 32–6' 2.12, pp. 25–7; 3.1, pp. 41–4.

Nance, R.M. 1939. 'Some Old Cornish Weirs'. *Old Cornwall*, 3.6, pp. 225–8.

Nance, R.M. 1948. 'The Cornish Rhymes of James Jenkins of Alverton'. *Old Cornwall*, 4.8, pp. 268–73.

Nance, R.M. 1949. 'William Allen's Cornish Rhyme'. *Old Cornwall*, 4.9, pp. 325–6.

Nance, R.M. 1951. 'Cornish Prophecies'. *Old Cornwall*, 4.12, pp. 443–53.

Norden, J. [1728] 1966. *Speculi Britanniae Pars. A Topographical & Historical Description of Cornwall*. [orig. London] Newcastle Upon Tyne.

Orchard, L.C.J. 1937. 'Some Notes on the Cornish Language in the Fourteenth Century'. *Old Cornwall*, 3.2, pp. 79–80.

Padel, O.J. 1975a. 'Cornish Language Notes: 3'. *Cornish Studies*, 3, pp. 19–24.

Padel, O.J. 1975b. *The Cornish Writings of the Boson Family*. Redruth.

Peter, T. 1903. *The History of Glasney Collegiate Church*. Camborne.

Polwhele, R. 1806. *The History of Cornwall*, Vol. V. London.

Pool, P.A.S. [1975] 1982. *The Death of Cornish*. Penzance.

Pool, P.A.S. 1990. *The Field-Names of West Penwith*. Hayle.

Pool, P.A.S. 1997. 'Zennor Bounds Revisited'. *Journal of the Royal Institution of Cornwall*, N.S. 2.4, pp. 37–41.

Pool, P.A.S. and O.J. Padel 1975/6. 'William Bodinar's Letter, 1776'. *Journal of the Royal Institution of Cornwall*, N.S. 7.3, pp. 231–3.

Price, G. 1976. 'A Note on Two Attestations to Late Cornish'. *Bulletin of the Board of Celtic Studies* 26.4, pp. 413–16.

Pryce, W. 1790. *Archaeologia Cornu-Britannica; or an Essay to Preserve the Ancient Cornish Language*. Sherborne.

Ray, J. 1760. *Select Remains of the Learned John Ray . . . with his Life by the Late William Derham*. London.

Ray, J. 1846. *Memorials of John Ray*, ed. E. Lankester. London.

Rowse, A.L. 1941. *Tudor Cornwall*. London.

Scawen, W. 1777 [orig. *c*.1678] *Observations on an Ancient Manuscript called Passio Christi . . . with an Account of the Language, Manners and Customs of the People of Cornwall*. London.

Smith, L.T. (ed.) 1907. *The Itinerary of John Leland in or about the Years 1535–1543, Parts I to III*. London.

Spriggs, M. 1998. 'The Reverend Joseph Sherwood: a Cornish Language Will-o'-the-Wisp?'. In P. Payton, (ed.), *Cornish Studies: Six*. Exeter, pp. 46–61.

Stoyle, M. 2002. *West Britons: Cornish Identities and the Early Modern British State*. Exeter.

Symonds, R. 1859. *Diary of the Marches of the Royal Army during the Great Civil War*, ed. C.E. Long. London.

Thomas, A.C. 1967. *Christian Antiquities of Camborne*. St Austell.

Toorians, L. 1991. *The Middle Cornish Charter Endorsement: The Making of a Marriage in Medieval Cornwall. Innsbrucker Beiträge zur Sprachwissenschaft* 67. Innsbruck.

Venn, J. and J.A. Venn 1922. *Alumni Cantabrigienses, Part I, From the Earliest Times to 1751*. Cambridge.

Wakelin, M.F. 1975. *Language and History in Cornwall*. Leicester.

Whetter, J. 1962. 'An Exchequer Court Case Relating to Gorran Haven'. *Old Cornwall*, 6.2, pp. 68–72.

Whetter, J. 1998. 'Gorran Historical Notes: Place-Names'. *Old Cornwall*, 12.2, pp. 39–40.

Whitaker, J. 1804. *Supplement to the First and Second Books of the 'History of Cornwall'* [by R. Polwhele]. London.

Whitley, H.M. 1882. 'The Church Goods of Cornwall at the Time of the Reformation'. *Journal of the Royal Institution of Cornwall*, 7.2, (no. 25), pp. 92–135.

Williams, N.J.A. 1995. *Cornish Today: An Examination of the Revived Language*. Sutton Coldfield.

NOTES AND REFERENCES

1. W. Borlase *Antiquities Historical and Monumental of the County of Cornwall*, London, 1769, p. ix.

2. G. Price (ed.), *Languages in Britain and Ireland*, Oxford, 2002, is a good survey of the history of languages in Britain. H. Härke, 'Kings and Warriors: Population and Landscape from Post-Roman to Norman Britain', in P. Slack and R. Ward (eds), *The Peopling of Britain: The Shaping of a Human Landscape*, Oxford, 2002, discusses some of the attendant social processes involved. I am drawing in this section on a discussion of speech community events by M. Ross, 'Social Networks and Kinds of Speech-Community Event', in R. Blench and M. Spriggs (eds), *Archaeology and Language I: Theoretical and Methodological Orientations*, London, 1997, pp. 210–61. For discussions of the notion of colonialism in the pre-modern period I am grateful to Chris Gosden.

3. Price, 2002, Chapter 6.

4. H. Härke, 'Population Replacement or Acculturation? An Archaeological Perspective on Population and Migration in Post-Roman Britain', in H.L.C. Tristram (ed.), *The Celtic Englishes III*, Heidelberg, in press; J. Hines, 'Britain after Rome: Between Multiculturalism and Mono-culturalism', in P. Graves-Brown, S. Jones and C. Gamble (eds), *Cultural Identity and Archaeology: The Construction of European Communities*, London, 1996, pp. 256–69; J. Hines, 'Welsh and English: Mutual Origins in Post-Roman Britain?', *Studia Celtica*, 34, 2000, pp. 81–104; H. Kleinschmidt, 'What Does the "Anglo-Saxon Chronicle" Tell Us about "Ethnic' Origins?"', *Studi Medievali*, 3rd series, 2001, 42.1, pp. 1–40.

5. Hines, 1996; Hines, 2000.

6. Hines, 2000, pp. 89–98. The quotation which follows is from p. 88.

7. Hines, 1996, p. 265.

8. Hines, 2000, pp. 98–102. The quotation is from p. 101

9. Cited in Härke, in press.

10. Price, 2002, Chapter 9.

11. Hines, 1996, pp. 265–6.

12. Kleinschmidt, 2001.

13. W. Stubbs, *Willelmi Malmesbiriensis . . . Rolls Series* 90, 1887, p. 148; Translation is in H.P.R. Finberg, 'Sherborne, Glastonbury, and the Expansion of Wessex', *Transactions of the Royal Historical Society*, 5th series, 3, 1953, p. 117. If ethnic cleansing appears too modern a term, perhaps we should resurrect 'driving'? Writing of this same event in 1818, 'D' in his 'Letters on the Ancient British Language of Cornwall', *Classical Journal*, 34–43, 1818–20, p. 442, compared it to 'The driving of the

inhabitants, as happened during the recent invasion of Portugal by Massena, and the expedition of Napoleon to Moscow'. The result is the same.

14. Finberg, 1953, p. 119; O.J. Padel, 'Place-Names', in R. Kain and W. Ravenhill (eds), *Historical Atlas of South-West England*, Exeter, 1999, p. 93.

15. Summarized in M. Spriggs, 'The Cornish Language, Archaeology, and the Origins of English Theatre', in press; cf C. Thomas, 'Settlement History in Early Cornwall: I, The Hundreds', *Cornish Archaeology*, 3, 1964, pp. 73–4.

16. Pertinent references to this period include: D. Hooke, 'Saxon Conquest and Settlement', in Kain and Ravenhill, 1999, pp. 95–104; M. Todd, *The South-West to AD 1000*, London, 1987, Chapter 10.

17. See J. Angarrack, *Our Future is History: Identity, Law and the Cornish Question*, Padstow, 2002, for a recent overtly Cornish nationalist reading of this history. In his Chapter 5 he alleges some serious and wilful acts of over-interpretation among historians of this period which surely deserve a response from those accused.

18. W. Scawen, *Antiquities Cornu-Britannick, or Observations on an Ancient Manuscript written in the Cornish Language*. From a manuscript in the Library of Thomas Astle, Esq. No publisher given, 1777, is the only published version, reprinted several times from a lost manuscript early version of the work, most accessibly by D. Gilbert, *The Parochial History of Cornwall*, 4 volumes, London, 1838, in Volume IV, pp. 190–221. For details of the extant manuscripts see entry for William Scawen by M. Spriggs in *New Dictionary of National Biography*, Oxford, in press.

19. Cf. J.R. Elliott Jr, 'Medieval Rounds and Wooden O's: The Medieval Heritage of the Elizabethan Theatre', in N. Denny (ed.), *Medieval Drama*, London, 1973, pp. 225–6; A.C. Cawley et al., *The Revels History of Drama in English, Volume I, Medieval Drama*, London, 1983, pp. xlii–xliv. W. Hals, *Lhadymer ay Kernow*, BL Add. Ms, 71,057, dictionary entry under 'Gwarry' makes the following interesting claim: 'However in the Latter end of the Reigne off Queen Eliz. Those plays were altogether suppressed by the Cornish Justices of the peace in open sessions by order or rule of Court'.

20. Gilbert, 1838, Vol. IV, p. 205.

21. As I argue at some length in Spriggs, in press.

22. Gilbert, 1838, Vol. IV, pp. 214–15.

23. F.E. Halliday, *The Legend of the Rood*, London, 1955, p. 11.

24. G. Price, *The Languages of Britain*, London, 1984, pp. 98–100. N.J.A. Williams, *Cornish Today: An Examination of the Revived Language*, Sutton Coldfield, 1995, p. 169 presents some interesting ideas on this.

25. Gilbert, 1838, Vol. IV, p. 206.

26. Gilbert, 1838, Vol. IV, p. 214.

27. N. Orme, 'Education in the Medieval Cornish Play Beunans Meriasek', *Cambridge Medieval Celtic Studies*, 25, 1993, p. 13.

28. The first statement occurs in H. Jenner, 'The Cornish Language', *Transactions of the Philological Society*, 1873–4, p. 178, and is repeated in his

Handbook of the Cornish Language, London, 1904, p. 11. The second quotation is from *Handbook*, p. 194. The 1873–4 publication is the first to go into detail on the 'spot references' that enable us to track where Cornish was spoken at particular times. Jenner accepted both the idea that Cornish was spoken in Devon in the medieval period and in Menheniot in East Cornwall in Henry VIII's time (see discussion later in the text).

29. R.M. Nance, 'Hints for Place-Name Study', *Old Cornwall*, 3.6, 1939, pp. 257–60.
30. This quotation is given in A.S.D. Smith, *The Story of the Cornish Language: Its Extinction and Revival*, Camborne, 1947, p. 6. Smith does not give a source for the quotation.
31. C. Henderson, *Essays in Cornish History*, ed. A.L. Rowse and M.I. Henderson, Oxford, 1935, p. 144n.
32. M. Wakelin, *Language and History in Cornwall*, Leicester, 1975, Chapter 4.
33. Wakelin's place-name evidence was from an unpublished study by J.E.B. Gover, 'The Place-Names of Cornwall', 1948, typescript in the Royal Institution of Cornwall, Truro.
34. M. Wakelin, 1975, pp. 74n and 77n.
35. J.G. Holmes, 'The Place of Cornish in East Cornwall, 700–1500 AD', unpublished paper presented to the 6th International Congress of Celtic Studies, Galway, Ireland, 1979; K. George, 'How Many People Spoke Cornish Traditionally?', *Cornish Studies*, 14, 1986. See Holmes this volume for further discussion of the issues raised in that paper.
36. George, 1986, p. 69. O.J. Padel, *A Popular Dictionary of Cornish Place-Names*, Penzance, 1988, pp. 30–1 expresses his reservations about the approach.
37. H. Abalain, *Destin des Langues Celtiques*, Paris, 1989, p. 170. The map is reproduced in D. Nettle and S. Romaine, *Vanishing Voices: The Extinction of the World's Languages*, Oxford, 2000, p. 137. It is not clear if this information is directly from Ken George and represents later adjustments to his 1986 views, as the exact source is not indicated. George is thanked in the acknowledgements of Abalain's book. A recent oral tradition may be the source, in the form '1400 Boscastle to Looe', as endpoint towns for each isobar are usually indicated on the map.
38. Williams, 1995, pp. 77, 79–90. The quotation is from p. 80. A more explicit statement on p. 77 gives the date as 'the middle of the sixteenth century'. In an earlier paper Williams had concluded more cautiously that the Padstow–Fowey line was the Cornish–English frontier in about 1535: N. Williams, 'A Problem in Cornish Phonology', in M.J. Ball et al. (eds), *Celtic Linguistics/Ieithyddiaeth Geltaidd: Readings in the Brythonic Languages. Festschrift for T. Arwyn Watkins*, Amsterdam, 1990, p. 259.
39. Williams, 1995, pp. 71–5.
40. P. Dunbar and K. George, *Kernewek Kemmyn: Cornish for the Twenty-First Century*, Cornish Language Board, 1997. N. Kennedy reviewed Williams's book in P. Payton (ed.), *Cornish Studies: Four*, Exeter, 1996,

pp. 171–81. A.P. Grant reviewed Dunbar and George approvingly in P. Payton (ed.), *Cornish Studies: Six*, Exeter 1998, pp. 194–9.

41. Dunbar and George, 1997, p. 159.
42. Padel, 1999; cf. O. Svensson, *Saxon Place-Names in East Cornwall, Lund Studies in English* 77, 1987.
43. Dunbar and George, 1997, p. 158. The map is based on original research by K. George, but the sources consulted are not given.
44. Padel, 1988, pp. 27–34.
45. R.M. Nance, 'When was Cornish last Spoken Traditionally?', *Journal of the Royal Institution of Cornwall*, N.S. 7.1, 1973, pp. 76–82. R. Lyon, *Cornish: The Struggle for Survival*, Tavas an Weryn, 2001.
46. H.S.A. Fox and O.J. Padel, *The Cornish Lands of the Arundells of Lanherne, Fourteenth to Sixteenth Centuries. Devon and Cornwall Record Society*, N.S. 41, 2000, pp. cxxv–cxxxvii.
47. O.J. Padel, 'Cornish Language Notes 3', *Cornish Studies*, 3, 1975, pp. 19–22.
48. Extracted from T.L. Stoate, *The Cornwall Protestation Returns 1641*, Bristol, 1981, pp. 30–1; T.L. Stoate, *Cornwall Hearth and Poll Taxes 1660–1664*, Bristol, 1981, p. 127.
49. D.J. North and A. Sharpe, *A Word-Geography of Cornwall*, Redruth, 1980; D.J. North, 'Towards a Framework for the Analysis of English in Cornwall', *Leeds Studies in English*, N.S. 19, 1988, pp. 203–230; D.J. North, *Studies in the Phonology of West Penwith English, Studies in Anglo-Cornish Phonology* 2, Redruth, 1991.
50. Fox and Padel, 2000, pp. cxxx–cxxxi.
51. References from John Leland 1538 in L.T. Smith, *The Itinerary of John Leland in or about the Years 1535–1543, Parts I to III*, London, 1907, pp. 179, 193, 203; Bosvenna from John Norden 1584, published as J. Norden, *Speculi Britanniae Pars: A Topographical and Historical Description of Cornwall*, Newcastle-upon-Tyne, 1966 [orig. 1728], p. 50.
52. See Map in S.L. Joyce and E.S. Newlyn (eds), *Records of Early English Drama: Cornwall*, Toronto, 1999, p. 462.
53. See Appendix 1 under 1349 and 1355.
54. Padel, 1999.
55. Todd, 1987, p. 274 for the quotation. Todd gives a good summary of the Anglo-Saxon penetration of the area pp. 267–75. W.G. Hoskins, *Devon*, London, 1954, p. 46 states that less than 1 per cent of Devon place-names overall are of Celtic origin.
56. R. Polwhele, *The History of Cornwall*, Vol. 5, Dorking, 1978 [1806], p. 4. and Vol. 3, Dorking, 1978 [1803], pp. 28–9.
57. G.A., 'Some English Place Names', *Cornhill Magazine*, 54, 1881, p. 569. For the discussion in *The Western Antiquary*, see I, Jan. 1882, p. 164; I, Feb. 1882, pp. 172, 199; I, March 1882, p. 203.
58. I. Taylor, *Words and Places*, London, 1864; 2nd expanded edition London, 1865. I have only seen the 4th edition edited by A. Smythe Palmer (London, 1909), but this follows the 1865 edition. In the 1909 edition, the

quotation is on p. 171. In the much reprinted Everyman edition (London, 1911), it occurs on p. 184

59. The only copy of this manuscript dates from 1750 and is in the hands of Henry Ustick (1720–69). It is now in the Royal Institution of Cornwall. The passage can be found in O.J. Padel, *The Cornish Writings of the Boson Family*, Redruth, 1975, p. 24, with Padel's useful footnotes on p. 35. The text was written at some time between 1675 and 1708, as discussed in M. Spriggs, 'The Reverend Joseph Sherwood: A Cornish Language Will-'O-the-Wisp', in P. Payton, 1998 p. 55. For the family of Harris of Hayne, see A. Pool, 'Harris of Kenegie', *Old Cornwall*, 4.7, 1948, pp. 224–7. The family connection with West Cornwall goes back to at least 1591, and the Cornish motto was perhaps adopted at about that time.

60. See W.C. Borlase, 'The Ustick Manuscript from the MSS. of Dr Borlase', *Journal of the Royal Institution of Cornwall*, 21, 1879, pp. 182–9. Jenner, 1904, p. 11, might just be referring to Taylor's claim, but he had read *Nebbaz Gerriau* in 1877 or 1878 and had then copied about half of it (which would have included the relevant section), even before its publication in 1879: see p. 32.

61. J. Loth, 'Reste de Brittonique en Devon au XIVe Siècle', *Revue Celtique*, 34, 1913, pp. 180–1, reports a possible instance of Brittonic but (he claims) not Cornish speech from fourteenth century Devon in a boundary document. This is referred to approvingly by Williams, 1995, p. 80, but Oliver Padel has pointed out to me that Loth's 'due Glas' in the bounds of Brentmoor is actually the latin 'duae' (two) and that there are other instances of renderings of latin *-ae* as *-e* in these texts. The word thus provides no evidence for the survival of Brittonic speech in Devon.

62. Williams, 1995, pp. 82–3. For 'Glas' see J.E.B. Gover et al., *The Place Names of Devon*, Vol. 1, Cambridge, 1931, p. 6 under Glaze Brook.

63. Quoted in Appendix 1 under 1602.

64. W. Hals, *History of Cornwall*, BL Add. Ms. 29762. When discussing the late survival of Cornish in Feock parish on fo. 76r, Hals cross references his discussion of Johm Moreman under Menheniot on fo. 176r where his sources are Prince and Hooker (see below). The implication of his cross-reference, and back reference to Feock and Creed where he gives supposed Cornish forms of the Communion service and the Creed and gives the Carew quote cited earlier (fo. 38r for Creed), is of previous Cornish language use. His next discussion, however, is of the recall of 'all Bookes of the Latine Service' (fo. 178r).

65. J. Prince, *Damnonii Orientales Illustres, or the Worthies of Devon*, Exeter, 1701, pp. 452–3. He is quoting John Hooker (alias Vowell), *Synopsis of Devon*, BL Harleian Ms. 5827, which I have not consulted. This is also quoted by W.J. Blake, 'The Rebellion of Cornwall and Devon in 1549' (Part 1), *Journal of the Royal Institution of Cornwall*, 18.1, 1910, p. 167. Hooker was a pupil of Moreman in Menheniot in the 1530s: see J. Youings 'The South-Western Rebellion of 1549', *Southern History*, 1, 1979, p. 115, where it is suggested that Moreman was responding to Bishop Voysey's instructions of 1538.

66. D. Defoe, *A Tour Thro' Great Britain*, London, 1742, p. 325. Also in the 1724 edition, p. 86 of Letter III. 'Southold', more correctly South Hole, is in Hartland, Devon.

67. R.M. Nance, 'The Cornish Language in the Seventeenth Century', *Old Cornwall*, 6.1, 1962, pp. 20–6. A.S.D. Smith, *The Story of the Cornish Language*, Camborne, 1947, p. 9, quotes a paper of Nance as stating that 'Some of the statements in Jenner's *Handbook* he would have altered himself if he had brought out a new edition; as I know, from having discussed these points with him'. Nance then goes on to dismiss the idea that Cornish was spoken at Menheniot in Tudor times or across the border in Devon in the late medieval period. Smith gives no details of the source for the paper by Nance.

68. Quoted in Appendix 5, p. 331 of W.J. Blake, 'The Rebellion of Cornwall and Devon in 1549' (Part 2), *Journal of the Royal Institution of Cornwall*, 18.2, 1911, pp. 300–38. D. and S. Lysons, *Magna Britannia: Cornwall*, London, 1814, p. iv citing Hooker also make it clear that he was 'speaking of the kingdom at large' in referring to Moreman's innovation of using English in the service.

69. See footnote 37 above for discussion of Abalain, 1989.

70. Holmes, 1979. These areas of English place-names were first delineated by N.J.G. Pounds, 'Cornwall's Eastern Frontier', *Old Cornwall*, 3.10, 1941, pp. 398–401.

71. Julyan Holmes and I were preparing our papers at the same time and I was able to consult his only at a late stage of preparation of this paper. From his paper I note additional examples of the 1100–1200 AD sound shifts which do not occur on my Figure 2 for the parishes of St Breock, Lostwithiel, Roche, and Treneglos. To his own lists I would add St Breward, Budock, Camborne, St Clement, St Columb Minor, Constantine, St Dennis, Gerrans, St Gluvias, Gorran, St Issey, St Just in Roseland, Kenwyn, Ladock, additional examples from Little Petherick and Luxulyan, Newlyn East, Probus, St Stephen in Brannel and Stithians. Only some of these occur in the eastern area with which he is immediately concerned. Additional sources are: C. Henderson, 'Some Old Names on Black-More', *Old Cornwall*, 1.6, 1927, pp. 1–5; P. Hodge, *The History of Cornish in the Parish of St Stephen in Brannel*, Gwinear, 1998; Holmes, 1979 and pers. comm.; R.M. Nance, 'Some Old Cornish Weirs', *Old Cornwall*, 3.6, 1939, pp. 225–8; O.J. Padel, 'Cornish Language Notes 1', *Cornish Studies*, 1, 1973, pp. 57–59; J. Whetter, 'Gorran Historical Notes: Place-Names', *Old Cornwall*, 12.2 1998, 39–40; Williams, 1995, p. 84.

72. The dialect words of interest include *mooldy* (St Ewe, and on north coast east to Gwithian) and *bannel* (only found in St Austell, St Ewe and St Dennis) for the south coast, and *widden* and *pig's crow* (both east to St Agnes) for the north coast; information from North, 1991, pp. 110–14. The -*n* to -*dn* and -*m* to -*bm* shifts on which the 1600 AD boundary is based in Figures 4 and 7 are listed in Appendix 2, with sources.

73. For Tregear see Appendix 1 under 1555–8. The idea that he was associated with Newlyn East comes from P.B. Ellis, *The Cornish Language and its*

Literature, London, 1974, p. 65, but no source is given for the statement. This idea is repeated by Williams, 1995, p. 75, again without reference, and is accepted by Dunbar and George, 1997, p. 62. The parish of St Allen is adjacent to Newlyn East. The southern end of the Holmes–George 1600 line was drawn to take in the 1595 reference to St Ewe (see Appendix 1).

74. See A.C. Thomas, *Exploration of a Drowned Landscape*, London, 1985, p. 36, quoted in Dunbar and George, 1997, p. 63. See also C. Thomas, 'A Glossary of Spoken English in the Isles of Scilly', *Journal of the Royal Institution of Cornwall*, N.S. 8.2, 1979, pp. 109–47.

75. For this latter point see reference to 'After 1640 Feock' in Appendix 1. The other references referred to in the text can be found there by year concerned.

76. C. Thomas, 'The Irish Settlements in Post-Roman Western Britain: a Survey of the Evidence', *Journal of the Royal Institution of Cornwall*, N.S. 6.4, 1972, p. 271.

77. We have good evidence of Cornish being known in Newlyn and Mouse-hole from this period, areas adjacent to the larger centre of Penzance, presumably where much of the fish from those ports would have been sold. See D. Barrington, 'On the Expiration of the Cornish Language', *Archaeologia*, 3, 1776, pp. 279–84; D. Barrington, 'Mr Barrington on some Additional Information relativee to the Continuance of the Cornish Language', *Archaeologia*, 5, 1779, pp. 81–6. See also Appendix 1 under 1756 to 1800 for further references.

78. Jenner, 1904, pp. 13–14, 21. He must have examined the Banks correspondence some time prior to 1874, as he also refers to it in *Transactions of the Philological Society*, 1873–4, p. 182, where he states he had examined the letter 'some time ago'. The source for the Spanish State Papers is given as BL Add. Ms. 28,240.

79. From J. Brooke, 'Open Workings', *Old Cornwall*, 12.7, 2000, pp. 22–3.

ON THE TRACK OF CORNISH IN A BILINGUAL COUNTRY

Julyan Holmes

INTRODUCTION

Politically and socially dominant languages can conceal the existence of a minority culture. For example, in the 1970s, new to the Cornish language and the wider 'Celtic scene', I was eager to try out what I knew of other Celtic languages—in particular, Breton. Despite its two million speakers, Breton was, for political reasons, almost invisible; even native speakers seemed to use French in public places. If one asked about the language, responses were not always dependable. In the Cornwall of 1700, a minority language also persisted, sometimes proudly, sometimes shame-faced, under pressure from what was (one might argue) an intolerant, centralizing elite. So, when Edward Lhuyd[1] asked similar questions about the Cornish language at that time, did he get an accurate answer? In this article, through examination of the historical shapes of place-names and other evidence, and by con-centrating on East Cornwall, I will argue that the Cornish language had a longer and stronger life than is sometimes suggested.

THE PROBLEM OF EAST CORNWALL

North and East Cornwall have tended to be sidelined by the quest for the 'last' native-speakers of Cornish. That quest has focused, naturally enough, on the Land's End peninsula, but this has had the effect of deflecting scholarly attention from other parts of Cornwall. A detailed account of the Cornish language in the eastern districts has not previously been attempted, and this article is the first to try to present a synthesis of existing and new knowledge to provide such an account. Hitherto, broad statements concerning the decline of the language,

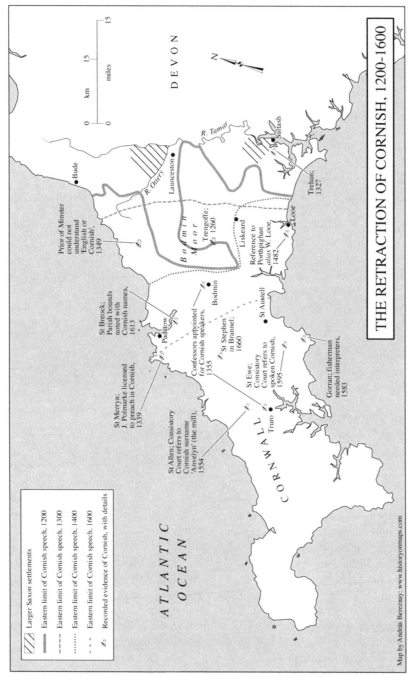

1. Map of East Cornwall, showing suggested eastern boundaries of Cornish 1200–1600.

THE RETRACTION OF CORNISH, 1200-1600

Larger Saxon settlements
Eastern limit of Cornish speech, 1200
Eastern limit of Cornish speech, 1300
Eastern limit of Cornish speech, 1400
Eastern limit of Cornish speech, 1600
Recorded evidence of Cornish, with details

ATLANTIC OCEAN

DEVON

CORNWALL

Bodmin Moor

R. Tamar

R. Otery

Bude
Launceston
Saltash
Trehan: 1327
Looe
Liskeard
Reference to Porthpighan alias W. Looe, 1482
Trengoffe: 1260
Prior of Minster could not understand 'English or Cornish', 1349
Bodmin
St Breock: Parish bounds noted with Cornish names, 1613
Padstow
Confessors appointed for Cornish speakers, 1355
St Austell
St Stephen in Brannel 1660
St Ewe: Consistory Court refers to spoken Cornish, 1595
Gorran: fisherman needed interpreters, 1583
St Merryn: J. Polmarke licensed to preach in Cornish, 1339
St Allen: Consistory Court refers to Cornish surname 'Anvelyn' (the mill), 1554
Truro

km
miles
0 15
0 15

N

Map by András Berznay; www.historyonmaps.com

even by fervent Revivalists like Morton Nance, have been rather simplistic: Cornwall was divided into an 'Old Cornish' zone in 'the North', where Cornish 'died out' by around 1200 AD, and 'the South', where features of Middle Cornish, such as the 's' form (for example, 'nans', a valley, replacing older 'nant'), prove the language survived later.[2] However, despite its simplicity, the principle is basically sound, but only if treated critically and used alongside other evidence, as it is in this article. The spread of this 't'>'s' feature and other dateable linguistic developments in place-names have been used on Figure 1 to plot boundaries for the minimum area of Cornish usage at certain dates, for this emblematic change in Cornish of final and medial 't'>'s' is the earliest reliable 'litmus-test' that we have for the continued use of the language in a particular locality. In the spoken language, this change took place in the eleventh or twelfth century. The earliest instance in place-names[3] is 1141, unless Rislestone' in Domesday Book, i.e. present day Rillaton, in Linkinhorne, is accepted. The 't'>'s' development is usually first recorded between 1200 and 1300, but sometimes much later. There are cases in East Cornwall where the 's' survives in the present-day name, even as far east as Rezare in Lezant. As the map demonstrates, I have linked these occurrences to make a base-line which I have conservatively considered the eastern boundary of Cornish *c*.1200 AD. The next, narrowly dated change, 'nn'>'dn', not found in place-names until the late sixteenth century, only shows up on the extreme western fringe of my map. Vowel changes are very dependent on orthographic practice but some are mentioned later.

REVERSIONS
Based on an assessment of the effects of bilingualism (or rather, of the juxtaposition of two language groups), I have drawn a slightly con-troversial conclusion. I consider that my data can be used to show not only the *earliest* possible date at which Cornish became extinct at a given point, but also a likely date for when it did fall out of use. I base this on the dates of 'reversions', i.e. where modernized Cornish forms of place-names, having appeared at some point, revert to older forms. These cases are listed, by parish and to the nearest century, in the appendices. The principal reason for these bizarre reversions must be the influence of English, as a second and ultimately dominant language. Cornish place-names in this area were almost always first adopted in English during the Old Cornish period. In English they ceased to evolve, which they continued to do in Cornish, as an integral part of the language. When Cornish was no longer spoken in a locality, the modern forms also dropped out of use, in favour of the form used in English. Ironically, they revert to obsolete Old Cornish, long disused

in the contemporary language! Names in use today are obviously not necessarily the 'best' or most modern form ever used by Cornish-speakers. A single exemplar can prove that a name in un-advanced, Old Cornish had in fact continued to evolve. This is clear proof that the language was spoken at this point long after the present map-form of the name would suggest. The pattern is shown by Middle Cornish 'Pennans' 1375, in St. Veep, found on today's map as 'Pennant'. Numerous examples will be found in the appendices. Most common in the east, the phenomenon is nonetheless found all over Cornwall; a selection of 'reverted' names includes Liskeard, Bodmin, Lanivet, Ladock, Restronguet, Redruth and Sancreed. All of these have attested 's' forms and constitute evidence for tracking down Cornish-speakers. Given somewhat limited data, these 'reversions' can only be a very approximate guide, but, as can be seen, date-lines deduced from them agree very well, firstly with the expected general retreat westwards, and secondly with other data, mostly the few 'spot-references' in Church and Court records.

MISLEADING FORMS

It is misleading, as some have done, to base conclusions on modern map-forms which frequently obscure the history of our language. Not only do they hide the 'reversions', described above, but in some cases conceal the very language of the original name. Cornish words can be re-interpreted, in weird and wonderful ways, as English. At Polperro, a mill called in 1565 'Tremylhorne' has ended up 'Crumplehorn'! Elsewhere, names are simply so corrupted as to be unrecognizable. Without older references, would we recognize that 'Marcradden,[4] in St Just in Roseland, derives from 'Mencrom(e)', a 'curved stone'. Only earlier forms provide the necessary clarification. For these, the best starting point is still J.E.B. Gover's typescript.[5] Most historical forms used here are from that source.

'IN CORNWALL IS TWO SPECHES'

The key to 'reversions' lies in the above statement by Andrew Boorde in 1542.[6] There has always been at least one other language beside Cornish in use here; English and Norman French are the most obvious incursers, but Latin, Breton,[7] maybe even Irish and Norse, have made their mark. When English-speakers colonized or acculturated parts of Cornwall, they named, or re-christened, settlements in the current Saxon fashion. Saxon names are heavily concentrated in two well-defined districts: one lies north and east of a line running from Millook (Cor. 'Porth Oy', 1481), through Poundstock, Week St Mary and Jacobstow, down the River Ottery to the Tamar, near Launceston.

Coincidence or not, the Ottery formed part of the 'county' border from 1086 to modern times. Saxon names here, often 'worthy' and 'cot', are identical in nature to those of North Devon and parts of Somerset.[8] They would seem to mark major Saxon colonization or acculturation in the area, for which the likely context is Centwine's claim, in 682, to have driven the Britons 'as far as the sea'.

A less defined area of heavily saxonized names lies between the Lynher and the Tamar. This might relate to land at 'Linig by Tamar', granted to Glastonbury in 710, by King Ine of Wessex.

It has been suggested that these two areas, especially the northern one, indicate an early ethnic boundary. When the Cornish king Gerent, in 705, probably as a gesture of appeasement, granted land at Maker to Bishop Aldhelm of Sherborne, it probably concerned transfer of revenue rather than land for Saxon colonization. *Linig*, on the other hand, as spoils of victory, does contain a number of Saxon names, mostly the later 'ham' and 'ton'. It is worth remembering that, until Athelstan's 'ethnic cleansing'[9] in the tenth century, a more extensive 'Cornwall', and with it British speech, stretched across the Tamar as far as Exeter. In most of south-east Cornwall, a high proportion of Cornish names extend to the banks of the Tamar. Taking all this into account, I infer that at the Norman Conquest Cornish was everywhere the majority language west of the Tamar, with the possible exception of the far north-east. Elsewhere, Saxon settlements, such as Newham, near Truro, were thinly scattered. Other settlements are indicated by the place-name 'Tresawson', i.e. 'Englishmen's farm'; there is one such in Lanreath. The very language of the name makes it plain that these were Saxon estates in solidly Cornish districts. But English names, or Cornish ones referring to 'sowson', saxons, do not have to be early; some may have been coined well into the Middle Ages.

Larger urban settlements, such as Bodmin, were quite late, at least tenth century. Launceston on its present site is post-Norman Conquest. Both towns must also have had substantial native Cornish populations. The suffixes 'ham' and 'ton', common in '*Linig*', the second area, seem to be later name-types. 'Ton' denotes, not an influx of settlers, but rather an administrative centre. It is often added to the existing name of a Cornish town. With Helston, 'Henlistone' in the Domesday Book, the first element, 'hen lis', is Cornish for 'old court', suggesting importance in pre-Saxon times. Helston in Kerrier was overwhelmingly Cornish-speaking until at least 1650, made clear by the Cornish street-names in use until then. The inhabitants referred to it as 'Hellas',[10] never bothering with the English 'ton'. Similarly with Rialton, 'Ryall' in 1420, and Launceston, twelfth-century 'Lanstavanton', and still 'called by the Cornish, Lesteevan', says Carew (see note 10).

'Stow' and 'stoke' marked Saxon religious centres. Presumably, these words were not used in Cornish, but I do not know of an example to prove this. The late colloquial version of 'Davidstow', 'Dewstow', given by John Norden, may contain a Cornish equivalent of 'Dewi', the popular form in Welsh of Dafydd (David). Jacobstow, 'Yacobstowe de Penalyn', 1270, was probably referred to in Cornish by the second, manorial, name. As with 'ton', these English names probably reflect ecclesiastical ownership and control, not the ethnic make-up of the local clergy. The tenth-century Bodmin Manumissions do show a roughly equal mix of population amongst the clergy, to judge from their names. This is complicated by the custom of some Cornishmen to adopt, or be 'honoured' with, Saxon personal names, e.g. the Alfeah Gerent found in the Bodmin Manumissions. All the same, if we take 'stow' to be equivalent to Cornish 'lan', we may note that Jacobstow, Morwenstow, Davidstow and Warbstow are in the north and east of Cornwall, the 'cot' and 'worthy' district, where Saxon immigration or domination was probably both early and concentrated.

BORROWING

Besides new formations, wholly or partly in the intrusive language, many older names, 100 per cent Cornish in origin, came to be used in English. Borrowed early, they are derived from Old Cornish, tenth-century or earlier forms of the names. 'Penquite', in Duloe, retained, at least among English-speakers, the final 't' of *Pencuit* (cf. 'Penquit', near Kingsbridge, in Devon, a very rare survival of Cornish in England; this name was probably 'frozen' at the time of Athelstan's tenth-century ethnic purge). Further west, e.g. in Kenwyn, the influence of Cornish-speakers meant that the form eventually adopted in English is the later 'Pencoose'. Borrowing and 'freezing' of names took place in other linguistic combinations. 'Grampound', from French 'Grand pont', was, in Cornish, 'Ponsmur', 1302, but never had a true 'English' name. 'Perranzabuloe' is the Latin of Cornish 'Pirantreth' (printed *Perankreth* on Norden's map, 1584). Thomas Tonkin's late seventeenth-century 'Piran-in-the-sands',[11] if ever actually current, did not catch on.

DIVERGENCE

As an integral part of the language, place-names develop just like any other words, *but only in the mouths of those speaking the original language.* So, even when speakers of both languages originally shared the same name, they drifted apart. In an environment of widespread bilingualism, minor divergences will have presented few problems (compared with such dissimilar couplets as St Blazey *alias* Landreth,

1601, or Mousehole/Porthenys), certainly no more than the comparable situation in Wales or Canada today. If people were aware of growing differences between 'their' form and that used in the other language, their attitude was likely to be have been contempt or at best irritation.[12] Certainly English-users would not normally have felt the pressure, consciously or unconsciously felt by Cornish-speakers, to up-date place-names. For that reason, the English language frequently preserved obsolete Cornish names. In the case of important manors, scribal conservatism may be another factor in the preservation of Old Cornish forms. Though these names will not have stayed 'fossilized' in the everyday conversation of local Cornish-speakers, English or French scribes, even if aware of 'corrupted' later forms, might have preferred to reproduce existing documents. Cornish words may, in any case, have been meaningless for them, a by-product of the reduced status of the native language. We must not be misled into talk of written and oral forms; Cornish-speakers were as likely to be literate as anyone else, and no doubt used contemporary Cornish in their own writings.

The noted Catholic scholar and poet John of Cornwall,[13] came from St Germans in the twelfth century. Ralph de Tremur,[14] a proto-Protestant priest from Lanivet, troubled Bishop Grandisson in the 1330s by denying transubstantiation. Both men were fluent in at least four languages: Cornish, English, French and Latin. It is likely that the Old Cornish vocabulary was adapted from a Saxon/Latin glossary, either at St Germans or in some other East Cornish priory.

SHIFTING PATTERN
Historically, names in Cornish may appear in any mix of Old and Middle Cornish forms. Occasionally Cornish and English qualifiers alternate, testifying to the shifting patterns of two language communities living cheek by jowl. A good example comes from St Kew where the estate of 'Tregoyt' is delimited in 1331 by 'nithera' (i.e. English 'lower'), but in 1350 by Cornish 'great' and 'small', i.e. Tregoyd-mur and -bian. Near Bodmin, Little Kirland is still 'Kirland Veghan' in 1525. In the appendices are a few other examples of active Cornish qualifiers, and also 'correct' Cornish spellings suggest that the names were written by persons used to writing in Cornish. Without corroborating testimony, dateable linguistic developments must provide the backbone of my theory.

As a rule, the language of the proprietor will have determined whether the contemporary form of Cornish was noted in records, but an overwhelmingly Cornish-speaking environment may anyway have forced acceptance of the contemporary version. Further west, where the latter situation lasted later, place-names are accordingly more likely, but not necessarily, fixed in their latest Cornish form. In the case of major towns, a contemporary Cornish name may have been kept in use by speakers in other parts: 'Loundres' 1710 (Bilbao Manuscripts[15]) for London, or 'Caeriske'[16] for Exeter, do not imply Cornish-speaking inhabitants in those cities. Even the Middle Cornish form of Bodmin, 'Bosvene',[17] does not in itself imply that its inhabitants spoke Cornish at that time, though place-name forms strongly suggest that some did. But when a later Cornish form is found for a less important place, it is fair to assume that it was used by Cornish-speakers, in that locality. It almost certainly proves the existence there of Cornish-speakers at a period contemporary with that form of Cornish.

Until Cornish was abandoned, two versions of a name were contemporary alternatives. The form in later Cornish was lost and replaced by that used in English, very often the same, but in an older form. Effectively, these reversions are no different from any other case where English replaced Cornish. A rock off Dodman Point hovers in the 1700s between 'Carrack Due'[18] (Moll's map, 1724) and 'Black Rock'[19] (Taylor, 1715); a stone on the Lizard is referred to on the Reskimmer Estate Book of 1812 as 'Men Mellon' *alias* 'Yellow Stone'. In both cases, the translations mark the last use of Cornish in their respective districts.

English spellings can be anarchic and in the early medieval period there are also problems due to French usages. One such is the 'h' used to harden 'c' and 't', giving an early form, 'Lyskerithe', 1308, of 'Liskeard'. Another factor is the frequent but irregular interchange between certain consonants, i.e. not the normal mutations of Cornish grammar. Some of these may be habitual in one language or the other, a few, (e.g. 'n'><'l') in both. Even the normal evolution of Cornish can create ambiguities: an 's' form of 'Ryt', 'a ford', is confusable with 'Ros', 'a heath', since the unstressed vowel tends to become neutral and indistinctly spelt. (Here, the 't'>'s' development, if confirmed, is crucial for dating.) Some alternations could occur at any period and so are irrelevant for dating, if vital for interpretation.

ORTHOGRAPHIC MARKERS

When we can identify, among the chaotic variations, certain developments, regular in Cornish, but not in English, we can trace the survival of the language. Whether dateable language developments are found, even in a district known to have been Cornish-speaking at the requisite period, may come down to the distribution of those elements which show them. Secondly, the longer the line of exemplars, the better the chance of finding significant forms. What matters is not when it is first recorded, but whether the development took place at all. There can, in place-names, be a delay of a century or more between when developments are thought to have affected the spoken language and when such changes are noted in written records. There does not seem to be a different time-lag in any one area so language developments can be safely used to plot the earliest possible date for the death of Cornish in a certain place. Rounded to the nearest century, these are shown, parish by parish, on the map, based on the list in the appendices.

A curious feature of some names is the false 'tre'. Often this is where Old English 'atte' has been altered to 'tre', giving us 'Trehill', 'Treforda', 'Treheath', etc., where the whole name was really English. Nicholas Williams[20] interprets this as marking a re-Cornicization of an area, but it does not necessarily mean a restoration of the language since English-speakers could equally well make an analogy with the many genuine 'tre's in the neighbourhood. Other words, too, such as 'kruk', 'a barrow', can be assimilated to 'tre'. The influence of 'tre' may account for 'Tywardreath', which is never noted as 'chi', although the later, Middle Cornish form is common around St Austell. Cornish-speakers may have adopted the known variant, 'Trewardreath', while English-speakers retained the fossilized Old Cornish 'ti' (or 'ty')

A SUMMARY OF DATEABLE LANGUAGE DEVELOPMENTS

Consonants
't'>'s'
The modern map shows a majority of 't' names in East Cornwall. Though appearing in the Old Cornish vocabulary, this change of final and medial 't/d'>'s' was not recorded in place-names until much later. A very early example, if the second part represents 'ryt', 'a ford', is in the Launceston Cartulary, where Trefrize in Linkinhorne (see note 3) is already Trevris in 1141. If these 's' versions do appear in documents, it strongly suggests that Cornish was in use at the place concerned until at least 1200. In fact, the development is often not recorded much before 1300 and so probably implies later survival.

'Pre-occlusions'
The 'pre-occlusions' 'nn'>/dn/ and /mm/>/bm/ first appear in literature, in the early 1500s, but in place-names not until the 1570s. Though the feature has not been found in the area of this study, it is common all along the South coast from St Austell, (Pedniddon) westwards. This development is absent from Tregear,[21] with one dubious exception ('mamb' for 'mamm', in Homylye XIII). In place-names, it is not found

until the late Tudor period, and so is a helpful marker of Late Cornish speakers.

Dialects?

The 'n'>'dn' and 'm'>'bm' feature seems scarce in northern mid-Cornish parishes (where other evidence[22] shows that Cornish was spoken in the appropriate period). This may, exceptionally, indicate dialectal differences, or, less likely, a particularly severe decline in the language's fortune in the late sixteenth century. Generally, I suspect that dialect was marked by subtle differences in vowel quality, (which orthography may not make apparent), and, most of all, intonation which in Cornu-English dialect still varies from one parish to another. Dialectal preference may underlie variations in Cornish syntax (such as 'wra'ma/ 'wrav vy' (= 'I do'), and hapaxes in vocabulary, like the unique 'enep' suffixes in Tregear's Homilies). Final proof awaits better knowledge of the provenance of manuscripts.

's'>'j'

The 's'>'j' development occurs mostly in the same situations as 'pre-occlusion', (i.e. after short stressed vowels), but appears earlier. It is found throughout the area of Middle Cornish, and may in fact coincide in date with 't'>'s'. It was earlier written 'ss', e.g. 'gansse'[23] = 'ganso', 'with him'. A softer sound, cf. the spelling 'Esse', in 1244, for 'Asshe', now Saltash. Later rendered 'g' it was assimilated finally assimilated to English 'j', and rendered 'dg' (e.g. St Jidgey<Villa de St Idi, 1169). The development is sometimes concealed by 'reversions' to an original 't'/'d', e.g. Ladock (Lagek, 1355). Elsewhere, today's 'ss' may in reality be merely an orthographic reversion; the spellings Trelissick, 'Trelegick' 1597 (Boazio map[24]) and Lelissick, Lanwolegyk, 1302, probably all originally represented the same soft 'j', even if modern speakers pronounce 'ss' as 's'. This consonant is presumably related to the palatization of 'ti', 'a house', to 'chi'.[25]

Vowels

It is when they are long and stressed that vowels are most informative, conforming to regular progressions, as seen:

1. with the neutral vowel, Old Cor. /ö/, >/eu/ >/e/.
   e.g. *mor* (great), represented later as *mur* and finally *mere* or *mear*.

2. The type of Long 'o' in 'Koes' (a wood), 'Goen' (a heath), 'Loes' (grey).
   /ui/> /oy/, /oe/> /ou/ (or /ow/) to /oo-e/

We might compare, from the Ordinalia, *anwous* (a cold), rhyming with *trous* (foot).[26]

The regular sequence is seen in these examples.

Cusgarne:	Coesgaran, 1380
Bodwin in St Teath:	Bossewoen, 1302
Mellancoose in Colan:	Melynencoys, 1335, Mellancowse, 1557

Long /i/ > /ei/ > /oi/

The grapheme 'ey' appears in the 1400s, but it may not always mark a diphthong. It is used in situations where it cannot have meant 'aï'. For example, Leyland wrote *deyth* for 'day', which Edward Lhuyd rendered *dydh*. The earliest 'ei/ey' digraphs in place-names are: 'Cheiensorn', St Martin in Meneage, 1435; 'Whele an Keye', Fraddon, 1529. Compare here 'treyhans harpys' in the Ordinalia.[27] This seems to show the same diphthong which occurred in the Great Vowel Shift of English and was certainly found by Edward Lhuyd *c.* 1700. Yet a similar sound change in the Bas Vannetais dialect of Breton is presumably not English influence. I know of no evidence for this sound change to have occurred, *in the living language*, in East Cornwall.

Long 'a'

It is difficult to determine whether the present-day dialect 'aa' was ever used in Late Cornish; it may instead be the result of former Cornish-speakers attempting an unfamiliar vowel sound. It is definitely inappropriate for some place-names: e.g. Chytane, St Enoder <tywar-don, 1296, where it is unlikely that 'aa' could be confused with /oː/. Other cases at variance with the dialect 'aa' are Crows an wra (Crows an wraughe, 1840) and 'bras' (big), regularly found in Late Cornish as 'brose' or 'brawze'. Contemporary examples, from different areas of Cornwall, are consistent with these being temporal developments, not regional dialects.

SPOT-REFERENCES AND OTHER EVIDENCE

1349: Following the Black Death, the Prior of Minster[29] ('Talcarn' in Cornish), appealed to the bishop because there were not enough parishioners to pay for a priest. He also said, tellingly, that none of the brothers could speak Cornish or English!

Place-name evidence exists for 'plen an gwarys' as far east as St Ewe and Gorran, further proof of the strength of the language, implying performance of Cornish miracle plays.

1355:[30] A confessor was appointed in Bodmin for both English- and Cornish-speakers.

1583: Gorran records of the Exchequer Court.[31]
1595: St Ewe Consistory Court.[32] Both these last cases refer to Cornish-speakers, taking the language up to late Tudor times. Place-name forms, including 'dn', give a similar date for Cornish usage, along the coast from St Austell to St Mawes. The bounds of St Breock, 1613, are in both Cornish and English, e.g. 'Mene Gurta', a 'staie stone'. Later still, the form of the language found in the bilingual bounds of St Stephen in Brannel, 1660, appears to match the date while field-names, listed by Henderson for Callendra, in Veryan, 1698, and Trefullock, in St Enoder, 1713, show the language at the same stage of development as contemporary documents in West Penwith. It would seem that in Roseland, Cornish was in use until the 1700s. To the north, evidence of Cornish-speakers east of Truro in the late Tudor period seems surprisingly scarce. Truro[33] itself was largely Cornish-speaking up to the Civil War, after which we find street-names referred to in English: e.g. 'Street Idden', 1652, becomes 'Narrow Street', 1667 (now 'Cathedral Lane').

INFERRED USAGE

There are various instances where, between Bodmin and the Tamar, the usage of Cornish is inferred from circumstantial evidence. These include Cornish names created for medieval estates, minor names and qualifiers for divisions of an estate The last two types do not long survive a change of language, when they are either translated or totally replaced. East of Bodmin, such names are less common.

It is important to exclude modern mine names, such as those that re-introduced 'wheal' into East Cornwall (or indeed West Devon). These names were not natural formations by habitual Cornish-speakers but introduced to share, by association, in the success of the great copper and tin mines of West Cornwall. Secondly, deliberate affirmation of Cornishness did not begin with Henry Jenner.[34] The enlightened and 'modern' Victorian writer William Bottrell[35] was responsible for Cornish names being given to Victorian developments around Mount's Bay. I have tried to exclude such conscious Revivalism and, where possible, filtered out a few 'freakish' cases when Middle Cornish forms re-surface exceptionally late, e.g. 'Boscaddon' (see Appendix 1) may not signify a late Victorian use of Cornish in Lanreath parish but is valid evidence, as a probable 'reversion', that Cornish survived there at least into the thirteenth century. I do not think that Cornish street-names survive for any towns east of Truro (which itself has a full set). This may support the idea that it was rural and coastal populations that retained the language longest, at least in mid and East Cornwall.

MINOR NAMES

Field-names and words used to distinguish separate parts of a property were more likely than larger properties to be recorded from contemporary oral information. Relatively few survive in East Cornwall. Copies of estate maps and field-name lists from Penwith, in the Charles Henderson collection at the Royal Institution of Cornwall in Truro, show that field-names do not survive long after the change in language. This may explain why 'ti', a humble house, is not found in the far east of Cornwall. One rare survival is 'Park Vinton,[36] i.e. 'spring field', in St Mellion. Elsewhere, typical remnants are 'Spernick', in St Pinnock, and 'Sparnock', at Liskeard, which both mean 'thorny'. There are cases, mostly large common fields, where a different name was used in the two languages, just as for villages and towns. An example is Gwelecrege *alias* Treworracke Field, in St Ewe.[37] Occasionally both names are still to be found: At Kingsand, on the O.S. map, the hill above the village bears the names 'Blackadown' and 'Minadew' (i.e. 'Black Hill'). At Doublebois, near Liskeard, an old sign names a cottage 'Gelly/ Copse'. Oliver Padel suggests a third case, in Poundstock, where 'Crowshire' possibly contains Cornish 'Crows', thus matching its English counterpart, 'Cross Park'. It must be more than coincidence that the sense of the Cornish has been transferred into English (see 'Shifting pattern', above).

Equally significant are a few 'tre' names which appear to be late foundations. Dr Padel mentions Trehan, near Saltash, where a William Hanna, bearing the name of the probable founder, is found living nearby within a few years of its probable foundation in the 1300s. Gover similarly links Trecollas (-colwes, 1401) with a John Calwys living nearby in 1361. 'Tre' was definitely an active element when Saxon settlements began to appear. As noted earlier, 'Tresawson', 'the Englishmen's estate', is found in several places, including Lanreath. Some 'tref's, like Trewolsta and Trevollard, are probably linked to Saxon personal names, Wulfstan and Aethelweard. At 'Trevelmond', the name may be the Norman 'Belmont'. This last suggests that 'tre' was still an active element in the post-Norman period. So does one hitherto unrecognized case.[38] In 1260, Roger of Deviock, member of the powerful de Luci family, granted 'Madoc's land' to John Smith, son of William Anglicus. In spite of his father's surname ('Englishman'), it seems likely that John was the smith after whom the property, Trengoffe, in Warleggan, was named. Polwhele[39] intriguingly mentions a deacon called 'Peter Jowle or Peter the Devil' in seventeenth-century Altarnun! If a Cornish-speaker, he must have come from further 'down Cornwall'. Similarly, the eccentric Sir James Tillie,[40] who coming from a St Keverne family, may be assumed to have spoken Cornish from birth. Having acquired the Coryton estate in the late seventeenth century, he christened his new house, near St Mellion, 'Pentillie'.

An interesting insight into the relationship between the two language communities is provided by the wardens' accounts for Camborne.[41] These bear witness not only to the currency of the language in the sixteenth century but also to the process of anglicization. There was clearly a campaign by the bishop to rededicate the church from Meriadoc to the newly fashionable Martin of Tours. When sharing the honour with Martin, the Celtic saint's name is generally spelt in an old-fashioned Latin form, Meriadoc(us), found in church records. But, when he stands alone, his champions, evidently Cornish-speakers, use the contemporary Cornish form of his name, Meriasek. The campaign on Meriasek's behalf did win, but, ironically, under his old Latin/Old Cornish (and, in fact, his *English*) name. More than likely, we owe the saint's play *Beunans Meriasek* to this very same in-fighting. A dry linguistic point, the development of 'd'>'s', is here a symbol both of the living language and an underlying, defiant insistence on Cornishness. Coming shortly before the 1549 Catholic rising, and bearing in mind that Thomas Stefyn (Stephyn), translator of Bishop Bonner's Homilye XIII, (see note 21), was a Warden of the Communion in Camborne, 1583–4, it may not be possible to extract the recusant factor from this dispute. Ruthless and insensitive destruction of ancient cults and customs did much to feed the fires of indignation.

LEGAL ARGUMENTS

There are other cases of the Cornish language and orthography being used to bolster legal arguments. Charles Henderson's history of St John's hospital near Helston[42] mentions a fourteenth-century case where the omission of final 'th' from 'meneth' is called to account. At St Columb, in 1522, John Tregian objected, in a dispute at the Star Chamber,[43] that 'There is no such place in Lambrobus (Probus) as Martyn's Field. There is however a parcel of land called Gwele Marteyn.'

DECLINE

The decline in Cornish-speaking must be primarily due to loss of prestige, with power of all kinds being transferred into the hands of English-speakers. Norman-French domination relieved this pressure for a couple of centuries. There is no evidence of French antipathy to Cornish. Peter Berresford Ellis[44] mentions studies[45] showing how the Black Death reduced the influence of the French linguistic minority in England. I suspect a similar negative effect on Cornish, most marked in the mixed language communities east of Bodmin. Certainly, the

heightened status of English as a legal language may have tipped
the balance between two languages previously of equally low status.
Relative numbers meant that English-speaking settlers always had
reserves across the Tamar. Then, in the fourteenth century, English
became the official language and *de rigueur* for social advancement.
Despite the flowering of Cornish literature which occurred in this
period, with the *Passion Poem* and the *Ordinalia*, there does seem to
have been a fairly rapid retreat. Bodmin Moor itself is something of a
blank space on the map but pockets may have survived post-1500 east
of Bodmin and on the south coast as far east as Looe.

I have added some references to the 'clay district' and the
Roseland which show seventeenth- and even eighteenth-century
survivals. Names showing dateable developments are listed by parish.
The absence of recorded 'reversions' does not prove that Cornish
ceased to be spoken at that place in that period, but it may be
significant where a relatively high proportion of unchanged forms exist
within the attested 1200 Middle Cornish dateline. The suggested map,
based on tracing dateable changes in the language, fits well with
'spot-references' and usage inferred from other evidence. If anything,
place-names probably paint a conservative picture.

CONCLUSION

This study demonstrates that Cornish-speaking communities persisted
in East Cornwall in the 1400s, at least up to a line from St Kew to
Looe. A century before, the boundary would have been a few parishes
further north. In the 1500s, there appear to have still been pockets
east of Bodmin and along the south coast between Fowey and
Looe. By 1600, the widely accepted Padstow to Par line is probably
correct, though the northern limit is unclear. The Dodman area and
Roseland retained the language as long as much of West Penwith. The
catastrophic decline which came soon after this followed a century of
Tudor and later Parliamentarian policies, ruthlessly employed to try to
produce a monolithic English state.

APPENDIX 1: Names with surviving 's'

Parish	Present name	Historic forms
Tintagel	Bossiney	Bothcyni 1259, Boscini 1288
Trevalga	Trewins	
St Kew	Lanseage	Nansceugy 1428

Cardinham	Trezance	
St Breock	Burlorne Tregoose	
Withiel	Withielgoose	
Lanivet	Boscarn	
Bodmin	Boskear	
	Nanstallon	
Treneglos	Scarsick	Rescardek 1346
St Cleer	Rosecraddoc	Rescaradec 1249*
Linkinhorne	Trefrize	N.B. very early 's', 1141, in Launceston Cartulary
Lezant	Rezare	
South Hill	Coskallow Wood	
St Germans	Lanjore ('j'<'s')	
Liskeard	Lestitha	Lanstinetha 1357
St Pinnock	Bosent	Bodcent 1306, Boscent 1327
Lostwithiel	Boslymon	
St Winnow	Bosmawgan	
	Respryn	Retpryne 1281
Fowey	Lescrow	N.B. Les < Res = a ford

Probable

Tintagel	Besloe	
St Minver	The Mouls	Mold 1766
	Smeath	earlier: Hensens/Hensent
St Gennys	Lansweeden	
North Hill	Tresellern	'alias Reselyn' 1689
Davidstow	Screws	Recress 1427, Trescrewes 1582
Quethiock	Treweese	both Treweese and Treweers contain 'gweres'= soil, c.f. Welsh 'gweryd'
Lansallos	Treweers	

Possible

Lanreath	Bocaddon	Boscaddon 1884 (*Simon's Directory*)

---

*This place, Ridkaradoch, *c.*1140 in Geoffrey of Monmouth's History, and Crathick Ford in the eighteenth century, later reverted to a form based on Middle Cornish

APPENDIX 2: Reverted names
with the date of last recorded 's' form, rounded to nearest whole century

Parish	Present name	Historic forms
? Pre-1300		
Linkinhorne	Rillaton	Risleston in DDB
c.1300		
Otterham	Tregray	Risgre 1296
St Teath	Bodwin	Bossewoen 1302
		('The Manor of Tremaruustel',
		W.M. Picken, *JRIC* Vol vvii ns
		pt 3 1975/6)
	Dannon	Deunans 1311
Lanteglos/Camelford		Nanseglos 1311
		(Langeglos 1610, Kip-Camden
		map)
Altarnun	Tregirls	Rosegrill 1260, Redegrill 1423
St Kew	Pendoggett	Pendewegoys 1302
Lanivet	Lanivet	Lanneves 1302 (*Assize Roll*)
	Reperry	Resperry
	Lesquite	Lostcoys 1320
	Retire	Restyr
Roche	Tremodret	Tremodres 1296
St Tudy	Lamellen	Nansmaylwyn 1280
Lostwithiel	Bodwen	Boswyn 1296
Egloshayle	Lemail	Nansmael 1280
	Trenant	Trenans 1306
St Mabyn		Nansdeui 1302 (lost)
Liskeard	Lamellion	Nansmelin 1298
St Pinnock	Liggers	Lozeard 1299, Lodegard 1290
St Sampson	Lantian	Nanstian 1302
St Austell	Pentewan	Porth Bensewen 1302
Possible		
St Martin by Looe	Bodigga	Bodcusuga 1256
Striddicks		Restreysek c.1300
c.1400		
St Mabyn	Becoven	Boscoven 1379
	Tresloggett	Treslogas 1428
St Kew	Penpont	Penpons 1435

Helland	Lecudden	Nanscothyn 1402
Lanreath	Trecan	Trescan 1284
	Trefrawel	Resfrawel 1380
	Lankelly	Nanskelly 1429
Lanteglos/Fowey	Bodinnick	Bosdynek 1396
Morval	Cutparrett	Coyspervet 1329,
		Gousparnet 1418
	Lanlawren	Nanslowern 1356
St Veep	Pennant	Pennans 1375
Boconnock	Boconnock	Boskinnek 1356

*c.*1500

St Sampson	Golant	Golenance 1454
St Neot	Lantewey	Lanstewy 1498 (Nandywy 1285)
Lanivet	Bodwannick	Boswenek *c.*1500
Liskeard	Liskeard	Lyskerrys 1375, Lescars 1478

Post-1500

Lanhydrock	Cutmadock	Cosmadeck 1547
Bodmin	Bodmin	Bosvene *c.*1400 (*Origo Mundi*, line 2399)
		Bosvenna 1590 (Carew)
Luxulyan	Bokiddick	Boskeddiocke 1621

Possible

Egloshayle	Trevillan	Rosevelyn 1569

APPENDIX 3: 's'>'j'

Parish	Present name	Exemplars of 's'>'j' development
St Issey	St Issey	Plugie 16th century (Oliver Padel, 'Plu names in the St Columb Green Book', *Cornish Studies*, 3)
St Issey	Canalidgey	Canelysy 1407
	St Jidgey	St Ide 1195
	Mellingey	Melynsy 1302
Little Petherick	Bolingey	Melyndy 1216
Scilly	Illiswilgig	Enniswelsick 1584
Luxulyan	Lampessick	Lampedgycke Wd (Henderson Calendar 19, p. 316)
St Just in Roseland	Trelissick	Trelegick 1587 (Boazio's map)

St Ervan	Bogee	Bosyuf 1340
St Columb Minor	Lanhainsworth	Lanhengewith 1706,
		Lanhynseth 1428
	Bejowan	Bosiwayn 1346
Ladock		Lagek 1355,
		alias Lasecke *c.*1580
St Austell	place-name now lost	Chi en Eruderor 1354
		(Tregrehan Deeds)
Padstow	Lelissick	Lanwolegyk 1302

Possibles

Cubert	Porth Joke	Porth Lajoacke 1630
St Enodoc		'St Inidgick' 20th century
		(oral information)
Lanteglos by Camelford		Langeglos 1610 (Kip Camden
		map)
Scilly	Molledgan	(if this is from *Melhwesenn*,
		'a snail')

APPENDIX 4: Chi

Parish	*Present name*	*Historic forms*
St Agnes	Chytodden	
St Austell		Chi en Eruderor 1354, Chi Pat,
		Chy an Grows 1403
		(both the last two from
		Tregrehan deeds)

Notes:
compare, from literature:
1. *Beunans Meriasek c.*1500, line 4100, begythya < besydha = to baptise
2. *Origo Mundi c.*1400, line 1657, na thyscryssough = do not disbelieve
        line 1869 dycryggyon = unbelievers

APPENDIX 5: Examples of Cornish usage in North and East Cornwall

Parish	*Cornish exemplar*	*Modern name*
Withiel	Hay Thu 1284	Black Hay
St Issey	Rosworek bihan 1250, -wartha 1314	Trevorrick
	(the name is also also found preceded by	
	English *Overe*, translating *wartha*)	

West Looe	Porthpighan (the 'small cove')	
	alias W. Looe 1482 (Trelawney Docs no. 11)	
St Eval	Trevysker veur, -vyan 1530 (E.C.P.)	
	= 'great' and 'small' T	
St Minver	Caryo meur, -byghan, 1346	
	= 'great' and 'small' C	
	Kaero porghel 1311	
	= 'Kaero of the pig'	
Boconnock	Menebrel wartha, -Woles, 1382	Menaburle
	= 'upper' and 'lower' M	

NOTES AND REFERENCES

1. Edward Lluyd, *Archaeologia Britannica*, Oxford, 1707.
2. See Oliver Padel, *A Popular Dictionary of Cornish Place-Names*, Penzance, 1988; p. 28 may refer to a paper I read on this subject at the Congress of Celtic Studies in Galway.
3. Cartulary of Reginald de Dunstanville.
4. Royal Institution of Cornwall (RIC), Truro, Henderson Collection, Cal. 16, p. 196.
5. J.E.B. Gover, 'Cornish Place-names', typescript in the Courtney Library of the RIC.
6. Andrew Boorde, *A Fyrst Boke of the Introduction of Knowledge* [1547], ed. F.J. Furnivall, London, 1870.
7. E.g. Luxulyan, the unique instance of the common Breton prefix 'Lok', a hermit's cell. Other possible Breton influences: Locrenton, near St Keyne, Lankerentyn 1311; dedicated to Corantyn, patron of Quimper in Brittany as well as Cury in Cornwall. Presumably the hermitage 'near Menheniot' in Polwhele's *History of Cornwall*, Vol. I & II, p. 130. Tarista, formerly 'Trerust', near Lansallos, appears to contain a rare Cornish word, equivalent to Breton 'rust', i.e. 'steep'. Killigorrick, in St Pinnock, 'Chilorgoret' in Domesday Book, 1086, probably contains the only example of Breton 'argoured', a wood. On Bretons in Cornwall, see A.L. Rowse, *Tudor Cornwall*, London, 1942, p. 95.
8. W.G. Hoskins, *The Westward Expansion of Wessex*, Leicester, 1970.
9. William of Malmesbury, *Gesta vegum Anglorum*, ed. Stubbs, London, 1887.
10. Richard Carew, *A Survey of Cornwall* [1602], ed. F.E. Halliday, London, 1969. p. 194.
11. Thomas Tonkin, *A History of St Agnes,* 1720; see *Journal of the Royal Institution of Cornwall* (*JRIC*), 7, 1975–6.
12. Carew, 1602.
13. John of Cornwall, *The Prophecy of Merlin*, ed. J. Holmes, Saltash, 2001.
14. F.C. Hingeston-Randolph (ed.), *The Register of John de Grandisson, Bishop of Exeter (A.D. 1327–1379)*, 3 vols, London, 1894–9, Vol. II, p. 820.

15. The 'Bilbao' manuscripts of Thomas Tonkin, *JRIC*, 21, 1922–5.
16. Nicholas Roscarrock, *The Register of the British Saints m/s c.1590*, ed. N. Orme, Exeter, 1995.
17. *Origo Mundi (OM)* first play of the Cornish *Ordinalia*, ed. Norris, Oxford, 1859, l. 2399.
18. Map by Hermann Moll, London, 1724.
19. Map by Thomas Taylor, London, 1715, first printed 1678.
20. Nicholas Williams, *Cornish Today*, Sutton Coldfield, 1995.
21. Homylyes, 13 in Cornysshe BM Add MS 46, 397.
22. Oliver Padel '"Plu" names in The St Columb Green Book', *Cornish Studies*, 6, 1978. For the Green Book of St Columb, see *JRIC*, 59 and Supplement, 1912.
23. *OM* l. 1373.
24. Boazio's map of Falmouth, 1597; copy at the RIC.
25. O.J. Padel, *Cornish Place-Name Elements*, London, 1980, p. 77.
26. *OM* l. 1121–2.
27. *OM* l. 1996.
28. Tonkin, 1720.
29. Calender of Patent Rolls 1909, Ed VIII, Vol. 10, pp. 247, 252.
30. Hingeston-Randolph, 1894–9, p. 1146.
31. Public Record Office, E134.30, Eliz/Hil.2 in *Old Cornwall*, 6.2, 1968–72.
32. See RIC, Henderson Collection, Cal. 10, p. 176.
33. Truro street-names: RIC, Henderson Collection, Vol. 1, Index pp. 104, 136.
34. Henry Jenner, *A Handbook of the Cornish Language*, London, 1904.
35. William Bottrell, *Hearthside Stories of West Cornwall* [1873] ed. Frank Graham, Newcastle-upon-Tyne, 1970.
36. RIC, Henderson Collection, Cal. 20, p. 234.
37. Charles Henderson, *Parochial History of Cornwall*, ed. G.H. Doble, Truro, 1925.
38. RIC, Henderson Collection, Cal. 5, p. 80.
39. R. Polwhele, *The History of Cornwall*, London, 1806.
40. RIC, Henderson Collection, Cal. 20, p. 131.
41. D. Thomas, 'Camborne Church Wardens', *Cornish Studies,* 6, 1978, p. 58.
42. C. Henderson, Records of St John's Hospital, Helston, *JRIC*, 22.3, pt 3, no. 75, 1928.
43. PRO, Star Chamber H.VIII XVII no. 209 r VIII.
44. Peter Berresford Ellis, *The Cornish Language and its Literature*, London, 1974.
45. Mario Pei, *The Story of the English Language*, London, 1968; Philip Ziegler, *The Black Death*, London, 1969.

SACRAMENT AN ALTER:
A TUDOR CORNISH PATRISTIC CATENA

D.H. Frost

INTRODUCTION AND ACKNOWLEDGEMENTS

The Tregear Manuscript was noted by Revd John Mackechnie of *Gaelic Without Groans* fame in 1949. It forms part of the Puleston papers, first described in *The Report of the Royal Commission on Historical Manuscripts, II* (London 1871), appendix, pp. 65–8. The work is a paper quarto, twelve homilies in Cornish bound together as BL Add. MS 46397, but with an additional work on the Sacrament of the Altar following them. It is to this latter work that I have devoted my attention, although clearly the whole is of great interest.[1]

When I began to study *Sacrament an Alter* (SA)—as the so-called 'Thirteenth Homily' of the Tregear Homilies has come to be named—I was all too aware of my inadequacy for the task of interpreting it. It appears to be a unique piece of Tudor Catholic apologetics, reduced to its essence—a compilation of patristic proof texts of eucharistic doctrine. My interest at first was primarily historical and theological, but it rapidly became clear that a fresh reading of the Cornish and Latin of the manuscript would be required, in view of the long-standing textual problems arising from the damaged folios. It also became clear that, unlike the other twelve Homilies, SA was not a translation of the work of Bishop Bonner and his chaplains under Queen Mary I. It was a quite different work—presented in both Latin and Cornish—which followed its own curious logic, but was clearly not a sermon at all.

Although my knowledge of Cornish—such as it is—is largely confined to its attested historical later forms, I have benefited from encouragement from all quarters. First and foremost Andrew Hawke, Nicholas Williams and Richard Gendall—although they each approach the subject from rather different perspectives—have aided me enormously, both with text and translation. Hawke's unpublished work on the text of the Tregear Homilies (TH) was my starting point, and I envisaged my whole project as supporting his wider endeavours. Ray Edwards and Keith Syed have placed at my disposal invaluable computer files and their expertise by e-mail. Audrey Randle Pool, Matthew Spriggs and a host of others have shed light on the historical origins of SA.[2] Above all, the work of Robert Morton Nance—both in the Bice transcript and in his papers at the Royal Institution of Cornwall—laid the foundations of understanding. As a result I feel that much of what I have put together is something of a team effort.

DEFINING THE TASK

The original plan for the task I was undertaking was a fairly limited and straightforward one. I was aware that Christopher Bice's transcription of Nance's work on TH, while an important basis for study, nonetheless pointed up the need for further work. As I have mentioned, Andrew Hawke's work in progress, established as part of the foundations of his proposed dictionary of traditional Cornish, had accomplished a great deal in this regard. But it seemed to me, Hawke and others that it would be useful to investigate the historical context of the work and, in particular, the sources (and references) for the patristic quotations. So I began.

Quite early on in this laborious but rewarding work—to be immersed in the Greek and Latin Fathers for days on end has its consolations—I became acutely aware of a problem. While the Hawke reading (which corrected many errors in Nance/Bice) had more or less established a sound text for the first twelve homilies, the 'thirteenth' (i.e. SA) required considerable further study. In fact it became clear that a completely new manuscript reading of this distinctive final piece in the TH jigsaw was the only safe way forward—with the help of patristic sources in restoring the damaged text—and this is what I needed to begin with, in order to make possible the second phase of my work.

This second phase would involve providing theological and patristic background to the ideas expressed in SA, as well as a commentary that would lead to a fuller understanding of its structure. I did not intend my work in any way to rival the full edition projected by Andrew Hawke, nor to overlap to any appreciable extent with the aims of the proposed four-column edition by Ray Edwards for Cornish Revivalists. Indeed I would make available my readings and notes to both in the hope that this would further the process of understanding. I hoped that by concentrating in great detail on SA, I would be able to shed light on the many problems with the text caused by deterioration of the manuscript, perhaps even restoring some missing portions. This has indeed proved possible, particularly with the later folios.

As a third phase of my work, I would seek to establish a possible *sitz im leben* or 'context' for the writing of SA. What was its relationship to the other Tregear Homilies and the circle around Bishop Bonner? What was its date and authorship? What sort of work was it—why was it, for example, not a homily like the other twelve? How did it come to Wales? All of these were fascinating questions deserving of time and study.

The work is still 'in progress', but I hope it will be both helpful and interesting to share some of the preliminary findings, some ideas on the source of SA, and a few interesting details that have come to light. I have tried to do this in a way that will not be off-putting to the non-specialist reader, but I would be happy to supply interested scholars with detailed evidence and appropriate references, as well as copies of the relevant parts of my work.

PRELIMINARY GENERAL FINDINGS

So far, I have more or less completed my revised reading of SA, and have traced and referenced almost all of the patristic quotations, allowing a clear picture of the nature of SA to begin to emerge. Most exciting of all, I believe I have found its source. A number of facts about the document now seem reasonably certain.

Firstly, it is clear that it is not by John Tregear, nor is it in his hand. Although bound with his work (and linked to it by certain marginal notes which we will consider later), it appears to display many features of later Cornish, and is certainly not a translation of Bonner's thirteenth 'homily' or dialogue. (Incidentally, the reason why there are only twelve homilies in TH appears to be that they were translated from an early edition—there were many printed—which lacked the true thirteenth. It may be possible to identify precisely which edition in due course, and I have plans in train to do so.) *Sacrament an Alter*, in other words, is something new and additional—a work in its own right—drawing from another source. The fact that it is in another hand and differs in language and style from TH has been known more or less from the outset, when it was discovered by John Mackechnie. Nance certainly made this clear,[3] along with the fact that some of the marginal notes in Homilies 11 and 12 are by the same author, but it does not seem to have been examined in detail for many years.

Secondly, it may have been the work of Thomas Stephyn. This is the name appended distinctively to Homilies 11 and 12, which are also distinctive because of the marginal notes added in the hand of the author of SA. It seems at least possible that Stephyn was claiming the authorship of the annotations by signing the homilies under Tregear —not least because the text of the homilies itself is written throughout in Tregear's hand. If so, Stephyn is the author of SA too. Charles Penglase has already suggested this possibility in his recent work on verbal forms in the Homilies.[4] There is more work be done in confirming the identification and exploring the career and background of Stephyn, as well as in finding out more about Tregear himself.

Thirdly, it is not a sermon but a catena. A catena is a collection or 'chain' of patristic quotations from the Greek and Latin Fathers of the early Church—in our case on the subject of the Blessed Sacrament. They were popular reference works in the Middle Ages, and made the theological patrimony of the Church widely accessible, albeit in limited ways. As I began to trace the patristic quotations, I rapidly discovered that apart from one or two isolated sentences—such things as *ema S. Austyn ow leverall* ('St Augustine says')—the entire work was made up of a recitation of patristic and biblical proof texts for the doctrines of the Real Presence, the Sacrifice of the Mass and Transubstantiation. It was not a homily at all. Even where the Cornish seemed in places to go beyond the Latin, it soon appeared—in almost every case—that it was merely translating more of the original than had been set down in the Latin extract. Nor did SA at first appear to be a wholesale translation of an existing source, such as parts of the *Catena Aurea* on the Gospels of St Thomas Aquinas, or the theological collections of Gratian, Ivo of Chartres or Peter Lombard. I found close links with some contemporary apologetics, however, particularly Bishop Cuthbert Tunstall's *De ueritate Corporis et Sanguinis domini Nostri Jesu Christi in Eucharistia.*[5] Nonetheless, this is not the direct source, and its listing of quotations by author points up the problem of the unusual and definite arrangement in SA.

Fourthly, it is probably from the reign of Elizabeth I. Bishop Bonner's Homilies were, of course, published in her predecessor Mary's reign, and it seems reasonable to assume that, in counter-balance to Cranmer's seeming contempt for Cornish at the time of the 1549 Rising in the reign of Edward VI, Mary's regime encouraged Tregear's translation of the first twelve into the language. This places TH some time between 1555 and 1558—probably later rather than earlier, as it was never printed.[6] SA has been thought to belong roughly to the same period. It is certainly later than TH—as witnessed by the marginal notes added to the latter in the hand of the author of SA. But on linguistic grounds it betrays a number of features which are characteristically late. Leaving aside (as possibly dialectal) the much-debated possible sign of pre-occlusion in *mamb* for 'mother', and (as possibly earlier but poorly attested due to the lack of surviving prose works) the use of continuous tenses of *bos* as auxiliaries as in TH and Welsh,[7] we have: the shift from 'e' to 'a' especially at the end of words (e.g. *leverall*); the appearance of *pecar* for *kepar*; the use of *ugy* for *usy*; of *inans y* for older *ynna y*; *rebta* for *ryptho*; individual spellings such as *marnance* for *mernans*; perhaps the early beginnings of a shift towards second person plural where second person singular would have been used before, and other examples. The fact that the text is appended to a probably already damaged TH, which looks as though it has journeyed far and under perilous conditions, only strengthens this impression. In other words, we seem to have here a recusant document from the reign of Elizabeth I.

Fifthly, as mentioned above, it is linked to Tregear's Homilies. Homilies 11 and 12 contain a certain amount of later marginal annotation by the same hand as the author of SA. This is important. Since I now believe that SA was not compiled primarily as a collection of quotations to back up the arguments of Homilies 11 and 12, it is significant that the author did go back over Tregear's translations of Homilies 11 and 12, providing them with these additional references. Obviously he was entrusted with TH at some point and wished to connect it even more fully to the great contemporary proof texts of Catholic eucharistic doctrine, in view of the similarity of argument in the last two homilies to other discussions he had studied.

Sixthly, it points towards continuing Cornish-speaking Catholicism well after the Reformation. Since SA was compiled after the reigns of Henry VIII and Edward VI at least—and almost certainly after Mary I—it suggests the survival of the Old Faith among some of those using the Cornish language despite the efforts of Cranmer and others. As Nance notes, the handwriting of SA, too, argues for a later date than TH. The seminarian in Valladolid (Richard Pentrey?) in 1600 who gave an address in the language is matching evidence that Cornish-speaking Catholics persisted, and had links with communities abroad where other scholars prepared works for their own missions.[8]

THE SOURCE OF THE TEXT

At this point it becomes necessary for me to explain exactly what the source of SA appears to be. It is a selective abstract of the patristic arguments in the 1554 Disputations at Oxford staged between the prolocutor of the Lower House of Convocation, Dr Hugh Weston of Lincoln College, and the deprived Archbishop Thomas Cranmer, along with similar examinations of Hugh Latimer and Nicholas Ridley. Weston was assisted in these disputations by other Catholic divines, including John Harpesfield, who wrote many of Bonner's homilies and whose doctoral examination formed part of the proceedings in which Weston invited Cranmer to take part.

The arguments and patristic quotations put forward in these disputations were recorded by notaries at the time, and then summarized for various interested parties as well as being worked up into an official report. Interestingly, a number of manuscripts survive.[9] The most cursory reading of these reveals that the patristic quotations in SA are precisely those of the Disputation at Oxford, in largely the same sequence within each portion of the arguments (although there are occasional jumps when material from Cranmer's Disputation is followed by the material from Ridley's Disputation etc.).

There is more. SA includes a few passages which are not directly taken from patristic authors. Virtually all of these are found—again in sequence—in the contributions made by the divines as they debated those particular texts on that particular occasion. This is surely conclusive. And the identification becomes even more complete when we realize that some of the remaining minor phrases we are left with as seemingly original from the author of SA—including such things as *Yma S. Austyn ow leverall* 'St Augustine says'; *whar an keth gerriow ma* 'upon these words'; *henna ew the leverall* 'that is to say'—are themselves often the very words used in the same place in the disputations.

It is possible to go even further than this, however. The text of SA appears to derive from the particular account of the Disputations of Oxford that is found in John Foxe's *Actes and Monuments* commonly called *Foxe's Book of Martyrs*.[10] We can assert this because the manuscripts are either (a) in Latin or (b) at least partially in summary form, and Foxe's full version—although it includes Latin (and sometimes Greek) versions of the patristic passages—gives an account of the whole debate in English, as well as full versions and translations of the patristic passages. On further study, it becomes apparent that these English translations have probably directly influenced those in Cornish. Thomas Stephyn (if it is he) writes his Cornish less classically than John Tregear, and more in a 'late modern' form. At the same time, however, he is less inclined than Tregear to borrow an English word when a perfectly good Cornish one will do. Consequently, when he does do this, it is significant that he choses the words of Foxe: *doubtys* for 'doubts'; *remaynea* for 'remaine'; *verily* for 'verely'; *touchia* for 'touch'; *recevya* for 'receaue'—all in exactly the same place as Foxe uses them. There are many telling examples of this, but for now one will suffice. At SA 63r.6 Thomas Stephyn has: *Rag henna te a recevest an Sacrament: mas in very ded te a obtaynest grace han gallus a nature a Christ.*[11] Foxe, reporting Weston, has: 'Therefore in a similitude thou receiuest the sacrament: but in deade thou obtainest the grace and power of his nature' (Foxe vi, 465; 1576, p. 1369).[12] While this is not exact in every detail, it explains the anomalous verbal forms in the Cornish perfectly. When each passage of SA is laid beside the corresponding passage from Foxe—something I hope to offer scholars for the first time in the full reading of the MS with notes that I am preparing—many such illuminating conjunctions occur.

Once we realise that SA is an abstract from Foxe, two further questions arise. Firstly, what can we deduce from the particular passages Stephyn choses? And, secondly, which edition of Foxe was he drawing from?

In answer to the first question, he quite selectively chooses the quotations advanced by the Catholic doctors in support of Catholic doctrine, and sometimes brief examples of their commentary upon them. For the most part he leaves alone the arguments themselves—not least because Cranmer in particular appears to acquit himself quite well in them. (I say appears, since we must guard against seeing Foxe as an unbiased, first-hand reporter on the proceedings, however convincingly his account reads.) Where SA does use Cranmer's words, it is by and large against him. In addition, the only substantial patristic quotation taken from Cranmer himself is given in a slightly different version, partly drawn from a quotation used in the Disputation with Ridley. This is significant, since virtually all the other quotations are given verbatim in SA. It is the exception that proves the rule.

As for the second question, I am presently working through the several editions of Foxe's work to see if any provide a better fit than my current working hypothesis. This is, that SA was written no earlier than 1570, since it certainly incorporates changes made by Foxe in that year. What is clear, however, is that the first edition of 1563 was not used. There are many proofs of this. Some are minor, such as *sufficiet* 1563, p. 945, *sufficit* 1570, p. 1598, *sufficit* SA 59v.5; *lectum aureum* 1563, p. 945, *lectus aureus* 1570, p. 1598, *lectus aureus* SA 60r.27; *nominis* 1563, p. 947, *hominis* 1570, p. 1599, *hominis* SA 60v.15. Others are major and substantial, such as the omission of words—*caro signatur* 1563, p. 947, *signatur* 1570, p. 1599, *signatur* SA60v.21–2—or indeed whole passages. In the quotation from St Ambrose, *De Mysteriis, 1, 9, 52* (PL 16, 406C) which begins with *De totius mundi* at SA 61v.3A, Foxe's first edition (1563, p. 952) continues only as far as *mutare naturas*. His edition of 1570 goes on from *Sed quid argumentis* to *affectus sentiat* (1570, p. 1603) and SA does exactly the same (SA 61v.7–22).

It is possible that a later edition was used, either that of 1576 or 1583, and increasingly the evidence suggests this. The later editions vary only very slightly from 1570 in the passages we are concerned with.

Furthermore, the edition of 1570 is the one that was made available as a large, chained volume, in every cathedral in the land. Such wide and free availability might suggest that SA could have been drawn from such a volume. One could imagine people being above suspicion, copying from a volume that observers must have believed was an entirely safe repository of edifying Protestant stories. The fact that such copyists may have been selectively writing out Catholic arguments for Transubstantiation, with patristic quotations to back them up, might have passed unnoticed by those who—like Foxe himself—would otherwise have been horrified.[13] However, it is likely that we shall be able to establish a firm date of at least 1576. Indications I have found so far include: *crebo* 1563, p. 947; *crebo* 1570, p. 1599; *crebro* 1576, p. 1364; *crebro* 1583, p. 1435 [*crebro* SA 61r.8] and *Home. 24.* 1563, p945; *Homel. 24* 1570, p1598; *Homel. 34* 1576, p. 1363; *Homil. 34* 1583, p. 1434 [*homele. 34* SA 60r.25]. Most decisive of all are the figures [1]383 at the foot of folio 65v(65a). They give the correct folio/page number for the 1576 edition of Foxe, for the material that immediately precedes them. It is for these reasons that while we can certainly date the Cornish of SA as being from 1570 at the earliest, I am increasingly sure that it is later than 1576.

It is interesting, however, that the Oxford Disputations lived on in the minds of at least some Cornish Catholics, in a different spirit from that inculcated by Foxe's fuller account. In 1554 they had served their limited purpose. Then they had asserted the return of the Church of England to full Catholic teaching on the eucharist, after it had been questioned during the Protestant years under Edward VI. In fact, shortly after the Disputations were concluded, a solemn procession and adoration of the Blessed Sacrament was held in the streets of Oxford. The author of SA and others must have held that memory, and the arguments that prepared the way for it, very dear.

Taking into account the change in the original translation of the passage cited by Cranmer, we can now reconstruct the bare bones of what probably happened: an initial copy was made from an edition of Foxe in or after 1576—possibly from a cathedral edition. Subsequently another copy was made of this, in which the Cranmerian quotation was amended and other minor changes made. Of course, SA may or may not have been this second copy itself. Either way, our author—while clearly learned—is rather more of a scribe than I had previously thought.

SOME INTERESTING DETAILS
Obviously what follows is a very small selection of the discoveries and detailed reappraisals that have made up the bulk of the work to date,

but I hope to be able, when it is finished, to make available in some form the whole body of research to those who would be interested. (In the following examples, the references are to the working edition of SA I have prepared.[14])

> *Cryst ny rug vsya trope k[epare e gerryow] dewetha* (SA 59r.1)
> 'Christ did not use a "figure" as his last words'
> [*Dr Oglethorpe:* No man of purpose doth vse tropes in his testament . . . therefore Christ vseth none here—Foxe vi, 450; 1576, p. 1362—from Cranmer's Disputation.]

vsya trope [k] is very difficult to read, and no comprehensive attempt has been made previously to make sense of this heading. For *usya,* however, the 'u' (in fact here a 'v') is clear, the 's' less so, the 'y' is reasonably clear and the 'a' is clear. In *trope* (a word in use in English since the 1520s for a 'figure' in the sense of 'figurative language' —*OED*) the 'r' is the difficult letter to see—it could be 'i' or 'e' instead. Possibly an alternative introduction inserted at the head of this page, where the folio is now partly damaged, this phrase is set so that the initial *I ma S. Austin ow leverall* of the main text could have been replaced when read by something like *Christ ny rug usya trope kepare e gerryow dewetha, kepar del uge S. Austin ow leverall etc.* 'Christ did not use a "figure" [i.e. figurative language] for his last words, as St Augustine says' etc. This accords well with the sense of the following passage. (For another use of *kepare e* see SA 60r.3—*kepare e lell ha meer inherita\n\ce.*)

> *begare a ra an ma\m\ maga e flogh gans e leath* (SA 59r.37)
> 'as the mother feeds her child with her milk'
> [*Dr Weston:* Like as mothers nurse their children with milke —Foxe vi, 452; 1576, p. 1363—from Cranmer's Disputation.]

begare a was previously mis-read as *be[ni]ell a* or *be ell.* Nance identified the word as being, possibly, '*bonyl*' (i.e. from *bo an eyll*)—'or else'. I believe it to represent *pecar/kepar*, which the sense also seems to require. What is intriguing, from a phonological point of view, is that it looks very much that its original form may have been *begar*—which may have been later altered to *ke[p]are.* Is it possible that *begar* might represent *pecar* (a late form of *kepar/kepare* found at SA 61r.17)? In any case, it seems to have been partly altered, the line through the 'b' hinting at a 'k'; the 'g' partly obscured (by a 'p'—no longer clear); the 'e' possibly being added later. However, it is arguable that the word may have been *kepare*—very imperfectly written and now irrecoverably obscured—from the start. I propose to discuss the case in detail in my notes on SA. It is not yet clear to me why there might have been such a shift or confusion between 'p' and 'b', or 'c' and 'g'—although it could be paralleled by the reverse confusion at SA 63v.10–11, where *th'agen sawya ny* ('to preserve us') is written *thaken sawya ny.*

> *a ve genis vrth an Worthias Maria* (SA 61v.27)
> 'was born of the Virgin Mary'
> [*Dr Young:*—was borne of Mary . . . was conceived of a Virgine—Foxe vi, 463; 1576, p. 1368—from Cranmer's Disputation, cf. St Ambrose, *De Mysteriis, 1, 9, 52* (PL 16, 406C).]

a ve genis vrth (=urth) an Worthias Maria and, below it, *a ve goris in crows, marow ha inclethis*, are phrases from the Apostles Creed. Permission was of course granted to teach this in Cornish in certain parishes, and it is exciting to think that we may have here a genuine survival of part of a version used. This seems the more likely because it differs slightly from Foxe's translation of St Ambrose. (Of course, the other liturgical phrase found in this passage—*hemma ew ow corf ve*—would have been said in Latin in the Canon of the Mass.) To these could be added other versions of well known liturgical prayers, which are alluded to in SA and might be of use to translators of the liturgy wishing to reflect traditional usage. (For example at SA 65v.21–22 we are given the basis for an authentic Cornish translation of *Agnus Dei, qui tollis peccata mundi* (to which chant in the Mass the passage alludes) i.e. *onne Dew, vge ow kemeras e ker pegh an [bys]*—'Lamb of God, that takest away the sin of the [world]'. The word for 'away' here represents *yn kerth/yn kerdh* and reminds us—as do other examples in SA—that in the combination 'rth' we find 'th' becoming silent by this period (unless, of course, representing the combination 'rgh' as in *Worthias* here.)

> *peiadow rag an bopell, rag meternath* . . . (SA 62r.18)
> 'prayer for the people, for kings . . .'
> [*Dr Young:* prayer is made for the people, for kinges—Foxe vi, 463; 1576, p. 1368—from Cranmer's Disputation.]

Capital 'I' and 'J' are not usually distinguishable in SA—but one or the other is employed here in *peiadow* where I have written 'i'. The word appears again at SA 63.36, where it is clearly *peiadow*. Although the first occurrence was read with an interpolated 's' by Nance, and indeed is not dissimilar to the 's' in *Jesus* below, the form of the topmost part

of the letter is characteristic. *Pejadow* therefore seems the likely pronunciation here. This is of interest not only for its confirmation of the
pronunciation of a word spelt more historically *pesadow* in TH, but
also as evidence of the use of 'i'/'j' for this sound in the evolving
traditional orthography. The sound may go back a long way—see
piyadow PC 334. (NB *meternath* (< *myterneth BM 2428* & *TH* <
myghterneth PC 785) gives analogous evidence of other shifts in pronunciation.) This passage is from St Ambrose, *De Sacramentis, 4, 4,*
14—PL 16, 439B.

> *an discipels ny\n\ go abel [y*ᵉ*]* p\er\thy *girreow age Arluth*
> Christ (SA 62v.36)
> 'the disciples were not able to bear the words of Christ their
> Lord'
> [*Dr Weston:* the Disciples could not abide the wordes of
> Christ—Foxe vi, 465; 1576, p. 1369—from Cranmer's
> Disputation; cf. St Ambrose, *De Sacramentis, 6, 1, 1* (PL 16,
> 454C).]

abel perthy—or just possibly *abel y*ᵉ *perthy* is a new reading. Previously
it had not been reported that there was a 'p' marked with a ligature for
er/ar before *thy,* and this section has been read as *an discipels nyng o*
abel thy gyrreow age Arluth Christ—translated something like 'the
disciples were not able for the words of Christ' or, better, 'the disciples
were not ready for the words of Christ' (Nance). Nonetheless *perthy,*
not *thy,* now seems more likely. The spelling *perthy* for the verb is
found in BM 2635. There is damage to the MS at the end of *abe[l]* and
at the beginning of *p\er\thy* and therefore just enough space for the
form *abel y*ᵉ *perthy,* which, however, cannot be clearly seen now—
although a minute part of the 'y' of the suggested *y*ᵉ may be visible.
ny\n\ go represents *nyns o*—and indicates the 'g' was being pronounced
as modern English 'j'. *Ne gesee* (SA59a.9—representing *nyns usy* or,
possibly, *nag usy* showing a late shift in the use of negative particles) is
another example of this division of words.

> *rag cressya agan corfow ny . . . tha creffe agen corfow* (SA
> 63v.18,21)
> 'to give increase to our bodies . . . to strengthen our bodies'
> [*Dr Weston:* he encreaseth our bodyes . . . the substaunce of
> our fleshe is increased—Foxe vi, 466–7; 1576, p. 1369—from
> Cranmer's Disputation.]

This is a translation of St Irenaeus, *Adversus haereses, 5, 2, 2* (PG 7/1, 1125). Nance believed the first of the verbs here to be **creffya* —presumably as a variant of *creffe (=*crefhe)*—but the double 's' is fairly clear and *cressya* (as found in CW 1255) would be much closer to the Latin verb *augeo* used here. With the second verb we clearly do have *creffe*. The addition of *consisto* to *augeo* (or of 'sustaunce of our flesh') was deemed to require a more specific Cornish verb, this time with the definite sense of 'strengthen'.

> *ema ran ow pedery fatla [. . .] ha gwyne, honora dew a bara*
> *ha dew a . . .* (SA 65r.4–5)
> there are some who think that [. . .] and wine, we honour a
> god of bread and god of . . .
> [*Dr Glyn:* Some there were which thought vs, in stede of
> bread and of the cup, to worshyp Ceres & Bacchus—Foxe vi,
> 492; 1576, p. 1380—from Ridley's Disputation.]

This renders in Cornish a passage from St Augustine of Hippo, *Contra Faustum Manichaeum, 20, 13* (PL 42, 379). A fairly free English translation, which unpacks the Latin, can be found in the Nicene and Post Nicene Fathers version: 'There is not the least resemblance between our reverence for the bread and wine, and your doctrines, which have no truth in them. To compare the two is even more foolish than to say, as some do, that in the bread and wine we worship Ceres and Bacchus.' 'God of wine' was therefore clearly the conclusion, but this is now lost. The version in SA, here reconstructed, reads: . . . *[Nonulli propter] panem et calicem Cererem [et Bacchum nos colere existimabant].* It is clear that, in the Cornish, [*in the Bread*] is missing and therefore something like [*erany in bara*]. Another possibility would of course be something like [*wreny in bara*] but it is a feature of Cornish Tudor prose (as exemplified in SA) that it more regularly uses *bos* as an auxiliary than *gul* in such a case. In doing so it is similar to modern Welsh. All of this illustrates the importance of considering the original patristic quotations, sixteenth-century versions of them, the manuscripts of the Disputations, and above all Foxe himself in reconstructing both Latin and Cornish phrases in damaged sections of the manuscript. (My reconstruction of the Cornish—here as elsewhere —is, of course, only conjectural. The form *esyn ny* is found in SA 65v.19, but the tail of a 'y' is visible too far to the right at SA 65r.4—not quite in the place we would expect for *esyn ny* but exactly right for *erany,* which is found in SA 65r.13.)

Pan[dra] lavirta ge? [An] host benegas e ma inter dowla an pronter (SA 66r.5)
'What do you say? The sacred host is in the hands of the priest'
[*Dr Weston:* Chrysostome againe, vpon the ix. chapter of the Actes. *Quid dicis? Hostia in manibus sacerdotis. &c.*—Foxe vi, 509; 1576, p. 1388—from Latimer's Disputation. Foxe gives no translation—cf. St John Chrysostom, *Homiliae in Acta Apostolorum, 21, 4* (PG 60, 170).]

The MS had become damaged here over the years, and two small fragments to the right of the folio appear to have become detached. When reaffixed, the smaller of the two was placed slightly below and to the right of its original position, leading to the erroneous reading *Acts Apostolis.* Another portion also became detached, and was even less well placed. Once these are readjusted, it becomes possible to reconstruct conjecturally something like—*Pandra lavirta/laverta ge? An host benegas e ma inter dowla an pronter*—with very little speculation. This may be evidence for another second sing present verbal form with -*ta.* The damage to the folio and incorrect placing of two fragments may also explain the loss of part of *Pan[dra].* The rearrangement of the fragments also has a bearing on the text just above. This was previously thought to represent *an owriek*—an allusion to the 'golden mouthed' St John Chrysostom. It is clearly *[ ]vs only angwra,* however, which could represent . . . *tus only a'n gwra.* This could fit with the marginal reference to St John Chrysostom, *De incomprehensibili Dei natura (seu contra Anomeos) 3, 40:* '*When prayer is made, it is not only men that make it*' etc.—a passage alluded to by Dr Weston in the Disputation with Latimer ('Likewyse both Augustine in the. 38 Psal. & Chrysostome, concernyng the incomprehensible nature of God, *Tomo. 3.* say: *Non solum homines etc.*'—Foxe vi, 509; 1570, p. 1626).

*ny\n\ gew dir hastenab apoyntis y*ᵉ worth an Apostelath (SA 66r.8–9)
it was not rashly ordered by the Apostles
[*Dr Weston:* I bring an other place of Chrysostome out of the same treatise, *Non temerè ab apostolis est institutum*—Foxe vi, 509; 1576, p. 1388—from Latimer's Disputation. Foxe gives no translation—cf. St John Chrysostom, *In epistolam ad Philippenses commentarius, 1, 3, 4* (PG 62, 204).]

Nance—in his manuscript translation in the Royal Institution of Cornwall—gives this as 'it is not in haste appointed from the Apostles', but the context and original show us that the *ny\n\ gew* (=*nynj yw*) is probably for *o*, and the abstract noun has a slightly broader meaning. Indeed, the ending of *hastenab* is noteworthy and seems to contain a suffix of abstraction, *-enab*. TH 2r has *hevelep, heveleb* but also *hevelenep* for 'likeness', which could lead us to suppose *eneb*, 'face' (C.Voc and Late Cornish, cf. Welsh *wyneb*) is found here; TH 16v has *methewnep* for 'drunkenness' where this might also be just possible. But what are we to make of TH34v *cotheneb* for Bonner's 'antiquity' and *hastenab* itself? In 'The Tregear Manuscript' *Old Cornwall*, 4, 11 (1951) p. 432, Nance indicates that he believes we are in fact dealing with a suffix for an abstract noun: '*Hastenab (hastenep)*, m., hastiness, haste; suffix *-enep*, -ness.' This is surely right, and parallels the Welsh suffix *-ineb* (as noted by Nance for *cotheneb*) in *claerineb, doethineb, ffolineb*. The *Geiriadur Prifysgol Cymru* (Cyfrol 2, Caerdydd, 1968–87) gives more examples and the two forms *-ineb* and *-inab*.

> *an keth Austin ma a leveris aferan rag e vam Monaca* (SA 66r.17)
> 'this same Augustine sayde masse for his mother Monica'
> [*Dr Weston:* the same Austine said Masse for his mother —Foxe vi, 509; 1576, p. 1388—from Latimer's Disputation.]

This was previously misread as *leveris a seran*. In his manuscript English translation, Nance gives: 'This same Augustine said a "seran" for his mother Monica'. Above the word 'seran' he has inserted the gloss 'prayer for rest for her soul'. The word thus made its way into subsequent dictionaries, and was supposed to relate to Latin *serenare*. On closer inspection, however, it is clear that the 's' is not an 's' at all, but an 'f'—i.e. *leveris a, fferan*, where *a, fferan* represents *aferan* or *offeren*—'Mass'. Thus *leverall aferan* is the exact equivalent of the English phrase 'to say Mass', a common Catholic expression to this day, meaning 'to celebrate the Eucharist'. It is pleasing to have confirmation of this usage (also found in BM 4419). The sense accords well with the appropriate passages in St Augustine's *Confessions*—where he describes how he took part in the offering of the funeral mass for his mother St Monica. (St Augustine of Hippo, *Confessions, 9, 12, 32* (PL 32, 775). 'When the body was carried to the grave, we went, we returned—without tears. Nor [did I weep] during those prayers which we poured out before Thee, when the sacrifice of our redemption was offered for her, as the corpse was placed beside the grave before being buried'. tr. Vernon J. Bourke, New York, CUA, 1953.)

LITERARY, THEOLOGICAL AND HISTORICAL
PERSPECTIVES

With much of the work on the new reading of the manuscript for SA completed, and the greater part of the patristic references traced, I am now turning my attention to the internal logic of the piece, abstracted as it is from Foxe's account of the Disputations at Oxford. Clearly—as noted above—it is still a *catena*, probably intended for teaching those who would be engaged in theological disputation. Now that we know its source, it is interesting to reflect on the rationale for the selections. I hope to outline the basic theological arguments behind both the Disputations and SA, although some of these melt away in the light of later scholarship, not least in reattribution, reinterpretation, and the discovery of earlier sources for some of the patristic quotations. Nonetheless there is much in what both Weston and Cranmer say that remains pertinent today.

It is also interesting to investigate the history of the manuscript as a whole, and in this area, too, I am currently undertaking further research. The Puleston family, from whom it came, may have claimed that it was confiscated from a Catholic house during the course of their assiduous support of Protestantism in the Penal Years.[15] I have discovered, however, from those researching the history of the families concerned, that there may be other explanations for this document finding its way into the Pulestons' possession. With the help of local Catholic historians, I have particularly been investigating the Edwards family of Plas Newydd in Chirkland.

I am now beginning to suspect that the manuscript came into the hands of the Protestant Pulestons of Emral through marriage, when the last heiress of the Edwards family, Catherine, married Sir Roger Puleston. If so, we may be able to connect Plas Newydd—a haven for Catholic priests, education and liturgy well into the Elizabethan years—with the story of this manuscript and the travelling priests who may have carried it.

When further work is done, it might be possible to suggest that Tregear's manuscript has known many travels—at least in Wales and possibly as far afield as Ireland, Belgium or even Spain—perhaps in conjunction with other manuscripts. It could have been in the custody of travelling priests, some of whom used the established sea crossings into Wales from Cornwall and the West Country, and the network of safe houses up to Chirkland and beyond. It had already had quite a history when, sometime after 1570, the annotations to Homilies 11 and 12 were made, and SA itself was compiled and added. Whether it left, say, the Edwards house after this—before its arrival at Emral—is a matter of conjecture.

To complete the story, I hope to append an account of John Mackechnie's discovery and collaboration with Nance in bringing TH and SA to light. I would welcome any light that could be shed on the Gaelic scholar's papers on SA—they do not appear to be in Canada with his books. Indeed, any insight into the career of Thomas Stephyn, or the history of travelling recusant priests of the 1570s in Cornwall, North Wales and the Marches, could be of assistance.

NOTES AND REFERENCES

1. A useful description of the MS as a whole is found in Brian Murdoch, *Cornish Literature*, Cambridge, 1993, pp. 129–30.
2. Among these I am particularly indebted to the staff of many libraries who went out of their way and beyond the call of duty to expedite my work, particularly at the Royal Institution of Cornwall (which holds the Nance Bequest), the Bodleian Library, the British Library, the Library of the College of St Cuthbert, Ushaw and, in later stages of the project, the Cambridge University Library, the Parker Library at Corpus Christi College, Cambridge, the cataloguing team at the Archbishop of Cardiff's Library ('Bishop Brown's Library') and my own college, St David's Catholic College, Cardiff.
3. In 'More about the Tregear Manuscript', *Old Cornwall*, 5.1, 1951, pp. 21–7.
4. Charles Penglase, 'The Future Indicative in the Early Modern Cornish of Tregear', *Etudes Celtiques*, 34, 1998–2000.
5. Bishop Cuthbert Tunstall, *De ueritate Corporis et Sanguinis domini Nostri Jesu Christi in Eucharistia*, 2nd edition, 1554. Tunstall wrote and compiled this work in 1551 under arrest, but by the time of its publication he was restored to his office as Bishop of Durham.
6. It is, however, conceivable that it was only ever intended as a written document: there was a market at this time for scribal copies of forbidden Catholic texts. See note 13 below.
7. E.g. *ema S. Austin ow leverall*.
8. Henry Jenner, 'A Cornish Oration in Spain in the Year 1600', *Royal Cornwall Polytechnic Society*, 90th Annual Report, 1923, cited in P. Berresford Ellis, *The Cornish Language and its Literature*, London, 1974. The Welsh Catholics on the continent were also active in the production of literature to support those at home. See Geraint Bowen, *Welsh Recusant Writings*, Cardiff, 1999.
9. These include the official report from Weston to Bonner among the Harleian MSS in the British Library (Harl. MSS 3642). Also surviving are short notes of the principal arguments in the Parker Library of Corpus Christi College, Cambridge. A longer document written in much greater haste and with many abbreviations—which therefore seems to me to be at least a candidate for something taken down at the time—is in Cambridge University Library, folios 13–29 of K.K.5.14. Ridley's notes are also in the British Library, Harl. MSS 422, art. 53, 60, 68.

10. The standard printed version—*The Acts and Monuments of John Foxe*, ed. G. Townsend and S.R. Cattley, London, 1841—commonly used for citation in the past is, like the *Patrologia Latina* and *Patrologia Graeca*, far from a modern critical edition. We are fortunate, however, that the excellent John Foxe Book of Martyrs Project at Sheffield University is steadily making its detailed work available, at http://hri.shef.ac.uk/foxe. In particular, their work on the sections dealing with the reign of Mary I is well advanced and already online as part of the projected full Variorum Online Edition of Foxe's Book of Martyrs. I had already completed my identification of the patristic texts in SA before I discovered this invaluable resource, which, had it been more widely known to students of Cornish, could have saved everyone a great deal of work. It is a great privilege to be of some small assistance to the JFP team by contributing some of the missing patristic references that I have been able to trace during the course of my own research.

11. Traditionally, SA has been referred to using a convention in which the folio number was used for *recto*, and that number followed by lowercase 'a' for *verso*—i.e. SA 63.3, SA 66a.10 etc. While far from presuming to cast this convention aside, I have preferred here to use more standardized references for ease of identification—i.e. SA 63r.3, SA 66v.10 etc. As yet, there is no published edition giving line numbers. My own system (which departs from Charles Penglase's in that I do not assign Roman numerals to titles) counts all full lines and title lines, but not marginal notes which happen to be written between lines. These may be identified with an additional 'b'—i.e. SA 61v.4b.

12. In citing Foxe, I usually give first the volume number (in Roman numerals) and page of Townsend and Cattley, and (invariably) the relevant year and folio number of the edition of Foxe, using the online edition of the John Foxe Book of Martyrs Project described above. By inserting this second reference as two figures separated by an underlined space—e.g. 1570_1604—into the URL for single pages of the Variorum Online Edition, the relevant passage may be easily reached. For this example the URL for the example would be: http://hri.shef.ac.uk/foxe/single/1570_1604.

13. Certainly such copyists existed, and indeed were in constant demand—largely due to the prohibition on the printing of Catholic works. See Bowen, 1999, p. 45.

14. For those with access to the manuscript, the first figure refers to the folio number—e.g. 59r = 59 recto (59) and 59v = 59 verso (59a)—and the second figure to the line number. I have included some lines of Latin marginal notes in this numbering scheme, where they traverse the whole page, or where they form significant headings, etc. Contractions are shown as characters between obliques, as the final 'm' in *ma\m*. Square brackets enclose damaged, lost or illegible material.

15. Again, see Bowen, 1999, p. 40, for one of the Pulestons writing in Welsh on the other side.

THE MEDIEVAL 'CORNISH BIBLE'

Malte W. Tschirschky

INTRODUCTION

In a French-language essay published in the journal *Etudes Celtiques*, Charles Penglase[1] claims that a Cornish translation of the Bible existed in the Middle Ages. He bases this claim on the so-called 'Tregear Homilies', a manuscript written between 1555 and about 1558 which consists of a translation of an English (Catholic) collection of sermons. Studying this Late Cornish[2] document, Penglase notices six passages with verb forms which obviously belong to the Middle Cornish period of the language and which appear, with one exception, only in quotations from the Bible. Penglase concludes that John Tregear, the translator of the manuscript, took the five remaining passages containing these constructions from a Middle Cornish version of the Bible then in existence and, furthermore, that this Middle Cornish Bible was still widely used and its language understood by the people of Tregear's time.

RESISTANCE OR REFORMATION?

Some of Penglase's statements in his essay, and the assumptions underlying them, are at least questionable. He declares, for example, that the translation of the Bible into Welsh was a kind of 'passive resistance policy'[3] by the Welsh people in response to their annexation by England. They were trying, he argues, to save their own language in the face of the threat of English domination, a threat that would lead, eventually, to the death of their language, and to the imposition of the English Bible and Book of Common Prayer. The Welsh Bible translation, however, has to be understood within the framework of Reformation history and was thus more a mechanism for the introduction of the (English) Reformation in Wales, substituting a vernacular translation for the Latin Bible, as had been done in England (witness William Tyndale's 1523–5 translation of the New Testament and subsequent editions leading to the 'Authorized Version'), Germany (Martin Luther's translation from 1522 onwards) and elsewhere. This substitution of languages in the Bible and also in the Prayer Book and church services was, as we know, among the grievances that stirred the Cornish to rebellion in 1549.[4] In Wales, however, the language substituted was Welsh, a means of bringing the Word to monoglot Welsh-speakers in a land where (in many areas) English-speakers were few.

As Gillian Brennan has argued, it was the achievement of a uniform religion (the enforcement of Protestantism) that had greater urgency than any other supposed or real design to achieve linguistic uniformity across the realm, although of course both intentions would be characteristic of centralist policy.[5] Penglase (who bases his sketch of the complex Reformation period solely on the opinions of Peter Berresford Ellis) ignores the 1563 Act for the translation of the Bible into Welsh,[6] a piece of legislation which demonstrated the primacy of religious over language matters in Tudor policy at that time. However much Tudor monarchs may have wished to do away with what they would have called 'provisional languages' in favour of English, the translation of the Prayer Book and Bible ordered by Parliament[7] actually had the immediate effect of *strengthening* the Welsh language, and was not at all primarily an act of resistance on the part of the Welsh.

Shortly after the passage just discussed, and in the same context, Penglase attributes generalized qualities and inherent patterns of preferred behaviour or acting to the inhabitants of Cornwall in a way that it is highly questionable. Penglase speaks of Tudor Cornishmen and women being 'less subtle than the Welsh' ('moins subtils que les Gallois') because translations of religious texts into their language in order to save it from a possible language death would have been opposed to their accustomed pattern of behaviour ('leur façon d'agir').[8] This tells us more about Penglase's world view (Michael Billing's term 'banal nationalism' comes to mind)[9] than it does about Tudor Cornwall. Far from the conservative Cornish failing to initiate their own translations, there was never a parliamentary enactment for a Cornish Bible or Prayer Book, perhaps because there were seen to be too few Cornish-speakers or (maybe) because Cornish was (as a result of the rising of 1549) already considered a dangerous rebel and 'Popish' tongue.

THE PENGLASE THESIS: A CRITIQUE
In this brief article, however, my main purpose is not to question Penglase's broad assumptions about the Reformation in Wales and Cornwall but to oppose the main thesis of his essay. My critique of his argument (outlined above), in which I do not deny the possibility of the existence of a Middle Cornish translation of the Bible *per se* but where I do strongly contest Penglase's inferences, can be divided into four main points. The first three emerge directly from Penglase's own treatment of his material.

Firstly, in at least two of the five specific cases discussed by Penglase, Tregear gives Bible quotations with the Middle Cornish verb forms first and then repeats the same passages using the constructions of Late Cornish; that is, he actually translates them into the Late Cornish variety.[10] If, as Penglase contends, the Middle Cornish passages in the text had indeed been understood without any problems by the Cornish-speaking audience, it would not have made any sense for Tregear to repeat the same quotations directly after their first, 'original' citation. Such a doubling is only necessary if the author wants to mention the quotation for some reason in its original language (or language variety) but cannot expect his audience to fully understand the original version standing alone. For example, while quotations from Molière or Goethe are usually translated into (Modern) English in present-day literature, those by Shakespeare and sometimes even Chaucer are not, the assumption being that contemporary English-speakers are comfortable with Shakespearean and perhaps even Chaucerian English but require translations of Molière and Goethe. This is contradictory to Penglase's assertion that the Cornish were familiar with the supposed Middle Cornish version of the Bible: if there ever was a medieval Cornish Bible, Cornish people by the mid-sixteenth century were probably not accustomed to hearing it being read out to them and would not understand its language easily. (In Cornwall today, one might observe as an aside, speakers of 'Modern' [based on Late Cornish] are not readily understood by speakers of 'Kemmyn' [based on Middle Cornish]).

Secondly, we know too little of the author/translator Tregear to tell much of his background,[11] but we can be reasonably confident that with even a modicum of knowledge of Cornish drama texts and some philological skills he could have modified the biblical quotations into a seemingly historical version of Cornish if he had reason to do so, and this may explain their apparently 'Middle Cornish' appearance. Penglase's own discussion allows for this supposition. To begin with, he rightly suggests that Tregear wished to create the impression of appealing to a higher authority but he concludes that this must be circumstantial evidence for the existence of a medieval Bible in Middle Cornish, a text that would inevitably have greater authority than any recent rendering: 'As the population was used to hearing the Bible in Middle Cornish, the medieval subtleties in these passages were to heighten the value of Tregear's quotations *which was surely his goal'*.[12] However, the higher authority to which Tregear in his translation of the homilies was appealing was more likely to be pre-Reformation Catholicism. The collection of sermons in question has to be seen in the context of Counter-Reformation policy. Here the use of a decidedly pre-Reformation language in a Catholic religious tract would neatly fit into the methods deployed by Counter-Reformation protagonists who often sought to demonstrate the continuity of the (Roman Catholic) Church to distinguish the older, established faith from the 'new' Protestant denomination. So Tregear surely had a motive to employ old-fashioned language.

Additionally, the one morphological form of Middle Cornish in the homilies which occurs outside the 'biblical quotations' (and is explained by Penglase as a 'residual archaism'[13]) hints at the fact that Tregear might have had to hand a working example (a medieval Cornish Bible?) on which he could have moulded 'historical' forms in other contexts, even if he had himself no substantial knowledge of medieval Cornish literature. Perhaps: but, as we know from the manuscripts that have survived today, Middle Cornish religious drama was still available at that time, and even if a translator such as Tregear did not have a good grasp of this earlier form of the language he may well have had access and exposure to such documents for comparative purposes. Again, Penglase has raised an interesting point but it does not in itself add to the argument in support of a medieval Cornish Bible, merely pointing as it does to the fact that if (as seems unlikely) Tregear had no knowledge of Middle Cornish there were extant texts that could help him.

To this may be added a further observation. In her discussion of the 'Tregear Homilies', Fudge briefly mentions the curious absence in the manuscript (observed by Nance) of pre-occlusion, i.e. a linguistic change illustrated exemplarily by the well-known word *pen(n)* 'head' which became *pedn* at some point in the history of the language.[14] Nance's solution to the problem (cited by Fudge) was to suggest that Tregear wrote in a dialect which had not (yet) been affected by pre-occlusion.[15] Another possibility is that he had learnt Cornish, not as it was used as the daily medium of communication in a living Cornish-speaking community, but on the basis of Middle Cornish, either directly from manuscripts which he studied as part of his religious work, or from a fossilized form of the language (which would

be closer to Middle Cornish) handed down in an area where Cornish
had long been in terminal decline and by then virtually extinct.[16] In
both cases, he would have been able to use Middle Cornish models for
verbal construction in his own translations. Be this as it may, we have
to accept that Tregear, in addition to his Counter-Reformation motive,
also had the ability to deliberately style his quotations in a seemingly
historical language variety.

The third major point is that in one of the five instances of biblical
quotation that he examines, even Penglase is not convinced that it is of
Middle Cornish provenance. He writes:[17]

> Il est à noter que Tregear n'*écrit* pas ce dernier passage en
> moyen-cornique. Il se borne à prêter une nuance médiévale à
> ce passage (qui cite Matthieu 16:13–19 et Jean 20:22–23) en y
> insérant des formes verbales du moyen-cornique, notamment
> les trois occurences de *rylly*. Il ne cite pas directement sa
> source, simplement il se contente de donner à ce passage
> d'origine biblique une saveur médiévale.

> It has to be noted that Tregear does not *write* this last passage
> in Middle Cornish. He confines himself to adding a medieval
> shade to this passage (which cites Matthew 16:13–19 and John
> 20:22–23) by inserting verbal forms from Middle Cornish,
> notably the three occurrences of *rylly*. He does not cite
> his source directly, he simply contents himself with giving a
> medieval flavour to this passage of biblical origin.

Here we have to ask, why would Tregear translate a biblical
quotation into Late Cornish and then rewrite the verbs contained in it
to make it sound medieval if he had a widely used and widely accepted
Middle Cornish Bible at hand? Penglase employs the word *écrire* 'to
write', which in itself suggests someone actively creating a text (writing
a translation), rather than merely rendering an established passage in
its original form. The same impression is conveyed a few lines before
the passage quoted above where Penglase asserts that Tregear used
Middle Cornish morphology in this instance '*because* it is a passage
from the Bible'.[18] In fact, what Penglase actually does here is
to acknowledge that Tregear deliberately reconstructed medieval
morphological features and employed them as a stylistic device in
order to make the whole text seem highly authoritative, only that on
this occasion (Penglase's fifth example) Tregear was not as successful
as in the other biblical passages. Unfortunately, this does not occur
to Penglase, who, despite the awkward evidence of this particular

example, continues to argue that Tregear has access to a medieval Cornish Bible. It is, after all, despite Penglase's insistence, not plausible that Tregear should quote from the medieval Cornish Bible in four instances and refrain from a direct quote in the fifth so as to be able to present his own attempt at a 'historical' translation.

Finally, it must be mentioned that, despite the apparent suspicion that existed in English circles of the Cornish and their language, there are indications that a translation of the Bible into Cornish was considered during the Reformation.[19] Again, this was part of the Reformation policy to allow and even encourage everybody to access biblical texts for themselves, either to read them (if possible) or to hear them being read in public readings and sermons. Thus Penglase's view that consideration of a Cornish translation was simply impossible in the political circumstances of the time needs some modification, although it remains the case that no translations were forthcoming.[20] Of course, a great many Cornish-speakers may have been killed in the slaughter of 1549 and its aftermath, and, whatever the level of ideological hostility to the language, that moves to translate the Bible and Prayer Book into Cornish did not bear fruit may have been due to the fact that by then (in the estimation of the ruling elite) Cornish had retreated to such an extent (geographically, numerically and socially) that a translation was not a pressing need, especially if many people had at least some knowledge of English, the preferred language. Moreover, that there was consideration given to translating the Bible into Cornish in the Reformation period is incompatible with Penglase's claim that a well-known, widely used and generally understood Cornish version had already existed since the Middle Ages. If we accept Penglase's hypothesis, there would have been no need for a new Cornish Bible translation, even if the language of the one in existence sounded antiquated by then.

CONCLUSION

Penglase is certainly correct when he writes in his conclusion that the 'historical' language of the biblical quotations in the Tregear Homilies was meant to heighten the authority of the sermons as a whole.[21] If Penglase's text is read only as a study on the use of archaic word forms to reach that aim (and the text invites us to do so)[22] it is quite convincing. As a whole, however, the hypothesis that a translation of the Bible into Middle Cornish really existed cannot be positively ascertained on the basis of morphological details in a single manuscript alone, and in that respect Penglase's argument is unconvincing. More-over, the absence of any other piece of corroborating evidence to prove that such a translation existed, together with the fact that not even a single copy of the allegedly widely used Bible has come down to us, casts further doubt on his thesis, as does the evidence that a translation was considered briefly in the Reformation period.

It is true that much, perhaps most of the medieval literature in Cornish that surely once existed must have been lost subsequently, but to explain the non-survival (if such it is) of even a single Cornish Bible out of the many copies that existed (according to Penglase) is extremely difficult, even if one tries to embed such an explanation (as Penglase does) within a paradigm of literature and language loss.[23] Again, one may grant that all copies might have been destroyed or lost (perhaps even as a result of Roundhead fury during or after the Civil War), but in the absence of any evidence in the first place, this is mere conjecture. If Penglase's observations on the verbal constructions in the Tregear Homilies are correct linguistically (an issue which I have not discussed here), then they have to be understood as a deliberate attempt on Tregear's part to historicize his text in order to heighten its value and authority. The summary, then, must be, not that a Middle Cornish Bible 'certainly existed',[24] fascinating as this thought is, but that probably none existed, and that despite Penglase's essay, we seem to have to put up with the thought that there never was a medieval Bible translation into Cornish. Nevertheless, hitherto unknown Cornish-language manuscripts are discovered from time to time (as in the recent case of *Beunans Ke*) and I would be delighted to be proved wrong by the discovery of a Middle Cornish Bible translation, not least as it would extend the corpus of historical Cornish literature considerably.

NOTES AND REFERENCES

1. Charles Penglase, 'La Bible en moyen-cornique', *Etudes Celtiques*, 33, 1997, pp. 233–43.
2. A different division of language periods than Penglase's would classify the text as very late Middle Cornish containing some features of Late Cornish, but this question cannot be considered here.
3. Penglase (my translations throughout): 'politique de résistance passive'; this and the following, p. 233.
4. Explanations of the so-called Prayer Book Rebellion range from the religious interpretation based on a Catholic point of view by Philip Caraman in his *The Western Rising 1549: The Prayer Book Rebellion* (Tiverton, 1994) and the social background Julian Cornwall stresses in his *Revolt of the Peasantry 1549* (London, 1977) to the account of the event as the 'Prayer Book War' between Cornwall and England (with its 'lethal influence on the Cornish language', p. 2) by Pol Hodge (*Cornwall's Secret War: The True Story of The Prayer Book War*, no place, 1999), to name but a few approaches. The most balanced and authoritative assessment is

that in Mark Stoyle, *West Britons: Cornish Identities and the Early Modern British State*, Exeter, 2002, especially chapter 1.

5. Gillian Brennan: 'Language and Nationality: The Role of Policy towards Celtic Languages in the Consolidation of Tudor Power', *Nations and Nationalism*, 7, 2001, pp. 317–38.

6. Cf. Peter Berresford Ellis, *The Cornish Language and Its Literature*, London, 1974, p. 63; Crysten Fudge, *The Life of Cornish*, Redruth, 1982, p. 26, and again Brennan, 2001, 326–7.

7. Cf. Norman Davies, *The Isles: A History*, Oxford, 1999, p. 493.

8. Both quotations Penglase, 1997, p. 233.

9. Cf. Michael Billing, *Banal Nationalism*, London, 1995.

10. Penglase, 1997, pp. 235–6.

11. Cf. Alan M. Kent, *The Literature of Cornwall: Continuity, Identity, Difference, 1000–2000*, Bristol, 2000, p. 52.

12. 'Comme la population avait l'habitude d'entendre la Bible en moyen-cornique, les nuances médiévales dans ces passages devaient augmenter la valeur des citations de Tregear, *ce qui était sûrement son but*'; Penglase, p. 238, my emphasis.

13. Penglase, 1997, p. 237: 'archaïsme résiduel'.

14. Fudge, 1982, p. 27.

15. Ken George, dating the occurrence of the pre-occlusion change to the sixteenth century, assumes that Tregear was a speaker of an older, more conservative Cornish who did not take over that change; Paul Dunbar and Ken George, *Kernewek Kemmyn: Cornish for the Twenty-first Century*, no place, 1997, pp. 62–3.

16. Fudge 1982, (p. 27) describes Tregear as knowing Cornish well, though it had not been his natural language: 'He may have been brought up to speak Cornish, but he was clearly educated by means of English, and this was the language which came to him most easily. His translations were a work of pastoral zeal; they did not spring from any living Cornish tradition.'

17. Penglase, 1997, p. 237, my emphasis.

18. Penglase, 1997, p. 237, my emphasis: 'Tregear emploie plusieurs formes du moyen-cornique *puisqu*'il s'agit d'un passage de la Bible'.

19. Ellis, 1994, pp. 62–4; in the same vein Kent, 2000, p. 51. Fudge 1982, (p. 26, following Ellis) mentions that in 1560, 'a conference held to study the laws of the new Anglican church moved a resolution, "that it may be lawful for such Welch or Cornish children as can speake no English to learn the Praemises in the Welsh tongue or Cornish language"'.

20. Penglase, 1997, p. 233.

21. Penglase, 1997, p. 241.

22. Penglase writes 'il [Tregear] *utilise* une autre forme du moyen-cornique', 'he [Tregear] *uses* another form of Middle Cornish' 1999, (p. 236); 'Tregear *se sert* d'un verbe en moyen-cornique', 'Tregear *makes use* of a verb in Middle Cornish' (ibid.); '*l'emploi* du moyen-cornique dans ces passages', '*the usage* of Middle Cornish in these passages' (p. 241, my emphasis throughout), just as if Tregear had the choice to use either

Middle or Late Cornish (which he would not have had if there had been a Middle Cornish Bible). The phrasing suggests that Tregear employed Middle Cornish in his translation into Cornish rather than that he just took it over from a Middle Cornish source text into his quotation; cf. my note above going in the same direction. Generally speaking, his inference from the evidence of the medieval language variety to the existence of a medieval translation appears to be a bit out of context in some places of the essay, almost as if he had added another hypothesis to it later, thus changing the trajectory of his study.

23. Penglase, 1997, p. 234: 'Bien entendu, tout comme le reste de la littérature cornique, celle-ci [la Bible cornique] a disparu en laissant peu de traces' ('Mind you, just like the rest of Cornish literature, this [the Cornish Bible] has been lost leaving few traces').

24. Penglase, 1997, p. 234: '[une Bible cornique] a sûrement existé'; again in his conclusion (p. 241): 'il paraît assuré qu'une Bible cornique médiévale a existé en Cornouailles même jusqu'au XVIe siècle', 'it seems to be certain that a medieval Cornish Bible existed in Cornwall even until the sixteenth century'.

REVIEW ARTICLE

PROPAGANDA AND THE TUDOR STATE OR PROPAGANDA OF THE TUDOR HISTORIANS?

Bernard Deacon

J.P.D. Cooper, *Propaganda and the Tudor State: Political Culture in the Westcountry*, Oxford University Press, 2003, hardback, 298pp., ISBN 019926 3876

The sixteenth century has undoubtedly become the principal battlefield of Cornish historiography. For almost half a century after A.L. Rowse's ground-breaking *Tudor Cornwall* the period lay relatively undisturbed, a quiet backwater where only local historians fished. Instead, attention became focused on more interesting events of the industrial revolution, mass emigration and de-industrialization since these seemed to be more relevant for understanding the contemporary situation of the Cornish people. As for the early modern period, the Tudors centralized, the gentry rose and the Cornish were, with some reluctance, integrated into English state and society. However, things began to change in the 1990s. In the context of a new interest in Cornish resistance to centralization, the Tudor period, from 1485 to 1603, began to take on greater importance.

In the later 1990s the half-millennial commemoration of Angove's rising of 1497 and the renewed threat of re-centralization accompanying top-down 'regionalization' stoked up a popular interest in the events of those years. Meanwhile, Philip Payton had argued that this was the period when Cornwall's 'first' or 'older' peripheralism of territorial and cultural isolation began to be broken down. A long process of transition, stretching into the eighteenth century, was one 'against which the Cornish reacted—in 1497, in 1549 and again in the Civil War'.[1] Enthused by this, Mark Stoyle picked up the baton and began to run with it. In a series of sparkling and provocative articles he began to put more flesh on Payton's interpretation. This culminated in 2002 in the publication of *West Britons*, in which he argued that a sense of 'Cornish ethnic identity' underlay Cornish 'politico-religious behaviour throughout the Tudor and Stuart periods' and 'underpinned the violent series of rebellions between 1497 and 1648'.[2] The Tudor period saw a visible identity of resistance in Cornwall to the encroachments of the Tudor state. The Cornish rose, not just in the period before 1550 but also in the 1640s, in a heroic but ultimately doomed series of desperate risings, struggling against their allotted role as a mere 'county' of England. Others have gone even further. These were the years when a heartless Tudor monarchy destroyed the Cornish language and the flower of Cornish (speaking) manhood in the killing fields that accompanied the 'Prayer Book War' of 1549.[3]

But this so-called 'Kernowcentric' perspective does not hold the field unchallenged. Recently, Mark Stoyle has predicted that a Kernowsceptic backlash may be just around the corner, one that would aim 'to thrust the historiography of early modern Cornwall firmly back into the box labelled "English local history"'![4] In fact the 'Kernowsceptic' interpretation was already well-established by the time he was writing his review article. Ian Arthurson's detailed studies of the 1497 risings had already placed them in a wider context of royal pretender manoeuvrings and high politics.[5] He had also argued for a 'south-west' framework for understanding the 'culture of rebellion' of those years.[6] From another angle, local historians of the Cornish gentry constructed a picture of a content and anglicized group in the Elizabethan and Stuart periods.[7] John Chynoweth even, over-ambitiously, strode into the fray with all guns blazing by constructing a 'theory of Cornish distinctiveness' from the writings of Rowse, Payton, Stoyle and Julian Cornwall. He then proceeded, at least to his own satisfaction, to demolish his Aunt Sally point by point.[8] However, this exercise was marred by uncritical and eclectic use of secondary sources and rendered unconvincing by the clearly romantic assumptions about 'Cornish distinctiveness' that Chynoweth had held and his obvious disappointment at not meeting them on the ground.

But 'Kernowsceptic' and 'Kernowcentric' historians alike have tended to unite in accepting the view that Cornwall, or the South-West, was a region of rebellion and resistance. Turning this representation of the people of the West, and particularly Cornwall, on its head, J.P.D. Cooper in his book *Propaganda and the Tudor State*[9] finds evidence that, on the contrary, Cornwall (and Devon) were havens of 'obedience and uniformity rather than rebellion and resistance' (p. 261). Most of the time subjects obeyed their rulers and, indeed, during the sixteenth century Cornwall was located 'within England's national imagination, as well as its administrative and judicial framework' (p. 3).

Cooper establishes his credentials as a 'Kernowsceptic' historian by adopting an explicit Devon and Cornwall framework. Nonetheless, he seems to be less than wholeheartedly committed to this 'regional' framework. This is a region which is not by any means a homogenous Devonwall but one in which Cornwall and Devon are much of the time discussed separately. Whole chapters, for instance those on 'Tyranny and Drama' and 'The Duchy and the Stannaries', are effectively reserved for Cornwall alone, while an epilogue self-consciously justifies the treatment of 'Cornwall and Devon together', admitting 'such a division requires a willing suspension of belief' (p. 252). Unlike in other texts, Cooper does not deny Cornwall's distinctiveness and he is aware of the modern sense of Cornish identity, albeit caricaturing it as 'separatist sentiment' (p. 4). But his admission that 'there was certainly something distinctive about the culture of Tudor Cornwall setting it apart from Devon and the rest of England' (p. 254) does not rest comfortably with his intent to combat the 'Kernowcentric' position. For this reason alone this is not the 'Kernowsceptic backlash' that Stoyle predicted. On the contrary, Cooper's intervention is an interesting one and, stripped of its normative assumptions, does offer us some pointers towards a more nuanced approach to the sixteenth century that might allow movement beyond the often stereotyped polarities of the current 'Kernowcentric versus Kernowsceptic' debate, all of which makes it a pity that Cooper's argument is fatally flawed, normatively, methodologically and empirically.

Normatively, he condescendingly dismisses the argument that Cornish popular politics in this period had an ethnic undertow as 'the nationalist school of Cornish history'. That may be so, but equally, Cooper writes from a recognisably English nationalist position that is well ensconced at Oxford University, from where this book emanates. Strange, therefore, though hardly surprising, that he fails to describe his own position as part of an 'English nationalist school'. An unreflective perspective from within this school of history leads him to ignore the corpus of work in Cornish Studies almost entirely, concentrating on just one article that appeared in *Cornish Studies: One* back in 1993.[10] The result is thus the same sort of tilting at windmills that we are familiar with from chapter 1 of Chynoweth's *Tudor*

Cornwall. More crucially, while apparently unaware of more recent work that has appeared in both *Cornish Studies* and elsewhere since 1993,[11] Cooper's approach also betrays a serious lack of historical imagination.

This is particularly serious given his attempts to identify the popular culture of the common people, something that requires a great deal more sensitivity to both text and context than Cooper is able to marshal. For example, arguing against Philip Payton's interpretation of *Beunans Meriasek*, that the audience would have read the play as an anti-Tudor text, with the Duke of Cornwall fighting for Cornwall against the tyrant Teudar, Cooper states that it is 'far from clear that a play audience would have identified itself with the county of Cornwall in this way' for 'allegiance to the shire was largely a thing of the future' (p. 78). Quite so, but he does not explore the possibility that people in Cornwall, perhaps especially those within the Cornish-speaking community, while lacking a modernist territorial identity, may well have possessed an allegiance to the idea of the Duchy of Cornwall. This institution in the early sixteenthth century just might have given rise to forms of allegiance that were very different from later 'county communities' but nonetheless rooted in place and in jurisdictional as well as territorial authority. Given the interesting role that Cooper later maps out for the Duchy in the production of English regnal loyalties, it is unfortunate that the possible meanings evoked by this institution in the early sixteenth century are not pursued. More generally, Cooper tends to adopt a very black and white, modernist view of identity, seeing it as a question of being either English or Cornish (see, for example pp. 144–145). Unwittingly occupying the same ground as the extreme Cornish nationalist, Cooper seems unable to appreciate that identities in the early modern period could be much more contested and fluid than this, with cultural and political identities perhaps 'nesting' in unexpected ways.[12]

Exploring issues of popular identity requires a certain degree of speculation and a theoretical awareness as well as historical imagination. And from the evidence of this text none of these are met with in abundance in the closeted ivory towers of English academia at Oxford. There English empiricism still reigns supreme. Such a historical approach leads to a 'failure-to-find fallacy'; if it wasn't written down then it simply could not have happened. Instead of adopting the sensible path, that the absence of evidence for a phenomenon does not necessarily mean that such a phenomenon did not or could not have happened, in the Oxford method the empirical vacuum tends to be promptly filled by the assumptions of the historical observer, a subjectivity strangely at odds with a purportedly 'objective' method. Thus the possibility that Arthur was still a folk hero in early Tudor Cornwall is discounted as 'there is little or nothing in the way of drama or literature to prove it'. This leads Cooper to disagree with Stoyle's claim that Henry Tudor 'aroused near-millenarian expectations among the Cornish people in 1485' (pp. 108–9). Whether he did or not, one wonders what Cooper would conclude now that we know that the newly discovered play of St Kea (*Beunans Ke*) has a strong Arthurian sub-text. This should alert us to the perils of being over-dogmatic in the absence of evidence when studying this period of history.

But, if the assumptions are unexamined, the approach partial, and the historical imagination limited, the underlying absence of critical depth fundamentally weakens Cooper's argument, even on its own terms. This is because it leads him to misrepresent and distort the evidence that he does find. This is particularly noticeable in two areas, though by no means confined to them. The first occurs when he is building up a case for popular loyalty to the Elizabethan regime and to the person of Queen Elizabeth I herself, while the second is found in his discussion of the state of the Cornish language. And, as we shall see, this latter, being crucial Cooper's argument, fatally undermines it.

A central plank of the book's overall thesis is that 'far from being a dangerous and restless borderland, Devon and Cornwall were integrated within the allegiance demanded by the English state, and were increasingly keen to celebrate the fact' (p. 51). To prove this, Cooper relies principally on evidence in churchwardens' and borough accounts for payments made to celebrate and mourn royal births and deaths, in particular through bell ringing. These, according to him, 'prove the existence of an earlier provincial culture of the celebration . . . of royal news' (p. 15). The death of Henry VIII in 1547 was thus 'conspicuously mourned by parishes in the south west' (p. 18). Yet, later on the same page, we are informed that 'unfortunately Cornish accounts for this year are scarce'. For scarce read virtually non-existent, as the only one mentioned is Stratton. One parish at the far northern extremity of Cornwall hardly seems sufficient evidence to conclude that Cornwall 'shared in the general reaction' of 'unprompted national mourning' in 1547 (p. 19). Moving on to Elizabeth's reign, we are told that 'by the 1570s, parishes in Devon and Cornwall were participating vigorously in the national culture of celebrating her ascension day' (p. 24). Cooper goes on to list eight Devon parishes before stating unequivocally that 'Cornwall, too, shared in this popular culture of loyalism' (p. 25). Yet the evidence from Cornwall comes from just three parishes: Antony (from 1579 onwards), North Petherwin and Stratton. Cooper fails to provide a map for his readers and appears to regard it as unnecessary to inform the more geographically-challenged among them of the location of these parishes at the very borders of Cornwall (North Petherwin was in fact administered as a part of the county of Devon at this time).

The only evidence from the whole of the rest of Cornwall comes from Camborne. But here we are told that 'the first definite reference to the culture of Elizabeth in Camborne comes rather later, in 1585' (p. 25). Camborne's tardiness in joining these government-inspired 'popular celebrations' could equally, of course, be read as a significant exception to the lack of any 'popular culture of loyalism' in the west into the 1580s. Cooper's claim that 'the accession day peals throughout Devon and Cornwall from the 1570s affirmed the loyalty of the distant region to the political centre' (p. 26) is supported by churchwardens' evidence from less than 2 per cent of Cornish parishes, and those all situated on the eastern land border. Such use of evidence is disingenuous at best and downright incompetent at worst. The reality, from Cooper's own evidence, could equally be that there is no evidence of a widespread popular culture of loyalism in Cornwall until the 1580s at the earliest. Gentry loyalism was another matter and it is not difficult for Cooper to find evidence for this.[13]

If the evidence used to buttress the central argument of popular loyalism is insufficiently sound to bear its weight, then so is the evidence cited in order to explain a limited culture of rebellion in Cornwall. For Cooper is forced to admit that the latter, had it existed, would have been found in the culture of the Cornish-speaking part of Cornwall. A chapter-length review of the play *Beunans Meriasek* begins confidently by attacking the 'political and anti-English reading' of Philip Payton. Yet the conclusion rather lamely comes around to the view that 'it cannot be denied that *Beunans Meriasek* might have had political overtones to an audience in and around Camborne when staged after the uprisings of 1497' (p. 81), a conclusion that seems to bear out Payton's original argument. Cooper is also forced to admit a linguistic distinctiveness that had 'important implications for the sense of Cornish identity, and the integration of the county within the rest of the kingdom during the Tudor period' (p. 70). Thus far he agrees with Mark Stoyle. He also admits that in 1549 the request for the translation of the English prayer book meant that there were 'still enough monoglot speakers of Cornish to turn the English prayer book into a political as well as religious issue' (p. 65). The distinctiveness of the culture of Tudor Cornwall rested on the continued existence of a Cornish language which could contain an 'anti-English feeling' (pp. 254, 256).

However, in order to square this conclusion with his argument on popular loyalty and obedience, Cooper then proceeds to assert that this anti-Englishness was already by 1549 'residual', found only 'in the remote west' and on the wane. 'Rather than constructing the river Tamar as a cultural dividing line between the English and the Cornish, we should think in terms of a recognisably Celtic society having survived only in the extremities of Tudor Cornwall' (p. 257). Taken on its own this is a useful warning against over-enthusiastic re-writings of sixteenth-century Cornwall in terms of twentieth- or twenty-first-century nationalism. But, continuing that 'plotting cultural maps is never an easy task, and we should be wary of claims that are too clear-cut' (p. 257), he then goes on to do exactly that. For, in order that his thesis should survive, Cooper must play down the extent of the Cornish-language community, following Richard Carew in despatching it to the 'uttermost parts of the shire'.[14]

The Cornish language, we are told, 'died east of Bodmin as early as the twelfth' century (p. 257). Only 'isolated pockets' in mid-Cornwall continued to use Cornish up to the Tudor period (p. 71). 'By the mid-sixteenth century, Cornish was little spoken beyond Penwith and the Lizard' (p. 65). These were 'both pockets of land . . . isolated from the rest of Cornwall' (p. 257). Indeed, his enthusiastic reduction of Cornish-speaking Cornwall leads him to go even further, to claim that only 'the parishes south and west of Helston had a particular identity' as displayed in the language, patronymics and a fragmented field system (p. 258). The absence of named 'rebels' in 1549 from Penwith and Kerrier Hundreds is, for Cooper, evidence that the leaders of the 1549 rising did not speak Cornish, as was the fact that the proclamation of the rising was at Bodmin: in his view, well to the east of the Cornish language.[15]

What evidence does Cooper employ to place the cultural divide between Cornish and English speaking communities so far west in 1549? The answer is, shockingly little. The principal secondary source cited is Crysten Fudge's *The Life of Cornish* (1982). Whatever its strengths, this popular introduction to middle Cornish was never intended to be a definitive academic text on the historical geography of Cornish. Much is also made of John Norden's statement, coined in the 1580s, that in Cornwall 'from Truro eastward it is in manner wholly English. In the west part of the country, as in the Hundreds of Penwith and Kerrier, the Cornish tongue is most in use amongst the inhabitants' (p. 71). Yet even Norden also wrote that 'of late', presumably that is in the generation before the 1580s, 'the Cornish men have much conformed themselves to the use of the English tongue', implying that there had been a recent language shift since the 1550s. Norden's phrase 'in manner wholly English' has been seized on uncritically by those who wish to argue Cornwall east of Truro had ceased to be Cornish-speaking by the 1580s.[16] But this is an awful lot of weight to be borne by just one ambiguous phrase.

Indeed, elsewhere in *Propaganda and the Tudor State* we are warned against relying on Norden, as he was non-resident, only visited Cornwall for a few days and relied heavily on drafts of Carew's *Survey* (p. 256). This, according to Cooper, ought to make us wary of Norden's account of the Cornish having a 'concealed envy against the English'. Critical of Norden when it suits his case, Cooper totally accepts his description of the state of the Cornish language, losing all powers of critical analysis in this latter area.

Other evidence (see Spriggs in this volume) strongly suggests that Cooper is just plain wrong about the Cornish language, not least his describing as 'fact' a situation that he has constructed purely to bolster his argument that the Cornish-speaking culture, potentially harbouring subversive and anti-English sentiment, was restricted to Penwith and the Lizard by 1549. Even in east Cornwall there is evidence from placename formation that Cornish was being used in places many years after the 1100s.[17] Turning to mid-Cornwall, Padel suggests that 'Cornish was in use in St Columb in the mid-sixteenth century'.[18] Meanwhile, in 1583, fishermen at Gorran 'could not speak or understand English', while in a court case it was claimed that two women at St Ewe were talking together both 'in Cornish and English' in 1595.[19] These citations, based on primary evidence and implying that Cornish was spoken in mid-Cornwall well into the sixteenth century, were available to Cooper, yet he chose to ignore them, instead concentrating on the speculations of John Norden, by his own admission a casual visitor. Other evidence he presents serves to compromise his own case. Thus he cites a production of a Cornish drama at Perran Round on Queen Mary's succession—a strange thing to do at a time when, he argues elsewhere in the book, no-one could understand Cornish in this district. This is followed by evidence for a play being performed in Penryn in 1587: to the east, not to the west of Helston. Finally, he notes that Carew was still describing the Cornish miracle plays in the present tense as late as the 1590s (p. 74).

The argument that Cornish was restricted to parishes south and west of Helston as early as 1549 (and if it was, there was surprisingly little change in the geography of the language between 1549 and Lhuyd's trip to Cornwall in 1700) is just not credible given the weight of evidence that points to language shift in Pydar and Powder Hundreds between 1550 and 1600.[20] Such a cavalier approach to the evidence, together with misplaced assumptions about language shift, make Cooper's characterization of the cultural geography of sixteenth-century Cornwall unreliable. Moreover, it is not difficult to find other examples elsewhere in this book of partial presentation of evidence. Thus we are informed that 91 per cent of the Cornish gentry took wives from 'within' Devon and Cornwall (p. 253). But what we are not told is that 80 per cent of Cornish gentlemen in Tudor Cornwall married Cornish-born brides and only 11 per cent Devonians.[21]

It is unfortunate that this book has so many empirical short-comings. For Cooper actually makes other points that could help move us beyond the often simplistic and polarized debate about sixteenth-century Cornwall. While not the first to raise the issue of cultural zones within Cornwall,[22] Cooper's observation that 'overlapping English and Celtic languages, law and religious practices' were contained in the one region is a fair one (p. 248). But of course the 'region' in question was the territory of Cornwall. It was Cornwall that contained both English and Cornish language cultures. Early sixteenth-century Cornwall was a land where a rough balance prevailed between these cultures. During that century, the pendulum began to swing inexorably towards the English language and, ultimately, the Cornish-speaking culture was almost extinguished. This Celtic culture could itself be viewed in larger geo-cultural terms, as the remnant of a trans-regional British culture looking to north and south, to Wales and particularly to Brittany. For Cornwall can be viewed as having been located at least since the ninth century on a cultural border-zone, influenced *both* by its maritime connections to other parts of Celtic Europe *and* by its land links to England to the east. Within Cornwall there has been and still is a fluctuating border, both socially and geographically, between English and non-English influence. Though the former apparently secured its hegemony in the seventeenth century, Cornwall's industrial revolution restored new links with Wales, this time economic rather than cultural, while in the twentieth century the Cornish Revival began to revive cultural links with the rest of the Celtic world. Cornwall is, therefore, a land of two historical traditions, one that looks towards England and the east and the other taking its inspiration from places to north, south and west. Celtic, industrial and family connections combine to point away from England and towards cultural cousins in Wales and Brittany and kin cousins in those of Cornish descent scattered across the globe during the emigration of the nineteenth century.

Cooper's argument about cultural zones could, moreover, be extended. He suggests there are two such zones in Cornwall, with the Cornish of east Cornwall linked more to 'the people of Devon' than to the Cornish-speaking western Cornish (p. 202). But, while he is right to note the cultural divide within Cornwall, the repercussions of which

demand a lot more serious research, he fails to apply the same argument to Devon. Devon appears as a homogenous unit, where many of
the elements of an independent regional political culture—a history of
insurrections, riots, piracy and tinning—also apply. But did they? And
did they really apply to the whole of Devon?

It seems, on the contrary, that such traditions were confined to
upland and west Devon. The 'rebels' of Sampford Courtenay and
the tinners of Dartmoor may imply that a cultural border, though
less sharp, can nonetheless be traced within sixteenth-century Devon,
separating the uplands and north-west Devon from the lowlands, the
large towns and southern and eastern Devon. Cooper, for example,
tells us that Devon retained a community of miners, a community that,
as in Cornwall, 'developed a sense of insularity [*sic*] and common
identity' (p. 189). Again this intriguing argument is disrupted by his
need to converge the experience of the two 'counties' in order to
construct a Devon and Cornwall region. For example, we are told that
tin was a 'major contributor to the economies of the two western
counties' and that production in Devon exceeded its fourteenth-
century peak in the mid-sixteenth century. That may be so but Devon
still supplied just a quarter of the tin production of Cornwall in the
1540s, a proportion that then declined to a ninth by the 1590s.[23] Here
again, Cooper misinforms his readers. He states that in 1521 Devon tin
production was 'about one half of the Cornish figure' (p. 190). But
even at this exceptional period for the Devon tin industry, its production, according to Lewis, was only 39 per cent of that of Cornwall.[24]
Tinning, while playing a major role in Cornish economy and society,
especially in that of western Cornwall, was relatively marginal in
Devon and restricted to particular locations. Cooper is forced to
exaggerate tin production there as he seeks to argue that the culture of
the Stannaries was not unique to Cornwall but also applied to Devon.

Nevertheless, if we ignore the manner in which the need to
conflate the experiences of Devon and Cornwall deforms the use of
evidence, Cooper makes what is perhaps the most interesting point
of the entire book in his chapter on 'Duchy and Stannaries'. Here, he
develops a convincing case that continuing regional distinctiveness
could actually work to make a place more rather than less 'loyal to the
Tudor centre'. More specifically, the Duchy played a key role in
providing both influence and income for Cornish gentry families in
the sixteenth century and in trying to protect the populace from the
risk of French and Spanish raids through the construction of coastal
fortifications. This led to the population looking towards the Crown for
its protection and fostered a sense of loyalty to the centre. And when
the Stuarts centralized the administration of the Duchy in the 1610s

and 1620s it was the second distinctive institution—the Stannaries—that had the 'greater impact upon popular loyalty to the monarchy' (p. 187). By the sixteenth and seventeenth centuries the perception of the tinners was that their 'liberties descended directly from the Crown' rather than the Crown having merely been the arbiter of pre-existing liberties (p. 199). As a result, tinners remained loyal to the Crown, while not offering obedience to the gentry, a combination that neatly explains both the royalism of the 1640s and the risings of the 1490s.

If this book stimulates some research on the complex links between Crown, Duchy and Stannaries in the sixteenth and early seventeenth centuries and the way these impinged upon popular loyalties, then its publication will not have been in vain. However, loyalism and royalism were fluid concepts in this period and a lot changed between the 1540s and 1640s, the meaning of 'loyalty' included. In view of this, any research taking these issues further will have to be a lot more imaginative, more alert to different readings and more sensitive to what the sources might be telling us than the reading that underpins *Propaganda and the Tudor State*. More generally, Cooper's book might have served to open up a debate about the binary tradition that underlies Cornwall's history and explains a good deal of the conflicts and tensions of the early modern period. Ultimately, it fails to address the subtlety of the Cornish condition because it is drawn by its agenda to enhance the role of one tradition at the expense of the other. In doing this it becomes just a mirror image of the approach that it condemns in other historians of Cornwall.

NOTES AND REFERENCES
1. Philip Payton, *The Making of Modern* Cornwall, Redruth, 1992, p. 65.
2. Mark Stoyle, *West Britons: Cornish Identities and the Early Modern British State*, Exeter, 2002, p. 1.
3. John Angarrack, *Our Future is History: Identity, Law and the Cornish Question*, Bodmin, 2002, pp. 174–6; Pol Hodge, *Cornwall's Secret War: The True Story of the Prayer Book War*, Truro, 1999.
4. Mark Stoyle, 'Re-discovering Difference: The Recent Historiography of Early Modern Cornwall', in Philip Payton (ed.), *Cornish Studies: Ten*, Exeter, p. 112.
5. Ian Arthurson, 'The Rising of 1497: A Revolt of the Peasantry?', in Joel Rosenthal and Colin Richmond (eds), *People, Politics and Community in the Later Middle Ages*, Gloucester, 1987, and *The Perkin Warbeck Conspiracy 1491–1499*, Stroud, 1994.
6. Ian Arthurson, '"As able we be to depose him" . . . Rebellion in the South West, 1497', in *Cornwall Marches On!*, Truro, 1997, pp. 22–8.
7. Anne Duffin, *Faction and Faith: Politics and Religion of the Cornish*

Gentry before the Civil War, Exeter, 1996; John Chynoweth, *Tudor Corn-wall*, Stroud, 2002.

8. Chynoweth, 2002, pp. 21–31. An earlier version of this appears in John Chynoweth, 'The Gentry of Tudor Cornwall', unpublished PhD thesis, University of Exeter, 1994.

9. J.P.D. Cooper, *Propaganda and the Tudor State: Political Culture in the Westcountry*, Oxford, 2003.

10. Philip Payton, "'A . . . concealed envy against the English'': A Note on the Aftermath of the 1497 Rebellions in Cornwall', in Philip Payton (ed.), *Cornish Studies: One*, Exeter, 1993, pp. 4–13.

11. See, for example, the chapters by Amy Hale and Alan Kent in David Harvey, Rhys Jones, Neil McInroy and Christine Milligan (eds), *Celtic Geographies: Old Culture, New Times*, London, 2002.

12. Colin Kidd, *British Identities before Nationalism: Ethnicity and Nationhood in the Atlantic World, 1600–1800*, Cambridge, 1999.

13. And see Chynoweth, 2002.

14. Richard Carew, *Survey of Cornwall*, London, 1811, p. 151.

15. This latter point is dealt with by Stoyle, 2002, pp. 23–4.

16. See also Duffin, 1996, p. 2.

17. Paul Dunbar and Ken George, *Kernewek Kemmyn: Cornish for the 21st Century*, Liskeard, 1997, p. 158. See also Holmes in this volume.

18. Oliver Padel, 'Cornish Language Notes: 3', *Cornish Studies*, 3, 1975, p. 22.

19. James Whetter, 'An Exchequer Case relating to Gorran Haven', *Old Cornwall*, 6, 1962, p. 69; A.L. Rowse, *Tudor Cornwall*, London, 1941, p. 23.

20. See Matthew Spriggs, 'Where Cornish was Spoken and When: A Provisional Synthesis' in this volume.

21. Chynoweth, 2002, pp. 91–2.

22. See Bernard Deacon, 'In Search of the Missing "Turn": The Spatial Dimension and Cornish Studies', in Philip Payton (ed.), *Cornish Studies: Eight*, Exeter, 2000, pp. 213–30.

23. G.R. Lewis, *The Stannaries: A Study of the Medieval Tin Miners of Cornwall and Devon*, Boston, 1907, pp. 253–4.

24. Lewis, 1907, p. 253.

NOTES ON CONTRIBUTORS

John Beckett is Professor of English Regional History at the University of Nottingham, where he has taught for more than twenty years. He has written extensively on British agricultural and urban history, and on the history of landed estates. Currently, he is preparing a study of the granting of city status to British towns over the past millennium.

Graham Busby is Senior Lecturer in Tourism Management at the University of Plymouth. He has published widely on rural tourism, sustainable development and tourism education, and is co-author of *Tourism: A Modern Synthesis* (2000).

Stuart Dalley was born and brought up in West Cornwall and was educated at the University of Exeter where he gained a first class honours degree in History and Spanish. He has recently completed an MA at the University of Bristol and is currently undertaking a History PGCE at the University of Bath.

Bernard Deacon is Lecturer in Cornish Studies at the Institute of Cornish Studies, University of Exeter. A frequent contributor to *Cornish Studies*, his most recent publications are *Mebyon Kernow and Cornish Nationalism* (with Garry Tregidga and Dick Cole) (2003), *The History of the Cornish People* (forthcoming, 2004) and *The Cornish Family* (editor) (forthcoming, 2004).

Brian Elvins, who died in 2001, was a specialist in nineteenth-century Cornish political history. An appreciation by Professor Edwin Jaggard of his life, work and contribution to Cornish Studies was published in *Cornish Studies: Ten* in 2002. His chapter in this volume appears with the permission of his widow, Elizabeth Elvins, and the assistance of his son, Jeremy Elvins.

David Everett is a postgraduate student at the Institute of Cornish Studies, University of Exeter, and is currently researching the life and work of Henry Jenner with particular reference to the Celtic Revival in Cornwall. He was formerly priest-in-charge at Treslothan, and holds an M.A. in Celtic Christianity from the University of Wales, Lampeter.

D.H. Frost is Head of the Honours Programme and a Member of the Chaplaincy Team at St David's Catholic College, Cardiff.

Julyan Holmes is a freelance researcher and writer who has published widely on the Cornish language and its revival, including guides to house names and personal names in Cornish. He lives in Liskeard, Cornwall.

Alan M. Kent is a Lecturer in Literature at the Open University. He has published widely on the literary and cultural history of Cornwall. He is editor of *The Dreamt Sea: An Anthology of Anglo-Cornish Poetry 1928–2003* (2002) and has recently co-edited a collection of newly discovered poems by Jack Clemo. In 1999, he was winner of a European Union script-writing award.

Patrick Laviolette is a Teaching and Research Assistant in the Department of Anthropology, University College London. His PhD thesis is entitled 'Meaning Towards Metaphor: Creating and Contesting Identity through Cornish Landscape Icons'. In addition to the anthropological and geographical study of British identities, his other research interests include the ways in which alternative forms of art, housing, sport and transport influence the material conditions of social movments and social relations.

Philip Payton is Professor of Cornish Studies at the Institute of Cornish Studies, University of Exeter. Amongst his numerous books are *The Making of Modern Cornwall* (1992), *Cornwall* (1996), *The Cornish Overseas* (1999), *A Vision of Cornwall* (2002), and *A.L. Rowse and Cornwall: A Paradoxical Patriot* (forthcoming, 2004). He is also editor of the annual series *Cornish Studies* and of *Cornwall Since the War* (1993) and (with Amy Hale) *New Directions in Celtic Studies* (2000).

Mark Sandford is a Research Fellow in the Constitution Unit at University College London. He has written extensively on issues of regionalism and is especially interested in the case of Cornwall. Amongst his publications is (with Paul McQuail) *Unexplored Territory: Elected Regional Assemblies in England* (2001).

Matthew Spriggs is Professor of Archaeology in the Department of Archaeology and Anthropology at the Australian National University in Canberra. He is a specialist in Pacific and Asian archaeology, on which he has published widely, but also has a research interest in the social history of the Cornish Language and its speakers.

Malte W. Tschirschky is a postgraduate student in the Institute of English and American Studies at the University of Frankfurt/Main in Germany. Holding the equivalent of a Master's degree in English Studies, Art History and Medieval and Modern History, he is currently working on his doctoral thesis on cultural aspects of Cornish nationalism. He is, amongst other things, anxious to raise the profile of Cornish Studies in Continental Europe.

David Windsor graduated in History and Politics at the University of Lancaster and then worked as a Local Government Officer for twenty years in London and West Cornwall. After six years with a Housing Association he took early retirement in 2000. He is now involved in a variety of voluntary work but has also carried out survey work for the Office of National Statistics and the University of Plymouth.